AFRICAN STORIES

by
Al J. Venter
and Friends

Protea Book House
Pretoria
2013

To Caroline: my anchor, my guide and my 'interpreter'.
Thank you darling.

BOOKS BY THE SAME AUTHOR INCLUDE:
Underwater Africa
Under the Indian Ocean
Report on Portugal's War in Guiné-Bissau
Africa at War
The Zambezi Salient
Underwater Seychelles
Coloured: A Profile of Two Million South Africans
Africa Today
South African Handbook for Divers
The Second South African Handbook for Divers
Challenge: South Africa in the African Revolutionary Context
Underwater Mauritius
The Ultimate Handbook on Diving in South Africa
Where to Dive: In Southern Africa and off the Indian Ocean Islands
War in Angola
The Chopper Boys: Helicopter Warfare in Africa
The Iraqi War Debrief: Why Saddam Hussein was Toppled
Iran's Nuclear Option
War Dog: Fighting Other People's Wars
Allah's Bomb: The Islamic Quest for Nuclear Weapons
Cops: Cheating Death: How One Man Saved the Lives of 3,000 Americans
How South Africa Built Six Atom Bombs
Dive South Africa/Duik Suid-Afrika
Barrel of a Gun: A War Correspondent's Misspent Moments in Combat
War Stories by Al J. Venter and Friends
Gunship Ace – The Wars of Neall Ellis, Helicopter Pilot and Mercenary
Guerrilla Wars – Conflicts in Southern Africa Since 1960/Guerilla Oorloë –Suider-Afrikaanse Konflikte Sedert 1960
Shark Stories by Al J. Venter and Friends
Portugal's Guerrilla Wars in Africa (due for release in the United Kingdom and the United States late 2013)

African Stories by Al J. Venter and Friends
First edition, first impression in 2013 by Protea Book House

PO Box 35110, Menlo Park, 0102
1067 Burnett Street, Hatfield, Pretoria
8 Minni Street, Clydesdale, Pretoria
protea@intekom.co.za
www.proteaboekhuis.com

Editor: Danél Hanekom
Proofreaders: Carmen Hansen-Kruger and Jerry Buirski
Cover design: Bruce Gonneau
Front cover image: Al J. Venter
Back cover images: Uganda skulls – Al J. Venter, Robert Mugabe – Al Venter collection
Typography: Zapf Calligraphic, 10.5 pt by Bruce Gonneau
Printed and bound by Interpak Books, Pietermaritzburg

© 2013 Al J. Venter

ISBN: 978-1-86919-842-8 (printed book)
ISBN: 978-1-86919-843-5 (e-book)

All rights reserved. No part of this book may be reproduced or transmitted in any form or by any electronic or mechanical means, including photocopying and recording, or by any other information storage or retrieval system, without written permission from the publisher.

CONTENTS

		PAGE
Introduction		1

CHAPTER

1	In Search of Doctor Albert Schweitzer	13
2	Angola's Tank Battle on the Lomba	27
3	Africa's Great Mercenary Tradition	51
4	Cairo – Heart of the Islamic Revolt	75
5	'Paddlebum' and the Rough Riders of the Rufiji River	91
6	The Future Role of Mercenaries on the African Continent	117
7	Rhodesia's War – Al Venter Looks Back	141
8	Questions and Answers with Adam Buske – A Professional Hunter in Africa	167
9	By Puma Helicopter across the African Continent	183
10	The Unanswered 'Hit' on Pelindaba in November 2007	205
11	Valentine Strasser – Africa's Vagabond King	223
12	Landmines – Hidden Killers	239
13	Female Genital Mutilation is now Worldwide	255
14	The Enigmatic Sarah Barrell	263
15	Portugal in Africa – Good Times for Some	273
16	Biafra's Aerial War of Attrition	287
17	Ghana: Contradictory West Africa	309
18	Uganda's Invasion by the Tanzanian Army and the End of Idi Amin	321
19	Operation Palliser – An Unusual British Deployment to West Africa	341
20	Lion Attack	355

21 The Central Intelligence Agency's Air War in the Congo	373
22 Fighting Horsemen on the Angolan Border	393
23 The Algerian Connection	401
24 The Great Zambezi River	425
25 A Witchdoctor in the House	441
26 A Week in an African Jail	453
Acknowledgements	460

INTRODUCTION

> When you have been born in Africa you are marked by Africa and wherever you go, you are a displaced person, for you have two identities.
>
> Mirella Ricciardi

Writing about Africa becomes easier after you've imbibed its dirty red dust a few times or have listened, transfixed, to the mellifluous sounds of the women from one village calling across the hills to those of another. And inhaled the delicious odour of raw wood smoke wafting up from the kraals below, almost none of which can be adequately described in words.

That delightful man, Alan Paton, captured it vividly in the opening paragraph of his *Cry, the Beloved Country!* when he wrote about a part of Africa that he truly adored: 'There is a lovely road which runs from Ixopo into the hills. These hills are grass covered and rolling, and they are lovely beyond any singing of it.' I have yet to find a more compelling start to any book I've read.

Of course, the continent has its problems. But we tend to dismiss them once the troubles have passed and then, more often than not, slot back into our everyday routines. This is not Europe or America, but things have never been so bad that us *wazungus* have stopped coming back. There are more foreign passport-holders living in South Africa today than ever before and long before you've closed the covers of this book, still more will have ambled through the arrivals concourse at Oliver Tambo International Airport. May it always be so.

Yet it was Africa's discord that originally put this scribe on his personal road to perdition on what early chroniclers would sometimes refer to as the 'Dark Continent'. I was young, impetuous and had travelled across a large chunk of Africa to hitchhike a lift on a ship travelling from Mombasa to Montreal, something you could do before insurance companies started to impose their impossibly draconian legal restrictions.

Afterwards, once I'd finished my studies in London, I headed home again to make a place for myself in South African society. But in those days – and here I'm talking about the 1960s – that was always an arduous journey, though the old Union Castle Line did

AFRICA

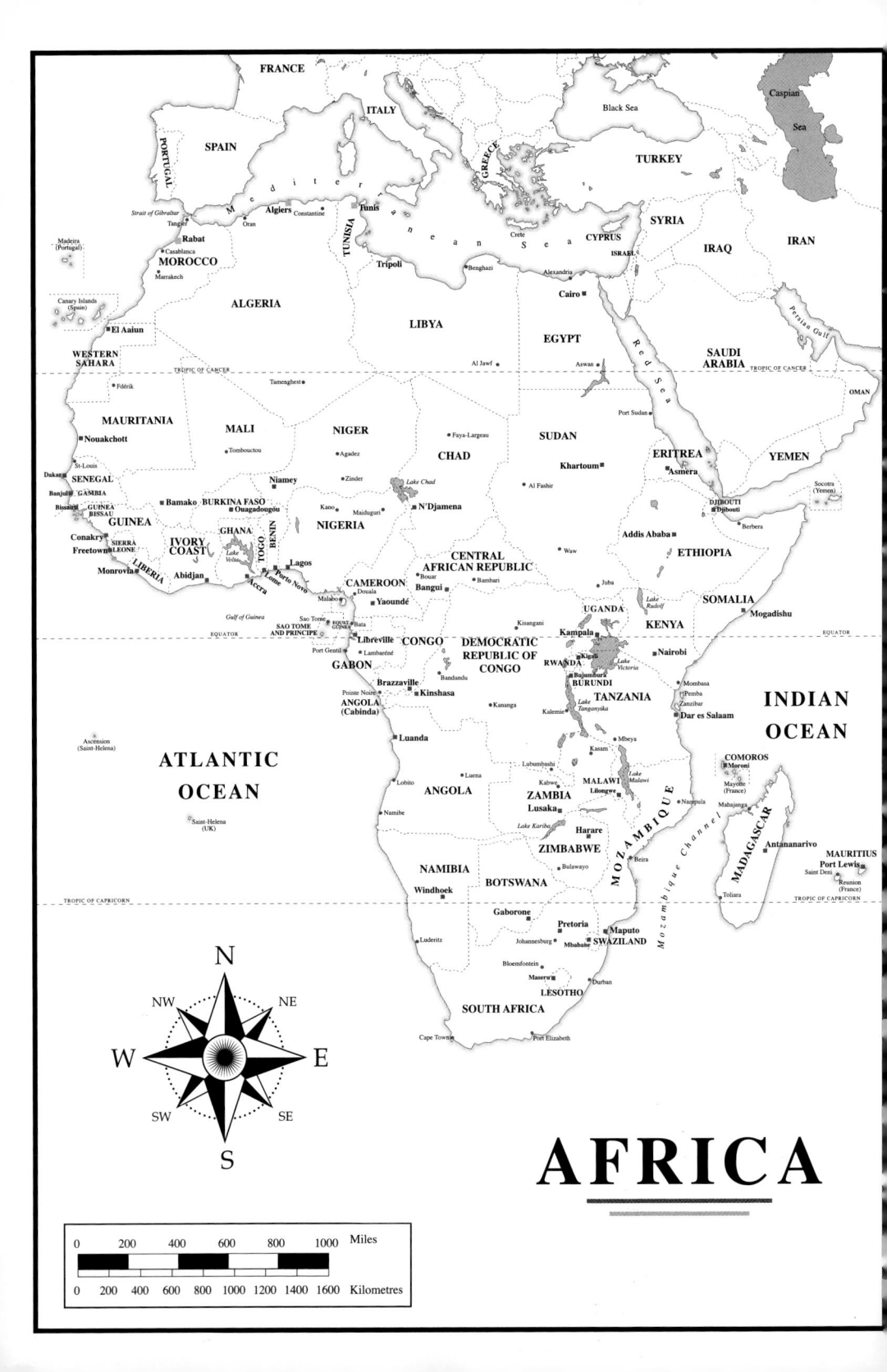

offer an alternative by sea, which lasted upwards of a fortnight.

It took us three days in a state-of-the-art, prop-driven Super Constellation passenger plane to travel from Heathrow to the then Jan Smuts Airport in Johannesburg, across the length of the African continent. We would get our heads down in nightly stopovers, usually in places that had an enormous appeal at the time, some with romantic names like Khartoum, Ndola, Kisumu or, depending on the airline – Douala in the Cameroons.

There were 80 passengers on board and we travelled at about 300 miles an hour in an aircraft that had been developed during World War II, originally built as Lockheed's answer to the venerable old Douglas DC-6.

In our eyes, the machine was a monster, most of us having grown up in the age of the Piper Cub or the Spitfire, because on home turf, we South Africans rarely saw World War II bombers like the Lancaster or the Boeing B-17 Flying Fortress. Yet by yesterday's standards, those antiquated aircraft were perfectly adequate for the journey, even if the Constellation's empty take-off weight was only about 30 tons, compared to more than 270 tons fielded by the Airbus-380 today.

To us simple souls, the journey was momentous, and, with air safety in its infancy, the 5,000 mile trip was not without risk. In those faraway days quite a few trans-African flights ended in disaster, but they were always rather jolly events, even if the privations we were subjected to were unimaginable by today's super-jet standards.

For a start, overnight stays in exotic locations – attended to by squads of immaculately clad Africans in their spanking white suits and red fezzes – were all part of a colonial tradition that went back almost forever. The flight companies did their bit by offering the passengers food and drink and, if we were lucky, that kind of frivolity could sometimes go on till the bus arrived to take us to the airport at dawn.

So too was the case with Kenya, in its heyday a delightful place, as chroniclers like Kuki Gallman, Mirella Ricciardi, Elspeth Huxley and Karen Blixen have told us. We called it the safari capital of the world, though the majority of the backpackers who transited Nairobi could rarely afford expensive outings into the wild.

The Kenyan capital was smaller, less sophisticated than Johannesburg and every bit as popular. But then that might have been expected, with the Nairobi National Park just half an hour's drive from the centre of town and boasting many of the attributes of modern society in a conurbation that was always regarded as on the fringe of the so-called 'undeveloped world'. For a start, it had the Donovan Maule Theatre where many British thespians spent a few months before moving south to the Republic, and customarily, a spell at the Alexandria Theatre.

In those days the Thorn Tree Restaurant – always popular on the front portal of the New Stanley Hotel, complete with an acacia growing out of the concrete – was the fulcrum of all social activity during the day.

After hours, the Norfolk Hotel took over, with the Delaware Terrace its favourite watering hole and very much a part of the old establishment backdrop. Hemingway used to drink there, so did his compatriot Robert Ruark and, long before that, Denys Finch-Hatton and his good buddy, the Honourable Berkeley Cole, an Anglo-Irish aristocrat whose namesake today lives on the Isle of Bute.

Interestingly, the Norfolk was the base from which many great adventurers began their exploration of the region and was also where American President Roosevelt began his world-famous African safari in 1909. He set off in pomp and style from the front steps of the hotel before heading out into the wilderness.

Over the years I spent a lot of time in Nairobi. The lovely Sally Church made it almost a home-away-from-home at her place on the verge of the foothills of Ngong, with the American adventurer Peter Beard and his mates living nearby at his primitive Hog Ranch. That was just a short stroll up a bush path where my son Luke was bitten by a night adder.

Peter, always the maverick, first came to Kenya as a teenager in the mid-1960s, by his own admission, 'infatuated with the romance of Africa'. Usually there would be Gilles Turle and his Somali girlfriend resident in the tiny tented village, though he has since moved to Lamu.

Peter had a few habits that could be quite disconcerting, including being an enthusiastic drug user who always seemed to have a joint lit, unless there were magic mushrooms or cocaine available. He had once been married to American supermodel Cheryl Tiegs, and had the reputation of being the lover of many famous women, including Lee Radziwill, sister of Jacqueline Kennedy Onassis. But that was to be expected as there were always lovely girls flitting in and out of his tent on the 45-acre estate which was within walking distance of the grave of Denys Finch Hatton. Those who have read *Out of Africa* will know that this British professional hunter and adventurer was a great comfort to Karen Blixen during difficult times.

Beard's worst excesses came from taking chances, something he did with abandon and which caused quite a few serious injuries, not always to himself. One of our mutual hunting friends, Terry Matthews, took him along on a game viewing trip and was almost terminally gored by a rhino because the hotheaded Beard was showing off in front of his friends. Then he almost copped it. In the mid-1990s, while photographing a herd of elephants on the Tanzanian border, Peter riled a cow elephant that charged.

The American monthly *Vanity Fair* recorded it as follows: 'As she tried to impale him, Beard – attempting to evade her tusks – hung on to her leg. She crushed him with her head, pressing him to the ground and fracturing his pelvis in five places as well as slashing his thigh. Other elephants crowded around, nosing him with their trunks. When Beard arrived at Nairobi Hospital, doctors warned that he was bleeding to death from internal injuries; as he was wheeled into the operating theatre, he had no pulse.

'But, after a long operation to piece his pelvis back together, using an external scaffold pinned to hipbones through the skin, the bleeding was stopped. The most immediate danger became the risk of infection: at the very least, Beard faced weeks in the hospital and up to a year of recovery. As shocking as it was, the news proved less than surprising to Nairobians, who long watched Beard's antics with a mixture of fascination and horror'.

As Terry Mathews said at the time, 'Peter was playing the fool with elephants 20 years ago, back when he was married to Cheryl. Everyone knew he was either going to hurt somebody else or hurt himself. Now he's done it.'

Peter Beard wanted to go into Uganda with me in March 1979, when I mentioned I was going to cover the Tanzanian invasion and, hopefully, the toppling of the crazy Idi Amin. It was a dangerous venture and Amin was eventually ousted, but Beard's often irrational actions had already made him suspect among us hacks so I declined with grateful thanks. Just as well too, because there was no saying how he would have reacted to the presence of 100,000 Tanzanian troops on the rampage.

Kenya in the old days, in contrast, was a marvellous place in which to simply savour the flavour of newly independent Africa.

I'd borrow a car from my old *rafiki* Mohammed Amin and head down to the coast, usually taking a short cut through the Tsavo Game Park. There I'd spend a week or a month diving in the warm waters off Watamu Beach, a stretch of coast that was splendid in its isolation. It was also a favourite of Jack Bloch, another old diving buddy who put Kenya's hotel industry on the map because he had a house there, and often as not we'd dive the Big Three Caves where the groupers were the size of Volkswagen Beetles.

Turtle Bay was safe in those days, in the true sense of the word. You could walk the length of the beach after dark looking for wayward moray eels that would lie on top of the reef at low tide and do so without the fear of being mugged. No longer: these days holiday homes in the region are plundered by the week if left unprotected.

Perhaps South Africa managed to teach Kenya a thing or two after all...

Nairobi was a convenient base from which to cover the rest of Africa. Apartheid had made many enemies for South Africa from the 1960s onwards and it was almost impossible to work in Independent Africa directly from the Republic, unless, of course, you were on the staff of one of the Fleet Street papers, the *New York Times* or one of the American news magazines. British journalist Jim Penrith was hired by the Argus Africa News Service and based there with his lovely South African-born artist wife Tatu for several years.

Peter Younghusband, who taught me a few of his newsroom tricks when we worked together in Cape Town, was on the staff of *Newsweek*, as well as the London *Daily Mail*, and he remained with them for decades. With his British passport, he had no problems. But simpler souls like me had to resort to guile to get our stories, which was why the Kenyan city became so useful to the peripatetic few from 'Down South'.

For a start, there were nightly flights to Nairobi out of Johannesburg – direct and non-stop – but even then passengers from South Africa had to have a reason for disembarking there. Though to be fair, the Kenyans had a solid grasp on the burgeoning tourist trade and did very little to interrupt the flow.

Still, British passport or not, there were times when I was questioned, sometimes with considerable scepticism about my so-called 'actual place of abode'. Which was when I embarked on what I thought was a clever touch of subterfuge.

No questions were asked on arrival at Embakazi Airport – later renamed to commemorate President Jomo Kenyatta – if your journey started in one of the former British Protectorates that included Swaziland, Lesotho and Botswana, and having visited Manzini often enough, I had a number of Swazi stamps in my passport.

After doing a little homework, I was able to persuade somebody in

Johannesburg to make me a set of Swazi immigration stamps – both entry and departure – complete with moveable date facilities. That meant that each time I left the old Transvaal for the north, I would simply stamp my passport with my new-found Swazi imprints and, to my delight, it worked like a charm.

The ruse went on for years, though obviously, were this deception to be blown, I'd have been in serious trouble and would probably have ended up in a Kenyan klink, or even in its notorious Kamiti Maximum Security Prison. In my business you quickly get to know the names of some of the prisons in which you never want to find yourself, and that includes Mugabe's Chikurubi, a hellhole called Black Beach outside Malabo in Equatorial Guinea, or Lagos's Kirikiri, arguably the worst of the lot.

Moving easily within the Kenyan expatriate community, the word eventually got out and there were quite a few Kenyan children at South African schools who would pop into my house to have their passports 'stamped', usually before they were due to return home. This tally included Angela, the delightful daughter of Daphne Sheldrick. The venerable Dame Daphne, as she is known today, still heads the trust named after her late husband David, a remarkable facility which has been a haven for orphaned elephants and rhinos for decades.

From Nairobi, the majority of the foreign correspondents who used the city as a base would shoot off into nearby trouble spots to report on the goings on. I entered Uganda a score of times from there, sometimes by road or small plane charter, occasionally by lake steamer out of Kisumu, but very rarely on commercial flights because Entebbe Airport had more resident government spooks than any other air terminal on the continent.

For much of this time Idi Amin was in control and his personally appointed 'Gestapo' could be ruthless. If a correspondent was even thought to be doing anything out of the ordinary, he or she could be arrested. Indeed, several journalists – including the American Nicholas Stroh as well as two Scandinavian journalists who tried to enter the country illegally across Lake Victoria – were murdered by that dictator's goons. You could hardly miss the bastards with their army-type swagger sticks and non-reflective dark glasses and it could be quite hairy. I deal with Uganda in some detail in Chapter 18.

Other destinations covered during this period included Somalia, though Mogadishu in the pre-revolutionary period was a rather pleasant place, with many of the original colonial trappings that remained behind after Italy had briefly subjugated the country still intact. Italian remained the country's second language for decades after World War II.

Apart from being remarkably laid back, Mogadishu in the old days had a huge expatriate community and much that was good about it, including several restaurants that were outstanding. That was unusual, considering that the Horn of Africa was always regarded as being on the edge of beyond. As any one of my colleagues who visited the place will tell you – out of earshot of his wife – Somali women were always stunning and, as we have seen more recently in many leading fashion magazines, they still are.

Most social activity took place on the city's lagoon where every embassy in the city had a stretch of turf where its nationals would hang out. The American Embassy was situated almost next door to the Russian one. Some were quite primitive, but there were invariably several with parties on the go.

That worked fine for many years until some Somali numbskull opened a camel abattoir a few miles up the coast. It would not have mattered had he not started dumping his offal into the lagoon, which, in turn, attracted every other shark in the Indian Ocean. Attacks became so common off Mogadishu that swimming was banned until the Americans invaded the country in 1992 and curiously, though they were still slaughtering camels up the coast, there were no recorded shark attacks during that brief period.

Communications in Somalia were always a problem, which included the roads with 14-year-olds behind the wheels of Land Rovers and no enforceable speed limit within the city itself. There was one public phone in Mogadishu's only post office in the downtown area, and indeed, it was very public because it had no private booth.

You had to stand in a long line to use it, never mind the throng behind, who could hear your every word.

In the 1960s and 1970s I would sometimes buy a decrepit old Renault-4 in Nairobi, usually for a song, join the Kenyan Automobile Association (to get the necessary carnet documents) and take the road south to Tanzania, Malawi, Zambia and Rhodesia and then onto home.

It was always an adventure, though things could be a little tight in Tanzania, for years officially at war with Mozambique, because *Mwalimu* Julius Nyerere had decided that all the whites in southern Africa had to go. Even though I was British, I still had to tread lightly because the Tanzanian secret police were everywhere.

Of course they knew who I was, and that I lived permanently in South Africa, but I was stringing for various overseas publications at the time including London's *Daily Express*, NBC Radio News as well as *International Defence Review* then headquartered in Geneva, which might be why they let me get on with it. I even formally applied for my visa to enter Biafra in Dar es Salaam, having to edge myself past a bevy of security police who asked a lot of questions in order for me to be able to do so.

Being a diver also helped. Because I'd visit all the famous dive spots up and down the coast, nobody took much notice of those of our ilk, except when I tried to take my diving gear across the frontier between Tanzania and Zambia. You try to explain to a uniformed official wearing a pistol on his belt (and who has probably never even seen the ocean) that this fairly large and heavy steel device in my trunk – a scuba tank, which for the uninitiated looks astonishingly like an aircraft bomb – is something that you actually strap onto your back in order to breathe underwater.

Ultimately, most roads in those faraway days tended to lead to Ian Smith's Rhodesia. Mozambique and Angola were already embroiled in full-scale guerrilla wars and it was only a question of time before hostilities jumped the frontier into what had previously been known as Southern Rhodesia.

Unlike most other African states then suffering many of the 'growing pains' that followed *Uhuru*, Rhodesia was a remarkably pleasant place, either for a vacation or to buy a house and live permanently.

War or no war, tourists couldn't keep away, which is understandable because the country had some of the best game parks on the continent, as well as the magnificent Victoria Falls and Lake Kariba. But then things only started to go off-kilter after the insurgents started planting mines in otherwise sacrosanct wildlife reserves like Wankie (Hwange today), Mana Pools and Gonarezhou.

Of all the foreign correspondent postings, Rhodesia was considered among the best. Accommodation and the cost of living were cheap, while locally resident journalists usually made a point of employing strings of servants which invariably included a cook, housekeeper, babysitters and a gardener, coupled to reasonably cheap liquor (even if some of it was 'home-grown'). Most importantly, the comms were good: You could lift the phone and call just about anywhere on the planet. To the majority of news folk posted there, you couldn't ask for better, even if some of these illustrious characters ended up, literally, drinking themselves into early graves.

Having come from all over the world to report, there was no question that this was a most unusual bunch, the majority outspokenly for the underdog and not afraid to say so, even though some were deported for taking too strong an approach. There is no question, in the words of another great British commentator Bill Deedes, that were Evelyn Waugh alive today and set his delightful satire on news gathering in Africa in this former British colony – instead of in pre-War Abyssinia – quite a few of them would have been appropriately featured in *Scoop*.

Salisbury, always a beautiful place, remained almost untouched by conflict throughout the war, though you could hardly miss legions of young soldiers in the streets, clubs and bars, nor the constant movement of helicopter gunships and other military aircraft flying across the city most times of the day.

To paraphrase the old aphorism, Rhodesia in its gloriously reckless heyday was, as some old timers like to recollect, the best of places. It was also the worst of times and attracted its share of oddballs. For the duration of this guerrilla struggle that ended with Britain handing the country to Robert Mugabe – a man who was to become the tyrant of his age – the country was a magnet for freebooting mercenaries from just about every country on the planet. There were even a few Seychellois troops fighting in the Rhodesian Light Infantry.

The American magazine *Soldier of Fortune* was also there and though I earned my crust working for a bunch of South African publications, I quietly got myself onto the masthead of this publication that covered just about every conflict to which access was allowed (or even disallowed). In fact, once I had made my mark, I went on to cover wars in other parts of Africa, the Middle East and even El Salvador. In the end, I earned enough hard cash from the proceeds largely of *Soldier of Fortune*, to build a rather lovely home for the family in Noordhoek in the Cape.

In Rhodesia, we mostly operated singly, or if there were any Yanks in the party, it would sometimes be in groups, invariably led by Colonel Robert K. Brown – owner, editor and publisher of *Soldier of Fortune*. He had served two tours of duty in Vietnam and his most distinctive feature was that he was almost as deaf as I am.

Others would follow in consort: characters such as 'Big John' Donovan, a reserve major and demolitions expert in the US Army, 'Fat' Ralph Edens, Dave McGrady (who afterwards graduated as a mercenary fighting for the Israeli cause in South Lebanon) as well as

Dana Drenkowski, a former United States Air Force pilot who had flown 200 missions over Vietnam in B-52 bombers and F-4 Phantoms. In Rhodesia, Dana spent a lot of the time at the Sharp End looking for what he termed were 'gooks'. That was before he became the only American ever hired as a mercenary by Libya's Muammar Gadaffi. Another famous Vietnam vet was Bob Boos, erstwhile editor of the magazine.

I devoted a chapter to Dana's adventures after he had been hired as a mercenary by Gadaffi in *War Dog*, among the most interesting of all my books. What was astonishing was that he had survived that episode, and against incredible odds. These days Dana works as a district attorney in California. It takes all kinds…

Soldier of Fortune's Bob Brown – for whom Dana also worked occasionally – was the original manipulator of circumstances, governments and those he came into contact with in any 'operational area', Rhodesia's included. He made no secret of the fact that he followed his own brand of what he liked to call 'participatory journalism'.

A lot of his effort went into creating counters – some of them quite outrageous – to radical causes. Brown either personally led 'unofficial' combat groups of his own people into these frays (it is against American law, curiously, for Americans to fight in foreign wars) or independently, he would send them into places like Afghanistan, the Sudan, El Salvador, Uganda, Rhodesia, Angola, the Congo, Lebanon, Mozambique, Burma, Laos, Chad, Nicaragua, Sierra Leone, Israel, Croatia, as well as a good few others that he'd rather I didn't write about.

From the late 1960s on, I spent almost as much time covering security developments in Rhodesia as I did with the Portuguese Army in Angola, Mozambique and Portuguese Guinea (or what the geography books today refer to as Guiné-Bissau). These were exhilarating times and though we weren't shot at all that much, we had our moments.

The biggest single problem we all faced was landmines. Travelling on gravel roads that only days before (or shortly afterwards) claimed their share of victims from Soviet TM-46 and TM-57 anti-tank mines that had been laid by the insurgents was never a pleasure. Nor were grim pictures of farmers, their families and innocent black civilians who had accidentally tripped them. And though we saw our share of vehicles blasted to scrap, let's just say we were lucky.

And we must have been, because we were to hear afterwards from those with whom we sometimes stayed along the way that after we'd driven off, a mine or two would be lifted along the self-same road we'd covered in order to move on to the next position.

On two occasions, years apart, the guerrillas – aware that there was a media presence at a nearby military base – tried to plant anti-tank mines along the roads we were to take the following morning. Both times, while inserting detonators, the mines exploded, causing human entrails to be splayed in a wide swathe across some of the trees nearby. It was both gory and sobering but the immediate lesson was that there is an inordinate length of intestines inside every one of us…

No reasons for these 'accidents' were ever given, though the word, years later, was that our old friend Colonel Ron Reid-Daly had possibly done the dirty. Most times he'd have some of his men 'doctor' ammunition caches that had been fingered by insurgents captured in battle. By Uncle Ron's own admission, the duties of his Scouts included destabilising the detonators of some of the mines uncovered in these weapon searches.

As he would explain, they would be 'tampered with' and the cache carefully covered again so that the guerrilla group replenishing supplies would not be aware that Rhodesia's Security Forces had been anywhere near the place.

CHAPTER ONE

IN SEARCH OF DOCTOR ALBERT SCHWEITZER

> Who can describe the injustice and cruelties that in the course of centuries they [the coloured peoples] have suffered at the hands of Europeans? ... If a record could be compiled of all that has happened between the white and the coloured races, it would make a book containing numbers of pages which the reader would have to turn over unread because their contents would be too horrible.
>
> Dr Albert Schweitzer

I was young, twenty-something and on my way to Europe. My route was overland, through Africa, all the way up the west coast to Dakar in Senegal.

Dr Albert Schweitzer – already on the 'Dark Continent' for decades – had been little more than a name to most youngsters of my generation. It had a familiarity about it of course, like Dr Spock or Carnaby Street.

I knew enough about *le grand docteur* – as they reverentially referred to him up and down this stretch of tropical jungle – to be aware that getting taken in at the hospital at Lambaréné for more than an overnight stay might be problematic. Simply put, the old man didn't like journalists and for good reason. For decades the literary world had harboured his harshest critics because of his supposed racial bias towards black people. Yet, the quotation above speaks for itself.

At the same time, everybody acknowledged that for all his real or imagined faults, this was a truly remarkable individual, one of the great minds of the 20th Century.

Born in 1875 in what was then still part of Imperial Germany, Dr Albert Schweitzer was first a German and then a French theologian,

The author went back to Lambaréné several times, the first occasion on his four-month trek through West Africa to London where he met the great man and spent time at his jungle hospital. On his departure, Dr Schweitzer inscribed a picture with the words, in German (and now badly faded): *Herr Albert Venter ... Gedenks ... in die Dezembertage, 1964 in Lambaréné ... Albert Schweitzer. 9 Dezember 1964.*

organist, philosopher, physician, and medical missionary. He was internationally recognised as an authority on Bach and his music, which he played at concert level.

In 1905, at the age of 30, he answered the call of The Society of The Evangelist Missions of Paris, a support group looking for a medical doctor to fill a position in Equatorial Africa. However, the committee of this French missionary society had its own ideas about who should go to Africa and told the aspirant that it was not ready to accept his offer. Basically, they considered Schweitzer's Lutheran theology to be 'incorrect'.

Amid a hail of protests from his friends, family and colleagues, the still young Schweitzer resigned and re-entered university as a student in a punishing seven-year course towards the degree of a doctorate in medicine, a subject in which he had little knowledge or previous aptitude. His rationale for this action was that he planned to 'spread the Gospel' by the example of his Christian labour of healing, rather than through the verbal process of preaching. He implicitly believed that this service should be acceptable within any branch of Christian teaching and he wasn't afraid to say as much to anybody who would listen.

Clearly, he was already recognised by many of his peers as a thinker. His credo for doing what he intended is fundamental and has been quoted often enough: 'You must give some time to your fellow men. Even if it's a little thing, do something for others – something for which you get no pay but simply the privilege of doing it.'

In 1912, armed with a medical degree, Schweitzer made a definite proposal to go as a medical doctor to work at his own expense at the mission station run by the Paris Missionary Society at Lambaréné. The tiny jungle village lay on the Ogoué (on some maps, the Ogooué) River, in what is today the African state of Gabon, then a French colony. But for that purpose he needed money, and by a series of concerts – he was already famous both for his Bach renditions and for his writing on the German composer, coupled to other fund-raising efforts – he was ready to equip a small hospital on a continent he had not yet set foot on.

In the spring of 1913, Dr Albert Schweitzer and his wife Helene set off by ship to West Africa. There was a coaling stop at Dakar and the next port of call, still more than a week away, was Port Gentil, today a major oil terminal. Still ahead lay a long river journey into one of the densest jungles on the planet with Lambaréné at the end of it. But that was more than 350 kilometres upstream, or roughly 14 days by raft.

An interesting bit of literary history is that Lambaréné has always been linked to the legendary Tarzan. Legend has it that Schweitzer's hospital on the Ogoué River was just northeast of the Greystoke cabin where, it was said, the original Tarzan was born. We've even had a book written about it by Marshall and Polling. Their biography provides us with amazing details which established the existence of a notorious cannibal tribe that locals will tell you today still survive in the remote interior.

During the course of Schweitzer's first nine months at his new posting, news of his medical prowess quickly spread. Up and down the river and as far south even as Brazzaville people were coming to him. He and his wife were soon inundated by patients, more than 2,000 of them in the first year – many of whom had travelled days, sometimes a week by dugout pirogues to reach the mission hospital. Throughout this period Helene Schweitzer was the only anaesthetist for surgical procedures that took place, and there were many. For this she used chloroform and papaveretum, a synthesized morphine derivative.

The rough-hewn wooden structures, in which the Schweitzers worked, alongside the fast-flowing Ogoué, are still there today and underscore the primitive conditions this couple faced. After briefly occupying a shed, formerly used as a chicken hut, they built their first hospital of corrugated iron, with two three-metre rooms used for consulting and surgery and additional adjacent dispensary and sterilising rooms.

Many of the structures, including the wards, were built on higher ground away from the river. These were all modelled on native huts of the region and comprised rough, partially trimmed logs. In those days – and during my first visit in 1964 – all these buildings were partially open to the elements and almost all faced a 50-metre path that led from the hospital to the river landing-place.

To the untrained eye, conditions were harsh. The only toilets available to patients and staff were a series of 'long drops' adjacent to the main path. In truth, it was primitive but it worked, which was just as well because there was no money for anything else, though that didn't stop him from being castigated in the European and American press for resorting to 'unsanitary' ablution facilities.

Undeterred by media attacks, he told a visitor to the hospital that his little corner of Lambaréné was a gathering place of people that needed help. Moreover, he said, nobody who came there had to live in a world all alone. 'Your brothers are here to help you.'

The great man had many notable qualities, but he probably loved his music most. This was something all of us who spent any time at Lambaréné were able to share.

Visitors who arrived at that cluster of musty, moss and fungus-covered, makeshift buildings on the banks of a great tropical river that most people have never heard about, would have sat through his modest solo performances almost every night after dinner. Plates would be put aside after the meal and we would be transfixed, often for an hour, as he played at what looked like the world's oldest foot-pedalled organ. Bach would compete with the noises of the African night and nearby mutterings from the cramped old wards stuffed with the diseased and the dying.

These were no concert performances and you didn't clap your hands when they were over. You sat in awe, almost prayer-like until he was done. Then you were thankful you were able to experience such an uplifting offering in one of the most unlikely environments. To this grand old man, his music was a form of prayer and he would say as much if asked.

One has to bear in mind that Bach, to the impatient generation of the 1960s, was a buzzword. To Albert Schweitzer it was a form of escape, and for good reason. Though only a simple medical man at heart, to the world outside he was supposed to be the greatest living example of someone who had dedicated his life to helping those less fortunate: Mother Theresa came afterwards. But even then, this man – driven by an inordinate reverence for life – could be bluff, even offhand sometimes to those he didn't know and he consequently had many detractors. What was always obvious was that he had little time for fools or idle chatter.

The problem in 1965, basically, was that in Africa, *egalite* – equality with its strong, unspoken racial overtones – had overnight become the shibboleth. A rather primitive hospital catering exclusively to uneducated people from the forest was never intended to be an enlightened version of some casualty ward back home.

Patients were brought to Lambaréné by their families, usually in the most basic of circumstances. Most would arrive in their home-made canoes paddled by male relatives because very few locals could afford a taxi, of which there was only a handful in any event in Gabon in the early days. Few dugouts even had outboards, and most used muscle to get about.

Once at the hospital, the tradition – developed over time, because Lambaréné never had the money or the staff to do otherwise – was that the patient was always encouraged to be accompanied by other members of the family who would share the load and cook, nurse or clean. It was a system that worked very well: the sick and the dying were tended by people they knew and loved in a primeval environment that was familiar to all.

I watched several of these entourages arrive, a canoe or two loaded to the gunwales with everything, often including a bicycle. There would be chickens, yams, the occasional gutted forest pig and bananas, inevitably, bunches of them and often a metre high. Somewhere among the utensils, beer and dirty rags that passed for clothing, there was something for the grand old man; pathetic offerings from a people who had just about nothing. These gifts were always made much of when they arrived, if not by either of the Schweitzers, then by members of his staff.

The doctor himself, invariably preoccupied with administrative matters and seated at his desk opposite the little gauze-covered window that kept out the insects, would see the newcomers approach, usually a low-slung speck on the water, distinguished by a succession of flailing arms.

A call would go out to his factotum, a Swiss woman volunteer by the name of Ali Singer, who must have spent half a century at Lambaréné and who is today buried in the little cemetery within yards of the man she served for so long. She, together with a somewhat stooped Schweitzer, would cross those few open metres of riverside to the landing to see what fate had brought them.

A single glance could usually tell whether there was hope. Without exception, every single patient was helped – or, more often than not, carried – up the rickety old wooden steps to the clinic and given the once-over by the old man, a tradition that was inviolate. To some it also seemed to be a curious start to therapy.

To be sure, by the time anybody arrived at Lambaréné from a jungle village a couple of days' hard push up or down the river, he or she would have exhausted every elixir that the local witchdoctor could pull out of his woven grass bag. Schweitzer, in these primitive regions, was usually the last resort. With blackwater fever, elephantiasis, malaria or syphilis – and, who knows, some early variations of Ebola that in those days would have slipped past medical science because Gabon was on the edge of the beyond – it was often too late.

No matter, Schweitzer the 'modern' medical man was meticulous. He would press and prod and peer and ask his questions, either in his heavily accented French or through an interpreter. Only then would he decide what to do next. If surgery was necessary, he wouldn't wait until the next day. He was the first to acknowledge that Africa can be unforgiving, and often the patient was cut open there and then and the tumour or whatever removed.

It was at such times that he might turn to somebody who had recently arrived from abroad to report on conditions at the jungle clinic, and offer a comment about making your own conditions for survival because there was nobody else to make them for you. As he said to one such visitor: 'It is necessary to grow into your ideals, so that life cannot rob you of them.'

The afternoon that I arrived, I had been preceded by half a dozen victims of a fairly serious road accident. Two members of their party had been killed and almost all the survivors – about six or eight of them – were drunk.

No, they told the *Gendarmerie* when they were ferried across town, they didn't want to go to the spanking new government hospital on the hill that overlooked Lambaréné town. They demanded to be taken to the old man. His services were free, weren't they? It was all bluster…

When this raucous, bleeding mass beached at Lambaréné, Schweitzer and *Mademoiselle* were waiting and the two Europeans did what they could for the injured before they packed them off. These people were government functionaries, he remonstrated and they could pay. Anyway, he added, his equatorial hospital was for other sorts of people and wasn't to be exploited. They should have known better, he added as an afterthought. Schweitzer was nobody's fool. But he was of the old school and that wasn't the way to win friends in an emerging, increasingly politically correct Africa.

To visitors, the Lambaréné mission clinic seemed to work well enough, but in other respects, it appeared to be barely functional.

The only running water seemed to come from a stream that flowed past the wards and was used to shift effluent, human or otherwise, into the river. Since then, of course, things have improved, but the water that you drink is still filtered in the old way, in a jug with a sieve, as it had always been in Africa before independence and, frankly, we weren't any the worse for it. Evian water in the more distant, darker reaches of the triple-tiered rainforest was unheard of in those distant days.

Our loos, like those of the patients, were perched on a hill adjacent to the bungalows. If you could focus through the hole in the bottom of the toilet, it was just possible to see nature – in the form of several million crawling maggots – deal with human waste the way it has done since time began.

To a first-timer, it was a bizarre experience and there were many visitors from our civilised world who were repulsed. Albert Schweitzer's primitive (but effective) crap houses were featured in a lot of glossy magazines, but as he himself was quoted often enough when questioned about them, 'there is always the bush, if you prefer…'

He was an individual of few words. A lot of folk who met him briefly but didn't have the time or patience to understand his foibles, thought him insufferable. My parting question to him on leaving Lamberéné late in 1964 was whether he had any regrets about the way he'd conducted his life, having survived 90 years and two world wars on this tormented planet.

He looked me straight in the eye and replied: 'Regrets are not something that I begin to consider. Nor have I ever. If I make a mistake, or if I take the wrong road, then I make sure that I don't do it again.'

To which he added moments later, 'and perhaps that is something that you yourself should consider, my young friend.'

Schweitzer was almost 80 when the famous British journalist James Cameron visited Lambaréné in 1953 and he was heard to comment about what he termed were 'significant flaws in the practices and attitudes of Schweitzer and his staff'. Cameron is on record as stating that the hospital suffered from squalor and was without modern amenities, and that Schweitzer had little contact with the local people.

Curiously Cameron never made public what he had seen at the time and according to a subsequent BBC dramatisation of the visit, he made the unusual journalistic decision to withhold the story. For personal reasons, or possibly because James Cameron viewed what was going on at Lambaréné in its broader human context – of lives being saved and people helped, with absolutely nothing being asked in return – he resisted the expressed wish of his employers to run an exposé aimed at debunking Schweitzer.

The American journalist John Gunther also visited Lambaréné in the 1950s and he was a little less circumspect. Gunther made a point of reporting what he termed 'Dr Schweitzer's patronising attitude towards black people'. He also noted the lack of Africans trained to be skilled workers.

After three decades in Africa, Gunther said that Schweitzer still depended on Europe for nurses, but what he did not disclose was that all those trained medical personnel gave their services for free, whereas any local Gabonaise taken on would, as a matter of course, have to be paid. Nor was there any mention of Schweitzer's constant battle, throughout his stay in Africa, to balance the books. There were always donations coming in – millions of dollars over decades, but the hospital grew substantially in size in this time and tended to the needs of thousands of people each year *for free*.

Almost every patient needed some form of medication and all that cost money...

Getting to Lambaréné in the old days was not easy. These days a morning flight will take you from Libreville, the capital, to a tiny airport on the primeval outskirts of this town.

You can also reach Lambaréné by road, but that sometimes means jousting with logging trucks whose drivers might be drunk or just bored enough to force you off the road for a bit of fun.

The first time I did the trip I went by boat from Port Gentil, at that stage a quiet backwater where ships bobbed at anchor in the roadstead. We were plagued by market mammies in dugouts and snakes on floating islands that drifted past on the water on their way to the open sea. Then it was a logging port and most of the houses that lined the waterfront were quaintly French Colonial. These days Port Gentil is to be avoided. It is a brash, expensive place and the accents are mostly phony American, which, it seems, comes from shipping oil wherever such activity takes place.

The boat that took me upstream in 1964 had probably been built by some French concessionaire at the turn of the century. It was low-slung and sluggish against the powerful current and possibly 25 metres long. More than a hundred of us were cramped into whatever space we could find. We shared that with baggage and such domestic animals as those who had crossed palms with low-denomination CFA francs could smuggle aboard. It was a harsh journey with no privacy and lots of jostle, noise and enough children to populate an orphanage.

Considering the privations – you squatted over the stern to relieve yourself – conditions weren't too bad. I travelled on the roof for much of the trip except when it rained, which was often.

What got me in the end was what many West African people call stinkfish, an everyday delight in places like Gabon, Nigeria, Ghana and elsewhere and frankly, the name says it all. Technically it is a form of salted, dried fish-biltong or jerky, only the climate is far too hot and muggy to allow it to cure properly. The result is a malodorous, festering *bonne bouche* that the only other European on board, a Peace Corps volunteer on vacation from Niger, confided would more than likely result in instant hepatitis B or typhoid.

I've seen stinkfish often enough since, quite often in some of the markets along the coast, but never again without gagging. On the boat, just about every square inch was stuffed with it. The stench, repugnant and nauseating, stayed with me for weeks.

Albert Schweitzer was the source of a great many legends and anecdotes, some kind, others unflattering. The most memorable was brought to my attention while I was at Lambaréné and centred on the keynote of Schweitzer's personal philosophy which was the idea of reverence for life, or in his own language *Ehrfurcht vor dem Leben*.

It took some years to emerge, but Schweitzer – viewing the carnage that resulted from the wars that blighted his life – strongly believed that Western civilisation was decaying. It had abandoned affirmation of (and respect for) life as its ethical foundation, he would declare.

Above all, as his biographers tell us, Schweitzer was a dedicated student of Christianity, though curiously, never a proselytiser. His *Quest for the Historical Jesus* remains a good seller throughout the West: now into its umpteenth edition. So too, with his *The Mysticysm of Paul the Apostle*. In these difficult times it is important to accept that what Albert Schweitzer had to say is as profoundly important in today's crazy times as it was when these pronouncements were made in the early part of the last century.

I was to see a very practical example of this reverence for life – *all life*, including all of God's creatures. We walked together to the leprosarium that had been built deep in the jungle some distance away from the main complex by a bunch of Japanese volunteer doctors. If the clinic and its accoutrements were primordial, this facility that cared for people suffering from leprosy was primitive in the extreme.

Along the way the old man suddenly stopped and indicated that I should do so as well. Then he pointed at a procession of army ants that had formed a lengthy column alongside and across the jungle path. In almost military style they were moving in line ahead.

'Be careful how you tread,' he warned in German ... 'we don't want to harm them in any way.' With that he stepped gingerly over the thin red line of ants.

Ethics, too, he is quoted as saying, are nothing but reverence for life. 'That is what gives me the fundamental principle of morality, namely, that good consists in maintaining, promoting and enhancing life, and that destroying, injuring, and limiting life are evil.'

More important, Albert Schweitzer was the first of the great religious 'caregivers', followed soon after by Mother Theresa. It says a lot that they were both awarded the Nobel Prize.

There was a lot more to Schweitzer than his primitive jungle hospital on the banks of the Ogoué River. All the original infrastructure is still there, though the old makeshift wooden structures by the river – together with his little clinic with its gauze windows (no glass in this jungle, except in the theatre) – have given way to a more modern edifice on the hill behind. He would sit contemplatively in his tiny study from where he was in a good position to watch pirogues arrive and issue instructions about what was to be done with the patients being brought in. Most times he attended to them personally.

There was one incident where he was moving some equipment and needed a hand. So he asked a man passing by to help, but was rebuffed with the comment that 'I am an intellectual *m'sieu* ... I don't do physical labour.' To which Schweitzer replied 'You are very fortunate, my friend. I have tried all my life to be an intellectual and I've never really succeeded ...'

Perhaps the most vicious barb aimed at Dr Albert Schweitzer while he worked at Lambaréné, was that he was a closet racist.

He was sometimes accused of being paternalistic or colonialist in his attitude towards Africans, and in some ways, his views did differ from that of many liberals and some of the more vociferous critics of colonialism. For instance, he implicitly believed that Gabon's independence from France had come too early. He pointed to the fact that the new African nation had been launched without adequate education or consideration of local circumstances.

One of the better-known Schweitzer quotes spoke along those lines in 1960, stating that 'no society can go from the primeval directly to an industrial state without losing the basic leavening that time and an agricultural period allow'.

The late Nigerian writer Chinua Achebe quoted Schweitzer as saying: 'The African is indeed my brother but my junior brother,' which resulted in criticism from Achebe, even though he acknowledged that Schweitzer's use of the word 'brother' at all was, for a European of the early 20th Century, an unusual expression of human solidarity between whites and blacks.

The fact is, as I was to observe during the week that I stayed at Lambaréné, Dr Albert Schweitzer was thrust into the vortex of the same kind of 'Heart of Darkness' that Joseph Conrad wrote about, only this was among the most unsophisticated – yet extremely complex – regions anywhere on earth, especially when compared to the continent on which he was born.

Schweitzer would almost certainly have regarded it an affront to have to justify his motives beyond the spiritual. And to this end, you need to carefully weigh his dictum: 'I consider my work as a medical missionary in Africa to be my response to Jesus' call to become "fishers of men", but also as a small recompense for the historic guilt of European colonisers.' That comment, simple and direct, can hardly be regarded as coming from a man who had been labelled racist.

The principle that Dr Albert Schweitzer did hold high was the belief – implicit and deep-seated – that present-day culture tends to divide people into two classes, and I quote: '… civilised men, a title bestowed on the persons who do the classifying; and others, who have only the human form, who may perish or go to the dogs for all that "civilised men" care.

'Oh, this "noble" culture of ours! It speaks so piously of human dignity and human rights and then disregards this dignity and these rights of countless millions and treads them underfoot, only because … their skins are of different colour or because they cannot help themselves. This culture does not know how hollow and miserable and full of glib talk it is, how common it looks to those who follow it across the seas and see what it has done there, and this culture has no right to speak of personal dignity and human rights …

'I will not enumerate all the crimes that have been committed under the pretext of justice. People robbed native inhabitants of their land, made slaves of them, let loose the scum of mankind upon them. Think of the atrocities that were perpetrated upon people made subservient to us, how systematically we have ruined them with our alcoholic "gifts", and everything else we have done … we decimate them, and then, by the stroke of a pen, we take their land so they have nothing left at all …'

As he said in the closing years of his life: 'A man does not have to be an angel in order to be a saint.'

Postscript: I went back to Lambaréné one final time a little more than 20 years ago to make a film on both the hospital and *le grand docteur*, long deceased, but very much alive in the minds of everybody in this still remote jungle outpost. This time I took my teenage son Luke and it was an experience for us both.

We stayed briefly in a rather posh hotel in Libreville, the capital, and found both the French Army and Israeli security personnel very much in evidence around the central city area where Gabon's president has his well-fortified and walled palace. Then, having hired a taxi and a driver, we set off along a fairly good, but unsurfaced road for Lambaréné, and we were almost all killed when our chauffeur overtook a logging truck at great speed in the face of another big vehicle coming from the opposite direction. At the very last moment, both trucks made a little space for us and we squeezed through.

There might have been inches to spare. I told the man at the wheel to pull over and promptly took over all our driving responsibilities. *C'est l'Afrique* …

Lambaréné in the late 1980s had changed little from my earlier visits. The leprosarium had gone, thanks to modern drugs, and a spanking new hospital, with modern surgical, x-ray and other space-age facilities had been erected on higher ground a couple of hundred metres from the river, though many patients, with their families in attendance, were still billeted in open wards.

We were welcomed cordially enough by two of the hospital's senior administrators, one of French extraction and the other, an American, but it was clear that strangers like a visiting film team were not welcome to stay, like in the old days. So, for the duration, we decamped to the town itself and stayed in the modest but comfortable Hotel Albert Schweitzer.

In the town itself, things were still very much as they had been in the past, with evidence of more river traffic than before, though the pirogues were all fitted with modern outboards that allowed them to move at speed against the current. Gabon's oil reserves had caused other changes and this resulted in a fairly affluent societal cross current, larger and more modern homes and more new cars than in most other African countries.

Not unexpectedly, there were more snakes around than we thought possible, considering the town was quite a busy little trading centre. They were everywhere we walked; in the grass alongside the hotel, lying alongside culverts on the roads around town and in the approaches to the river. Local people ignored them, which must sometimes have been difficult because some of these reptiles were more than three metres long, and I was told, deadly poisonous. Who knows how many people die of snakebite along this stretch of river each year?

Having made our movie, we decided to head back to civilisation on the river and though it involved a bit of haggling, we eventually paid the master of a dilapidated old oil barge to take us on board for the day-long run to Libreville. The barge was basic – there were no cabins, no ablution facilities, no nothing, with only a wheelhouse over the head of the helmsman. We took our own food and sat on the open deck all the way to the sea.

It was one of the most exhilarating experiences of Luke's life – all of our lives, in fact – watching the jungle that hung over the water like a gigantic green curtain slip by and simply imagining the creatures that inhabited this incredibly verdant stretch of real estate.

Judging solely by the sounds that echoed back at us from the darker depths of the interior, there must have been a lot of animals because their calls were constant: birds, monkeys, chimps, elephants and the rest. Curiously, though we never saw one, there must also have been a lot of hippo, but they remained elusive for the duration.

I took a photo of the river as the sun dipped over the horizon at sunset and, once developed, the picture that emerged was like one of those images from early paintings left behind by the explorers of another epoch. It was quite beautiful and I ended up using it on the cover of one of the great books to emerge from that era, Chris Munnion's *Banana Sunday*[1]. As the Africa correspondent for London's *Daily Telegraph*, Munnion covered this beat, and more's the pity that his book is no longer in print.

Chris, dear fellow that he was, has gone on the long walk, but the river is still there, and for those with more than a modicum of an adventurous spirit, this is one of the great African experiences still awaiting.

And it is cheap too: the river journey cost the four of us only $100, but don't expect anybody at Schweitzer's old hospital to accord you any kind of welcome, not unless you arrive with a wallet stuffed with cash.

1 Chris Munnion, *Banana Sunday*, Ashanti Publishing, Rivonia, South Africa, 1992.

CHAPTER TWO

ANGOLA'S TANK BATTLE ON THE LOMBA

DAVID MANNALL TELLS US HOW SOUTH AFRICAN ARMOURED VEHICLES KNOCKED OUT SOVIET TANKS

'... a series of bitter fights in South Angola – known as the Battle of the Lomba River – took place between 9 September and 7 October 1987 ... SADF and UNITA forces prevented the Angolan Army (FAPLA) – which had already suffered heavy losses – from crossing the river. The Soviets withdrew their advisors and left (what remained) the Angolan Army without senior leadership. By 29 September the South Africans had gained the advantage and launched Operation Modular, a significant armoured offensive. Four days later – on the southern bank of the Lomba River near Mavinga – they attacked and totally annihilated a FAPLA armoured battalion.'

From 'The Battle for Cuito Cuanavale': Wikipedia, the free encyclopaedia

A maxim coined by Winston Churchill during the Boer War: 'The most exhilarating experience in the world,' Churchill said, 'is to be fired at with no effect,' to which Colonel Robert K. Brown, owner and editor of *Soldier of Fortune* magazine, added '... and to fire back.'

That day, 3 October, would end like no other during our operational tour of Angola in 1987. What the Wiki website did not say, was that following several hours of hard fighting – in which a couple dozen Angolan tanks were destroyed – the enemy fled. Government soldiers abandoned their armour, vehicles, BM-21 rocket launchers, artillery and, as they left the battlefield, many discarded their uniforms and dumped their AKs into the river. Some battle!

Clockwise from right : First pass home after 'basic training', my uniform looking as fresh as me. More confident, now 90 mm gunner and qualified armoured car driver, proudly sporting School of Armour flashes. Long hair courtesy of time in 'The Bush', happy to be home on the day conscription ended and the war within began.

Known as 'Operation Modular', we were awake by three in the morning. Our weapons, vehicles and personnel were all battle-readied for what we'd been told was likely to be a pretty significant contact with the Angolan Army. The last time we'd engaged that same Angolan brigade – a contact that lasted about an hour – their combat ability hadn't been regarded as much of a threat to us, either by guys on the ground or our commanders towards the rear.

Sure they'd lobbed grenades and RPGs, and yes, there'd been one fatality on our side – which happened because the infantry boys had been deployed alongside our vehicles, and we all knew that humans make for soft targets, but that was about it. What I wasn't aware of when we started out on 3 October, was that by the end of that day, we'd have ended up killing or wounding a very substantial number of the enemy.

As before, as with every previously planned engagement – which was largely ranged against FAPLA government forces – I liked to ensure that my boots, socks, underwear, tank-suit and the rest were all 'super' clean. It was very much a personal matter. As my mother always said – 'if you have an accident, it would be nice when you got to hospital for the nurses not to have to undress a dirty you.'

At the same time, I had absolutely no intention of pegging-off, even though each one of us accepted that there would be casualties. We'd been warned that it would be no ordinary skirmish: indeed, we'd been hurled into a grim and proper war and an awful lot of people were getting killed, even if there were something like 15 or 20 times more of their soldiers dying than our own. Obviously, the stakes were high.

But I'm running ahead of myself. I should mention that in those far-off days, I was a pretty laid-back guy. That said, I took no chances when preparing for battle. As a section leader, others would rely on the decisions I made, which made me uncomfortably aware that were I to get it wrong, I'd have to live with the consequences, especially if one of our own guys were to get into trouble.

Our tactics were all pretty basic. My vehicle was part of a squadron of a dozen Ratel infantry fighting vehicles (IFVs) that included two command cars – my own and one other – and my call-sign was Three Two Alpha (32A). As a group, we were labelled Charlie Squadron and our emblem, proudly emblazoned on the frame of each vehicle, was a clenched black fist, clutching a bolt of lightning.

Roughly two hours before dawn, all dozen vehicle commanders checked communications and confirmed battle readiness. Then, abruptly, an order came down the radio-net: 'All vehicles start.' There was a surge of emotion as I realised we'd moved one more step closer to engagement.

I passed the order down to David our driver and he hit the starter. The powerful ten-litre turbo-charged engine – the Ratel's is housed in its own protective steel cocoon just three metres behind where I was positioned – switch-kicked into action. Within moments the forest around me burst into a cacophony of deep rumbling roars as hydraulic systems kicked in.

Then, the order: 'Charlie Squadron, move out'. I relayed the instruction to my crew: 'OK, guys, we're underway ... let's go.'

After two months in an extremely active combat zone, we'd all become a pretty well-oiled fighting unit, though I hadn't worked continually with the same people all year round, because some of the guys with whom we'd trained had been replaced. Others had become ill or moved on during our time in the operational area, colloquially known as 'the border': thus, the Border War.

It was no secret that my driver, an extremely capable lad, had arrived into my charge not exactly enthusiastic for what lay ahead. He wasted little time in demonstrating abhorrence for just about everything military. In fact, he despised the army and, as with quite a few of the conscripts, hated its impersonal, intrusive and multifarious authority. But as second-in-command of the little troop of four Ratels that made up our section, they took their orders – as relayed down the line – from me.

Our gunner Herbert Zeelie – whom everybody knew as Herb – was an equally remarkable fellow. He had been one of the least *paraat* or disciplined members of the unit during our training phase. But with some additional coaching since he'd joined my crew, he'd already proved himself more than capable, responding promptly and unquestioningly to orders. That day, as I was to discover, he would demonstrate bravery and accuracy many times in the heat of battle, which was a lot more than could be said for those across the line who opposed us.

As planned, Charlie Squadron was at the head of the battle group that went into contact. The ghostly green shadows that appeared on our NVGs, or, more appropriately, night-vision goggles, initially offered only sketchy, speckled images of the world around us, at least until our eyes adjusted to their use. But I could clearly make out the protective steel casing of the IFV ahead, always by the single tiny

From left: Final preparation before crossing into Angola. Call-sign 33 won't come back. We found a speedy tyre replacement service deep in Angola. However, I would've needed six of those monster run-flat tyres after 3 October, had my vehicle still been serviceable.

penlight perched precariously on its rear. I could also distinguish trees and other potential hazards, though I had to adjust to what was still a very new dimension.

The first time we were issued with those sophisticated NVGs I was astonished at the amount of detail they displayed, sometimes in total darkness. Indeed, they magnified so much light that if someone dragged on a cigarette 20 paces away, it was as though they'd switched on a torch or even used a cigarette lighter. The luminosity that resulted would sometimes temporarily blind me, so I couldn't imagine going into battle wearing goggles because the muzzle-flash from a 90 mm cannon would spew flames two-metres deep on either side of the gun. Bang, and with a set of NVGs in place, you're blinded!

Nonetheless, cumbersome as they were, night-vision goggles were the best means of 'safely' navigating some of the heavily forested regions of south-eastern Angola after the moon had disappeared over the horizon before dawn. Headlights simply weren't an option: the enemy would in any event hear us coming and if we offered them an option of being able to spot our lights, they would be able to range their shots. There was no question that they were aware of our presence because they could hardly miss the noise our engines made. And let's face it, it was uncomfortable knowing that there would be a massive force awaiting our arrival, guns primed.

As if in a choreographed ballet sequence, the squadron moved out in echelon, our advance marked by the distinctive high-pitch whine of the turbochargers spooling up to assist in-line six-cylinder engines that pushed our 20-ton armoured beasts through the soft African soil.

By then I was in my usual position on board the IFV, standing on my crew commander seat, waist and upper body protruding out of the turret and going through the usual preparatory drills. This was also a time for communicating with other IFV commanders, each one of us directing and guiding our drivers – like the rest of our crews – hunkered down deep towards the front of our seven-metre-long vehicles. Our job was to alert the man at the wheel of any potential hazard as he slowly navigated a path across a difficult and primeval land.

David, after months on the job, was by now an expert at manoeuvring our Ratel through the bush and he responded readily to my directions. Most times he simply followed rows of deep ruts carved into the soft, desert-like sand by troops of vehicles immediately ahead. Herb, the 90 mm gunner, didn't have much to do, so he just sat back and waited, though a snatched snooze was definitely not a part of it.

There was no question in the minds of any of us that all this was for real. Skirmishes and contacts we'd encountered in the preceding months were all part of an ongoing learning curve and we hadn't missed the reality that these short, sharp firefights had gradually increased in intensity as the Angolan Army tried to secure a foothold on the southern banks of the Lomba River.

For a while FAPLA had been intent on reinforcing their in-theatre forces which, our commanders reckoned, already totalled something like 10,000 troops, never mind the several hundred armoured vehicles like ours. There were also five or six squadrons of T-54/55 Soviet-built main battletanks, in the argot, MBTs.

The build-up had been significant. We'd been made aware of increased political pressure from Fidel Castro and Cuba's Soviet sponsors in the preceding months to make inroads into the 'Deep South', all of which led to increasingly aggressive counterstrikes on our part. What we were also told was that the Angolan Army was utterly committed to annihilating their prime objective: the UNITA rebel command under Jonas Savimbi in southern Angola. His force was composed of elements of the 3rd Regular, 5th Regular, 13th Semi-Regular and 275th Special Forces Battalions, plus several thousand more guerrillas operating independently in the bush.

As the operation progressed, we'd been warned that we would eventually come up against a fully mechanised tank brigade that had earlier been dispatched to circle around the source of the Lomba and been spotted by reconnaissance elements sent in to spy the terrain. As before, enemy size and strength were both problematic, as was their deployment. Not long now, we'd been assured by some of the sceptics in our ranks, everything would be disclosed...

Being on the ground in hostile enemy territory, we were not to know that two months previously FAPLA's 21st and 25th light infantry brigades – as well as its 47th (armoured) and 59th (mechanised) and 16th brigades – had already moved out of Cuito Cuanavale in their bid to launch the biggest Angolan Army offensive of the 21-year war. Additionally, these ground forces had the advantage of solid air support, almost all of which came from their airbase at Menongue. Enemy air assets included Soviet Sukhoi and sophisticated MiG-23 fighter-bombers, the majority deployed in ground-attack roles.

As fighters, we were centred on the 61 Mechanised Infantry Battalion Group, a unit of the South African Infantry Corps. While classed as mechanised infantry, it was a motley collection of infantry, armour and artillery, haphazardly interspersed as tactics and the terrain demanded. Interestingly, the unit had originally been formed in 1978 as Battle Group Juliet in South West Africa as a force to prevent attacks on the region from SWAPO guerrillas in southern Angola and saw its first action in Operation Reindeer in early May 1978. Months later the battle group was renamed '61 Mech' and became part of the regular order of battle.

Now, almost a decade later, an enormous Angolan strike force had reached the northern banks of the Lomba River near Mavinga and we were ready for them: there had been others before, but nothing with this kind of armoured clout.

Our immediate shortcoming was that the South African Air Force (SAAF) had no aircraft that could match squadrons of Soviet jets that had been deployed throughout the south, in large part because Pretoria had been stopped from acquiring any by a United Nations-imposed arms embargo. And anyway, the fighting that would take place was almost an hour's flying time from our own airfields in Ovamboland and Caprivi.

We'd been told that if Cuito Cuanavale was lost by FAPLA, the next closest comparable outpost would be Menongue, roughly 300 kilometres from Mavinga and almost half the distance again from UNITA's headquarters at Jamba in the extreme south-east of this vast country.

By then, our own forces were approximately 500 clicks inside Angola, and, to my surprise, it wasn't all the kind of arid country we'd expected. Angola, far from being desert-like, had some huge forested areas, some of which might even be described as jungle, with visibility sometimes down to less than 50 metres. The trouble was, this was hardly adequate for the kind of mechanised warfare in which we were to be involved. We'd been trained to accurately pick off targets at more than 2,000 metres, so somehow, we'd have to improvise. But then, so too would FAPLA.

Conversely, some of the large trees that speckled the countryside were enormous and offered the singular advantage of excellent air-cover for our oversized vehicles from Angolan war planes. This was important in another respect: during this politically sensitive cold-war period, Pretoria actively denied that there was any kind of South African military presence in Angola. In fact, they told Washington, London as well as the United Nations, our infantry fighting units and the thousands of men who supported them, were simply not on Angolan soil…

As our squadron got closer to the Angolan battle lines across the way, the mood on the radio-net became tense. There was no more idle banter, no jokes and certainly nothing that was not essential. In the three hours after we'd pulled out of our temporary base at four in the morning, our minds had suddenly switched to operational mode. Looking back on those distant days, and specifically that morning of 3 October as dawn finally broke over our moving convoy, I recall feeling curiously positive. I was prepared, my mind calm and quite confident that the crew would do what was asked from them.

Fuck! We'd been training for this event long enough and were thoroughly familiar with our equipment, all of which had been primed for the impending action. Also, we'd already had a few contacts with advancing FAPLA units the month before, though none of these earlier sorties had been decisive. What we'd learned from our intelligence people was that an entire Angolan brigade had massed near the confluence of the Lomba and Cuzizi Rivers, with a plan, it was suggested, to cross back over to the northern banks, possibly because our earlier attacks had put their wind up.

From intelligence available to us when we'd been given our battle orders the previous day, we'd been warned to expect a lot of resistance. As one of the senior officers expressed it: 'FAPLA's 47th Brigade has their backs to the Lomba River and that means that should they take a beating from us, they'll not be able to withdraw from the contact area which, as we've seen, is a frequent Angolan tactic...'

By then, battle-group leaders had made the decision that our unit – Charlie Squadron – would form the front line of the formation, while Alpha and Bravo anti-tank companies (our 90 mm contemporaries from the infantry unit) would form up on our flanks to prevent encirclement by enemy forces. Overall, the formation would resemble an oversized U-shape, with 20 mm infantry Ratels working in tandem with 81 mm mortar IFVs – as well as command vehicles – all active within a strategic pocket created by the 90 mm formations.

Just after sunrise we arrived at our staging point. There we disengaged from our support vehicles and fanned out into our pre-arranged battle formation, all the while relying increasingly on radio contact to ascertain our positions relevant to each other. We began moving forward, tentatively at first, anticipating contact at any moment, even though we'd been advised that the main body of the enemy force was still a couple of thousand metres ahead.

Chapter 2
Angola's Tank Battle on the Lomba

Clockwise from top: The 20-ton Ratel made good speed on tarred roads, but Angola had none, so progress was often grindingly slow, further hampered by MiG bombing runs and landmines.

Civilisation at last! The first morning in demobilisation camp after 90 days in theatre. Many beers were soaked up on arrival the preceding night.

61 Mech gate flash – the camp consisted mainly of tents, but thankfully had a swimming pool.

After about an hour, our progress was halted by a command from the captain. By then we were probably about a kilometre from the enemy but because of thick bush, they remained unseen. It was then agreed that our UNITA allies from one of their infantry platoons would move forward on foot, establish the rough positions of the waiting forces, engage briefly and then withdraw. Once enemy locations had been ascertained, our artillery batteries to the rear would start lobbing 155 mm shells over our heads and only then would Charlie Squadron take the lead and push ahead. In this instance, as we were only to discover afterwards, it was FAPLA's entire 47th Mechanised Brigade.

As a point of reference: It remains my understanding that a brigade is at least three times the size of our battalion. More salient, these brigades bristled with some of the most modern equipment that the Kremlin could provide, along with some of the most high-ranking Soviet officers ever to conduct warfare outside USSR's borders. More salient Ratels were never intended for direct confrontation with armour.

35

The brigade that waited for us that beautiful spring morning comprised at least two squadrons of a dozen T54/55 main battle tanks, fortunately not the newest in the Russian arsenal. They were backed by multiple squadrons of infantry fighting vehicles, very much like our own, like the BTR 60 with mounted multi-barrelled ZSU-23 heavy machine guns that could easily rip a Ratel apart with a single salvo, something that happened occasionally, with loss of life.

Looking back, it was perhaps just as well that we didn't know what lay ahead. We were certainly close enough to the line of fire to observe squads of scrawny, battle-hardened UNITA troops dressed in what seemed to be rags, with their AK-47s, RPGs and the very occasional Stinger anti-aircraft rocket suddenly materialising from the bushes around us and stalking forwards toward the enemy. Within 20 minutes the chatter of gunfire ahead had become intense: there was no turning back now.

Another ten minutes passed and still more UNITA combatants ambled past our positions after their brief firefights. Some were so nonchalant in their approach, they might have been on a morning stroll. Nervously, I gave these black-skinned warriors a grin and an optimistic 'thumbs-up'. We shared no common language, other than the international hand signal for 'everything's OK'. But for us, things were definitely *not* OK. More chatter on our radios suggested that we were finally about to engage.

Then it came: 'Charlie Squadron, we're holding for the artillery bombardment' said the captain on our radio-net. And within moments came the crumps, and still more crumps with the occasional hollow 'thwump!'.

None of us could miss the almost ceaseless flashes of exploding munitions less than 200 metres ahead of us as dead-eye mortars and long-range artillery hurled a coordinated ripple of explosions onto nearby enemy positions. A minute or two passed and my headset crackled back to life: 'Charlie Squadron, let's move out.' The dreaded order came through in Afrikaans, first language of the SADF. As a crew commander, I was required to constantly monitor three radio channels. These were squad-net (my little group of four Ratels), troop-net (used by each of the Lieutenants that controlled the movements of their troops of 4 APC-90s), and of course, I was in constant communication through my helmet mike with Herb the 'deadly gunner' and David our driver.

'Okay boys, this is it, let's move out. Herb, prepare to fire,' I ordered and we began our slow forward movement, all the IFVs of

Chapter 2
Angola's Tank Battle on the Lomba

Charlie Squadron in close formation, everyone else behind us. It was just after nine in the morning, five hours after we had first set out and for the following seven hours nothing happened behind our fighting group that didn't warrant consideration: my field-of-focus narrowed sharply towards everything immediately ahead and the rest of Charlie Squadron fighting alongside our machine. Our troop of four Ratels had become the fulcrum of our very universe.

Fellow combatants, or those of you who have experienced severe trauma like a vehicle accident, will know the meaning of everything suddenly going into distinct slow motion in those precious critical moments between life and death. Time becomes suspended, normal rules of reality are fuzzy and things you might normally accomplish during such intense duress afterwards seem impossible to have been achieved under normal conditions.

So too, for me. After 18 months of preparation, the Battle of the Lomba River kicked off with the sun at arm's length over the horizon. Before I knew it, it was four in the afternoon. By then our Ratel – and those around us – had been in contact with dozens of Angolan tanks, but curiously it didn't strike us that we were fighting against pretty impossible odds. Lieutenant Adrian Hind, our squad commander, had been killed by enemy fire, his crew seriously injured and his Ratel destroyed, but on the opposite side of the battlefield, an entire FAPLA armoured brigade – tanks, APCs and the rest – were annihilated.

It was actually much worse for the Angolan Army. By the time the battle had conclusively turned in our favour, their survivors – after losing most of their two dozen tanks – were beaten back into a rapid retreat, hundreds of their troops left behind dead and their wounded screaming for help. There were also more than a hundred

Left to right: Fire-and-move through high-speed open terrain. UNITA officers occasionally led tactical briefings because we worked very closely with their troops on the ground.

Above: Blinding muzzle-flash during night-fire training.

Left: Heavy going for our convoy at the start of the rainy season in November 1987.

FAPLA vehicles abandoned, their occupants relinquishing some of the Soviet Union's most prized and modern equipment. Among the items captured was a completely intact SAM-8 missile battery, an astounding intelligence coup because this weapons system had never before been seen by western intelligence services.

'Capture one of these SAM-8 launchers, the loader and its control vehicle and you've paid for the war,' some 'big-cheese' general told us during a pre-war pep talk. Altogether there were three SAM-8 batteries taken, although some of them a bit worse for wear, at least one ended up in the hands of American weapons specialists within weeks, a special flight having been dispatched to Pretoria by Washington to fetch it.

During the initial phase of the battle on the morning of 3 October, our entire formation moved forward with the IFVs of C-Squad spaced about 30 to 40 metres apart. My troop number 32 was arrayed to my left, with 31 and 33 arrayed on the right.

First moments of actual engagement came just moments after a warning on the radio, 'all units ... be advised ... enemy snipers emplaced in the trees'. Moments after I'd acknowledged, the battle commenced. It started with the staccato chatter of light machine-gun fire and, while trying to seek out the source, the bush directly ahead burst into life. I was faced with a ferocity of fire I'd never experienced before.

It took only moments to accept that enemy forces seem not to have dug themselves in as usual. Most of the opposing troops had taken cover behind some of the larger forest trees and we suddenly found ourselves right in the heart of the kill-zone. Our units were less than 200 metres from the nearest enemy concentrations and, within moments, all manner of carnage erupted. Months of drills and training abruptly kicked in. The rest of the day happened as if in a dream, surreal almost. We were simply going through the drills, my brain working at hyper-speed, identifying, evaluating, targeting, manoeuvring, and surviving.

Despite earlier 'ripples' of our own multiple rocket launchers and artillery fire, which had been used to soften the target area, we were faced with a well-established enemy front line no more than 200 or 300 metres directly in front of us. All enemy positions were well camouflaged and lay concealed within a dense tree line. Behind that, FAPLA gunners were laying down a barrage of fire that ranged from concentrations of AK-47 and RPG-7 barrages to intermittent 100 mm tank and artillery salvos. I could see men moving around ahead of us, their muzzle flashes etched sharply against the dark forest backdrop and could clearly identify silhouettes of hard targets.

It was recommended that we enter combat 'hatch-down'. The problem with this approach was that to identify targets using periscopes or through the two-inch thick green glass surrounding the commander's hatch was just too inefficient for rapid target acquisition. The upshot for me was that earlier I had established the best way to survive and that was with my head and half my body out of the hatch so that I could better see what was going on in the bush around us. I'd only just drop down when the crackling poc-poc-poc against the Ratel's mainframe told me that we were taking hits: the noise resembled a popcorn machine rattling on the body of the APC. That happened often enough because there were enemy emplacements – dozens of them – all around us and we could hardly miss the 'swoosh and blast' of the hundreds of rocket-propelled grenades as they whizzed past, some exploding into the trees ahead and others self-destructing at 900 metres behind our positions.

War, as anybody who has experienced real combat will tell you, is quite often punctuated by some furiously intense moments of lunacy contrasted by periods of downtime that can sometimes go on forever. In our case, explosives were being hurled in all directions as an incalculable amount of weaponry was fired at our positions which, at best, could only be regarded as improvised as we never had any real cover. Throughout the exchange, we faced a curtain of bombing, with the ground alongside my Ratel constantly kicked up by large-calibre explosions. Even the air we breathed was putrid and thick with cordite; for a while it seemed as if we'd been bracketed by a cacophony of blasts.

Retaining a good squadron formation, we gradually began making forward movement, always jockeying position, never staying in the same place for longer than was absolutely needed. Our job was to identify the next target, release perhaps a couple of 90 mm shells, and then move on. We never remained static in one spot for longer than 60 seconds.

During those first two hours we endured an intense amount of enemy fire from the tanks, and a lot more from small arms, RPGs, mortars and whatever else the enemy could bring to bear. I noticed that there were several Angolan Air Force MiGs buzzing overhead and reported this back up the chain of command, as if they didn't already know ...

'Fuck boys, we got planes overhead!' was my unfrilled message to headquarters. But there was no time to be distracted by enemy aircraft because I had to remain focused on what was immediately ahead. In the hours that followed, I would continually snatch quick glances into the trees – for snipers – and into the sky, my Browning 7.62 mm turret-mounted machine gun always ready to pick off anything 'soft'.

This pattern was repeated hundreds of times as the battle progressed. 'Tank 250, 11 o'clock ... fire when ready,' I ordered. Herb quickly traversed his barrel onto target and *boom* ... another shell on its way. Because the two forces were ranged in battle so very close together, our shells would most times strike targets dead ahead within a fraction of a second.

'Yes! Fucking good shooting, Herb!' I'd shout down the mike. Then I'd tell the gunner to lay another one there to make absolutely certain!'

BOOM! And the next round was also true. There was no time for congrats because we'd move swiftly towards another position in what had already become a hazardous game of hide and seek: us hiding and popping off shots and enemy tanks desperately swinging their turrets about while searching for something static to shoot at.

Then another target would appear, this time, perhaps, a personnel carrier. 'Gunner,' I called. 'Load HE (High Explosive) ... target 300 metres ... 12-o'clock ... *fire when ready!*'

The blast from our recoil was like a wallop in the nose, almost like getting slapped in the face by a heavy wet towel and something that we could never get used to.

'Target eliminated.' I called. Then after a moment or two: 'Next ...'

We would repeat the process over and over again, which is how it went for my well-drilled crew, one fluid fire-and-movement after the other, or as somebody else described it, like a well-calibrated machine.

What a phenomenal bunch of guys they were and we didn't regard it as peculiar that there wasn't anybody in my squad who was older than 21…

Looking back on these events, years later, it became clear that we probably needed a lot of luck to survive such a massive onslaught. But we were aware too that we could improve our odds by eliminating a target each time one came into view, which was often. An enemy tank or a BTR would appear, I'd indicate position and range, the gunner would zero in and that was it. Then we'd move to a new spot and wait for something else to happen.

It might have been dangerous, but it was actually exciting as hell. We were playing games with our lives and until you've actually tasted that kind of risk, there are those who reckon you haven't lived. Fact is, you certainly can't explain that kind of experience to somebody who hasn't been there…

At some point during the early stages of battle, the Ratel to my left – 32 Charlie, or in the lingo 32C – Lance Corporal Bobby R screamed over the troop-net that he was having problems with his gun man. His voice sounded desperate when he called: 'My gunner won't shoot, *my gunner won't shoot!*' he called, several octaves above his usual tone.

I immediately asked whether his gun had jammed. But no, Bobby said, when he came back online, the man had frozen, simple as that. Moments later he added something about the guy being paralysed with fear, and that too, was something that happened occasionally and in every war…

Bobby came back: 'I have one of their tanks targeting me at my 12 and the gunner is refusing to hit his fire-switch.'

'Okay Bobby, we've got you,' I replied.

My instruction to David, my driver was immediate: 'Forward 11 o'clock … 40 metres.' Then I told Herb to give me a HEAT round – High Explosive Anti-Tank – which he knew meant that we were going to go after the T54/55 that was threatening Bobby and his crew.

'*Now!*' I screamed into the mike.

Unlike our buddies who served in the South African main battle tank, the 'Olifant', we had no dedicated or auto-loader in the 90 mm

Spoils of war, a few of us Charlie Squadron lads pose with a T-55, like a day at a theme park.

Ratel. So between the gunner and the crew commander, we would load our rounds directly into the breech from the 29 bombs arrayed in place inside the turret. Still more bomb-bays inside the vehicle held the remaining payload – and that meant another 42 bombs – but they were not accessible from inside the turret. The only way we could replenish turret stocks was to exit the APC and pass each bomb up into the turret where it would be stowed. But that was all pretty time-consuming because the rounds were large and the turret a somewhat constricted place.

It was a lot worse if we had to reload while under fire, which happened often enough because every one of the TFVs was a critical component in the uncertainty of what was going on all around us. We were trying to destroy enemy assets and they ours, and as with any battle, numbers mattered.

With 32 Charlie, it was impossible for the crew commander Bobby to try to help and possibly reach over the breach to hit the fire-switch. Had he been able to do so, he would have had his arm torn off by the breech which had a vicious recoil that reached back half-a-metre towards the innards of his machine.

While my crew was shifting our position and loading the tank-buster round, I continued to maintain my chest-high position out of the turret. Meanwhile, I searched intently for the FAPLA tank that

Bobby said was targeting his Ratel. Then I spotted it in some thick bush, off towards our flank. I actually found it in seconds, but in such circumstances time does seem to stand still. Meantime, I was pouring a stream of fire from my mounted 7.62 mm machine gun into the T54/55, desperately hoping to distract its crew and also to help Herb locate the target, which is why tracers are so valuable.

'Gunner,' I called. 'Watch for my tracer rounds … target 250 … behind that tall tree, 10 o'clock … fire when ready.' The target tank had already fired one round at Bobby's Ratel, but missed, and it was obvious that another would follow.

'Fire now, fire now!' I ordered and an enormous blast from our 90 mm followed. 'Bomb away and on target,' Herb called, though he didn't need to because the explosion that followed said it all.

'You fucking beauty, Herb!' I got back on the radio and called it in, 'Three Two, this is Three Two Alpha, we've eliminated 32 Charlie threat, now get that fucking gunner outta here.'

It wasn't long before 32 Charlie was withdrawn from the front line and we never saw that gunner again. Bobby returned to the fray later in the day with a replacement. What was really ironic was that Bobby's gunner – the troopie who froze at a critical moment that might have cost the lives of everybody on board his Ratel – had been outstanding in all his training phases throughout the year.

I put it all down to an interesting lesson in life…

For the rest of the time, we continued pushing forward, sighting and eliminating targets and, as always, a lot of it was touch and go.

Since the start of Operation Modular (or Moduler as it was known), we had never been tested quite like this. In fact, there was no contact we experienced that had lasted anything as long. Nor were there ever such high-value targets. It seemed that each time we knocked out something significant – like one of their battle tanks – another seemed to pop up out of nowhere and replace it. Three hours into the battle and we were still coming under intense bombardment.

Still, while we were coming up against a solid wall of enemy armour, Charlie Squadron was more than holding its own. But by then some of the crews – including my own – were beginning to run low on turret ammunition, which was when our commandant ordered a tactical withdrawal. We pulled back about a click, well out of sight of the enemy but close enough to our support units to replenish bombs, refuel and grab a bit of grub from a ration pack. There was almost no time to compare notes with my fellow crew commanders, though some of us were able to exchange a few words.

Then, within the hour we were summoned by the big brass, told how well we were doing and ordered back to the front line.

Meantime, the enemy had not been inactive. They'd reinforced their lines and the afternoon session immediately began with more contacts from T-54/55s and what was obviously a more organised defensive line. We got straight back into our routine drills, moving, firing, moving, improvising, and on the move again.

There is an expression in several languages that if you give an infinite number of monkeys an infinite number of typewriters, one or more of the works of William Shakespeare would eventually emerge. In our case, despite our superior training, an awesome number of projectiles were being thrown at us. Some of the larger calibres would have cleaved through a Ratel with enough kinetic energy to kill everybody. Indeed, that happened during the course of the war and obviously, casualties followed.

While the enemy was clearly badly trained or tended to lose focus whenever they came under concentrated fire, their guys were at a distinct disadvantage in other respects when compared to us. Many of them were undernourished and, from what we'd experienced, the majority were inadequately trained. In some cases, some of the FAPLA troops were unwilling to fight for a cause they did not really understand.

In truth though, they were still a potent force and this ongoing battle was far too closely fought for them not have some success. The longer we fought, the greater the chance the enemy would score hits.

So it happened that in the ongoing fog of exchanging fire that afternoon, a call came through the squad-net that one of the Ratels – it was identified as 33 – had taken a hit. Moments later somebody else reported that the strike was 'direct'. That was serious.

'Fuck! What's the situation? The crew?' I demanded.

Our captain came back sharply, his voice stressed. 'Confirm hit, vehicle immobilised ... some of the crew sitting on the ground alongside.'

The incident was critical because there was enemy everywhere around us. But just then we had a few problems of our own, and the crippled Ratel was too distant for me to do anything about it. An infantry APC commander moved forward in an attempt to rescue the crew, confirming at the same time that the IFV had been blown apart. Literally, as if somebody had used a giant can opener to split it in half, which sometimes happens with 'thin-skinned' armour.

I never witnessed the incident which took place a couple hundred metres to our right, though shortly afterwards confirmation came through that we'd lost second lieutenant Adrian Hind. Also, his crew got mauled, one of his men losing an eye and some fingers, while a former school pal of mine, Graham, earned himself a bravery award for leaving his vehicle, sprinting across open ground to the stricken 33 and returning with a lifeless Adrian Hind who died shortly afterwards.

There was some chatter about how and why one of the enemy tanks had managed to target 33, but I prefer to believe that the tank got lucky. One needs to bear in mind that there were a lot of enemy tanks in the vicinity and any one of them could have popped up in the dense foliage and lobbed a shell. A direct hit from their 100 mm guns meant tickets for whoever took the strike.

We, on the other hand, in order to cripple or disable a main battle tank had to ensure not only a good shot but an outstanding one. It had to be delivered either directly onto its tracks, or even better, fired into the seam between its turret and hull. It didn't take any of us long to discover that a Ratel-90 could take four or five shots to kill a tank.

Fortunately, while we were deployed in Angola, Herb, our gunner, never had that problem. We worked to a set pattern that if you missed with your first two shots you shifted your Ratel into another position. In turn, that forced the enemy gunner to have to 're-acquire' his target. But, if you remained static, it was pretty fundamental that we would then be offering our enemy too many chances to eventually get one of his shells onto target.

The right flank of Charlie Squadron took some time to recover from the loss of momentum caused by the loss of Troop 30's command

Left to right: The beast wallowing, after the rain. My friend Corporal Venter catching a quick half-time bite to eat.

unit, whereas on the left flank we continued to make good progress. We pushed hard against the forces arrayed against us, but we'd suddenly acquired so many targets since the lunch break that we were again beginning to run low on bombs in the turret. I didn't need to be told that if this epic battle continued for much longer we'd need to pull back from the front line to replenish. However, any idea of leaving the other crews – my brother's-in-arms – to fight on without us, was to my mind, anathema.

I may have been fearful of what lay ahead at the start of the day, but just then, while we were immersed in battle, there was no way I was leaving the rest of the gang without me by their side.

This state of affairs also presented something of a conundrum, because I was aware that the other crew commanders were also running short of ammo. But unless we were given the order to withdraw within the next five or ten minutes, 32 Alpha would be fending off T-55 tanks on its own.

So I chose my moment just after hitting the last hard target in my field of fire, when I called back on the radio: 'Three Two, this is Three Two Alpha, I'm going to need to withdraw to replenish my turret.'

'Three Two Alpha affirm!' came the response from the troop commander who was obviously both stressed and focused on his own field-of-fire. I instructed David to begin a rapid withdrawal, keeping my head out of the turret to monitor his reverse: we didn't just then need to run into something large, like one of the big forest giants or worse, get stuck down to our axles in a bomb crater.

The reloading exercise, I knew, would require me to be out of the vehicle for several minutes: I'd work fast, but every shell that passed from outside would have to be secured inside by the gunner. That meant that we'd need to find somewhere relatively secure: we couldn't be left exposed and technically unarmed while completing the process. The immediate problem was that the further we retreated, the longer we'd be out of our fighting line and that meant leaving the guys to face the enemy without us. Every single one of our guns counted!

With bombs, shrapnel bullets and the rest whizzing and pinging everywhere, we'd only reversed about 20 or 30 metres when, inexplicably, David slammed on his brakes. The Ratel slowed right down and I didn't like it. 'Keep going, keep going, Dave ... *move!*' I shouted loudly through the mike, telling him that the terrain was clear and that there were no obstacles in the way.

'OK, Corporal,' he responded. He'd hardly begun to resume his

Chapter 2
Angola's Tank Battle on the Lomba

Friends from UNITA with a recoilless gun. They had a lot more vehicles for their rag-tag army after 3 October.

pull backwards when a huge explosion suddenly rocked our Ratel. Something massive – we found out afterwards that it was a heavy-calibre mortar – had detonated just a few metres behind us. Shrapnel splintered onto the upper surface of the IFV as well as into the hub of the spare wheel locker that was usually positioned on top of the engine hatches and, in the course of events, seemed to absorb a lot of hits.

I didn't know it yet, but I was lucky, seriously so. Although I'd been monitoring our reverse manoeuvre with my head out of the turret, I was shielded from the full impact of the blast by the thick steel hatch-cover which had been locked into its customary 90-degree upright position behind my head. Had David not momentarily slowed our reverse, that same mortar-round would've landed directly on the front of the vehicle, or possibly even on top of it, where I would have had no hatch-cover protection. It was that close!

We continued pulling back, but about 150 metres later I called down to the driver. 'Okay David,' I said into the mike, 'there is no real safe place to do this, but we've got to replenish. So stop now.' Realising that we had neither cover nor protection from the crazy maelstrom of battle taking place just a short distance away, I ripped off my helmet, jumped off the turret and almost cat-like, landed on the ground three metres below where I'd been perched.

I couldn't miss a bunch of black streaks down the side of our vehicle: scorch marks from some of the shells that had glanced off our mainframe. I wasted no time in opening the heavy steel door that covered external ammo stores, selected the appropriate ordnance, unlocked their bomb catches and passed the seven kilo bombs up to Herb in the turret. One shell at a time, we worked at hyper-speed, he locking the bombs away in their dedicated racks while David reached round from his cockpit to clear expended shell casings which cluttered the floor of the turret.

Good operational practice dictated that we hurled the casings out of the turret, but in the lunacy of the preceding hours, we'd not always had the time to do it because Herb's hatch always remained locked while the fighting went on. I would've been the only one able to do the job and that wasn't always possible given my multitude of tasks, target-spotting in particular.

As soon as we'd replenished the turret ammo, I told the other two that we should get back into line: there was no time to hang about in the rear. Also, with all that open ground around me, I was keen to return to the relative safety of my turret, obviously the safest option. While replenishing our ammo, several enemy shells exploded around us and the Ratel shuddered from some of the bombs that detonated nearby. Still, clearing the casings was a priority – if they were not removed, we risked having one or more trapped under the gun mechanism and that would have meant not being able to rotate our turret onto target.

Moments later we were back in line: the entire operation – it felt like an hour at the time – had taken something like six minutes...

By the time we'd returned to our original position in the formation we immediately began to take hits from a group of Angolan infantry who'd just exited a Soviet BTR-152 troop carrier which was a bit smaller than our Ratels and were usually fielded with 14.4 mm heavy machine gun mounted on the cab. Most of the enemy had taken cover behind a large tree which also shielded their vehicle.

I was about to order a first strike on their vehicle when I noticed a black dot travelling towards me, coming in almost in slow motion. In a moment the dot got larger but I already knew that I had an RPG-7 headed straight at us. There was no time to think. My legs buckled beneath me as I dropped into the turret. I looked upwards as the distinctive green grenade spun away missing my hatch-cover by inches. That was close!

No time to consider the implications, I called down to Herb on the mike: 'New target acquired!' I shouted. 'Load HE, large tree,

300 metres, follow my tracer-rounds … fire now!' He did, hitting the tree trunk squarely and obliterating half the cover the Angolan troops were using to shelter under.

'OK, good shot … tree gone! Let's take their vehicle … load HEAT … fire when ready!' And that he did, with only a handful of survivors fleeing back towards their own lines.

A moment later I felt a sharp pain in my back: I'd been hit. Scary at first because one doesn't know the extent of a wound, I quickly realised that I was OK. I'd taken a piece of shrapnel and Dion, the squadron medic, extracted it later that evening. That little piece of metal later became another memento of war.

Shortly after I got hit, call-sign Three Two started calling down the troop-net, 'I'm taking direct fire … tank … but I can't locate the target.' That was my troop leader: he had adopted the closed-hatch approach after he'd taken a shrapnel wound to his shoulder. But it did make for tricky target location and he was now dangerously exposed.

I responded immediately: 'Shit boys, we're not losing another vehicle today, let's go get this bastard.' The crew was with me all the way and followed instructions without question, even though we'd already survived a good six hours' madness. The number of close calls or near misses had been impossible to calculate and by then, what the hell, we knew we were invincible.

'Three Two, this is Three Two Alpha … we're moving in on your position from your 3 o'clock. Now.'

Finding the enemy tank had suddenly become my only focus, but as with most things, it becomes easier with practice. I reckon it was less than a minute before I spotted a barrel protruding from some heavy bush and, moments later, the muzzle-flash from a 100 mm cannon. By then I was almost behind that piece of enemy armour and had a full view of the rear of a Soviet T-54/55.

I told David to move us a little further down range to ensure that Herb had a decent sighting of the target. With a HEAT round locked and loaded, I told our gunner to hold everything.

'Gunner new target acquired: 11 o'clock … 200 metres. Follow my tracer … I'm aiming at his turret seam, and make this shot count, Herb, because we've got to slot him before he gets off another shot at Connor's Ratel. Fire when ready!'

The recoil from our shell resulted in the usual sensation of being punched in the face but when I checked a second or two later, I was able to report a bull's-eye. The tank had taken a mighty hit and then, to my surprise, its turret flipped right off the main body of the tank,

Charlie Squadron, 61 Mechanised Battalion, scruffy and battle-hardened deep in Angola, October 1987.

all three or four tons of it. I'd heard of this happening, but never actually seen it for myself.

'Three Two, this is Three Two Alpha,' I reported over the net. 'We got that fucker...'

A few weeks later we began to see some of the propaganda leaflets used against FAPLA. One of these showed a broken Russian MBT with its turret lying upside down alongside. I can only believe this wrecked T-54/55 to be the same unit we'd cleaved open that afternoon. Months later I was told by one of our officers that I was to be nominated for a bravery award for this action and some other bits and pieces in combat, but like some of the other guys who were commended, we never heard anything further.

C'est la vie. I'm alive, and those for whom I was responsible, had survived. That means a lot when we'd eaten a few shovelfuls of shit together and emerged intact at the other end.

Others hadn't been so fortunate.

CHAPTER THREE

AFRICA'S GREAT MERCENARY TRADITION

Mercenaries – hired guns – are in a class of their own. Though there have been thousands of these freebooters active in scores of wars on almost all continents since the end of World War II, very few have made their mark. Manuel Ferreira, an erstwhile SADF Military Intelligence member/operative, worked with Bob Denard in the Comoros Archipelago, a clutch of several islands strategically positioned at the northern entrance to the Mozambique Channel. Ferreira tells us something about mercenary lore...

The most prominent of the mercenary bunch – in the English-speaking world – is Colonel Mike Hoare, 'Mad' Mike to those who know him well. The appellation originally came from the East Germans who despised this former British Army captain for curtailing vigorous Soviet efforts at Congolese dislocation in the 1960s. Wikipedia describes him as follows:

> Hoare was born in India. He spent his early days in Ireland and was educated in England. He served in North Africa as an armour officer in the British Army during World War II. After the war, he completed his training as a chartered accountant, qualified in 1948 and emmigrated to Durban where he ran safaris and became a soldier-for-hire in various African countries.

The name Mike Hoare will always be linked to the Congo in that difficult period following this troubled African country's independence from Belgium. His first mercenary action was with 4 Commando in Katanga in 1960/61: this southern province tried

GP troops on parade in Moroni. (Photo: Manuel Ferreira collection)

to break away from the authority of the central government in Leopoldville (Kinshasa today).

Three years later, he was hired by Moïse Tshombe, the Congolese Prime Minister, to lead the 300-man 5 Commando, composed almost entirely of South Africans[1].

His most distinguished role came soon afterwards, when Hoare and his men – together with Belgian paratroopers, a bunch of Cuban exile pilots flying Harvard trainers, as well as CIA-hired mercenaries – worked in concert in a desperate bid to save the lives of 1,600 civilians, mostly Europeans and missionaries. The operation took place in and around Stanleyville (Kisangani) and was dubbed Operation Dragon Rouge by its planners. Sadly, many of the victims who were taken hostage by the rebels were murdered.

On a totally different mercenary tack is former South African Air Force Colonel Neall Ellis, today regarded as the world's most famous mercenary aviator. Still flying support missions in Afghanistan, Ellis over the decades has seen action in a dozen wars on three continents. He is also the man whom General Sir David Richards, the British Chief of Defence Staff – in a private note to this author – called 'a great man'[2]. That followed the activities of Sir David, then a 'lowly' brigadier – in countering the actions of a large rebel army that was trying to overthrow the government of Sierra Leone. Many of these actions are detailed in Neall Ellis's biography, *Gunship Ace*.[3]

Finally, there is Colonel Bob Denard, a French military professional who turned the fortunes of aspiring mercenaries sideways by taking over an independent African state. Denard invaded the Comoros island group four times and successfully ruled the independent Republic of the Comoros for more than a decade in what some saw as his personal fiefdom. It is worth mentioning that his story follows the tradition of that excellent film directed by John Huston called *The Man Who Would Be King*. Although the two main characters in the movie were Sean Connery and Michael Caine, Denard, a real-life French mercenary who took an island state and kept it for himself, is even more flamboyant than anything on screen, because it really happened.

South Africans were involved there as well. Eventually a number of clandestine operations linked to Black Africa, Israel and the Falklands War – many of them emanating from Pretoria – could be traced back to this island group.

Moroni, the Comorian capital under Bob Denard, whose private life was often as tumultuous as his military interventions, headed the three-island *Union des Comores*. It was to become a simmering cauldron of intrigue and subterfuge. The end came in 1989 when Denard was removed, this time at the behest of French President François Mitterand. The Élysée Palace sent a powerful naval force to the island group from La Réunion and he was evacuated to South Africa by a French Para group.

A few words about the Comoros, a curiously remote and independent African outpost north-west of Madagascar in the Indian Ocean. Desperately poor, it has embraced a blizzard of languages and boasts an exotic history that goes back centuries. There is a fourth island, actually two with several associated islets, neatly linked across a narrow stretch of water and listed on the charts as Mayotte, but it decided in 1974 to remain French. Like Tahiti, Martinique and Guadeloupe in the Caribbean, it chose not to seek independence from France and it is still administered directly from Paris as an overseas department.

Interestingly, Mayotte is scheduled to become the outermost region of the European Union in January 2014.

With a population of less than a million, the independent Union of the Comoros is not only the third smallest African state, it is also the southernmost member of the Arab League. That means it has three official languages Arabic, French and Comorian – a language based on several dialects derived from Kiswahili and that is spoken throughout the archipelago.

Diminutive, its brief history following independence from France in 1975 has been chequered. Army rebellions were followed by coups d'état and much turmoil resulted, which is why the country's history is among the most complex of all the world's developing countries. A lot of this dislocation stemmed from Islamic influences, one of the reasons why, for a time, it called itself the *République Fédérale Islamique des Comores*.

The following timeline provides some of the answers. Its first president, Ahmed Abdallah, declared his country unilaterally independent on 6 July 1975.

Eight months later, French mercenary Bob Denard – with clandestine support from Jacques Foccart, the *éminence grise* of post-war French politics, and a specialist in covert operations in Africa – overthrew Abdallah in an armed coup and replaced him with Prince Said Mohammed Jaffar. He didn't last very long and was ousted by Ali Soilih, who was a virulently anti-French radical socialist. Paris suspended all aid to the island state and Denard left the islands because of what was termed at the time 'incompatibility of ideals...'

In May 1978, Denard returned to overthrow President Soilih and reinstate Abdallah, again with the support of the French, but this time the Rhodesian and South African governments were also involved.

Soilih's brief rule was characterised by some of the most brutal actions launched by any African tyrant and seven additional putsch attempts did not help. Soilih was finally forced from office and killed in May 1978. While in power, he told his people that he had been divinely blessed by Allah to rule and was himself akin to the Prophet Muhammad.

He tolerated no opposition and murdered his opponents at will. When his people protested, he had them gunned down, which was what happened at the massacre of Comorians in Majumba and again at Iconi. Meantime, Soilih maintained that he took his instructions directly from Allah and it wasn't long before the consensus was reached – both on the islands and in France – that the man had gone totally off his trolley. Obviously, the French had to do something and they prepared Abdallah, the country's original ruler, for a comeback. Meanwhile, somebody from French Intelligence had been visiting the Denard home.

Chapter 3
Africa's Great Mercenary Tradition

The Frenchman's second coup is worthy of a movie in itself. Its theme and modus operandi feature strongly in the book *The Dogs of War*, written by British author Frederick Forsyth about a mercenary seaborne invasion very much along the lines of what actually happened. Codenamed Operation Atlantis, there is no question that both Monsieur Foccart and the French government were involved.

Denard and a group of his trusty lieutenants scoured a number of European harbours in search of an old but still seaworthy ship that they could use in what was to become a classic 'one-ship' invasion. They found the rust bucket *Antinea* in a French port, gave her a paint job and made her seaworthy before setting off down the African coast in April 1978. With Denard was his little clique of 46 handpicked 'volunteers' – many of them having seen action with him in the Congo and against the Egyptian Army in the Yemen. Four sailors were hired to ensure that Denard and his men reached the Comoros.

The men had been well equipped – obviously by the French government – with a range of automatic weapons, mortars and other war matériel which would be used to overthrow a legitimate African government. A great deal of attention was given to planning en route: each day the men would hone their fighting skills and become thoroughly acquainted with the hardware they would be using to achieve these aims.

The ship rounded the Cape and then turned sharp left before heading into the Indian Ocean. After 33 days at sea, the invasion group arrived off Moroni harbour on the night of 13 May 1978. The men had spent a day off one of the other islands because the skipper took a wrong turn en route to Grande Comore. The otherwise competent captain had to ask a local for directions to Moroni and he was taken into custody to avoid him alerting the authorities. He was released in the capital after the invasion.

There is no question that what Bob Denard set out to do was precarious. Had things gone haywire, his relatively small group of insurrectionists would almost certainly have been put up against a wall and shot by Soilih's people. In the end it was preplanning that did it and Denard's small band of warriors succeeded in completing the task at hand in little more than two hours.

Having gone ashore clandestinely in several small boats, his men first overcame troops guarding the port. They then neutralised the local militia before mortaring a nearby army barracks, which caused almost all the Comorian soldiers to flee. President Soilih, with nowhere to go, sought refuge in the palace under his bed where

South African Military Intelligence member/operative Manuel Ferreira worked with Colonel Bob Denard in the Comoros archipelago.

he was found, naked and in the company of two young women. He was taken into custody and later killed, though nobody ever claimed responsibility.

Denard immediately had all political prisoners released from the island's jails, made a public declaration over state radio that he was acting on behalf of the 'oppressed' people of the Comoros and, within days, he and his men gained control of the two remaining islands, Anjouan and Moheli. By then, as previously arranged, President Abdallah was on his way back from Paris. Meantime, as Stage Two of the deal, contact was established with both Rhodesia and South Africa and Denard created his famed *Garde Présidentielle*, the Presidential Guard or, as the men knew it, the GP.

Denard remained the de facto ruler of the island group for the next eleven years and, with the help of a substantial group of French and South African nationals, built the GP into a formidable force of 500 highly trained Comorian soldiers. Manuel Ferreira, multilingual in English, French, Portuguese and Afrikaans, was at the fulcrum. In time, he formed close ties with the man he often fondly referred to as *mon colonel*.

Chapter 3
Africa's Great Mercenary Tradition

This new order didn't come without its requisite share of hiccups. There were several attempted coups by opposition groups, some of them clandestine units with foreign funding from countries that resented the presence of a mercenary force in the Indian Ocean. Then, towards the end of November 1986, and quite unexpectedly, President Abdallah was murdered. Denard meantime had converted to Islam and taken one of the island beauties as a wife. His first marriage had been to a Jewish girl in Morocco, followed by a torrent of liaisons and the birth of several children before his only other actual marriage on Grande Comore.

In 1989, French forces invaded all three islands, bringing to an end both Denard's rule and his by-now rickety relationship with South African Military Intelligence. Two weeks later, he and his men, under escort, were on their way to South Africa. He stayed on in Pretoria until February 1993, when he returned to face trial in France.

But Denard wasn't quite done with the islands. In 1995, he launched Operation Kachkazi, his final coup in the Comoros. Loyal to his former black GP colleagues, he returned in strength and, with some popular local support, released some of his old colleagues and friends who had been jailed by the new order.

France soon put an end to that putsch with French naval and marine detachments invading Grande Comore. Denard and his band of merry men were again arrested and ousted.

Colonel Bob Denard, born in April 1929, was conscripted into the French Army on leaving school. After a circuitous route, he became the international community's most famous, indeed notorious, 'War Dog'.

Part of it, say friends, was inherited because he came from a family with strong military ties: Denard Snr had served as a soldier in the French concession in China.

Having spent time with the French Navy in Indochina and in French Algeria, the still youthful Denard got himself a job as a policeman in Morocco – from 1952 to 1957. But even there he got into trouble and served more than a year in prison for involvement in what was termed 'an attempted attack against the Minister of State, Pierre Mendès-France'. Acquitted in 1957, he was repatriated to France.

His role as a staunch anti-communist was soon recognised in Paris and Denard was called on to take part in several covert operations. In the process he handled several government-funded 'jobs' in support

Colonel Denard during his final passing review of his loyal *Garde Presidentielle* (GP) troops before handing them over to the commander of the French force that was airlifted into the Comoros to oust him. That action forced Denard to fly into exile in South Africa. (Photo: Manuel Ferreira collection)

of *Françafrique* (a term referring to France's sphere of influence in her former colonies).

Denard began his mercenary career with secessionist troops in Katanga in December 1961, making a name for himself thereafter by rescuing a number of white civilians who had been encircled and taken hostage by a brutal bunch of revolutionaries. They called themselves the Simbas (lions) and their headquarters during the course of Operation Dragon Rouge was in Stanleyville.

This was no 'spontaneous' anti-government rebellion. The Simbas had good backing from the Chinese and some Cuban irregulars, including Che Guevara. Opposing 'pro-Western' forces were tacitly backed by the CIA and Belgium. Denard was in charge of his own unit of French mercenaries called *Les Affreux* (literally, 'The Terrible Ones'). Later, on behalf of Tshombe, Denard helped put down an attempted coup by Katangan separatists in July 1966. At one stage, he was wounded and flown out with a group of more seriously wounded men to Rhodesia in a hijacked civilian aircraft, regarded today as the first recorded instance of the hijacking of a commercial passenger aircraft.

His final role in the Congolese debacle was when he sided with Katangan separatists and Belgian mercenaries led by the mercurial Jean 'Black Jack' Schramme in a revolt in eastern Congo. Following a string of successes against the largely disorganised Congolese army and air force, the dissidents were bottled up in Bukavu, in the extreme eastern part of the country. Taking matters into his own hands, Denard invaded Katanga with a force of 100 men on bicycles in an attempt to create a diversion for a Bukavu breakout, but that episode ended in disarray.

The Frenchman is known to have operated or participated in conflicts in Biafra, Yemen, Iran, Nigeria, Benin, Gabon, Angola, Congo/Brazzaville, Zaire, Libya, Chad, Ivory Coast, Mauritania and the Comoros.

According to Frederick Forsyth – who was in Biafra at the time – Denard went to the enclave, by then completely surrounded by Nigerian forces, took one look at the odds and told the rebel leader Ojukwu that he and his men wanted out. The Biafrans had no option but to put them onto the first aircraft back to Gabon and, as Forsyth recalls, he didn't bother to return the hefty cash advance that he and his men had been given by the rebel command.

From 1968 to 1978 he was employed in support of the government in Gabon where he was temporarily based and from where he carried out military actions on behalf of the French government in Africa.

While Denard might have been involved in a raid against Guinea in 1970, he was certainly involved in the failed 1977 coup attempt, codenamed Opération Crevette, in Dahomey (today's Benin). By all accounts the attempt was betrayed from the inside because opponents of the Denard group were ready for them at Cotonou Airport. Although Jacques Foccart denied personal knowledge of the attempted coup after its failure, he did recognise that it had been backed-up by the Togolese leader Gnassingbé Eyadéma, Houphouet-Boigny of the Ivory Coast, Omar Bongo of Gabon and Morocco's King Hassan II, all of whom were strongly allied to France at the time.

One of Denard's more interesting mercenary episodes involved himself and some of his colleagues working with a secret British Special Air Service group in the Yemeni mountains to the north of Sana'a, countering Egyptian Army and Air Force efforts to subjugate the country. The Brits were led by Colonel Jim Johnson, who gave the author a first-hand account of much of what had gone on in the Arabian Peninsula at the time. Johnson had kept back some magnificent photographs of a campaign that lasted for three years and which very effectively thwarted Nasser's efforts at Arab domination of a significant corner of the Middle East.

Notably, it was a campaign where the British worked hand-in-glove with the Israelis (who supplied some of the support aircraft), the Jordanians (responsible for liaising with all the players) and the Saudis who funded the operation. Jim Johnson recalls flying to Amman in a chartered plane and sitting directly behind Jordan's King Hussein and Moshe Dayan, Israel's most famous wartime general. As he recalls, the two men were involved in a series of 'animated discussions' throughout almost the entire flight.

Johnson's most successful efforts involved sabotaging Egyptian war planes in night raids: it happened so often that Nasser eventually pulled his forces back from the eastern side of the Red Sea[4].

Speaking of some of these events in later years, Bob Denard said that it had never been dull ... one interesting episode followed another.

'My thirty years of the mercenary life brought me into contact with men of courage and idealism, men with often princely qualities who risked their lives, many dying for the cause they had adopted as their own, men who offset by far those who thought the mercenary life an easy road to riches and glory or whose actions at times brought us into disrepute.'

In 1979, the French Secret Services put Denard in touch with Pretoria, and he held talks with the Chief of Military Intelligence, General P.W. van der Westhuizen. The South Africans were eager to engage because it was held that the Comoros might help South Africa break out of its isolation and gain access to the Mozambique Channel together with the airport at Moroni on Grand Comore island, which they subsequently rebuilt so that it could take large aircraft.

According to Manuel Ferreira, South African Military Intelligence agents visited Moroni and inspected the *Garde Présidentielle* and its installations. A few days after their return to Pretoria, Denard was informed that the South Africans were ready to help. In return for funding the GP, the South Africans requested that they be allowed to establish a permanent Electronic Warfare (EW) station on the islands and President Abdallah approved the request.

Pretoria's presence on the Comoros would last until January 1990 and throughout, all South African military projects launched from there were classified Top Secret. Even today, very little is still known about them.

Over a decade, South Africa helped the Comoros with economic and rural development, funded and created a farm, engaged in road construction, provided humanitarian assistance, built holiday resorts and much more. The South African Department of Foreign Affairs also opened a mission in Moroni and appointed a permanent representative. Ferreira tells us that South African military personnel serving on the Comoros were accorded the rank of second lieutenant in the GP, with the commander of his group a full lieutenant.

'In the first years of our presence on the Comoros, personnel were

Chapter 3
Africa's Great Mercenary Tradition

issued with GP military cards bearing false identities and tours of duty usually lasted three months. The electronic warfare station was operational 365 days a year and the entire central and northern Mozambique as well as Tanzania was 'targeted' by the EW station, FRELIMO and South Africa's African National Congress being the main focus.

'South African military doctors were also permanently deployed with the GP and responsible for all medical care concerning GP personnel. More serious cases were flown to Pretoria and admitted to a closed, secret ward at 1 Military Hospital which was staffed by personnel with top-secret security clearances.

'Military Intelligence also sent South African military instructors to the Comoros to train the GP and selected members were sent to South Africa to attend various military courses. A fairly large group of Comorian troops was sent to Tempe, the military base outside Bloemfontein in the Orange Free State for training as paratroopers.

'In 1989, a small group of specialists from South Africa's crack Reconnaissance Regiment (Recces) trained GP soldiers and the Deputy Chief of Staff: Intelligence, General Joep Joubert, flew to the Comoros for the graduation ceremony. From 1988, a full-time Military Intelligence liaison officer was permanently stationed in Moroni.

Denard's mercenary forces haul out some heavier stuff for a review – in this case a rear-mounted Dshka 12.7 mm heavy machine gun. (Photo: Manuel Ferreira collection)

'About then, Pretoria's Foreign Affairs representative in Moroni, became outspokenly critical of the GP and of Denard. He eventually became such a problem that we were ordered by Pretoria to target him, which meant that every time he picked up his 'phone and spoke to his bosses in Pretoria, we taped everything'.

'The diplomat was eventually expelled by President Abdallah, but by then, Denard had become a lot less visible and active in the day-to-day operations of the GP. His deputy, Commandant Marques, took over, though we still saw Denard almost daily, usually at lunchtime in the officers' mess. It was almost a ritual with him, making a point of shaking hands with each of us and wishing us a friendly *bon appétit*.

'Bob Denard, whom we had come to appreciate with time, was the ultimate officer and gentleman!'

Over a lengthy period, this rather distinguished Frenchman, who, by then, was already something of a legend in military circles, was to become more entangled in Pretoria's macabre machinations in Africa north of the Zambezi. Working from some of his personal correspondence, Ferreira tells us of an interesting event that, until now, appears to have slipped through the cracks.

As the Falklands War between Britain and Argentina escalated, Pretoria instructed Denard to arrange a secret landing of two large cargo planes at Hahaya, his island airport. Pretoria sent a C-130 loaded with military equipment for the Argentine Forces and Denard recalled that the instructions were that everything had to be offloaded and transferred to a DC-8 that had a Panamanian registration. He wasn't told what the contents were, but the inference was clear: the Frenchman was responsible for overseeing its safe transfer.

Denard: 'The work was almost complete when one of my officers called "Take a look, Colonel!" as he opened one of the containers. I could easily see the shape of a missile, before my officer closed the container. I knew that Armscor was not capable of manufacturing such a weapon. As the DC-8 taxied out and took off, I realised that the South Africans were being used as a relay by either France or Israel.'

Not long afterwards, authorisation was granted for a request by General Van der Westhuizen that a South African Airways Boeing 737 be painted in Air Comoros livery. This plane would fly the Nairobi route, assuring the South Africans liaison with Dar es Salaam, the Seychelles, Mauritius, Lilongwe in Malawi, Jeddah in Saudi Arabia, as well as facilitate the transport of pilgrims to Mecca.

'I emphasise that this route would not have been possible without

Chapter 3
Africa's Great Mercenary Tradition

At the unit's GP base 'Charlie' – South Africans Tony & Ian. (Photo: Ian C. Highley)

the GP, which undertook the security of the international airport of Hahaya.

'Another operation saw me arranging for Comorian passports to be issued to South African agents in order to allow them to take delivery of five Dakota DC-3 aircraft in New Zealand.'

A while later, General Van der Westhuizen who was succeeded as Chief of Staff, Military Intelligence by Vice Admiral Dries Putter, told Denard that he wasn't able to increase financial support for his island operation. But, he assured the mercenary leader, he would be a lot more cooperative than his predecessor. He said that more Comorians would be allowed to go to South Africa for 'quality instruction in transmissions and mechanical matters' as well as a lot else besides. It was then that a section was sent to Tempe for the Parabat course.

'The Admiral also furnished us with enough munitions for our requirements. Despite financial difficulties, the GP managed to preserve its prestige with the population and maintain the highest standards of all units of the Comorian Forces.

'Pretoria's Secret Service then informed me that because of the United Nations arms embargo against South Africa, they were

The Comoros island group has always been a delightful tropical resort with idyllic beaches, coves and hidden inlets. Moroni harbour, though primitive, would have been a major drawcard had it been situated in the Mediterranean.

experiencing difficulties in purchasing weapons for the Angolan rebel movement UNITA. That guerrilla movement, led by Swiss-educated Dr Jonas Savimbi, was the main anti-communist force opposing the MPLA-led government in Angola. I went to work and after making contact with some arms merchants in Hong Kong, we found the weapons in China that UNITA urgently required.

'It was interesting that China's leaders in Beijing, regardless of the arms embargo and of UNITA's lack of enthusiasm for Chinese political ideology, were willing to trade. It was an excellent opportunity for them to take a swipe at the Soviets – who supported the MPLA. Even better, the South Africans were willing to pay good money, and that always talked loudly in the weapons trade.

'My position on the Comoros enabled me to furnish South African agents with the passports they used to move between South Africa and Hong Kong as well as Switzerland in order to finalise the deal. I assured their protection in Europe, undertaken by a GP member who had served in the Rhodesian Army. Obviously, I also kept my old bosses informed: throughout the negotiation process, I was able

Chapter 3
Africa's Great Mercenary Tradition

to brief *Direction Générale de la Sécurité* (DGSE), the French External Intelligence Agency and it wasn't in their interests to do anything to hinder me.'

As Manuel Ferreira commented years later, it was small wonder that the AK-47s issued to Comorian troops were Chinese manufactured.

Ferreira recalls the day he first met the famous Frenchman.

'I was sitting in my office getting ready to join Denard's bunch when the telephone rang. A female major from Counter Intelligence said she wanted to see me. Her office was just a couple of floors above mine in the Liberty Life Building, Headquarters of Military Intelligence in the heart of Pretoria.

The woman told me that MI had a few of questions for me. This happened just days before my departure for the Comoros, the first of many deployments to those beautiful islands.

"What passport do you use?" she asked.

"Mine," I replied.

'She was shocked. "You can't use your own passport. I'll have to issue you with another one."

'I argued that there wasn't time for a new passport to be issued. I'd have to use the one already in my possession and with my name in it.

'"What's your cover story?" the Major asked.

'"I am a Belgian businessman," I replied.

'At least she liked that answer.

'Then she queried; "Who in your family knows that you are going to the Comoros? Who will take you to the airport?"

'"Just my wife and my mother," I told her.

'Again she was shocked. "That's a breach of security!" she argued.

'Patiently, I had to explain to her that my mother also worked at Intelligence Headquarters and in the very same division where I had my office, and that my wife had also been in the Defence Force for many years. I also mentioned that as a nurse, she was in regular contact with Comorian patients.

'The major still wasn't happy. She spent the next 15 minutes telling me what I could and could not do. I almost felt like a primary school kid being berated by a boring teacher. I was about to tell her a few home truths, but then thought the better of it and let matters lie … counterintelligence personnel can sometimes be annoying in the way they go about their jobs, and this was one of them.

'Finally I went to the airport and flew to the Comoros, excited that

Main entrance to Colonel Denard's *Garde Presidentielle* military headquarters at Kandani (Photo: Vitor Mosca) and left, Colonel Denard formally introduces outgoing CSI Admiral Dries Putter and new CSI Lt-Gen 'Witkop' Badenhorst to GP officers. (Photo: Capt H – courtesy of Manuel Ferreira)

I was about to meet a man whom I admired enormously. His friends and adversaries would label him The Great Pirate, or the Greatest Dog of War of All Time. To me, the name Bob Denard said it all.

'We landed at Hahaya Airport, north of Moroni and, as I disembarked, the humidity hit me. It was mid-summer in the Southern Hemisphere and it was like stepping out of the aircraft into a sauna bath. The colonel's troops patrolled the entire area, both in the airport and its environs.

'I was fetched from Hahaya and taken to the camp where I saw a couple of familiar faces, which was when everyone told me about the great New Year's party that would be held that night for the Presidential Guard. And so it was, an enormous occasion, with everybody going to the *Centre Nautique* – the officers' mess of the Presidential Guard – for a gigantic New Year's party.

'When we got there it was already dark and I could see that entire area was surrounded by dozens of heavily armed black troops.

'"What's going on?' I asked. "Is Bob worried about an attempt on his life?' Apparently not, came the reply. This was how things were done on special occasions.

'On entering the mess, I caught my first glimpse of the man when he was pointed out to me, sitting alongside his lovely Comorian wife. There was no question: he radiated a commanding presence.

'It was quite an occasion, with the best of French cuisine, seafood and Dom Perignon champagne. As the clock ticked towards midnight, the party became more rowdy. While some of Bob's men began to get a bit out of hand, he spent the whole evening sitting quietly next to his wife at the head of the table.

'I got to know Bob Denard a good deal better with time and we had several other enjoyable functions in his company. I also discovered that despite that raucous New Year's party, the colonel was actually a quiet man who never indulged in the kind of braggadocio behaviour one might have expected from somebody with his reputation.'

In retrospect, it became clear to us all that the professional Colonel Bob Denard had made much of his life.

This mercurial private soldier had his own three islands, an army that he personally commanded and to top it, the man was simply irresistible to women. To those who met him for the first time, the Frenchman could be utterly charming. He was also living proof that bravery, secrecy and loyalty remain the keys to survival in whatever war or battle you are involved.

There are those who will add that he was also able to give a pretty good account of himself in a court of law, for he was to spend a lot of his time – particularly in his later years – countering accusations that were probably well founded, but that lacked that final essential ingredient: proof. It helped, of course, that much of what he had achieved came with the backing of French (and for some time, the South African) intelligence establishments.

At the end of the day, everybody involved always got their requisite pound of flesh…

On the military side in the Comoros, it was all fairly straightforward. The SADF paid something like US$6 million a year towards the GP budget. That meant that cooperation – and those bits of military intrigue in Africa in which the SADF was involved – invariably went off reasonably well. There was the occasional glitch, but that was rare, because the colonel was very much a 'hands-on' person. In a nutshell, he knew and understood Africa.

At one stage, says Ferreira, the GP had a group of Recces under the command of a commandant (lieutenant-colonel today) teaching the GP Special Forces a few unconventional tricks. At the end of the course, several South African generals and other senior ranks visited the Comoros to attend the graduation ceremony.

Then, in order to deflect some of the attention from himself – there were strings of journalists and other spooky characters constantly visiting the islands – he announced his retirement and appointed his right-hand man, Dominique Malacrino (alias Commandant Marques) as head of the GP. About then, things started to become a little uncertain.

Nominally, Denard was still in full charge of the military and he continued to enjoy great political influence, but there were people – both locals and foreigners – who wanted him ousted. Also, with changes of government in France, some of his supporters either moved on or retired and there was no question that the New Guard was both suspicious and resentful of this non-politically correct individual who, after all, was still categorised as a mercenary.

In a bid to make his case more legitimate, Denard the soldier and Comorian political leader, converted to Islam. Clearly, it was the sensible thing to do since the island group was preponderantly Muslim. He assumed the name of Saïd Mustapha Mahdjoub and it was then that he took a local wife, who was at his side at all public events.

Meantime, France began to put pressure on the South African government to force the Frenchman and his mercenaries out of the Comoros. What was more, they had the political and military clout to do so, since many of the aircraft in the South African Air Force – both helicopters and jet fighters – had come from France.

Ferreira: 'The crunch came when the South African diplomatic representative in Moroni, a man by the name of Roger, called a press conference. The order had come from Pik Botha, the South African Minister of Foreign Affairs, to publically denounce Denard and demand not only his immediate departure but also his entire largely white foreign contingent of mercenaries.

'Obviously there were some serious ructions in Pretoria. It rankled at all levels that Botha had taken things upon himself and acted without consulting the South African Defence Force. We were aware that our military people did not approve and, as a consequence, there was a lot of friction.

'Undeterred, Denard immediately retaliated and had the South African representative expelled from the country. Shortly afterwards a new man was appointed in the Moroni post, but then things went even more sour when a South African citizen who had been working for the Southern Sun Hotel conglomerate on the islands was arrested by a bunch of GP soldiers at the airport for taking photographs. He too, was deported back to South Africa.

'Not long afterwards, a flash signal came through from Pretoria. A Lear Jet was about to land on the Comoros. On board, it said, was the top structure of the South African Defence Force.

'The South African top military brass – including the Chief of Staff Intelligence, Lieutenant-General *Witkop* Badenhorst – spent several days cloistered in meetings with Colonel Denard. Clearly, he was told that severe political pressure was being exerted on them for him and his men to quit the islands.

'Not long after this high-level group had returned to Pretoria, we received an ultrasecret signal from Pretoria that our military liaison officer had to personally hand-deliver to the colonel. Part of the bad news for Denard was that his budget was being cut by 50 per cent for the following year.'

By now, Denard was facing pressure from all quarters, including from certain indigenous factions within the Comoros itself. Life was being made increasingly difficult for the man and Denard was literally fighting for his survival as well as for any future role that the GP might have had on the archipelago.

The next phase, according to Manuel Ferreira, was seminal to Denard's future role on the islands.

He tells us of 'Foxtrot', also French and a captain in the *Garde Présidentielle*. Additionally, he was in charge of all matters relating to security of the president and of his personal bodyguards. Foxtrot's house was right next to the Presidential Palace in Moroni.

'Foxtrot was actually a very pleasant chap and mixed a lot with us South Africans. He'd spend most of his spare time either playing chess with the guys or attending our braais.

'As usual, that particular Saturday night, Foxtrot spent several hours at the base with us. As he was leaving, I asked whether he would be around the next day. "No, not tomorrow," he answered, explaining that his men would be, as he phrased it, "conducting night exercises." This was his exact answer.

'I confess that nothing seemed peculiar about his retort. After the recent departure of the South African Recces, night exercises by the GP sounded genuine. In fact, it was something we might have expected.

'Then, that next evening, Sunday night, just before I went to bed, all hell seemed to be breaking loose from the direction of the presidential palace. There was a lot of shooting and we could see tracers arching across the sky from Moroni. I said something to my comrades that it was probably Foxtrot and his night exercises."

'The next morning, as usual, I was the first up in the Interception Operations centre. As I entered, I heard our military liaison officer calling me frantically over the radio from his home, outside Moroni: "Manuel, nobody is to leave the base, the president was killed last night!"

'Bob Denard acted with alacrity. Obviously disconcerted, he accused the Comorian National Army of launching an attack on the presidential compound. Moreover, he wasn't wrong because the *Forces Armées Comoriennes* and its chief, Commandant Ahmed Mohammed, had staged a coup and ended up murdering the president. He immediately dissolved the national army and had some of its officers arrested.

'That was when France gave Denard and his men an ultimatum: they were to leave the Comoros with immediate effect.

'Of course, the colonel refused. His immediate reaction was to promise to "fight back to the last man". That was his view of retaliation against a possible sea and airborne invasion by the French.

'From then on, every single day, we were to see French warships patrolling along the horizon off Moroni. There were also regular French reconnaissance flights over Grande Comore, usually at very high altitudes. GP troops were deployed at all strategic points along the coast and artillery guns were positioned in Moroni itself, facing the sea. The colonel was taking the threat very seriously indeed, but he was obviously aware that this was not something that happened overnight. The French had substantial resources to hand and they had to take a while to muster ... most of it had come from the island of Réunion, which remains staunchly under the tricolour. A series of discussions followed, but Denard was adamant. He was not going to surrender.

'Meantime, the order came from Pretoria that all SADF personnel deployed with the GP were to break off all contact with Denard's people. We were prohibited from entering their main barracks or to eat at their officers' mess, something that had been the norm for many years. Even our army medical doctor officer who operated out of the main GP barracks was ordered to vacate that position.

'Following Pretoria having made its decision to break with Denard – it was all Pik Botha's doing, of course – I was asked by our military liaison officer, to go to the main GP barracks and pick up 30 crates of beer that we had ordered a while back ... they had already been paid for. Because nobody else had the courage to show up, I took the initiative to fetch it all. But then, while loading the crates, my comrade Daniel, a veteran French mercenary who was on the Comoros with the colonel from Day One, came closer. He never said a word, but just gave me a filthy look, which, I suppose, said it all.

'You could hardly miss the resentment. We South Africans had shafted a close friend and ally. And that, after all the colonel and his men had done in the interests of the Republic ... as one of them phrased it: "now that we need you more than ever, you desert us."

'For the first time ever in my life, as a solid South African patriot, I was seriously embarrassed.

'It was the same old story of treachery on the orders of foreign powers. Pretoria had dropped its old friend in the dwang, very much as it had done with the whites in Angola and Mozambique who had asked Pretoria to give them a hand and declare a unilateral declaration of independence in 1975. The same happened soon afterwards with the Rhodesians. They too were dropped in at the deep end on Washington's orders. Now it was Denard's turn...

'Although we did halt all contact with the GP, Colonel Denard kept up his sides of the bargain until the end. His military guards remained on duty at our base to the end, with our rations delivered daily from the GP mess.'

The rest is history. The inevitable did not take long to happen. French forces invaded, not in Moroni, but at the airport, with the deployment of crack Paras brought in by helicopter. These troops then advanced towards Moroni and the GP barracks. After brief discussions and to avoid a possible bloodbath, the French agreed that Denard did not need to surrender and could vacate the islands in a dignified manner with his white officers in tow. It was done with customary French *savoir-faire*, gentlemen's agreements all round...

Denard then handed his Comorian forces over to the French commander at the airport, after a final passing review of his loyal troops. He and his men were allowed to board a commercial SafAir C-130 aircraft, fully armed and in uniform. Once airborne and on their way to Waterkloof Air Force Base on the outskirts of Pretoria, they removed their fatigues and handed over their weapons to the South African crew.

Years later, in 1995, Denard was still man enough to show the world his true calibre. He invaded the Comoros once more, took

Head of the South African contingent was Military Intelligence WO Charles Robinson who worked with the Comoros mercenary unit under Colonel Bob Denard as a full GP Lieutenant. Robinson originally served with the Royal Navy, the Rhodesian CIO, SA Navy, Military Intelligence and the Comoros GP. (Photo: Manuel Ferreira collection)

over in a couple of days and freed some of his ex-GP soldiers who had been jailed by the new order. He was totally loyal to his troops and they adored him.

The French wasted little time on this occasion and again invaded the island, arrested the colonel and escorted him back to France. There he was charged with the murder of President Abdallah Abdermane. When the matter eventually came to trial, Denard claimed that a faked coup was undertaken by the GP that night so that this could be blamed on the regular army, which would then be forcibly disarmed. It had all been carefully planned beforehand, he told the judges. He further maintained that President Abdermane had actually agreed to the faked coup and, at 00:10 hours on 26 November, had signed the order to disarm the regular army. Seconds later, he lay dead in his pyjamas. The simulated coup had gone terribly wrong, Denard claimed.

While the court maintained that it could not believe this version of events which led to the death of a serving president, he and his deputy Marques were acquitted. The prosecution had failed to prove its case, the reason being that a key witness, Manuel Ferreira's good old friend and comrade 'Foxtrot' could not be traced...

As Ferreira wrote afterwards to his colonel, 'Bob, I don't give a shit how the President died. The fact is that only you, Marques and Foxtrot were privy to exactly what happened that night. All three of you were in his room when he was shot. You and Commandant Marques were acquitted and that's all that matters to me.

'Moreover, you and your highly disciplined GP created the longest period of peace for the islands, during which time you oversaw the establishment of democratic institutions. You also helped develop the country's economic infrastructure, facilitated the creation of companies and jobs, promoted rural development, encouraged the building of roads and propelled the improvement of humanitarian conditions in a world where people had suffered relentlessly under a succession of rulers with little notion of transparent, compassionate governance...

'I salute you, *mon colonel*...'

Last words

Michael Rocord, French Prime Minister from 1988 to 1991 under President Mitterand, admitted in Washington in January 2000 that Colonel Bob Denard had been in a 'relationship' with the DGSE, the French External Security Agency. He disclosed that there was complicity between the French State and the plot to overthrow President Abdallah.

Five days before his assassination in November 1989, President Abdallah had sent a letter to President Mitterand, informing him that he had raised the question of the Comorian island of Mayotte in a memorandum to Javier Perez de Cuellar, Secretary-General of the United Nations.

Mayotte was then – and is still – the only part of the Comorian archipelago that remains under French control, an issue that has been consistently and vehemently contested by all governments of independent Comoros, ever since the island group achieved independence from France. It continues to be a matter that is both emotional and contentious among the majority of Comorians, including quite a few who continue to live on the twin islands that make up French-dependent Mayotte.

A final note too, from Manuel Ferreira, who today lives a quiet but industrious life in the Southern Cape with his family: 'After my period of service with the *Garde Présidentielle* came to an end, I went on to serve a few tours with the Zaire Secret Services under President Mobutu Sese Seko.'

But that, he says, 'is a story for another day ...'

1 Mike Hoare's book *Congo Mercenary* has been on the best-seller lists for decades.
2 General Sir David's exact words in the letter were: 'Neall Ellis is a great man: I and everyone in Sierra Leone owe him much.'
3 Al J. Venter: *Gunship Ace: The Wars of Neall Ellis, Helicopter Pilot and Mercenary*, Casemate Publishers, United States and Britain (with a South African edition published by Protea Books, Pretoria).
4 Duff Hart-Davis: *The War that Never Was*, Century, London, a division of Random House, 2011.

Former South African Air Force helicopter gunship commanders Arthur Walker and Neall Ellis took these photos while flying chopper support missions for Somalia's Puntland Police Maritime Force (PPMF). The unit was commanded at the time by Colonel Roelf van Heerden. A 40-year-old, French-built Alouette helicopter, still airborne, formed the basis of Puntland's anti-piracy operations and, top, the Panamanian-registered *Iceberg 1*, one of the ships attacked by pirates and its crew members held hostage for three years. Most of the men on board were rescued as a consequence of Van Heerden's efforts. The helicopter remains operational and is armed with a single Soviet-era PKM belt-fed 7.62 mm machine gun. Colonel Van Heerden is writing a book about his Somali adventures.

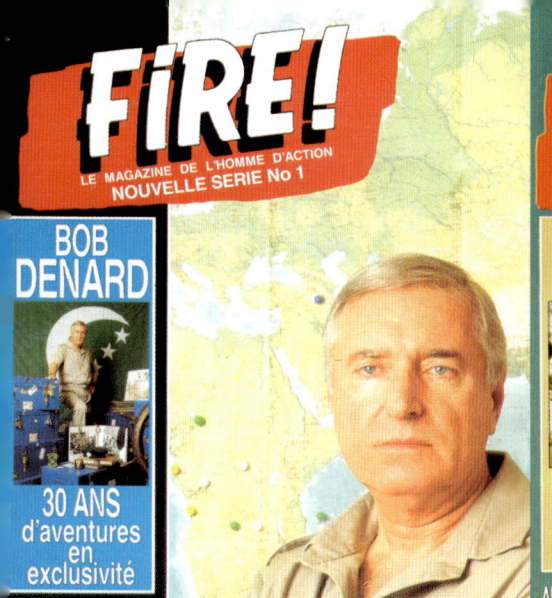

FIRE!

LE MAGAZINE DE L'HOMME D'ACTION
Nouvelle SERIE No 1

BOB DENARD
30 ANS d'aventures en exclusivité

- ASTRA A-70
- LES PARAS AU ZAIRE
- LE «RAID GAULOISES»
- LES ARMES DE POING DES «FEDS» US

FIRE!

LE MAGAZINE DE L'HOMME D'ACTION
Nouvelle formule No 3

BOB DENARD
30 ANS d'aventures: LE YEMEN

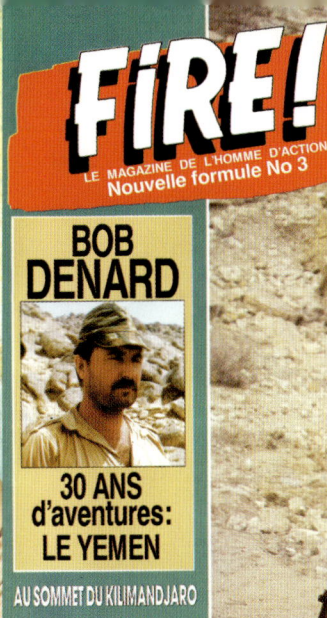

- AU SOMMET DU KILIMANDJARO
- COUTEAUX «HILL KNIVES»
- LE GLOCK «AMPHIBIE»
- DAN WESSON «SUPERMAG»

1ère année - Bimestriel N° NS 3
MAI-JUIN 1992

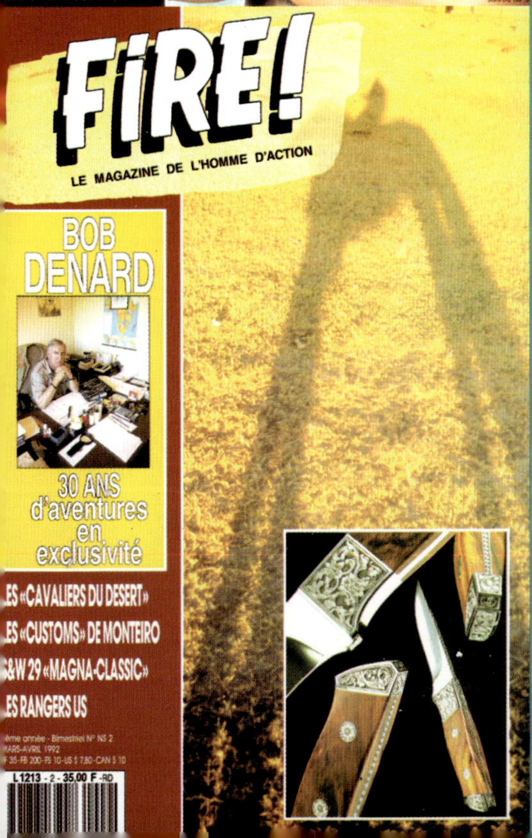

FIRE!

LE MAGAZINE DE L'HOMME D'ACTION

BOB DENARD
30 ANS d'aventures en exclusivité

- LES «CAVALIERS DU DESERT»
- LES «CUSTOMS» DE MONTEIRO
- S&W 29 «MAGNA-CLASSIC»
- LES RANGERS US

1ère année - Bimestriel N° NS 2
MARS-AVRIL 1992

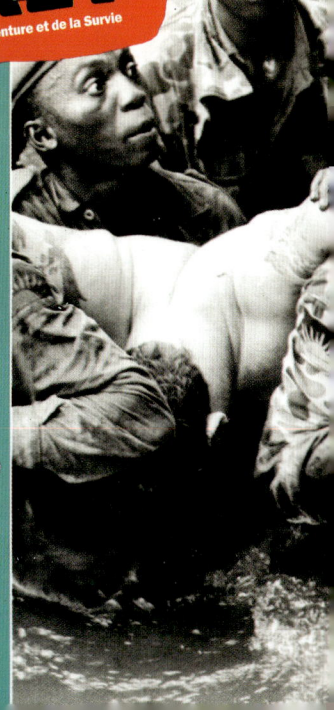

FIRE!
CHASSE, TIR, NATURE

Le Magazine de l'Aventure et de la Survie

BOB DENARD
30 ANS d'aventures: LE BIAFRA

- RAID MOTO «ANGOLA 91»
- CZ 75 «VECTOR CUSTOM»
- JEFFERY .600 Nitro-Express

Exclusif
NORIEGA - DEA

1ère année - Bimestriel N° NS 5
SEPTEMBRE-OCTOBRE 1992

Colonel Bob Denard, one of the most famous mercenary commanders of his era, fought in numerous conflicts, including against President Gamal Nasser's Egyptian Army after he had decided to subjugate Yemen. The British government decided to counter that move and sent in an SAS force commanded by Colonel Jim Johnson, who hired Arab and French mercenaries to sabotage Egyptian strongholds, airports and aircraft (Photos from Fiona Capstick's and author's collections). The bottom photo, courtesy of Leif Hellström, was taken when Denard was involved in the Congo.

A variety of views of war in Africa, mostly from the author's collection. Top shows black troops undergoing training, pre-teen soldiers in Uganda (bottom left) and in Angola, UNITA'S efforts at unconventional rail transport. The Mi-8 (centre left) is in the livery of the South Sudanese Air Force and was taken by Peter Wilkins while working in that country on behalf of Durban's Starlite Aviation.

A variety of shots from the Congo, courtesy of the Leif Hellström collection, showing the various air assets used against both the United Nations and anti-government rebels. The bottom photo depicts one of the WW2-vintage Trojan trainer/ground-support aircraft provided by the CIA and flown by Cuban expatriate pilots from Miami.

The beautiful old slave castle at Elmina in Ghana, today a national museum (Photo: Author) and below, some of the Cuban pilots who flew in the Congo in the 1960s after they had been hired in Miami for the task by the CIA. Bomber pilots were also recruited by Langley. (Photo: Leif Hellström collection)

Some of the Rhodesian troopies who fought with Darrell Watt in the rebel colony (top photos); the two centre pictures are from Neall Ellis and were taken in Sierra Leone and, below, Ellis's Mi-24 helicopter gunship fires a salvo of rockets at rebel positions in a jungle village in the interior. (Photo: Author)

After Executive Outcomes had been ousted from Sierra Leone, Cobus Claassens, who had previously served in the South African Army, stayed on and helped create an anti-piracy unit in the tiny West African state. Here, top, he and his men intercept a suspected smuggler in open waters beyond Freetown (Photo: Author). Below shows aircraft working for the Red Cross delivering food to Biafra's starving millions. (Photo: Leif Hellström collection)

CHAPTER FOUR

CAIRO – HEART OF THE ISLAMIC REVOLT

The Egyptians have a unique way of dealing with problems. They like to sweep them away in bursts of enthusiasm that often defy logic: Nasser in opposing the colonial ethos; his successors in opposing Israel and the seemingly irrational break with the Soviets at a time when Cairo was almost totally alienated from Washington ...

Much has changed in the forty-something years since I first visited Egypt not very long after Israel's destructive Six Day War, termed the Third Arab-Israeli War by some historians, or in Arabic, *an-Naksah*; 'The Setback'. The consequences of that disaster continue to have enormous ramifications in the contemporary Middle Eastern approach towards people of Jewish origin.

Indeed, still more is changing in that country right now. My November 2011 visit to the great Arab city, known for many centuries as *al-Qahira* – Cairo the Victorious – followed the much-publicised uprising that finally unseated President Hosni Mubarak. That ended a three-decade rule that was notable for its close links with Washington and, of considerably more consequence, a demonstrably acquiescent Egyptian attitude towards Israel. Had I returned home a week later, I would have been there to observe another round of violence that erupted in el-Tahrir Square and elsewhere in the country that left more than 40 people dead and wounded thousands.

The insurrection, as we all know, went on for months and though Egypt's ruling class at first scoffed at the possibility of the dissidents gaining any kind of advantage, it soon became clear that the revolt had the support of the masses. As in Tunisia, followed by Libya, the writing, as the old adage goes, was on the wall, an aphorism that originally had its origins in the hieroglyphic Egypt of old.

One of the more disturbing disclosures to emerge after President Mubarak had departed the scene, was that even as security forces pressed their violent crackdown on protestors and people were being killed and wounded, the United States continued to send ammunition to Egypt. This was disclosed by Amnesty International on their website on 7 December 2011.

The rights group said that one shipment carried at least seven tons of chemical irritants and riot control agents such as tear gas, and was destined for the country's Interior Ministry. It was one of three shipments that came from Combined Systems, an American company that specialises in these restrictive agents. Amnesty disclosed that many of the cartridges and grenades picked up by protesters in Cairo's Tahrir Square – which had become the heart of the demonstrations – bore the company's trademark.

Though I had been to Egypt many times over past decades, including while making five television documentaries on the country, its people and its cultures – both Muslim and Christian Coptic – nothing could have prepared me for some of the changes that greeted me this time round.

The Nile, beautiful in places and especially so in dilapidated Cairo has entranced generations of visitors. This is the view from one of the few five-star hotels still operational in the city. (Photo: Author)

Chapter 4
Cairo – Heart of the Islamic Revolt

By November 2011, the seat of pharaohs, caliphs, imams and the *sha'b* – the masses – seemed to have undergone a metamorphosis like no other in its 5,000-year history. Over millennia, civilisations had come and gone, Alexander the Great had arrived as a conquering hero and so, too, had the Caesars. The intrusive arrival of Islam happened 1,400 years ago and, thereafter, there was Napoleon Bonaparte, British colonial rule, as well as two world wars.

In one way or another, each one of these historical episodes left their imprints, some of them indelible. But everyday society remained little changed and it stayed that way until the 20th Century and the onset of an age of modern communications. Almost overnight, a new form of religious Jihad had taken hold and these days it was the turn of Egypt's Muslim Brotherhood to win acceptance by the people.

Like their cousins in Lebanon, the even more radical Hizbollah (to whom the Brothers are politically linked – even if the one is Sunni and the other preponderantly Shi'ite) the radical clerics in Egypt are not only the most efficient proselytisers in the Middle East, they are also the most powerful political force. Their efforts among Egypt's poor and dispossessed are exemplary, in large part because their workers – almost all of them unpaid and, quite remarkably, incorruptible in an extremely corrupt society – are active within a large section of the population that has little or nothing. Moreover, they ask for nothing in return. It is all the "Will of Allah" they tell the supplicants and when that happens, people take notice.

More worrying – to the West and, in particular Washington and Jerusalem – is the Brotherhood's subtle promise of possibly reverting to age-old traditional Koranic traditions that include Sharia and, possibly, the abolition of all things Western. Also, it is ironic that a Western style of democracy brought to power the *least* democratic of all the parties involved in the 2011/2012 general elections.

It was in August 1969, a little more than two years after the Six Day War that I first travelled overland through Egypt, one of a tiny band of Westerners who saw fit to visit a country then still caught up in a vortex of ongoing hostilities with the Jewish State.

Weeks before, while settled in a small hotel on the outskirts of Addis Ababa in the early hours of the morning, I listened on the tiny portable radio that I carried in my luggage to a broadcast on Voice of America's Africa Service. Reception was patchy, but there was no missing the emotion in the voice of a commentator in Houston who spoke of somebody called Neil Armstrong just having set foot on the surface of the moon. Like much taking place in those early years of

The grim, unsmiling face of Sheikh Omar Abdel-Rahman – formerly head of Egypt's *al-Gama'a al-Islamiyya*, and today serving a life sentence for sedition in the United States – appears everywhere in Cairo's streets. Egypt's Muslim Brotherhood government has approached Washington numerous times to have him released from prison and sent home. (Photo: Author)

uncertain adventure and experiment, I was transfixed.

I was equally enthused to arrive soon after that in Khartoum, the Sudanese capital city and was about to begin my long overland journey up the Nile. Ultimately my destination was Cairo and the first leg – one of several by train – was interrupted by the kind of two-day sand storm to which only the Sahara Desert can subject the unsuspecting. Having eventually reached the sprawling desert rail terminal town of Wadi Halfa, then slowly being engulfed by the waters of a rising Lake Aswan, we were shifted, en masse, on board a paddle steamer that took us three days to reach Aswan.

It was not an easy journey. Like other non-Arabs, I was subjected to lengthy interrogatory sessions by officials wherever and whenever we were stopped. Abu Simbel, then not yet raised because of the rising levels of the dam, was all but devoid of tourists, as was Luxor and its historical Valley of the Kings.

It was also curious that though there were people suspicious of this youthful British traveller moving about Egypt on his own, I never felt threatened. Attacks on unarmed tourists by religious zealots only came years later. At the same time, local people were reluctant to be drawn into conversation with a Westerner, largely because security police and the armed forces were just about everywhere.

The last part of my journey was in a luxurious mahogany-panelled coach, a legacy of the British Raj and crammed with Egyptian army and air force personnel. As the only Westerner on board, I was regarded with a curious measure of friendly misgivings, with just about everybody asking me, almost in as many words, what the hell I was doing there.

That stopped abruptly after I'd raised an arm and, in total astonishment, gesticulated towards a bunch of World War II-era barrage balloons over one of the towns that we were passing through at the time. An obviously-concerned Egyptian Air Force officer with whom I had been talking suggested that I look elsewhere whenever our train passed any kind of military establishment or army convoy that included armour, of which there were a lot. Point taken...

Then, at dawn, came the monolith that we all know as Cairo, one of the high points of my life as a foreign correspondent.

Not nearly as crowded or as noisy as the 26 million residents of the greater city make it today, the place was a serpentine, contradictory kind of place that tended to stultify the senses. It took me a while to understand why Cairo, a thousand years ago, had nowhere to go but up, and why, even then, there were suburbs crowded with 10- and 12-storey tenement buildings.

The traffic forty years ago wasn't nearly as dangerous as it is today, but there was already an intrusive armed security presence on every street corner and alongside every public building. These days one gets the impression that there is not a foreign embassy in the Egyptian capital that does not have strong-points at its gates that are manned by soldiers: the Syrian Embassy opposite the King Hotel in El Dokki on the west bank of the Nile seemed to have a full company of troops guarding its environs during my most recent sojourn.

Following recent Israeli military adventures, immediate impressions during my earlier visits was of a great city under siege, with concrete and sandbagged blast protecting walls in front of all the entrances of most large buildings. In places, it was almost reminiscent of old movies of London during the Blitz.

Meantime, there have been significant changes, among the people especially. Forty years ago there were many more *galabiyas* about than one sees today, modern Egyptian males are apparently more comfortable in Western garb than in the long-flowing, simple robes that the people of the Nile always seem to have preferred. So too with the Tarboosh, the Turkish fez that one hardly ever sees in contemporary Egypt.

During earlier visits, there were not nearly as many beards among the men or, among the women, the *niqab*, and the conservative headscarf that is the most radical Islamic all-black attire that covers women's bodies from head to toe with only the eyes showing. These recent developments also reflect a Muslim Brotherhood influence.

For the majority though, basic lifestyle has changed little over the decades, with *dukkans* everywhere, selling anything from desert dates to orange juice and toothpaste. There also seem to be almost as many sidewalk cafes with their hubble-bubble-smoking patrons as *milayas*, the traditionally worn long hair-covering shawl customarily preferred by women of Islamic persuasion. In November 2011, I ended up spending quite a bit of time, usually for breakfast and for evening drinks at one of the nicest not-so-little coffee bars in the Middle East.

Cilantro, on Messaha Square, not far from where I was staying, might almost be regarded as Cairo's answer to the kind of hangout in Paris's St-Germain-des-Prés that, in its day, was frequented by the cognoscenti of another era – Arabic versions of Gertrude Stein, Scott Fitzgerald and James Joyce. A heady crowd, including many of the country's budding politicians, gathers there each evening.

The place is invariably crowded with students, most of them enthusiastic young men and women who wouldn't be out of place in one of the dives off London's Great Russell Street or near one of New York's better-known universities. Cairo's youthful intelligentsia is a diverse, friendly bunch, always willing to help and, once engaged in conversation, astonishingly well informed about the world around them; certainly far more so than the average American or British undergraduate. The truth is, with immediate prospects that are both

The Syrian Embassy in Cairo has been the focus of almost daily protests by expatriate groups campaigning against the regime of Damascus President Bashar-al-Assad. The author stayed in an adjacent hotel and was a witness to many of these demonstrations. (Photo: Author)

forbidding and threatened, these people take life seriously, almost all of them intent on making something out of what had previously been nothing.

It is a little incongruous though, as charming as Cilantro is, that the coffee shop lies only a stone-throw from one of the main El Dokki shopping areas. Along one area, butchers predominate and there are hundreds of carcasses of freshly slaughtered sheep tethered to their overhangs on the pavement outside their shops: you actually have to step lightly to avoid blood dripping onto your head. And then, a few yards away and corralled in makeshift pens, are scores more of these animals waiting to have their throats cut in the tradition of Hallal. It matters little to these people that they allow the lifeblood to flow into the city drains.

There have been some notable changes. In November 2011, I was hardly ever pestered by what had previously been legions of beggars cajoling for *baksheesh*. The nation today is prouder, more resigned to its destiny, and to beg for money would be regarded by many as unseemly. It still happens of course, as it did in the old days, but now the practice is mostly restricted to street children and vagabonds.

The most striking change, I was to discover, was in communications, a facet that in the mind of the average Cairene has made the globe a good deal smaller than before. Television, the Internet, Facebook etc., were, as Egyptians have discovered, an inseparable link to the world beyond the Nile, Arab ones included. With the social media, these people now get the kind of information that was unthinkable at the time of my first visit.

In 1969 the average Egyptian lived life more or less as he and she had always done. King Farouk and those before him had come and gone and the country was ruled by its leaders almost as the kind of personal fief that might have been in place when Tutankhamun was placed in his gilded tomb in the Valley of the Kings. Fallaheen peasants – by far the bulk of the population – accepted their lot and paid their taxes as the uncomplaining, disposable Serfs that they were.

There was no possibility of them ever being able to question the authority of those in control. Islam, when it arrived 1,400 years ago, simply reinforced these tenets, as Prophet Muhammad, peace be upon Him, had willed it. Allah commanded all, said the Imams of old and, as ancient tradition dictated, nobody dared question the Word.

In the late 1980s, about twenty years after my first visit, I returned once more to Egypt, this time to make a series of documentary films and though not a great deal had changed, the masses, as always, remained pitifully impoverished. But some forms of change had arrived, television especially.

Though Egypt started its first TV broadcasts a few years after the end of Hitler's War, only the wealthy and the connected could afford to link up and watch a paucity of earlier programmes that eventually went on to make Cairo the broadcasting capital of the Arab world. Slowly, inexorably, more people were able to buy TV sets, more often than not in the great expanse of Egypt outside the cities, but on a cooperative basis so that costs were shared by the rural community. A village in the interior would elect a committee that would collect money from their locals to buy an aerial and a set and it would be placed in the middle of the village where everybody would gather after dark and watch the evening's offerings, which more often than not included football matches.

I was able to observe this from up close while filming in a tiny commune north-east of Cairo, not very far from Damietta, a provincial capital. We'd spend two days recording the antics of a couple of potters who were making amphora pots that the village women would use to collect water from the river. These two artisans, like their forefathers, used the same Nile mud that scores of generations of amphora-makers had resorted to and their skills were essentially the same. The only visible progress was a single bulb that provided light in the almost primeval hut near the water's edge where they spent their 11 hours a day producing the 30 or 40 jugs that were later baked in a kiln.

All else was by hand, including the stone wheel attached to a primitive traction device that they drove with their feet: it powered the revolving wheel before them on which the two men shaped the mud, a messy business, but under the circumstances, effective.

They'd work for an hour or two and take five minutes for a smoke outside in the sun. It was hard going in damp and debilitating conditions that obviously didn't make for old bones. But these simple, devout people didn't complain because they knew no better. Their fathers had spent their lives in similar conditions, as had legions of their antecedents before them.

But there was a single notable difference to the routine. Come sunset, the two labourers would wash their bodies in the clear waters of the Nile and head home to their modest dwellings in their village where food was waiting. That done, they would head for the town square where the TV was already blaring the day's news. And though our subjects might have been regarded as backward by the occasional outsider, like ourselves, who passed through, these good folk were soon able to accept that hard as their lives were, the world did not end where the only road into the interior petered out in the desert on the edge of town.

With the reluctant assistance of our government-appointed Arab minder and translator, we were able to answer their questions about the civil war then raging in not-too-distant Lebanon, and even to offer an opinion as to whether President Ronald Reagan was a good man or possibly evil.

Obviously, it didn't take long for Israel to enter the equation and everybody was surprised to learn that I had actually visited that horrific 'den of vipers', which raised suspicions that I might be a Mossad spy. This was something, courtesy of the Egyptian broadcasting system, they were also familiar with.

All that took place almost a quarter century before my last visit in 2011 and in the interim, changes have been even more radical. An event had taken place, not only in Egypt, but in several other Islamic countries during a period that the media had dubbed 'The Arab Spring'.

In short shrift, a series of unconventional revolutionary steps were taken by the formerly despised masses to depose a bunch of dictators that had ruled too long and far too much in their own self-interests. Egypt's President Mubarak and Colonel Muammar Gadaffi of Libya were among the more prominent of the oligarchs that were unseated.

Egypt's uncertain future rests on several issues that threaten to unravel and, in the process, possibly push the country in the direction of more radical elements eager to snatch the initiative. The Muslim Brotherhood has been quick off the mark and has moved into an unassailable front-ranking position in the struggle.

Political slogans apart, the Brotherhood will be faced with the same problems that dogged the last government, the most pressing being Egypt's economy.

Though the Brotherhood maintains that it is a largely moderate political force and would be able to contain the Islamic zealots within its ranks, not everybody is so sure. The accusation that the movement is biding its time and paying what is termed 'lip service' to democratic principles has become commonplace within the country's media, and it will stay that way until the Imams decide that a free press is not in the interests of Egyptian Society, something that also took place in Iran after the Mullahs took over.

Groups of protestors often gather in their hundreds and the Egyptian Army is on permanent standby in adjacent streets. Demonstrations rarely lead to violence though. (Photo: Author)

That the Muslim Brotherhood holds powerful sway over the majority of the population is without question.

Even before Mubarak was deposed, the movement had its agents active in every corner of the country. Moreover, it enjoyed a significant advantage that in the short time available, its strengths became unassailable: unlike almost all the other Egyptian political parties, the Muslim Brotherhood had no need to explain to the majority of the population who they are. Nor did they have any need to detail their objectives.

Everybody in the country was aware that the movement is totally committed to the masses – and that sentiment refers to *all* Egyptian people, as it is detailed in its manifesto. This document also stresses that its actions, from the supreme administrative top, all the way down to the lowest level of serfdom, are dictated by Koranic Law.

How all this is likely to be implemented, leaders like Mohammed Badie – the ultra-conservative, eighth supreme leader of the Muslim Brotherhood, and his predecessor, Mohammed Akif – are not prepared to say. But what alarms Egyptian secularists, liberals, Christians and other minorities, is that once the Brotherhood achieves a majority of seats in the Egyptian Assembly, it will impose on the nation rigid and regressive religious laws that in all likelihood might ultimately compare with the worst of those of Afghanistan's Taliban.

Though these words are harsh, the fear is real enough to have caused many of Egypt's better heeled commercial and industrial leaders to make interim plans for themselves and their families to live in more equable political climes. London and Paris are among the most favoured destinations. One of the reports carried by The Associated Press after the elections stated that in the nine months, following the departure of Mubarak, a quarter million Egyptian Christians had left the country and that more were making interim plans to leave because they feared for their lives and those of their families, children especially.

There are a number of pointers with regard to future actions that are likely to be taken by the Muslim Brotherhood command.

One of these involves the link with Israel, and by inference, with the United States, which, since the signing of the Camp David Accords by Egyptian President Anwar El Sadat and Israeli Prime Minister Menachem Begin in September 1978, has contributed more than US$60 billion to Cairo's coffers.

It says much that Sadat was assassinated three years later by dissident Egyptian Army soldiers who totally opposed any links with the Jewish State and that the power brokers then – more than 30 years ago – were Muslim Brotherhood, one of whom was Ayman al-Zawahiri, who has always taken the radical Qutb line of thought that every society, Muslims especially, is worthy of Jihad.

The cell – originally established by al-Zawahiri before he went into exile – eventually evolved into the Egyptian Islamic Jihad, which holds even more extreme views than the Brotherhood, while the so-called Qutb Doctrine stems from Sayyid Qutb, a hardliner who was imprisoned for a decade and propagated the concept that a revolutionary vanguard is honour-bound to defend 'True Islam'.

It is interesting that the Muslim Brotherhood has always declared that any link with the Jewish state would, as the Book dictates, be *mamnu*: forbidden. Significantly, al-Zawahiri today heads al-Qaeda.

A lot of what will take place in the Middle East over the next few years – politically and economically – is likely to be predicated by several factors, the most important of which is the Egyptian economy.

Population growth, coupled with employment – or, more likely, the lack of it – will undoubtedly follow. This has become manifest over the past decade as the Egyptian pound has lost good value compared to previous years. Should this trend continue, all these issues together are likely to have a profound long-term effect on the nation's growth and, should there be a serious downturn, political disenchantment will unquestionably follow.

While many of those involved in such an imbroglio are obedient followers of the faith, the more immediate, more pressing need for every one of them is to put bread on the table. And when this is not forthcoming, as in Iran, dissidence, no matter what the leaders – Muslim Brotherhood or otherwise – say, is likely to result.

European and American economists are obviously concerned about what is going on in this corner of the Middle East, primarily because the Egyptian economy is not only stagnant, the collapse of the tourist market – because of sporadic violence and revolts – has created critical conditions in many spheres.

The unofficial unemployment rate, I was told by one of the political leaders (who was unable to back up his comment with statistics – because there are none in present-day Egypt) is now heading towards the 25 per cent mark and growing: this in a society where the labour force has increased from 9.5 million to more than 25 million in the past three or four decades. Egypt's population has increased to 80 million in the same period.

Part of the problem lies with a 1950s-era Nasserite guarantee that there would be state employment for every university graduate in the country. Yet, when the government announced a decade ago that it was hiring 170,000 people, the move sparked protests that left dozens injured. The mass job offer, it turned out, was aimed solely at more recent graduates and left thousands of older bureaucrats-in-waiting in the lurch, some of whom had been waiting for state jobs since 1985.

These developments were all the more remarkable because Britain's *Economist* a short while before had dubbed Egypt 'the very model of a modern emerging market ... the International Monetary Fund's prize pupil'.

Then the economy was burgeoning, with registration of private cars up almost fourfold in two decades. Literacy, meanwhile, had improved by half again in the same period (from 42 to 61 percent) and it continues to grow in large measure because of the number of female graduates.

A Chatham House report that appeared in 2011 encapsulates it adequately when it declares that Egypt's financial problems today are linked to the neoliberal economic policies of the Mubarak era which were seen as closely tied to corruption and crony capitalism.[1]

Egyptian troops encountered during the author's visit late 2011 were an ordered and disciplined security element around Cairo, always neatly turned out and polite to enquiries by strangers like myself. As can be seen on the following page, Egypt's weapon of choice is the ubiquitous Kalashnikov. (Photos: Author)

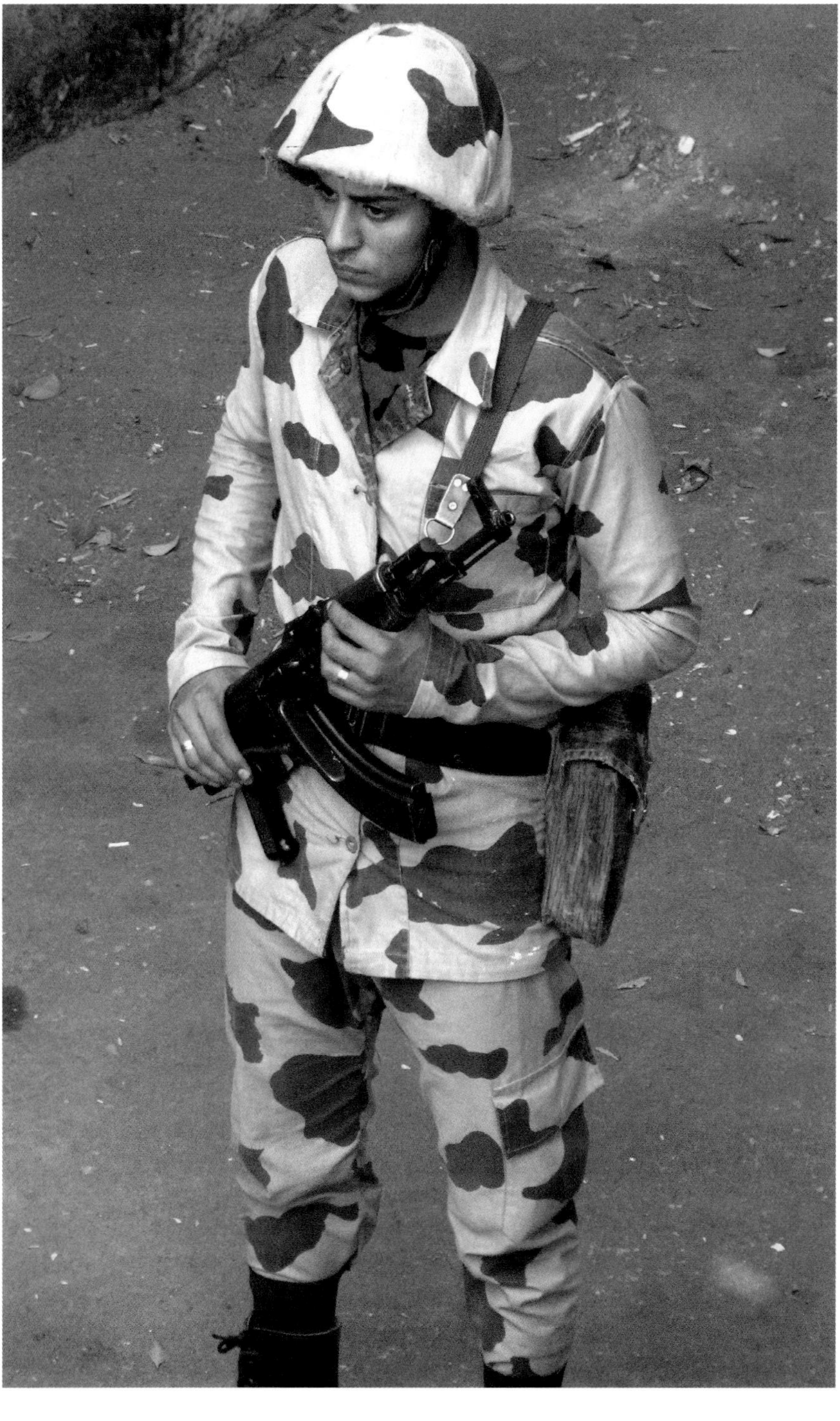

The report makes some startling comments linked to the high economic growth rates with an average GDP growth of six per cent in the last few years of Hosni Mubarak's rule. This was linked to increased foreign direct investment, attributed largely to the economic policies of a technocratic cabinet headed by former Prime Minister Ahmed Nazif.

It goes on: 'The cabinet's reforms were argued to have created an environment that was favourable to business and attractive to investors. This helped propel Egypt into the international spotlight as an emerging market of choice. On this basis, some of the participants felt that a number of the financial-sector reforms had been praiseworthy. Reforms to the banking sector were cited as an example of a successful policy which is now bearing fruit in the transitional period.

'However, one important complaint was repeatedly raised: high growth rates did not lead to an equitable distribution of wealth between rich and poor. In fact, there were marked indications of increasing inequality. Liberalisation policies and free-market reforms, involving a diminished role for the state, were said to have failed to meet Egypt's developmental needs.

'One speaker said that only ten per cent of Egyptians have bank accounts today, a figure that has changed little since 2005.'

It says a good deal that 'bread, freedom and social justice' was one of the cornerstone slogans from Egypt's 2011 revolution, 'dramatically highlighting the importance of economic development – or the lack thereof – in instigating high levels of resentment against the former regime. Participants saw a reappraisal of economic policy as a crucial step towards meeting the demands of the revolution.'

Walk about the streets of Cairo today, especially in the vicinity of many of the seats of higher conventional learning (as opposed to hard-line Islamic religious instruction) and there are almost as many girls as boys to be seen among student groups flocking the streets after lectures. I spoke to many of them when the opportunity availed, which was not easy in a society where single men do not talk to unmarried women, or girls in the street, irrespective of your motive.

What then has brought about this change? In the Arab world, Egypt still boasts the second biggest economy after Saudi Arabia and Cairo remains it's most powerful political and military influence. The ancient axiom still holds true: if Egypt sneezes, the rest of the Arab world catches a cold...

Part of the answer lies in what the *Economist* more recently termed 'Egypt's growing pile of woes,' which, it warned, 'carried the risk of spontaneous combustion'.

It goes further, because the other, more dominant aspect remains Israel, a festering conundrum that simply refuses to go away. The general consensus in Cairo today is not whether Cairo and Jerusalem will remain on nodding terms – their respective diplomatic missions are still in place – but rather, whether it is possible for the two nations to hold onto the shaky liaison they, under American patronage, have succeeded in establishing over past decades.

Part of the motivation is hard cash. One of the clauses of the Camp David Accords is that both nations receive $3 billion a year while peace is maintained. And while Israel is today one of the seventh or eighth wealthiest countries in the world, Egypt is among the poorest and even the Muslim Brotherhood would think twice about losing that kind of enticement.

1 Chatham House, London: MENA Programme: Egypt Dialogue Workshop Report: 'Egypt's Economy in the Transitional Period': September 2011.

CHAPTER FIVE

'PADDLEBUM' AND THE ROUGH RIDERS OF THE RUFIJI RIVER

In sub-Saharan Africa there are few river systems as wild, untamed and as unforgiving as that of the Rufiji in southern Tanzania. To add to its mystique, the whiff of history almost overwhelms those visiting the area for the first time. Veteran African historian and former professional hunter Hannes Wessels gives us another take on this imbroglio.

East Africa has attracted its share of distant visitors for millennia, not only from the Middle East but also from China. Numerous legends – some apocryphal, others for real – detail a variety of expeditions to the eastern fringes of the Indian Ocean. Pliny the Elder listed a few, so did Herodotus, and some involved destinations all the way south to Mozambique and beyond.

Indeed, in his scribblings, the Greek historian Herodotus talked about several expeditions out of Egypt. He actually mentioned the Sofala Shoals in Mozambique, the word having Yemeni origins: *sufala*, suggesting shoals or shallows.[1] Related documents record a maritime disaster that involved what has been termed the 'Eudoxus' a 2,000-year-old wreck found near Cape Delgado on Tanzania's border with Mozambique, which it was said, could have been heading towards Cape Rhapta, the name given by the Phoenicians to the Rufiji Delta.

There is evidence of even more distant 'foreigners' having visited these outposts. Even today you still find shards of ancient Chinese pottery among the ruins in Kenya's Gedi, only a short stroll from Watamu's beautiful beach, south of Malindi. Add to that a mystery that embraces the so-called 'royal dog' of Madagascar, a breed called the 'Bichon'. Their spread is linked to Phoenician maritime peregrinations and possibly other ventures out of the Mediterranean

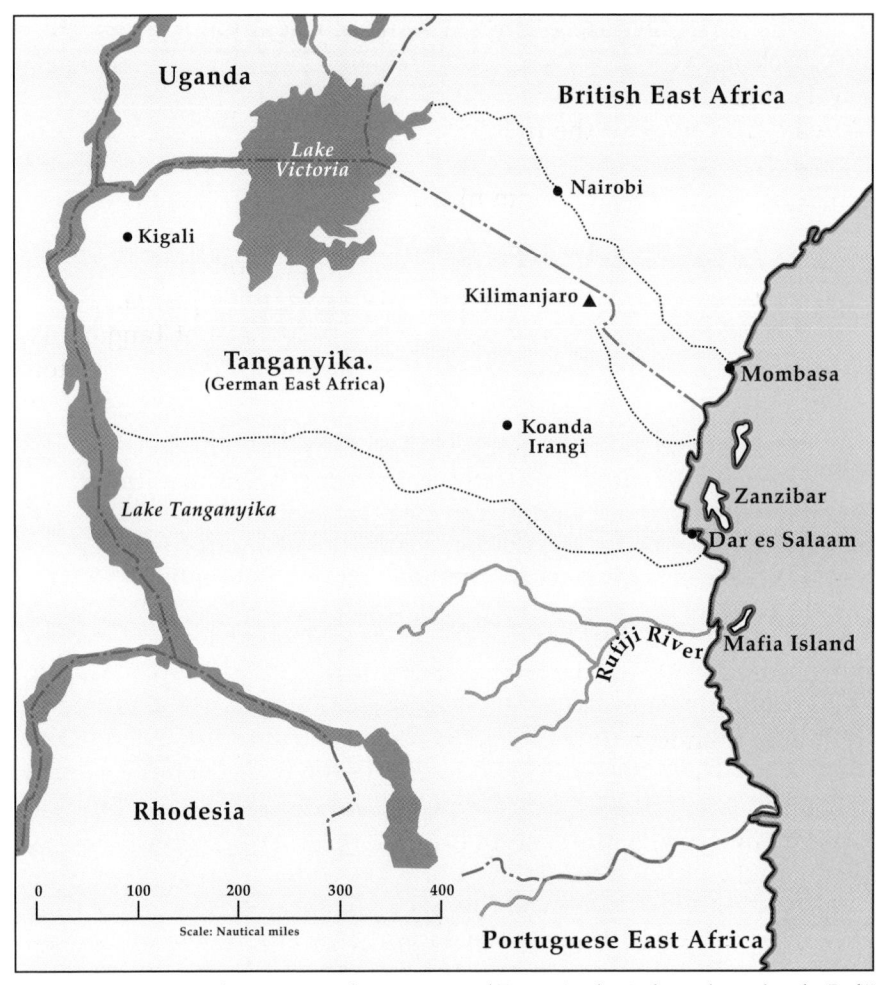

Originally a German colony, Tanganyika was renamed Tanzania after independence, but the Rufiji is still where it always was, running strong in the south of the country.

at a time when our forefathers were running about Europe in skins.

Similarly, there are cats on Lamu Island in Kenya, with many of the traits shared with those depicted on Egyptian hieroglyphics. It says much that no Phoenician worth his salt would dream of going to sea without having at least one cat on board.

But it is the 'Rhapta', a settlement in the Rufiji Delta that concerns us here. Our earliest colonial history – and that includes the Arabs who came to Africa in search of ivory, gold, precious stones and, of course, slaves – are known to have sailed up this river into what is today Central Tanzania, or Tanganyika, as it was once called. The records show that they collected cargoes of all the items mentioned,

Chapter 5
'Paddlebum' and the Rough Riders of the Rufiji River

as well as spice, incense, gum and some of the animals which they took back as gifts for the leaders that originally sponsored these wanderings. It comes as no surprise that early Europeans who visited Africa weren't the first to ship chimpanzees home to amuse themselves and others.

The Sultan of Oman – from his expatriate seat in Zanzibar – sent his surrogates up this same river to find these goods, which were brought back to the island and then shipped on the returning monsoon across the Indian Ocean to the Arabian Peninsula.

Fast forward to the 19th Century and the conquest of Tanganyika by forces loyal to Imperial Germany, and it was the murky waters of the Rufiji that once 'ran scarlet' with the blood of those killed in what is recorded as the Maji Maji rebellion against Kaiser Wilhelm's rule. *Maji*, in Swahili means water, and local tribesmen believed the bullets fired by the German Mausers turned against them would dissolve into a kind of vapour. They couldn't have been more wrong.

Following some initial setbacks, the German forces – in what they referred to as *Deutsch-Ostafrika* or German East Africa – recovered and proceeded to wreak havoc on those who had the courage to challenge their rule. But then, Tanganyika's coastal Africans – the warlike Makonde people especially – were always a recalcitrant lot.

Shortly before World War I, an illustrious German by the name of General Von Lettow-Vorbeck arrived in Tanganyika and he was to make his mark in a succession of East African battles that he fought against the Allies for the duration of hostilities. Already an accomplished strategist, he commanded the only Imperial German force that never capitulated. At the end of the war, he marched his men across the frontier into what was then listed as the British colony of Northern Rhodesia and ordered his *Schutztruppen* to lay down their arms.

Paul Emil von Lettow-Vorbeck – he died in 1964 – commanded what is regarded today as the single greatest guerrilla operation in recent history. It was also the most successful. For four years, with a relatively small army that never exceeded 14,000 men – roughly 3,000 Germans and 11,000 Africans – he held in check a much larger force of 300,000 South African, British, Belgian, and Portuguese troops.

Among these was a large South African force commanded by former Boer leader Jan Christian Smuts: the German general ran rings around him as well, which was surprising because Smuts was no stranger to unconventional war.

The South Africans suffered badly for the duration of that campaign, losing more men through illness and tropical disease than in battle. That story is detailed in a marvellous book titled *For King and Kaiser*, written by Gerald Lange. It is worth mentioning that these exploits have not gone unnoticed by Hollywood. Aspects of the Von Lettow-Vorbeck saga features in a 1993 episode of the television series *The Young Indiana Jones Chronicles*.

A poignant reminder of this clash of arms is the grave of Sir Frederick Courteney Selous, one of Africa's great explorers and hunters, on the banks of the Rufiji River. It was during that campaign that Selous – whose name was subsequently adopted by a crack Rhodesian counter-insurgency unit – was killed by a German sniper while reconnoitring the lower reaches of the Rufiji. Typical of the level of chivalry of the time, General Von Lettow-Vorbeck, clearly devastated by the news, called an immediate truce to mourn the passing of Sir Frederick, whom he called a great adversary. He wrote a letter of condolence to the Selous family in Britain and declared himself distraught that he would never get to meet the man whom he acknowledged as a great fellow officer.

The Rufiji has many other secrets. Some surround the final moments of the 4,000-ton SMS *Königsberg*, a German Navy cruiser that was intended to have sunk numerous French and British ships then plying the Indian Ocean at the start of the Great War. In fact, she only managed to send one Allied ship to the bottom before engine failure forced her to seek refuge among the mangroves in the Rufiji Delta in 1914. The *Königsberg* was joined in exile by her supply ship, the *Somali*.

But for the determined efforts of the remarkable South African big-game hunter 'Jungle Man' Hannes Pretorius – then a major in the British Army – she may never have been discovered. Braving hippos and crocs, he swam across the Rufiji at night to report the position of the enemy ship to his superiors.

What only emerged later was that the cruiser's engines were in a sad state. Most of it had to be dismantled and sent overland to Dar es Salaam by truck and ox-wagon for repairs, no easy task when there was a war to cope with, and some of the parts having to be shipped from the original factory in Germany.

The British wasted no time to use this disaster to its own advantage. After Major Pretorius had pin-pointed the cruiser's position at its riverside hideout, the cruiser HMS *Chatham* moved down the East African coast late in October 1914. Two additional British cruisers, HMS *Dartmouth* and HMS *Weymouth* arrived a month later and

Chapter 5
'Paddlebum' and the Rough Riders of the Rufiji River

blockaded the Rufiji Delta. *Chatham* at one stage opened fire at some distance and set fire to *Somali*, but it failed to hit the *Königsberg*, which promptly moved further upstream.

Finally, two shallow-draught monitors—HMS *Mersey* and HMS *Severn* were towed all the way to East Africa from Malta. They headed for the Kenyan port of Mombasa – first traversing the Suez Canal and then the length of the Red Sea before they reached the Swahili Coast. Aided by a squadron of four primitive bi-planes brought in from South Africa, the British warships engaged the *Königsberg* in a long-range duel, with the aircraft acting as spotters for the British gunners. It took a couple of days, but the six-inch guns on board the monitors finally did the trick and reduced Kaiser Wilhelm's warship – the same one, ironically, that had once taken him on a state visit to Britain – to scrap.

What was left was only finally salvaged in 1964, well after Tanzania's independence.

Eighty years later, a youthful Michael Rowbotham, another remarkable white African – but only by self-adoption – studied the charts that detailed the river's meandering course. Scion of a blue-blooded martial family and related to King Edward III, his upbringing was typical of that experienced by members of what the establishment likes to refer to as 'Landed Gentry'.

This historical photo and those on the next page are of the wreck of the Imperial German Navy cruiser SMS *Königsberg*, sunk in the Rufiji Delta by Allied action early in World War I. Wilbur Smith based his book *Shout at the Devil* on this action. (Sourced at *Bundesarchiv*, Germany)

Sent to Holyrood School in Bognor Regis, a stint at Cheltenham, acknowledged as a 'breeding ground for men who had fight to the death for King and Empire' followed. The school was as good as its reputation. Cheltenham produced more recipients of the Victoria Cross than any other establishment in Britain or the Commonwealth. Within those tough confines Mike Rowbotham's nickname of 'Paddlebum' – Boater's Backside – materialised and stuck.

Leaving school, the war in Europe was already gathering pace. Ordered to report for duty at the Brig of Don in Scotland, he was posted to the Argyll and Sutherland Highlanders as a private, but it was a short stay before he entered an officer cadet training unit. Rowbotham eventually emerged as a subaltern, having earned a commission in the famed 51st Highland Division of the Gordon Highlanders – 'The Jocks'.

A distinguished unit, their claims to a special place in military history came with the routing of an Indian garrison that fled on hearing that their attackers wore nothing under their kilts.

For 'Paddle', though, more serious stuff was waiting. Sent across the Channel to the town of Goch in France, he experienced his first brush with the Reaper when American planes bombed his unit in error. Some of the most intense close combat of the war resulted, causing the unit to take nearly a thousand casualties before the final German surrender, by which time they were on the outskirts of the naval base at Bremershaven.

The war over, the Gordons were quickly dispatched to Tripoli in Libya to deal with a domestic insurrection, and there, young Rowbotham was given an insight of what life was like in East Africa from some of the men who had passed through the region before the war. Discharged from the army with the rank of captain, he spurned the prospect of a degree at Cambridge and, instead, secured a berth on a liner heading for Mombasa.

'Riding the train from Mombasa to Nairobi, I heard a lot of talk of

Chapter 5
'Paddlebum' and the Rough Riders of the Rufiji River

the man-eating lions that had taken a liking to meat from India and brought the railway construction to a halt, obviously long before my time. But I knew then, that I would never live in England again.'

His first job was managing a farm in Molo, to the west of the Rift Valley and he soon made a bunch of similarly-minded pals who were in search of African experiences. He also met Tony Bentley, one of the best-known professional hunters in East Africa: one thing led to another and he began an apprenticeship under Bentley and another of his associates, universally known as 'Bullshit' Bonham. A great raconteur, Bonham was reputed to be the most foul-mouthed of all the hunters in the British colony.

For Rowbotham, these were exciting times and included lengthy spells in the bush as well as wild cavorting sessions in Nairobi. When not carousing at the long bar of the Norfolk Hotel with Harry Selby, Robert Ruark and some of the girls from what was already known as 'Happy Valley', he'd end up in one of Nairobi's many clubs, the Muthaiga included.

As he recalled years later, there were a few streets, dusty, dirty streets, one of which was Government Road. At one end there was the railway station and at the other, about a mile away, was the Norfolk. They ran horse races along this stretch, using Somali ponies as mounts, from the station to the Norfolk, where riders would party after the race. Weekends were often spent at Malindi, then a delightful little coastal village that included the Eden Roc Hotel and the local club, a one-roomed affair like so many clubs in the East African Sticks, but certainly one of character.

The owner's wife was June Carbury, who had already carved a dubious niche for herself as the gin-soaked wife of Lord Errol, a leading member of the 'Happy Valley' set. Drunk or sober, the Carbury woman would never mention anything about the murder that was to become the subject of a book and a film titled *White Mischief*.

The prime suspect, many thought, was the beautiful but steely-faced Lady Delamere. June was in the house at the time of the crime and was said to be the only person who knew the truth. It was no secret that 'Lady D', as the governor's wife was known, was pretty useful with firearms, attested to by another associate, the well-endowed Peter Leth, to his cost. When Lady Delamere tired of him, she shot him, missing his heart by perhaps an inch, rang the police and told them to 'collect a would-be suicide who is making a mess on my carpet'. This they did, but they were delayed by a puncture along the way.

Peter Leth would stay with me in Rhodesia, and he would often repeat the story, probably because he felt he was far enough from Kenya to not be targeted again.

Then there was an equine-faced woman called Claudia Slaughter, a great party girl who would socialise wildly and often end up smashed. She almost certainly knew of Peter's reputation of being extremely well-hung – in fact, we all did – and at one of these thrashes she approached him and said, 'Oh, Peter darling, I'm far too drunk to f... you.'

To which he replied, 'Claudia, dear, I'm not nearly drunk enough to go to bed with you.'

Another great character was the inimitable Lady Astor, the first woman ever to sit in the British Colonial Legislature. Her full name was Lady Sidney Farrar and she was acknowledged by all to be immensely capable and a very competent farmer in her own right. She left Kenya after it achieved independence in 1954, headed south to Rhodesia where she settled and eventually died in Zimbabwe.

Lady Astor despised the great Winston Churchill with a passion. The story that still persists is a comment she made to the Prime Minister in the House of Commons when she said, 'Mr Churchill, if you were my husband I'd put poison in your drink.' His retort was even more direct: 'Lady Astor,' the great man replied, 'if you were my wife I would drink it!'

It wasn't long before Mike Rowbotham put down something resembling roots and married a girl called Ann. The occasional hunt called and he couldn't settle down, leaving the running of the farm to his wife.

Kenya in the post-war days was attracting its share of international interest with Ernest Hemingway a regular, like the rest at the bar of the Norfolk, together with an increasing number of wildlife films being made in the country's bush. It didn't help that Mike was occasionally hired either as a consultant or as one of the hunters needed to keep an eye on the set in a land where there were lion, leopard, elephant and rhino in abundance. These jaunts also gave him access to any number of pretty young actresses struggling with what were termed 'irrepressible urges' following the onset of what was referred to in the trade as 'khaki fever'.

But then a big-horned buffalo flattened 'Paddlebum' and left him with several holes in his anatomy. The outcome was that he was suddenly less enthusiastic about hunting.

He recalls that it has been a bitterly cold night, as only those who live above the escarpment in East Africa might understand. 'We were hunting up Ikomo way, a region to the west of Serengeti and left the camp in the dark ... it was original storybook country in the southern catchment area of Lake Victoria, where the falling rains start their long journey down the Nile to the Med.

They had a long way to go, he told somebody, to Fort Ikoma and beyond. The stronghold itself, clearly lovely in its day and overlooking the escarpment, was already in ruins, a massive stone structure that had been built by the Imperial Germans before the war with more mambas and cobras peering out from among the rocks than anybody thought possible.

'Paddlebum' takes up his story:

'We were motoring along the edge of a thick grove of bush that screened the Grumeti River from the plains. Game was everywhere – zebra, Thompson's gazelle, hartebeest, Grant's gazelle, impala, topi, ostrich, in fact, the entire range of East African wildlife and all of it standing well clear of the bush because the big cats had not yet settled for the day.

'Then suddenly, in the half-light we spotted them, three enormous black shapes. Though they were still a good 500 metres from our vehicle, there was no mistaking that distinctive, hunched buffalo shape. They must have heard us, but were unable to get direction as the breeze was in our favour.

'I drove my hunting car straight into the bush to conceal our presence, got out and used my binoculars to view three of the biggest buffalo I had ever seen. My client was nonplussed; he already had a buff together with an excellent bag, but the buffalo on the right was outstanding and I knew it would almost certainly rank high in Rowland Ward's *Records of Big Game.*

'By now, we were well-secreted in the bush and there was time enough for me to give my client my thoughts. He should grab this opportunity, I urged, because it was something that wouldn't happen again. He agreed, reluctantly, and I could see that the man was nervous.

'My plan was simple; we'd move in such a way that we'd ambush the buffalo as they got to the thick bush where we were waiting. He agreed, and made himself comfortable. As the sun rose, the three huge beasts started to move towards the river and we were able to position ourselves immediately ahead of them. But the animals were in no hurry and anyway, they weren't aware of our presence.

'They must have been about 100 metres away when I asked the

client to hold out his hand: it was trembling, and this worried me. Frankly, I anticipated the worst, but this was no time for nerves and we certainly weren't about to change our minds because the animals were almost on us.

'My gun bearers – three local fellows called Maina, Kiprotich and Kilbrono, with whom I hunted for many years – were squatting behind us totally alert to the risk; they were appreciative of what was about to happen and obviously hoped that the client would shoot well. They knew that he didn't like me to back him up.

'In a worst-case scenario one of the buffalo might be wounded and we'd have to go after it. A wounded buffalo in that kind of thick, almost impenetrable bush could be dangerous. Meantime the buffs were moving forward and when they were about 50 metres from us, I pointed at the largest in the bunch and whispered: "Keep your shot, low … aim for the heart."

'Moments later I told the client to shoot. He lifted his rifle, took aim but then nothing happened … the man was transfixed with fear.

When the trio were still about twenty-five yards ahead, I again whispered, urgently this time, that he should shoot. Whether the lead buffalo heard me or noticed any movement on our part, I don't know, but they broke into an immediate gallop and veered off to the right, presenting my client with an easy side shoulder shot: a well-placed bullet would break bone and penetrate the heart, ensuring a kill.

'The first two buffalo crashed straight into the thick bush and finally, a shot rang out. I saw the buffalo falter as it was hit, but was unable to tell where. At this point I leapt forward and let fly into the wavering bush with my double .470. I had hopes that I might take down the animal or at least draw blood, which would make following its spoor that much easier.

'We heard the buffalo galloping down a game trail, through some thick, springy bush that grows so profusely on the banks of that river and then, quite suddenly, there was silence. All we could hear were the calls of some laughing doves that had been alarmed by our firing.

'I told the client to relax. He should come out of his hiding place and sit on a fallen tree trunk and have a smoke, I suggested. This would allow time for the wounded buffalo to separate from the others and, if he was fatally hit, succumb.

'While the client smoked, I discussed the situation with the gun bearers and all agreed that the buffalo was lightly wounded and

Chapter 5
'Paddlebum' and the Rough Riders of the Rufiji River

that it would probably take the rest of the day and God knows how much tedious tracking for us to catch up with it. What we didn't know just then was that we were wrong in all our assessments and that's unusual because normally we can judge such situations with remarkable accuracy and then act accordingly. Had we been correct in our assumptions, we'd have known what to expect.

'After a wait of about twenty minutes I asked the client if he wanted to company us in the search for the wounded buffalo, something us professional hunters simply have to do – it's the law – and anyway, it is only right, in terms of sportsmanship. The client knew he wasn't required to accompany us while we tracked wounded game, but said he would come anyway. With that we went into a thicket that was about as dense as it gets.

'Within a short distance we found our first traces of blood. A little further there were tracks that suggested that the wounded animal had separated from the other two. This was hardly an ideal situation because it presented an extremely dangerous situation: others wounding buffalo in the past had died for less.

'We pressed on anyway, following a light blood spoor of a buffalo moving at a fairly good speed. We also observed that it hadn't paused in its flight: it was obviously looking for the thickest bush cover.

'Later that morning – and miles from where the animal had been walking – we found ourselves in the kind of heavy bush growth

One of the castles built in Tanganyika's interior by Imperial Germany. This one stands desolate and abandoned in the Serengeti. (Photo: Author)

Since most of the Rufiji River flows through country adjacent to the Selous Game Reserve, the two adventurers constantly came upon herds of buffalo, elephant and buck. (Photo: Darrell Watt)

that could only be described as exceptionally thick: we needed to literally squeeze ourselves between clumps or walls of dense bush. Suddenly, the gun bearer Kiprotich stopped: as the lead tracker, he had walking directly ahead of me. He'd obviously spotted our quarry and flattened himself against the wall of vegetation.

'I forced myself past him and saw the hindquarters of a buffalo lying down several paces ahead in front of me. No vital parts were visible as its head, chest and ribcage were hidden behind foliage and there was obviously no chance of my placing a bullet correctly in the animal's heart. Moreover, the situation was further complicated because we couldn't wait for the buffalo to move.

'I did the obvious, crouched down and drove a raking solid shot into the hip-joint of the animal, the idea being to immobilise it.

'But no such luck. The huge beast leapt to its feet, swung around to face me and charged head up, grunting as it came. In a moment I stood and fired the remaining round left in my double, hitting the animal in the right place when it was still barely an arm's length from the end of my rifle. Then holding the rifle across my face and in front of me for protection, everything went blank.

'The animal had been struck by the last bullet, as I'd hoped, but in its dying moments, it charged on with its huge bulk providing momentum. The next thing I recall was looking up as I lay paralysed on my back, seeing the buffalo's feet flailing about above my face. Then it collapsed beside me and uttered a final last groan, something buffalos do when dying.

'Meantime, I couldn't move and that worried me. My gun bearers carried me to the shade of a large tree, for the sun was now at its highest. The client returned, viewed the carnage and was totally at a loss as to what to do next.

'We rested in the shade for a while, before I could be assisted to our hunting car that had been driven to the edge of the bush some distance away. That was when my gun bearers told me that I'd been hurled high into the air when the buffalo hit me, and that my rifle was totally shattered on impact with the animal's enormous horns. I don't remember any of this, but I had to take their word: the shattered rifle testified to their account.

'Considering what I'd been through, my injuries were surprisingly light. I'd suffered two impacted vertebrae from leaning forward to receive the blow, a cracked skull and, overall, a pretty bad bruising. But at least I was alive. The head, skin and front feet were taken from the animal and placed in the hunting car and now, presumably, form part of the German client's collection of trophies in Europe.

'Then with great care, my men carried me to the vehicle and we all slowly drove to camp.

'There must be a God that takes care of those who don't deserve it, for, as luck would have it, Tony Henley brought his safari into the same area later that day. Crossing the river further down, he noticed my car tracks heading in the direction of the Mansira where we were camped.

'It's an unwritten rule that incoming professional hunters liaise with other professionals using the same area and he duly came to camp, only to find me in bed. Fortunately, a charter flight had been arranged from Nairobi for the following morning to bring photographic equipment to Tony's English client, so early the next day I was placed on several mattresses in the back of the five-ton safari truck and driven to the Seronera airstrip and flown to Nairobi.

'While I had a lot of pain in my back and other quirks, I couldn't have been that badly hurt because they never even bothered to X-ray me at the hospital. My wife's father, a surgeon, came to my ward, took one look at me and told my doctor, "Listen, you'd better X-ray this fellow." So they did that, and came back to me with the news that I had a broken back. "And what's more, my father-in-law said on a subsequent visit, "can't you see that his eyes are all over the place?"

'They X-rayed me again and found I also had a cracked skull – a bloody great crack all the way down my head. "You could clearly feel it with your finger," he told them. So he just took me away in a pick-

As with most of Africa's larger rivers north of the Limpopo, it is impossible to travel far without encountering 'pods' of hippo either in the water or along the banks. These are dangerous animals, taking a larger toll on human life in Africa than crocodiles. (Photo: Caroline Castell)

up to the Nairobi War Memorial Hospital where I stayed another four or five days, after which Ann took me home.

'I lay in bed for about a month with the curtains drawn and then it wasn't long before I was up and about again, but it was quite a few months before I was able to tackle my next buffalo hunt, though with a lot more respect than before for the great animal that provides us with the greatest of challenges.'

All these East African adventures had taken place in the early 1950s at a time when most people living in Kenya were not aware that there were several serious security issues unravelling. Kenya's largest tribe, the Kikuyu, had never really managed to settle down after World War II and the first time that news of a tribal uprising was to come to the attention of the young hunter happened while he was in the bush. Almost overnight, Kenya went onto high alert.

Mike Rowbotham was on safari in the Ngorongoro Crater with members of America's famous DuPont family, when an emergency message was transmitted throughout East Africa. It stated that a national emergency had been declared by the colonial government and that all able-bodied men in Kenya were to report immediately for duty. The gist of it was that a black nationalist leader by the name of Jomo Kenyatta, who had lived, studied at the London School of

Economics, and worked in Britain during the years 1931 to 1947 – and even married a white woman – returned home to head a political grouping known as the Kenya African Union or KANU. He was subsequently instrumental in creating a terror group that was called Mau Mau.

Though war was never officially declared in Kenya – like the Malayan Campaign, it was labelled an emergency – thousands of British troops were drafted into Kenya to counter the rebellion. Together with the Royal Air Force, British security forces were involved in an extensive guerrilla war that lasted several years. Ultimately, superior tactics, numbers and ruthless counter-insurgency measures (some so brutal that they would never be countenanced today) resulted in government forces gradually whittling away at enemy resources. But not before a number of settlers were murdered in terror attacks.

A good deal of anti-Mau Mau motivation came from the settlers themselves, many of whom were fluent in the Kikuyu language and were formed into clandestine pseudo groups that were used to infiltrate Mau Mau gangs in the forests.

While the whites lost only 14 – some under the most gruesome conditions of being buried or burned alive – thousands more innocent black civilians were murdered by Kenyatta's thugs. Those insurgents not killed in operations, were arrested and placed in concentration camps, mostly in the north of the country.

Kenyatta himself spent seven years in detention, almost all in a fly-blown camp at Lodwar in what was then called the Northern Frontier District. During this period he was given a bottle of liquor a day, in the hopes of some colonial officials that he would drink himself to death. But they hadn't quite got the measure of this wily old African politician.

At the end of it, Kenyatta was released and, despite objections, both in Britain and Kenya itself, he went on to lead Kenya to independence as the country's first elected president.

It was to be expected that many members of the East African settler community rejected Whitehall's new African dispensation which was regarded by most as little more than appeasement. At issue was the future of their farms, the education of their children, and medical facilities for all. Over time they were proved right, because Kenya today is a bankrupt shadow of the prosperous little colonial outpost it was before and these days is involved in a low-intensity war with Islamic Jihadists operating out of Somalia, its northern neighbour.

In retrospect though, the move towards *Uhuru* was sensible and just. Within a decade almost four dozen other black African states – some British, others French or Belgian – had joined the independence trail that had first been forged by Kwame Nkrumah in Ghana in the late 1950s and Tanganyika's Julius Nyerere a few years later.

In Kenya itself, London insisted that many settler farms be sold to the new black government (at prices that were regarded, even by some of the critics, as reasonable). What the new owners did with those farms was their business, but at least the trappings of independence were complete. In contrast, a large number of settlers refused to yield and this group included Mike 'Paddlebum' Rowbotham.

After an official visit to London on behalf of the soon-to-be-dispossessed white farmers, 'Paddlebum' and three of his co-conspirators – one of whom had taken to naming his animals after newly appointed heads of government – were expelled from East Africa. Rowbotham went on to seek sanctuary in Ian Smith's Rhodesia, pleased indeed to discover a more resilient people then in the process of girding for a political fight not unlike that fought by his old mates in the Aberdare Hills. Only this uprising was to develop into a full-blown guerrilla war.

As history has proved, Africa again prevailed and after a bitter seven-year military struggle, the Rhodesians, while putting up a brave show, were eventually stymied by limited human and material resources. It was the numbers game all over again, as was to happen in South Africa a decade later.

After Mugabe took over and renamed the country Zimbabwe, Rowbotham found himself living on a farm outside Harare, the capital. But conditions were fraught, both domestically and politically, with the guerrillas who had been involved in the war demanding more settler land for their efforts. Meantime, Rowbotham had been aware that a bunch of enterprising operators in Zimbabwe had started several commercial canoeing operations along the length of the Zambezi River and he decided that perhaps the time had come to do the same along the wild waters of the Rufiji in Tanzania.

In order to establish the company, 'Paddlebum' teamed up with two young men from very different backgrounds. Hannes Nel, a tough-as-teak young Afrikaner, was complemented in a curious way by Nick Wilson, who, like Mike Rowbotham decades before, had come to Africa from England 'for the sun, the bush, the animals and the wild open spaces of Africa.'

Wilson had made his way south by road through Egypt, Eritrea and across the Sudan into Kenya. He stayed a while and then went on

Chapter 5
'Paddlebum' and the Rough Riders of the Rufiji River

to Tanzania and sought a way not only to settle, but possibly to start a safari business. Rowbotham's initial entreaty to join him on the Rufiji sounded exciting, and like Nel, Wilson accepted a partnership in what was clearly a very uncertain enterprise for no other reason than that nobody had done anything like it before along that stretch of the Rufiji.

Rhodesian-born Hannes Nel, the son of a farmer, had lived all his life in the bush and, like Wilson, the challenge was enormously appealing. Young tourists were heading to Africa in droves, the majority in search of adventure. Obviously there were dangers in the isolated southern reaches of Tanzania, but both young men reckoned that with the new business on its feet, they could make a killing. Anyway, neither of them allowed such obstacles to intrude.

With a flippancy that comes easily to the kind of English eccentric that emerged in post-war Africa, 'Paddlebum' initially ignored the warnings of some of the hunters who had worked the southern reaches of the great Selous Game Reserve that abutted onto the Rufiji watershed. Somebody suggested that some kind of aerial reconnaissance might be prudent to establish the number and extent of rapids, swamps and other obstacles, but Rowbotham dismissed all that as a waste of good money.

There was no question that the Rufiji basin had animals galore and that this would be part of the appeal that would attract tourists, what nobody mentioned was that on the river itself there was a surfeit of aggressive crocodiles and hippo, and snakes everywhere, never mind lion, leopard, buffalo, elephant and hyena.

The biggest impediments, it transpired, were rapids to be encountered along the length of the river. Depending on the water level, particularly during the rainy season, some of these cataracts were enormous. But none of these problems were envisaged, never mind planned for, while firearms, radios, first-aid kits, anti-venom snakebite kits, flares and the like were dismissed by Rowbotham as 'junk.' After several nights of hard drinking in bars along the way, this intrepid little band of adventurers set out from Dar es Salaam for the bridge on the Ruaha River.

Hannes Nel: 'We got to the bridge and Mike, immaculately dressed, as always, emerged from his truck and folded out a canvas chair. Sitting there in grand style, he told us that we were to go to the village of Utete, about 300 kilometres away: it was as simple as that, he declared and we didn't argue. Meantime, our kit consisted of a canoe, two rather dilapidated sleeping bags that were strapped to make for easy stowage, some cans of food, together with a few utensils in a wooden box. There was also a single panga, or machete, a couple of knives, some vegetables, cigarettes and a camera.

'Find the grave of Frederick Selous,' was 'Paddlebum's' specific instruction. To which he added: 'then check out some campsites and do a reconnaissance. I expect a full report when I see you next.'

That was it, said Hannes. When he asked Rowbotham whether he could borrow his sponge, a somewhat treasured item that his boss used to clean his car, Mike simply glared at him but allowed him to take it anyway, with the warning: 'Just don't you fucking-well lose it!'

'Mike Rowbotham didn't move from his chair while he watched us load our supplies into the canoe and looked on solemnly as the current swept us downstream. "Don't forget my sponge," were his parting words as we waved goodbye. There was no question in my mind: there were some interesting times that lay ahead.'

Barely out of Mike's sight, the two men were buffeted by a spate of shallow rapids and it was then that they were to discover that the Rufiji's otherwise placid course could sometimes change by the hour. It was fast-flowing in some places, and then the river would widen and the flow would slow enough in the shallows to let them walk alongside in the water and sometimes, even to circumvent rapids.

'I knew the Zambezi,' remembers Hannes. 'Crocs on that river were a problem but tended to avoid you. Not these buggers.

'They would spot our canoe heading downstream and come straight at us. From the first day we were beating them over their heads with our paddles to keep them at bay … it was terrifying, I'd never seen anything like it … but then they'd probably never seen a canoe before.'

As Nel remembers, it was obvious that these great animals, some four or five metres long, had absolutely no fear, either of the canoe or its contents. It was also worrying, he said, that the hippos were equally belligerent. 'That was an even bigger problem because there were many hundreds of them and females with offspring became the real nightmare in the end.'

Both men conceded that with those conditions prevailing, they were terrified from the start, but by then the bridge from where they had launched, including 'Paddlebum' and his car, were miles behind them and the two explorers could little more than continue down the river.'

'I think it was day three when there was a steep drop in the river leading to a succession of rapids, quite big ones, actually,' Wilson recalled. 'That was when we found a fairly quiet stream along the north bank of the Rufiji where there was a waterfall and we were able to lower our canoe to calmer water below. Then, out of the swirling waters below, we found our path blocked by huge pods of angry hippos that moved aggressively towards the newcomers.

'We obviously weren't too eager to retrace our steps, so we decided to go for it. We waved our arms, banging the sides of the boat and screamed and, at first, the hippos were bewildered. But that quickly gave way to aggression and they came at us with the kind of aggression we hadn't seen before. No doubt about it, an Olympic Gold would have been a cinch,' Wilson declared.

'Paddlebum' Rowbotham, in the meantime, had returned to Dar es Salaam and was not aware of any of these events. Nor, by all accounts, was he overly concerned.

The safari along the Rufiji proceeded at a steady pace and the two men were constantly facing new threats.

Wilson recalls a rather large crocodile coming up from behind and nudging the boat one morning. 'I looked around just in time to see it about to clamp its jaws on Hannes's arms when he was looking the other way. I shouted and Hannes snapped his arm back, which was when I bashed the blighter on the nose with my oar.

'But it kept on coming, snapping again at Hannes's arm, biting the oar, even though he kept on belting it as hard as he could. Meantime, I was paddling like hell up front. Finally he managed to poke it in its eye and the croc gave up.' It was experiences like these, Wilson admitted afterwards, that caused them to become almost inured to fear, which was perhaps just as well because, as he says, there was never a time when we weren't in real danger.

Day seven brought a different kind of threat to the expedition. Moving at a good speed downstream, they were met by the kind of roar that suggested that there was whitewater ahead. As they approached that set of rapids, a spray emerged in the sunlight that created a marvellous rainbow over the water.

'We carefully weighed our options. It would be at least two days of hard work to porter everything around the rapids across some pretty tough bush terrain, so Hannes suggested that we try and run them. We decided to toss a coin instead, only we used one of our knives.

'The knife "said" run and we took off at a heady pace through the foaming water. Hannes did a great job steering, while I was trying to bale out water faster than it was coming in.

Photo: Darrell Watt

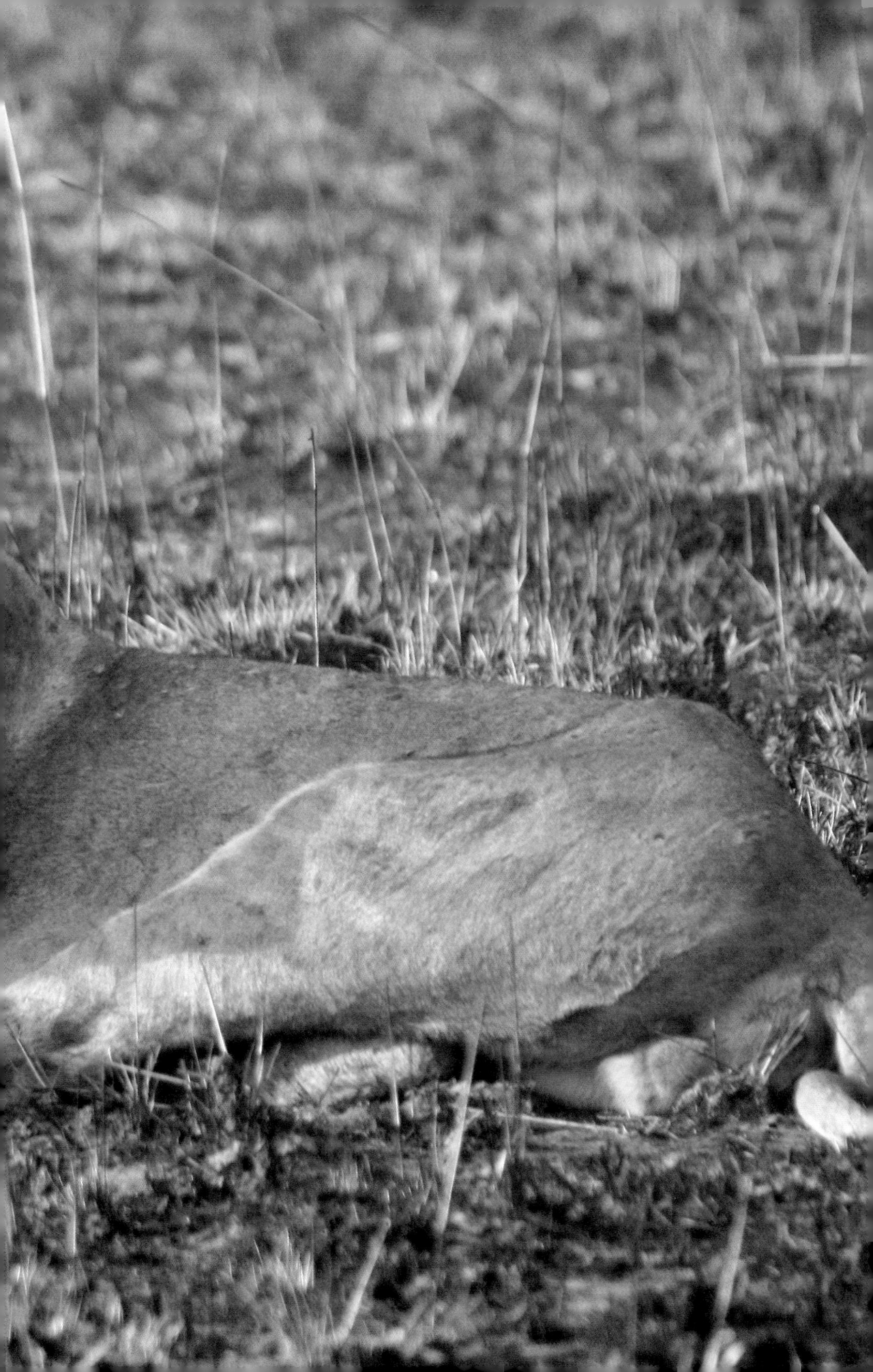

'Then, quite suddenly, we hit something that resembled a giant maelstrom and before we knew it, we'd capsized. There seemed to be little point in us hanging on, so I baled out, surfaced and called to Hannes. By now, he had the rope that we used to tether the canoe in his teeth and when he opened his mouth to reply, the boat simply disappeared.

'With both of us in the wash, we just had to go with the flow. I eventually made it to a pool where I could grab a rock and pull myself out of the water. I realised that I'd lost sight of Hannes, but a short time later, he came up behind me. It was a huge relief...'

There was no question that both men were exhilarated to have survived an experience that should have spelt more serious consequences, but they were also conscious, acutely so, that while they were alive, they were totally alone in an otherwise hostile environment. Between them they possessed only a pair of knives. 'Hannes had a blade strapped to his calf and had kept his shorts while I had taken the precaution of stringing my knife onto my belt. But I also had my shoes and a shirt.

'From where we had emerged from the water, we caught sight of our wrecked canoe on its belly on the far bank of the river. To recover it would have meant swimming the Rufiji and, without question, the crocodiles would have done something about that. On the face of it then, our kit was lost. Later that afternoon, with the two men sitting disconsolately under a tree and pondering the uncertain future that lay ahead, one of the sleeping rolls drifted into view: it consisted of a canvas cover that was sturdily bound by webbing straps and brass buckles.

'Inside was a roll of foam, a blanket and a mosquito net, and also, to our relief, an old Bic cigarette lighter that must have fallen out of my pocket while asleep the previous night. The flint worked, but it had no gas.

'We were cheered by this small act of providence, of course, so we cut up the bag and fashioned two simple smocks, some foam-lined shoes for Hannes and pushed the rest into a backpack that was also in a bundle and which held the mosquito net.

'With what was left of the only blanket between us, we shaped and cut something resembling an arrow and secured it to a large piece of driftwood in the hope that if an aerial search were ever to happen, the pilot would spot it.

'Our biggest problem then was we didn't have a clue where we were, or even how far down the Rufiji we had paddled. Our only real option was to start walking and that was really tough going. It wasn't long before Hannes's feet were lacerated by sharp stones

Chapter 5
'Paddlebum' and the Rough Riders of the Rufiji River

and thorns but he staggered on, never complaining. All day long we were hammered by tsetse flies, and could only joke about how many pints of blood the two of us contributed to keeping the bloody parasites alive, not to mention that a tsetse fly bite can be painful and there were an awful lot of them.

'But we struggled on, Hannes with his bloody feet and obviously, acutely aware of many predators in the bush. By day two we both started feeling the effects of not being able to eat anything and drinking unfiltered water from the river.

'After a couple of days our stomach pains worsened, and we tried to settle that by rifling a bird's nest for its eggs which we ate raw and then, using the mosquito net, catching a couple of fish. But it was all rather slim pickings.

'The first two nights on the river weren't all that bad because we managed to make a fire by rubbing the old Bic lighter to get it warm and it barely managed to produce a flame. The third night it rained, the Bic wouldn't work and it was as miserable as hell. Freezing cold, totally dark and with no moon, we buried ourselves in the sand to try to keep warm but were immediately attacked by sand fleas. Whatever skin remained was exposed to the elements and covered by mosquitoes. It was a horror of a night, seemingly without end. Then we were faced with a charging hippo coming at us in the dark. We leaped out of our sandpits, yelling, brandishing our knives and finally turned him away, but only at the last moment.

The fourth day was a watershed because it also provided us with our first big meal. Trudging along the riverbank, we looked down and I caught sight of a crocodile in a pool below. It wasn't very big by their standards, barely two metres, but to us it presented an option: food. The creature just lay there, half submerged and staring at us, its mean eyes protruding just above the water.

'We only had one thing in mind: eat or die. But how were we to catch the blighter?

'Hannes suggested that I distract it while he jumped it from behind and stabbed it in the brain. I said I've got a better idea: he distracts it while I jump on its back and knife it. We argued a while and then decided on Hannes's Plan 'A'.

'Sun-bronzed, blonde, blue-eyed and heavily muscled, Hannes pounced from the riverbank like some sort of primeval Tarzan. He landed squarely on the croc's back and, with a mighty blow buried his blade into the beast's head. Somehow though, he seemed to have missed its brain because the animal went berserk and sent him flying headlong into the pool.

'With the water churning and an extremely angry croc snapping and convulsing, I took the initiative and followed Hannes into the water as well, the two of us slashing it with our knives and eventually stabbing it into submission. By the time the deed was done, the water all round us was red with the croc's blood and we were exhausted.

'We spoke about the attack afterwards and the fact that there really was no alternative: for us it was literally kill the croc or die. Lying there immediately afterwards and panting wildly, Hannes asked, "Do you think it's dead yet, mate?" I replied that I fucking-well hoped so or it was going to be a lot of fun trying to skin the bastard.

'I was ready to eat the meat raw, but Hannes insisted on cooking it, which obviously made good sense because crocs are reptiles. Frantic rubbing of the lighter yielded no flame. Using a pile of elephant dung as a shroud, I tried to get some dry grass alight with the flint, but to no avail. I even ended up punching the pile of crap with my fist in frustration and it must have released some methane as I gave the Bic a despairing flick and a small blue flame lit up our lives.

'The tail cooked-up beautifully and we ate well. There were many trips to our improvised bush toilet after that lot, but amazingly the only thing I eventually got sick of was Hannes's jokes.

'The nights after that little episode were long. Our muscles ached, huge swarms of mosquitoes overwhelmed our sleeping torsos and throughout, we were tired, cold and utterly uncomfortable. Sleep always came, but in spurts, interrupted by the occasional nearby roar of lions or the cackle of hyena packs that somehow must have been aware of our presence.

'Utterly defenceless and in a constant state of pain, a peculiar fatalistic nonchalance eventually overwhelmed us. What will be, will be, we told each other.

'On the morning of the sixth day, having just set out, I heard a thunder of hooves nearby. I looked to my right and saw a waterbuck heading straight for me, followed a short distance behind by a large male leopard. The big cat stopped dead in his tracks at this interruption and glared at me, which was when I thought, now what? If it came for me, I was a goner, so I just stood there and looked into its yellow eyes, so close I could detect a pungent odour emitted by its spotted pelt.

'Hannes came shuffling up behind me, head down, oblivious, bedraggled, tattered and torn. The leopard took one look at him and, I would imagine, was a little offended at the nonchalance of the unexpected new arrival because it shook its head and slunk away

Chapter 5
'Paddlebum' and the Rough Riders of the Rufiji River

into the bush in disgust. That evening, a quick swim took us to an island refuge and it was our best night's rest so far.

'Our single biggest problem that emerged as the days passed was trying not only to maintain hope that we would eventually be rescued, but also the need to keep our spirits from sagging, an issue that gradually became more critical. Just about all of it stemmed from the fact that we really had no idea where we were or, for that matter, how much longer we could last. Was anybody even aware of our plight?

'Hannes was still managing to walk, even though he had only a flimsy covering over the soles of his feet, which looked terrible. Sometimes it resembled a huge open wound and there was no question that he was finding it more difficult to walk each day. Obviously, there was the additional threat of infection and, if that happened, we both knew we would be sunk.

'We constantly tried to be cheerful, but with time, even our jokes became strained. There was no question that we were in Shit Street up to our necks, with the reality looming that there was a good chance that we wouldn't actually make it.

'Then, on the morning of day twelve, deep in the African wilderness, we suddenly came upon something we both recognised from some aerial photos we'd studied back in Dar es Salaam: these were expansive open water pans set away from the Rufiji. We knew then that we weren't very far from Mbuyu Camp and salvation.

'Like the river, the pans were croc- and hippo-infested, but if we took the long route round, it meant an extra two days of hiking. That wouldn't do, we both agreed, because fatigue, exacerbated by bad foods or no food at all, had suddenly become a factor. Out came the trusty knife again and we tossed for a decision. The result sent the two of us diving headlong into the water and swimming for our lives. It took a little while to reach the other side, but with our hearts pumping and utterly exhausted, we made it. All we could do was hug each other.

'Twelve days against pretty tough odds and alive, Hannes commented: "That was certainly some achievement. It was the kind of exhilarating sensation that you only experience once in a lifetime, if at all."

'It didn't take long before we stumbled rather than walked into the camp and the first people to see us were some American tourists. They were shocked because we really were a sorry spectacle: barely any clothes on our backs, covered in mud and, all over, enormous welts, bites, sores, scratches, bruises and Hannes's feet oozing blood.

But we were smiling!

'Once we settled down and were given some food and drinks, I felt as if I had just woken from an extraordinarily long dream, and a bad one at that! The Americans asked whether our car had broken down? "No," we replied, "we lost our canoe."

'A day or so later an aircraft took us back to Dar es Salaam and civilisation. Thrilled, we scrubbed, ate and drank ourselves stupid. By mid-afternoon we were asleep in a room at the old Agip Motel when the door burst open and in marched the dreaded 'Paddlebum'.

Sartorial, in double-breasted blazer and cravat, flushed from a boozy lunch at the club, a strange look appeared on his face. From disdain and a mixture of anger that we had botched the operation, he mellowed briefly; could see that we'd obviously had a tough time. He sat himself down at the end of one of the beds and assumed the role of inquisitor.

'"Gentlemen," he said gruffly, "in your own time ... situation report if you please!"'

'We were totally awake by then and set about telling him about our adventures. We'd been shipwrecked, we smiled, but he didn't react. We explained how, after losing the canoe, we'd walked semi-naked and starving for eight days halfway across the Selous Game Park, with every African predator, insect and reptile in creation for company.

'Nor did he react when we told him about our struggle with a crocodile that became our first real meal, or when he heard about our encounter with the leopard.

'Finished with our long tale of woe, Mike stood up and pulled himself erect at the foot of our beds. Then, hands clasped behind his back "Paddlebum" looked down at us imperiously. There was complete silence as he drew a deep breath while we waited for his reaction.

'"And I suppose you lost my fucking sponge too!" he barked.'

1. Read more: The Phoenician in East Africa: http://phoenicia.org/phoeEastAfrica.html#ixzz1kZTdARWK. Also, http://phoenicia.org/phoeEastAfrica.html#ixzz1kZTFfhjh, and http://phoenicia.org/phoeEastAfrica.html#ixzz1kZSjkGos

CHAPTER SIX

THE FUTURE ROLE OF MERCENARIES ON THE AFRICAN CONTINENT

It is an ugly word, mercenary. Hardly the rough and tough of the quotidian, it conjures up images of mindless brutality and the murder of innocents. To others, it is a call to arms. In Africa, these hired guns and their gunships have not only helped save countless lives, they have changed the course of contemporary history, as they are now doing in countering piracy in the Indian Ocean. Another example is Sierra Leone where during the course of a civil war in the 1990s a single Mi-24 gunship twice drove rebel forces from the gates of Freetown. Thereafter, South African mercenary pilot Neall Ellis joined British Forces – then commanded by Brigadier David Richards (today General Sir David Richards) – and turned the war on its head.

Before that, a South African mercenary force that flew Angolan Air Force MiG-23s – as well as Mi-24 gunships – ended a 30-year civil war in this much-disputed West African country.

One of the ironies of the present military campaign in Mali, with French and British troops ranged against a fairly large guerrilla force linked to an organisation called AQIM – Al-Qaeda in the Magreb – is that this war could have been cut short.

In February 2012, a sizeable force of mercenaries negotiated an US$80 million deal with the former president of Mali to counter a Taureg rebellion that threatened the government. Apart from a moderate-sized ground force that would tackle the rebels on home turf, the aviation side included two Mi-24 helicopter gunships and four Mi-17 armed support helicopters.

"MERCENARIES? I ASKED FOR MISSIONARIES!"

Cartoon that appeared in a Durban newspaper following the abortive Seychelles mercenary invasion by Colonel Mike Hoare and friends. It was dedicated to Peter Duffy who served with Hoare in the Congo and who subsequently, with the rest of the conspirators, spent time in a South African clink for trying to overthrow a legitimate island regime.

The private military company (PMC) involved in this venture had originally been offered six Vietnam-era Huey Cobras by an unnamed country at $1 million each. It was decided to go for helicopters of Ukrainian origin instead.

The deal for acquiring these aircraft had already been signed and money was about to change hands when Captain Amadou Sanogo, an unknown low-key officer who headed a dissident junta in the Mali Army, launched a mutiny that toppled the Bamako government.

Almost simultaneously, AQIM routed the Malian army and seized the north of the country. Curiously, though military assistance was offered by several African countries, the Sanogo regime rejected all offers. He was also initially opposed to French involvement in countering this revolt, but since almost $1 billion has been offered in military aid by Western nations for the Mali army, the captain – who likes to compare himself with the 'liberator' General De Gaulle – has since moderated his stance. That makes sense, since about a fifth of the money is scheduled to go directly under Captain Sanogo's control.

Chapter 6
The Future Role of Mercenaries on the African Continent

Much of what goes on in this country that fringes the Sahara is unreported, including the extensive use of gunships by the French Air Force to drive the Ansar Dine Islamic group from all the towns they captured earlier into the remote Ifogas mountain range of the desolate north. In September 2012, while delivering food to soldiers of the Mali army, a United States C-130 cargo plane coming in to land at a forward operating base was struck by machine-gun fire from the rebels. Nobody was injured and the plane made it safely back to its original destination in Bamako.

Recent reports out of South Africa suggest that several Western nations are looking at a private military option, ergo mercenaries, to replace their troops once the Mali security situation has been stabilised.

The insurgency in Mali is not unique. As we go to press, guerrilla wars are being fought in more than a dozen African states. Almost all centre on the exploitation of commodities that include minerals, oil, precious stones, hardwoods and food resources. Among these is coltan, short for columbite-tantalite, a black tar-like mineral and a vital component in a vast array of small electronic devices like cell phones and iPads and found in significant quantities in the Congo. That country possesses about 80 per cent of the world's raw coltan deposits, with Russia holding most of the balance.

Eeben Barlow (third from the right) one of the founders of the mercenary group Executive Outcomes, with some of his Angolan and South Africa associates. Former Special Forces operative Nick du Toit – who spent five years 'in a living hell', in Equatorial Guinea's notorious Black Beach prison – is on his left. (Photo: Peter Duffy)

Three South African mercenaries at Sierra Leone's military headquarters at Aberdeen, outside Freetown: bearded Cobus Claassens stands between Raymond Archer and Simon Witherspoon. The Soviet-built Mi-24 helicopter gunship used by Neall Ellis to smash rebel units is visible on the landing pad above them. (Photo: Cobus Claassens)

The Central African Republic was recently invaded by a rebel army that originated in Chad and the Sudan. Having taken the diamond fields around Bria in the north, this rag-tag but well-equipped unconventional force – with the backing of mercenaries from the Sudan, Egypt, Nigeria, Chad and, more recently, the Ugandan rebel movement Lord's Resistance Army – has all but overwhelmed government forces.

Interestingly, the CAR rebellion is an almost copycat version of recent bloodshed in the equally commodities-rich Eastern Congo.

Elsewhere, conflict has enveloped parts of Somalia and its Kenyan neighbour, while the Sudan remains unsettled.

Before that, West Africa's Mauritania announced that it had killed AQIM leader Tiyib Ould Sidi Ali in a raid launched by its armed forces. The Algerian-born Ali was wanted for a failed bombing attempt in Nouakchott, the Mauritanian capital. Ali is known to have been responsible for an attack on the Israeli embassy in 2008 and was plotting more violence in the region.

Nigeria, too, has come under fire from Islamic fundamentalists in an ongoing wave of brutality that knows almost no par in contemporary Africa. The extent of that insurrection has already been classed as a low-level guerrilla war by America's State Department.

Tens of thousands of people – both Muslim and Christian – have died in pogroms that centre largely on differences on religion as well

Chapter 6
The Future Role of Mercenaries on the African Continent

Some of the images that emerged from the failed Seychelles mercenary invasion, including a newspaper cutting, the Air India boeing that was hijacked to bring the South African mercenaries back to Durban, and its pilot and one of the aircraft's stewardesses. (Photos: Peter Duffy's collection)

Stewardess and her mercenary hijacker swop memories

YOGIN DEVAN

Not in her wildest dreams did Air India first class cabin stewardess, Ulka Kothare, believe she would one day sip French champagne in the warm Durban sun with her former hijacker.

But this week when she came face to face with Durban photographer Peter Duffy, she recalled he was one of the "most friendly hijackers" among the mercenaries aboard the hijacked Air India flight from Seychelles to Durban in November 1981.

Mr Duffy served 21 months of a five-year sentence for his part in the hijacking.

Over lunch this week, Mr Duffy and Ms Kothare — she arrived in Durban on a scheduled Air India flight this time — exchanged their own experiences of the hijacked flight more than 12 years ago.

Duffy was among 45 mercenaries under the command of Colonel Mike Hoare who had landed at Mahe Airport on the Seychelles to seize control of the island.

Captain Umesh Saxena who was at the controls of the Air India plane happened to be at the right time at the right place as far as the hijackers were concerned.

When the coup went all wrong the mercenaries used the Air India plane to escape.

Ms Kothare reminded Mr Duffy how she and her colleagues had been "initially scared" when the plane was hijacked. However, after a while the mercenaries' relaxed manner had set them at ease.

She also related how some "thirsty" mercenaries offered to pay for alcoholic beverages with their travellers' cheques.

"We could not accept the travellers' cheques and gave them the drinks without charge. We were scared if we refused them drinks, they would become agitated."

She also recalled how she and her colleagues attended to the shoulder gunshot wound of one of the mercenaries, Charles Dukes.

Mr Duffy told the smiling stewardess he looked forward to a "reunion party" with the crew in Bombay with Captain Saxena as the chief guest.

HIJACKER AND HIJACKED: Peter Duffy and cabin stewardess Ulka Kothare recall their experiences. *Picture: Grant Erskine*

as the country's oil rights, in part because Nigeria now supplies the United States with about a quarter of crude oil needs. Before he was killed in Pakistan, the al-Qaeda leader Osama bin Laden swore to end Nigerian oil shipments to America. In this, he and other political dissidents have been partially successful.

Washington, London, Paris, Moscow and Beijing are all aware of the threat potential of these military struggles, especially since Africa is booming and foreign investors are throwing money at the continent on an unsurpassed scale. Yet, with this largesse has come a measure of insurrection and dislocation not seen in Africa since the 1970s and 1980s.

Apart from offering military aid, technical expertise, as well as training facilities and personnel, there is little the major powers can do to counter this kind of dislocation on the African continent. With the exception of Mali, none of these countries are willing to commit to having their own troops go in and bring a measure of order to ongoing chaos: the spectre of body bags shipped home from Iraq and Afghanistan remains stark in the minds of their politicians.

All of which makes particularly appropriate the comments of William Shawcross – the author of *Deliver Us From Evil*. He declared that 'if we want to put the world to rights and we're not prepared to risk our own forces in doing so, then we should consider the employment of private security forces'. He added that if the South African mercenaries had been allowed to do the job they were intended for, before they were kicked out of Sierra Leone in 1996, 'a lot of children would still have their hands today ...'

In truth, *US News and World Report* seemed to have had it right when it declared on 30 December 1996: 'Want peacekeepers with spine? Hire the world's finest mercenaries.'

There is no question that the level of violence in Africa is escalating. The threat factor in some areas, specifically the Congo, is real enough to have an effect on commodity market prices.

The international community is aware of these problems, underscored by US counterterrorism officials paying much attention to an increasingly dangerous incubator for extremism.

Former Assistant Secretary of State for Near Eastern Affairs David Welch told the House Foreign Affairs Committee that 'the threat from al-Qaeda's presence in the region is significant, very dangerous and potentially growing in a couple of cases'. In other interviews, senior American government officials talked about recent developments in the impoverished region of North Africa, the Sahara, and the grasslands to the south known as the Sahel. The consensus was that this vast area has the potential for violence.

It is no secret that much of the sophisticated military hardware sent to Libya to topple Muammar Gadaffi – including SAM ground-to-air missiles (MANPADS) and some of the most advanced artillery systems in Moscow's arsenal, like the quad-barrelled ZSU23/24 – have found their way into the hands of some of those exporting revolution to other African states. Almost all weapons used by Taureg guerrillas in Mali, for instance, originated in Libya.

The African Union is trying to do what it can to stem the tide, but its resources (and available cash and the ability to provide trained soldiers) are limited. Also, the majority of African troops recently deployed in the Congo were either badly trained or almost totally unmotivated in the face of a crisis that resulted in tens of thousands of innocents being forced to flee. While the AU has done reasonably well in Somalia, its record elsewhere in Africa is dismal.

Chapter 6
The Future Role of Mercenaries on the African Continent

So too with the Central African Republic, where Gabon – its nearest neighbour – fully aware that the capital of one of its closest allies was about to be overrun by rebels, offered a meagre 120 soldiers in support.

The bottom line is that in any counter-insurgency, it is essential to recognise the dangers of 'incremental escalation'. The historical lesson that has been learned empirically since World War II is that 'trailing' an insurgency typically condemns almost all counter-insurgency efforts to failure. We've seen that happen in the Congo, Nigeria, Eritrea, Sudan and a host of other African states facing insurrection. And of course, in Afghanistan...

For all that, there is a feasible and accessible counter to some of the African military adventures currently being embarked on by a host of largely anti-Western guerrillas active in Africa today. These groups are a diverse lot, their methods as varied as their ethnic or national origins.

In Mali, for example, there are combatants from many countries, including Saudi Arabia, Egypt, Nigeria and even a few Afghans. Interestingly, several 'volunteers' from Chechnya have been spotted in rebel ranks. The only common denominator among them is that all are devout followers of the Prophet.

Strategists on both sides of the Atlantic have consistently voiced the opinion that many of Africa's wars could be given short shrift with the use of helicopter gunships flown by freelance professionals. British military historian John Keegan told me before he died in 2011 that it was a pity that the West did not look more positively at the kind of potential that a well-equipped, motivated and trained mercenary force has to offer, particularly in Third World conflicts.

Though disruptive efforts to oust the Egyptian Army from the Yemen between 1962 and 1970 was very effectively run and coordinated by Britain's Special Air Service, with Colonel Jim Johnson in command, French and Arab mercenaries were also employed. The Egyptians took so many losses that this insurgency was eventually labelled 'Nasser's Vietnam'. (Photo: Author's collection)

It was his view that helicopter gunships were the best means of stopping mindless and primitive carnage. He was also enthusiastic about the use of hired guns to counter some of these threats and made the point that people tended to forget that General Charles Gordon [of Khartoum] served in the Middle East as a mercenary. 'Moreover, he did so both under the Chinese Emperor as well as under orders of the Khedive of Egypt,' were Keegan's words.

A more recent comment came from General Sir David Richards, Britain's Chief of Defence Staff who, in a personal note to this author, declared that the role of Neall Ellis, the South African helicopter gunship pilot who fought under his command in Sierra Leone, was exemplary. His words were succinct: 'Neall Ellis is a great man. I and everyone in Sierra Leone owe him much.'

The reason why General Sir David Richards has been outspoken about the world's most famous mercenary aviator, is because Ellis was able, single-handedly and over a period of several months, to keep the anti-Freetown rebels off balance with his lone and antiquated Mi-24 helicopter gunship. He continued to do so until the British Army and Royal Navy were able to step in and bring that war to a close.

Former SAAF helicopter gunship pilot Arthur Walker took this photo of wounded Somali servicemen while serving with the Puntland Police Maritime Police Force. It followed an Alouette strike early in 2013, against pirates who had been holding hostages on board a ship.

Chapter 6
The Future Role of Mercenaries on the African Continent

Financing a mercenary force is not cheap, but it hardly compares with the manner in which the United Nations has been able to squander resources in almost all the military operations in which the world body has been involved in Africa.

In Sierra Leone, the mercenary group Executive Outcomes was paid something like $30 million to force Revolutionary United Front rebels to the negotiating table within about six or seven months of launching a vigorous military counter to the RUF terror campaign. In contrast, the UN's budget for its first six months in this remote West African state – where their people were faced with exactly the same security problems as the South African freebooters – exceeded a quarter billion dollars, or $1.5 million a day!

There was another significant anomaly. Executive Outcomes rarely had more than 100 men in the field and, at most, three operational helicopters. The UN contingent in Sierra Leone at one stage totalled 16,000 troops from 16 different countries…

Which raises the question: what does it cost to mount a helicopter strike force in Africa with modest support elements?

Mercenaries come from all over. In the Rhodesian War there were many Americans who served in regular as well as unconventional forces fighting the guerrillas, like this pair of bounty hunters who were paid for insurgent kills. Dana Drenkowski (left) flew 200 Vietnam missions in B-52 bombers and F-4s before being hired as a mercenary by Gadaffi. His 'partner in crime' is Jim Bolen. (Photo: Dana Drenkowski)

The short-lived West African Republic of Biafra was one of the first in modern Africa to use mercenaries within its ranks. Some went there after having fought in the Congo. French freebooter Robert Denard commanded a group that flew into the jungle airstrip at Uli one night and promptly left 24 hours later, in part because Biafra was a more brutal war than anything they had experienced before. At Pretoria's behest, South African Colonel Jan Breytenbach and some of his men were also involved, having come into the beleaguered enclave through Gabon. (Photo: Author's collection)

Chapter 6
The Future Role of Mercenaries on the African Continent

One of the white mercenaries who fought in Biafra was Belgian Marc Goosens who had served as a career officer in the Belgian Army. In 1964 he went to the Congo as Belgium's chief military advisor with the rank of colonel and attached to the Congolese Army. In Biafra, he served as a major and was killed in the battle for the riverside city of Onitcha. A leader by example, Goosens was worshipped by the men he led and when he was killed in action, they carried his body back from the front. He was acclaimed a hero and buried with full military honours.
(Photo: Author's collection)

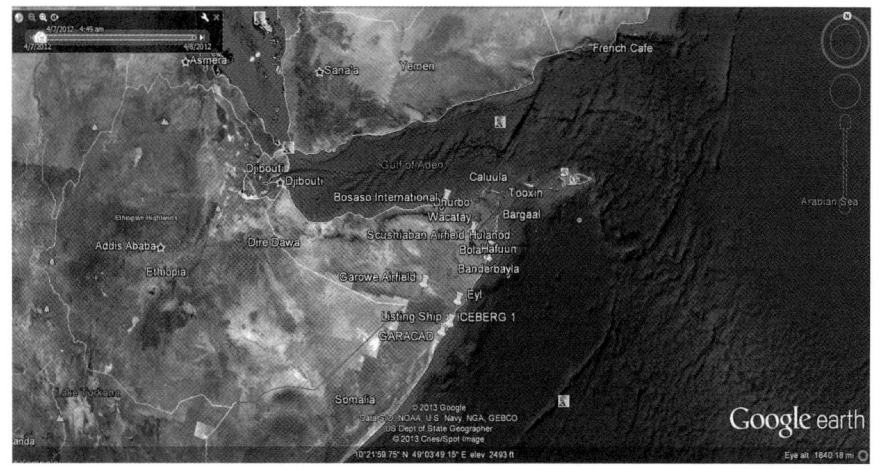

Google Earth photo indicating the area of operations of Somali-based mercenary pilots in the north-east of that troubled country. The most effective efforts being made to counter these actions come from a part of Somalia that has declared itself independent from the Mogadishu government and calls itself Puntland. The Puntland Police Maritime Force – originally created with CIA support and funds – has its main base at Bosaso on Puntland's north coast. The location of the freighter *Iceland 1*, hijacked by Somali pirates and held with more than two dozen hostages for three years, can also be seen.

According to Neall Ellis, three or four Russian Mi-24s would be more than adequate in any strike role if deployed in the kind of insurgency now facing countries like the Central African Republic or Mali. In addition there would need to be a couple of Mi-17s for logistical backup and troop-ferrying roles.

Also, there is hardly an African country without a medium or small helicopter wing and these could be employed for the purpose. If not available, helicopters can be legally acquired by countries offering appropriate end-user certificates. Without the right papers though, it is almost impossible to acquire such weapons.

Gunships – whatever their role – do not come cheap, especially since prices have gone up in recent years. Five years ago you could buy a used but serviceable Hip for about $6 million. Today, a good quality Russian Mi-8 – with a modicum of spares – is going to put the buyer back about $10 million. Currently, most come from the Ukraine.

A fully serviceable Mi-24 (Hind) gunship sells for less, but the cost of spares, in all departments, can be crippling.

An additional outlay is aircrews. During the recent Mali insurgency, the word on the mercenary grapevine was that freelance gunship pilots were being offered $1,500 a day, with copilots fractionally less. In Somalia, the lone pilot flying the Alouette III

OPÉRATION MARINE

AFRICA

MS. CABO VERDE chalutier de 52 mètres Pêche en Islande
MS Antinéa chalutier de 73 Mètres. Terre Neuva

1969 OPS BIAFRA : MS. MI CABO VERDE
Transport de Munition Cherbourg Libreville – Walvis Bay Libreville
La Rochelle : 5 Rotations de 21 Jours de Mer Aller. 22 Jours Retour

1978 OPS COMORES MS ANTINÉA
Lorient – Las Palma, 7 Jours de Mer Las Palmas MORONI 28 jours de Mer Total 35 jours.

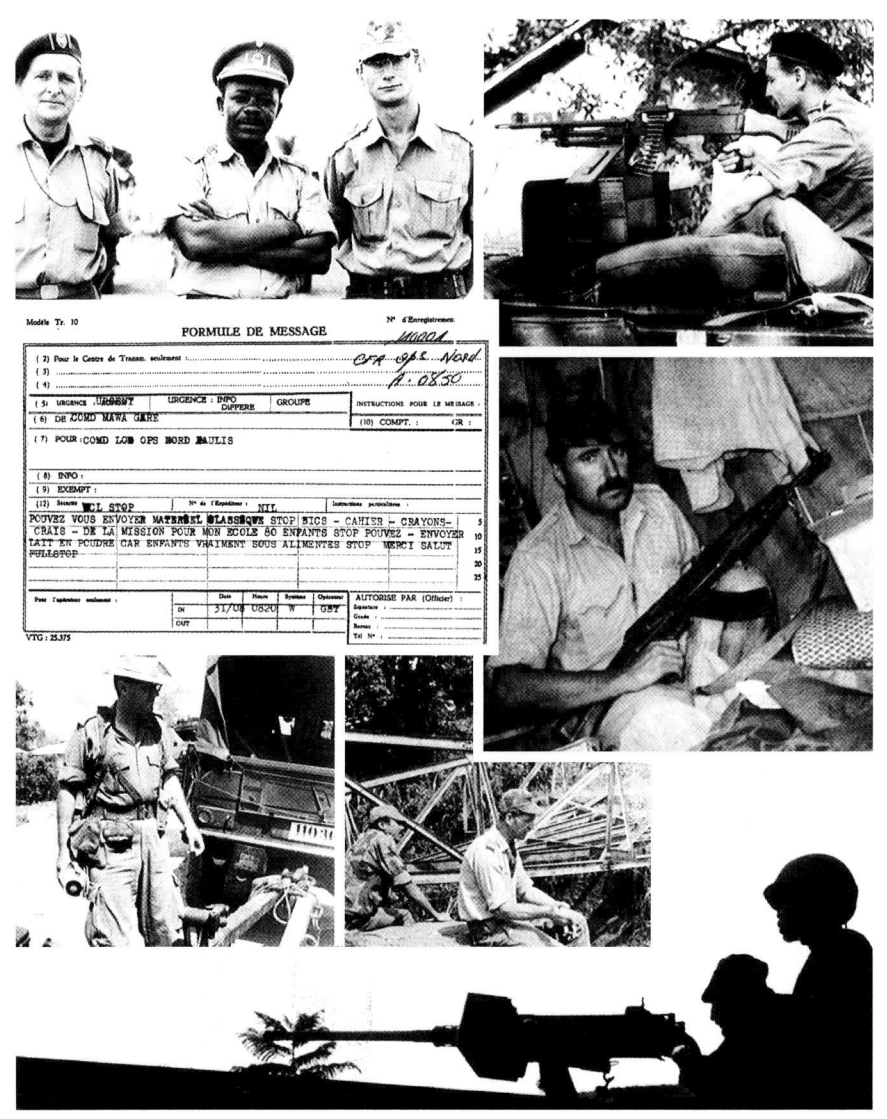

Previous page: French mercenary leader Colonel Denard's hand-drawn map of some of his African maritime operations, including Biafra (1969) and the Comores Archipelago (1978). On this page there are various images of the 1960s Congo debacle which involved South African and European mercenaries. (Map courtesy of Fiona Capstick; photos from author's collection)

bought by Somalia's Puntland Police Maritime Force (PPMF) – currently countering pirates operating off the Horn of Africa – earns roughly the same as some of the better-paid American helicopter pilots in Afghanistan. In the Horn of Africa he flies the single Alouette gunship on his own, with a gunner manning the machine's RPD automatic weapon on board.

Ground crews are essential to maintain these aircraft, which can sometimes be a crippling expense for a poor African nation that faces an insurgency.

While flying operationally in Sierra Leone, Ellis had the services of a bunch of Ethiopian technicians, many of them Russian or American trained. As he commented when I flew with him in West Africa, 'these fellows are real professionals, often going with us into combat situations to keep things ticking over'. He reckons that a six-ship chopper wing would require at least a dozen engineers to keep the helicopters airworthy.

Add to that travel costs, suitable Western-style accommodation and food as well as adequate, if improvised, medical backup, and costs are likely to escalate markedly. Mercenary air wings rarely offer search-and-rescue facilities: if you go down, which was the case in Sierra Leone, you are on your own.

Additionally, as with Executive Outcomes in both Angola and Sierra Leone, aircrews tend to use small fixed-wing planes for spotting or logistical purposes, especially if some of the 'hot' areas are some distance from the main bases of operations.

A notable success involving 'freelance aviators' more recently was the rescue of 22 sailors who had been held hostage by pirates on board the Panamanian-registered freighter *Iceberg*[1] for three years off the coast of Somalia.

Several members of the crew had died during this period and others were savaged and tortured by their Somali guards. The *Iceberg*'s chief engineer had had his ears cut off because he 'did not listen'; then they crushed his leg with a steel bar so that he could not escape.

Aware of the fate of these men, the government of Puntland, a semi-automous entity that had originally been part of greater Somalia but which had decided to go it alone after the central government collapse some years ago, tried to negotiate with the pirates several times. Each time their entreaties to release the prisoners were rejected.

Finally, in December 2012, a small group of South African mercenaries in the employ of the Puntland Maritime Police Force attempted to rescue the prisoners. About 20 ground troops that included a Puntland detachment and led by former Executive Outcomes veteran Rudolf van Heerden, launched the attack. The effort was backed by a single Alouette III helicopter gunship with a Soviet-era PKM machine gun mounted at the port door flying top cover.

Colonel Bob Denard with some of his 'trophies'. The ship's wheel came from the HMS *Antinéa*, a rust bucket in which he and his men sailed from Lorient in France to Moroni, with a brief stopover in Las Palmas. (Photo: Fiona Capstick)

Having brought some heavier weapons – including a Soviet 82 mm smoothbore B-10 recoilless gun as well as RPG-7s to bear – the onslaught ended 12 days later when the pirates, using mobile phones, called their leaders to negotiate a truce through diplomatic elements in the Yemen. The Puntland government agreed to exchange the hostages for the freedom of the pirates who were holding them.

This was the first time an independent military group had rescued a group of hostages from captivity while still at sea.

This development has injected a deadlier threat into the scenario. With al-Qaeda-linked al-Shabab forces having been driven out of their safe havens in southern Somalia (as a consequence of military ground and action by African Union forces), Puntland is now experiencing a surge of Islamic-backed terrorism.

Own sources indicate that there are now an estimated 300 al-Shabab guerrilla fighters in Puntland and that their ranks include a number of Egyptian Jihadists.

Washington is aware of this development. For much of the time under review, security in breakaway Puntland was handled by Bancroft Global Development, a military training group funded by

Chapter 6
The Future Role of Mercenaries on the African Continent

the United Nations and the US State Department and headquartered jointly in Washington DC and Mogadishu. Bancroft provided training in a range of military services, from bomb disposal and sniper training to handing out police uniforms. The terror group has moved into this area adjoining the Red Sea.

Meantime, another American firm has been tasked to run security operations in Puntland and indeed, the anti-pirate attack took place under its auspices.

The assets of the PMPF are modest. Prior to Bancroft pulling back to Mogadishu, a pair of upgraded Mi-17s was ordered, but these were put on hold and never delivered.

The force lacks the support of the original 120 expatriate combatants fielded by Bancroft until the group was disbanded last June following United Nations pressure. Involved then was former US Navy Seal Erik Prince, founder and owner of Blackwater International, who for the Puntland operation had partnered up with Lafras Luitingh, a former South African Special Forces operative and original founder of Executive Outcomes. Twenty private military contractors remain, all part of the PMPF air-wing infrastructure.

Still at the unit's Bosaso air base, a small town in the north of

Mercenary 'Flying Column' en route to Stanleyville in the north-east Congo at the height of the Simba rebellion. The relieving force which ended up saving hundreds of prisoners held by the rebels had little in the way of armour and were regularly ambushed. (Photo courtesy of Leif Hellström)

the country about 500 km east of Djibouti is an Antonov-26 with a rotating Russian crew. This aircraft is used for bringing in supplies, troop rotation as well as to drop fuel and equipment to PMPF elements on distant operations. This includes dropping 44-gallon drums of fuel at sea for the three Zodiac RHIBs, fast craft fitted with 400hp Volvo twin-screw inboards and 12.7 mm DshKa heavy machine guns mounted on their prows and deployed for anti-piracy operations by the PFMF.

Jet-A1 is also dropped by parachute for the Alouette helicopter when needed.

Additionally, the PMPF has at its headquarters at Bosaso three new Ayres Turbo Thrush crop-spraying aircraft armed with four-barrelled mini-guns capable of firing 4,000 rpm, as well as US-supplied underwing air-to-ground rockets.

Adapted for close-air-support roles and labelled 'Vigilantes', the aircraft were originally developed for anti-narcotics crop-spraying roles in Colombia at the behest of the US Department of State. Clearly, the machines are a useful adjunct to the limited airborne capability of the PMPF.

Another aviation element routinely seen at the airbase at Bosaso is a pair of military Mi-17s with upgraded 2,500 hp engines. No photos are allowed near the place and the crews – one of the pilots is a woman – have no contact with those linked to the PMPF, except senior military officers within the Puntland government.

Interestingly, the pair of Mi-17s have been completely modified to include Western avionics, which, by some accounts, is a first for the Russian helicopter. Its original clamshell rear doors have been removed and a ramp installed, very much in line with what was originally sported by the French-built Super Frelon helicopter, in all probability to allow for the mounting of automatic weapons that can be fired out of the rear. The two Mi-17s use the same shooting range for training as the PMPF helicopter, which lies a short distance from Bosaso.

It is significant that a major al-Shabab cell was recently uncovered near the town and that the base has come under attack several times in recent months.

The presence in Puntland of increased numbers of al-Shabab fighters was underscored weeks ago when local residents reported an Arab dhow, purportedly out of the Yemen, that had entered one of the lagoons along the northern coast and unloaded a cargo. This contraband was hurriedly buried and the boat fled when curious locals started to approach.

Chapter 6
The Future Role of Mercenaries on the African Continent

In a search the following day that involved the unit's helicopter, as well as PMPF ground forces, a cache of arms was uncovered, but it was obvious that only part of the cargo had been unloaded.

It consisted of 120 RPG-7 launchers but no grenades. Also found was a quantity of B-9 ammunition, but no barrels (the B-9 is of Soviet origin and slightly smaller than the B-10 recoilless gun).

Other munitions recovered were 220 RPG-7 rockets and, clearly for improvised explosive devices, 40 kg of TNT, 20 electric detonators incorporating the latest technology, four rolls of Cortex detonation wire as well as 20 kg of ammonium nitrate in sacks – it looks like fertiliser but can be very effectively used in IEDs.

There were also several boxes of AK and PKM ammunition as well as hand grenades.

In another recent development, an American private military company offered its services to equip Kampala with a moderate-sized helicopter strike force for deployment in its Somali-based security operations against the al-Qaeda-backed al-Shabab terror

In Africa – and much of the Third World – Russia's Mi-24 (Hind) gunship is still regarded as one of the most effective counter-insurgency weapons in the armoury of any defending nation. At roughly $6 million apiece for a serviceable model, they are comparatively cheap compared to Western gunships, are rugged, reliable and easily serviced. This one, flown by veteran mercenary aviator Neall Ellis, worked hard at countering rebel advances in Sierra Leone. (Photo: Author)

movement. This operation was not linked to the Puntland operation, but indirectly would have worked on security issues in tandem.

Zone 4 International, an Atlanta-based American company submitted a proposal [below] to the Ugandan Peoples Defence Force (UPDF) for the lease/purchase of three Mi-24V (Hind) helicopters to support that country's AMISOM operations in Somalia. It included several options for an ACMI (aircraft, crew, maintenance, insurance) lease and aviation/mission-support services. The machines were delivered shortly afterwards.

The company declared that since Uganda was substantially contributing to the United Nations Somali security mission in the Horn of Africa, the intent was to offer the UPDF an 'unmatched military capability' that could be presented to AMISOM/UN by the UDPF, the idea being to increase their mission effectiveness and reduce direct threat exposure to African Union (AU) ground forces in Somalia. That offer was subsequently accepted by the United Nations.

The Mi-24V helicopters were to be configured in a multirole capacity and used for strikes against al-Qaeda-linked enemy units, force protection, medical evacuation, troop transport, emergency airlift, aerial surveillance as well as intelligence gathering.

Zone 4 International also offered aviation and mission support services to include (but not limited to) the provision of highly experienced English-speaking crews, field maintenance, and operational support. In addition, at the request of the UPDF, the company was willing to provide full mission support capabilities for the deployment and sustainment of the air group such as construction of a forward operating base (FOB), static and mobile force protection, and logistics solutions to ensure 24/7 mission readiness.

Mi-24V specifications

Three crew, eight passengers (or four medevac stretchers)
Propulsion: 2 Turbo shaft Klimow TV3-117VM engines
Speed: 335 km/h (181 knots)
Service ceiling: 4,500m/14,764 ft
Range: 500 km
Empty weight: 8,340 kg. Maximum: 11,500 kg

Available armament (ordnance not included)

Yak B 12.7 mm – four-barrelled nose gun (Gatling)
NSV 12.7 mm x 107 mm crew-served weapon

UB-32 launch pods for S-5, 57 mm unguided rockets
Optional avionics and equipment included GPS Garmin-155XL and ALFA-2031 night-vision goggles (NVG).

The company stated that it had access to five Mi-24V helicopters, all under zero time overhaul, which could be operational within 90 days. The helicopters were all manufactured in 1986 and had never been deployed in combat, had been inspected by staff and deemed in excellent condition. Mission ready, the machines could be delivered, subject to export/import requirements, within three months.

Concept of operations

The company offer was of the nature of a self-sustaining concept of operations (COO) which included the following:
- Mobilisation
- Deployment to theatre
- Operations management and control while in-theatre
- Sustainment while in-theatre
- Handover of asset ownership

Technical offer

Operating roles included, but not limited to, day and night air operations available 24 hours a day and seven days a week for the insertion/extraction of AMISOM troops, passenger flights, cargo transport, on-call aero medical evacuation (medevac), search and rescue, and reconnaissance flights.

Fixed wing

1 CASA 212 multipurpose and reconnaissance aircraft.
ACMI Lease of CASA 212 aircraft equipped with forward-looking infra-red camera and night-vision optics. The primary mission role: to offer forward observation capability aircraft and personnel on encroaching hostile threats.
Additional mission roles at the request of AMISOM would include, but not be limited to:
- Forward observation and aerial intelligence-gathering for AMISOM forces
- Medevac
- Troop and cargo movements
- Aerial drop operations

Crews

The company would hand-select experienced English-speaking crews with the pilots-in-command (PIC) having a minimum of 500 rotary flight hours, four sets of pilots, weapons systems officers and three flight engineers for each Mi-24V. Crews would be vetted by Zone 4 International and undergo refresher flight training and ground operations training prior to deployment to Somalia. Additionally, crews would attend high-risk advanced operator training at the company's Tactical Training Centre in Serbia. Training would include medic life-saver courses, tactical pistol, and escape and evasion training.

Proposed crew requirements for Mi-24Vs: four pilots, four weapons systems officers, three flight engineers/medics, two ground engineers. Total operational complement: 13.

Maintenance and spare parts

The Mi-24Vs were finally delivered to Entebbe Airport in Uganda with combat stores that included spare parts and tooling equipment. This included TV3-117 spare engines, one set of main and tail rotor blades, parts, petroleum oil lubricants, and avionics. Maintenance conducted on-station to include (if required):

- Daily service check
- 300 hour check
- 500 hour check
- Engine/APU change
- Minor maintenance
- Airframe patchworks

Insurance

All aircraft were registered to carry hull, third-party liability, war-risk and crew insurance.

Operations staff – Forward

Zone 4 offered to appoint a programme manager (PM) experienced in military helicopter operations in areas of high risk. This position would be an on-site post and have direct oversight of the operation and assets. In addition, the PM would act as liaison between the UDPF and AMISOM forces and have a full understanding of the AMISOM mission and the Rules of Engagement (ROE). He would be backed by an operations specialist with strong military experience.

Operations staff – Rear

Administrative and logistics coordination support would be conducted by the company offices located in Nairobi, Kenya and Atlanta, GA.

Operational base

The main operational base was to have been constructed at specific [deleted] coordinates adjacent to Mogadishu Airport.

This field HQ would be built on hard earth with a 1200 x 30 metre airstrip suitable for rotary and fixed-wing aircraft with an aircraft parking enclave 70 x 70 metres located [deleted]. This operating base would be able to accommodate up to 30 persons to include prefabricated housing units, potable water, plumbing, electricity, environmental control units, dining facility, washroom, apron lighting stands, expeditionary runway lighting system, up to 1,000 metre earth perimeter (in wire mesh containers) and watchtowers with illuminating spotlights.

Cost

The price for one Mi-24V flight hour was listed as $7,500 while a single CASA 212 flight hour was quoted at $2,000.

Minimal monthly guaranteed hours (MGH) and contract period

The minimal guaranteed hours per Mi-24V helicopter was set at 50 flight hours each. For the CASA 212 the stipulation was set at 60 hours, all aviation assets with contract periods of 24 months.

Monthly payment for a CMI lease purchase of three Mi-24Vs

Item MGH Rate per Flight Hour Total Cost (three helicopters)
Mi-24V:
- 50 flight hours x $7,500.00 = $375,500: TOTAL $1,125,000
- Monthly payment for CMI Lease of the CASA 212: $120,000

Total monthly payment for aviation services $1,245,000

24-month cost of aviation/long-term transport services:
- $29,880,000
- Aviation operating base stand-up cost: $2,000,000

Total programme cost for 24 months: $31,880,000

> NOTE: The Uganda government did not avail itself of Zone 4 International's personnel offer, maintaining that it preferred to use its own aircrews. The result was that all three Mi-24s crashed in Kenya while in transit to Mogadishu in 2012.

Soldiers of Fortune often find themselves working in unusual places. American mercenary Dave McGrady signed up with the Israelis to fight with the South Lebanese Army against hostile Islamic Arabs – the forerunners of today's Hizbollah – in the Shi'ite-dominated south of that embattled land.

CHAPTER SEVEN

RHODESIA'S WAR – AL VENTER LOOKS BACK

> More than three decades ago, a South African magazine group published a series of four 24-page colour supplements in their magazines on the war in neighbouring Rhodesia: two in English went into *Scope* magazine and the other pair into their Afrikaans counterpart. There is a rather interesting series of events as to how this all eventually took place, because it almost happened by accident...

I was reminded of that tiny chapter of African history when I met 'Lottie', or more respectfully, the Princess HSH Charlotte Maria Benedikte Eleonore Adelheid et omnes sancti Prinzessin von und zu Liechtenstein, widow of former Rhodesian Minister of Defence, P.K. van der Byl. That was at the launch of P.K.'s biography in London late in 2011. South African author Hannes Wessels had spent a year putting the book together, obviously with good support from Lottie and the family.

It was the mid-1970s and I'd been in Mozambique watching the exodus of the Portuguese Armed Forces and many Portuguese nationals who decided that perhaps their time in Africa had come to an end.

It struck me, driving to the Rhodesian border from Tete – a big town on the Zambezi River, now all but lawless because the Portuguese garrison had abandoned the place – that the average South African knew almost nothing about the escalating guerrilla war then being waged along their northern borders. Most weren't too interested in what was going on anyway.

Shortly after I'd checked in at Salisbury's Monomotapa Hotel, I lifted the phone and called the office of the Rhodesian Minister of Defence. It was a wild chance because it was almost five in the

Though the Rhodesians lost many good men in their insurgencies, the overall death toll on the government's side was comparatively light when compared to casualties in conflicts like Vietnam and Algeria. It hit home hard when one caught sight of funerals such as this one in Salisbury for a troopie that had been killed in action.
(Photo: Hannes Wessels collection)

afternoon, but, I thought, what the hell! Who should pick up the phone but the Defence Minister himself...

In as few words as possible, I told P.K. that I had just returned from Mozambique and that one of my immediate impressions was that most South Africans were largely unaware of what was going on just then in Rhodesia. I pointed out that conflict had enmeshed every sector of his country's infrastructure and, possibly out of ignorance, there weren't too many people south of the Limpopo who cared a damn.

I suggested that I might be able to remedy that situation by doing a series of reports for the magazine group for which I worked. In characteristic P.K. fashion, the Minister said that I should come over to his office.

'Now?' I asked, perturbed.

'Yes, of course, *right now!*' was the command.

'But I'm not dressed, Sir. I've just arrived from Mozambique ... I'm filthy ... been travelling all day ... I'm still in my shorts, T-shirt and takkies ...'

'Never mind that,' he replied gruffly. 'You make your way to my office in Milton Buildings and I'll tell the guard to expect you. Take a taxi – it'll be quicker ...'

By the time I got there, I had kind of formulated a plan, having come up with the idea of the four colour supplements. It was an enormous imposition, of course, because I had absolutely no authority to negotiate on behalf of Republican Press in Durban on something that would clearly involve the outlay of hundreds of thousands of rands, never mind the staff that would have to be involved, coupled to several months of work.

Once I'd laid the concept before him, P.K. – always the moving force in such issues – thought it was a splendid idea. He would speak to Prime Minister Ian Smith, he said, and in the meantime, I should make arrangements to get Boet Hyman and his family – the owners of *Scope* – to come to Salisbury as soon as possible.

'Think you can do that?' he asked as he turned towards me, eyebrows raised. 'Of course I can, Sir. No problem at all,' I lied.

I called Durban first thing the following morning and told Jack Shepherd-Smith, my editor, that we'd been *invited* to do a series of supplements on the Rhodesian War and asked whether he would speak to the Hymans. *Scope Magazine* was their flagship publication and, obviously, were it to happen, this would be an enormous undertaking. It could also be quite profitable for the group because, as the saying goes, like sex, war tends to sell ...

Jack acknowledged that there was a marvellous scoop in the offing, which, in fact it was, because, until then there had been sparse coverage of the Rhodesian military struggle in the South African media.

One thing led to another and it wasn't too long before the entire Hyman family flew to Salisbury and met with P.K., together with other members of the Rhodesian government. On disembarking from their aircraft at Salisbury Airport, they were greeted with much fanfare by the head of Rhodesian Protocol. Three or four months later the supplements were out and were being distributed throughout South Africa.

Rhodesian African Rifle troops on patrol in the Mtoko area. (Photo: Author)

It was perhaps just as well that it happened like that, because the reports that appeared were certainly a wake-up call for many of the people down south.

Unsavoury things were taking place along our nearest northern frontiers that would ultimately have significant consequences for us all, even though our own Border War was already in full swing in South West Africa (Namibia today) – and that war lasted 21 years…

Interestingly, before I left P.K. at his office, he had invited me to lunch at his home the next morning, in part to discuss some of the detail and what such a venture would actually entail.

Somehow, I'd given the minister the impression that I was very much a part of the Republican Press hierarchy and it probably never occurred to him that I was little more than a lowly paid staff scribbler. Fortunately, I'd already covered a few African conflicts, including Biafra and the Portuguese conflagrations, so I had a fairly good idea of most implications. More to the point, he accepted immediately that this would be no ordinary military assignment: the four journalists involved in obtaining material for the supplements would have to spend time embedded with Rhodesian units at various locations.

The Van der Byl home in the Rhodesian capital was a delightful old Cape Dutch structure near the middle of town and, for his own purposes, P.K. had invited Wikus de Kock, a fellow-minister in the Smith cabinet, to join us.

But halfway through the meal, I collapsed. In fact, I almost fell with my head in a plate of oxtail stew. I didn't know it yet, but I was coming down with malaria, and fast, something I'd probably picked up during my sojourn along the Zambezi Valley. I'd spent several nights in Tete and while there, had been half eaten alive by mosquitoes. In a bid to help, P.K. asked Wikus to search in his booze cabinet for a bottle of *witblitz*, a high-powered Afrikaner moonshine that can singe hair.

'Pour him a stiff one, Wikus,' he said, but it didn't help. It was obvious to them both that they had a very sick man at the lunch table. The Rhodesian Minister of Defence ended up driving me back to the Monomotapa Hotel in the back of his posh British limo and told the receptionist – or rather, ordered her – to get me a doctor. 'Pronto!' he declared. 'Can't you see the poor fellow is ill?'

An hour later I was admitted to Salisbury's Andrew Fleming Hospital and, indeed, the dreaded lurgie had struck. The onset of fever was so bad that the same night Republican Press flew my then wife from Johannesburg to be at my bedside: the doctor in charge believed I wouldn't see the next light of day.

I obviously did, but it being malaria, it took me a couple of months to come right.

The rest is history, because the following excerpts appeared in the supplements:

RHODESIA'S WAR – AL VENTER LOOKS BACK FROM THE FIRST OF THE *SCOPE* 24-PAGE REPORTS: JUNE, 1976

ALMOST a year has elapsed since **SCOPE** *published two exclusive reports on the Rhodesian War. Then, hostilities were restricted mainly to the area between Mount Darwin and the Zambezi Valley with sporadic activity farther west.*

Six months ago a second front was opened, which can be divided into two broad regions. One is the eastern zone stretching from Nyamapanda (the Mozambican border post leading to Tete) to Umtali and including the Inyanga and Vumba mountain regions.

The second area of hostilities stretches from the city of

Umtali south to the South African border. This region includes the tea, coffee and sugar estates around Chipinga, the giant Hippo Valley sugar plantations, the Gonarezhou National Park, the Nuanetsi farming district and a fairly large tract of territory stretching inland towards the main rail and road links with South Africa just north of Beit Bridge.

One independent estimate has put the area in dispute between security forces and insurgents as about the size of Natal, running in a long swathe from the Zambezi to the Limpopo. It is thought that there are more than 500 terrorists active in the east and south-east.

Conditions within the war zones are serious. Recent developments include a terrorist contact in the hills overlooking Umtali. A group of four or five insurgents were spotted in May by a security force patrol and chased across the Mozambique frontier.

Pump houses in the Hippo Valley Estates have been mortared, a bank was blown up south of Inyanga and a variety of government, civilian, and military targets rocketed. These attacks are over and above daily onslaughts on farm homesteads and what is probably the most concerted land mining campaign yet launched in Africa.

On average, two civilian and military vehicles are lost to mines each day, although recent security force measures have resulted in large quantities of landmines being lifted in daily clearing operations which span all major untarred routes in the operational area. All roads are now classified red, amber or white, according to the level of terrorist activities.

There have been other changes. Terrorists are now adopting some of the measures employed by the Vietcong in Vietnam.

One of these includes the use of poison spikes and a variety of booby traps, all intended to maim or kill the pursuer, but which, more often than not, result in injury to civilian blacks, their livestock or wild animals.

Recent intelligence sources have indicated that much of the planning, logistics, supply, battle tactics and day-to-day thinking employed in the war against Rhodesia stems from a substantial body of foreign regular army officers stationed along the Rhodesian border in Mozambique.

These are reported to include staff officers from the Zambian, Tanzanian and Mozambican Armies acting on behalf of the Organisation of African Unity. There are also a few Cubans, some Vietnamese veterans and a variety of East Europeans, including Russians, East Germans and Bulgarians. The Arab States are represented by Algeria and Libya. There is evidence of this new participation in the way targets such as the Rutenga rail link and the petrol station at Inyazuru are designated for attack and the manner insurgents move directly to these 'soft' targets. The intention, basically, is to spread havoc over as wide an area as possible.

In Mozambique and Zambia this operation has been termed the 'Third Force' by the joint ANC command, and four southern African presidents are personally responsible for co-coordinating the activities of the Zimbabwe Liberation Army (ZLA); Presidents Nyerere, Kaunda, Machel and Sir Seretse Khama.

The inclusion of the Botswana President is not all that surprising since Sir Seretse has regularly met with the three other presidents in working sessions on the war. This information substantiates recent reports that Botswana may be considering cutting the Rhodesian rail link which runs through her territory.

The man most severely affected by the continuing war is the Rhodesian farmer.

Three years ago, shortly after the first serious attacks out of Mozambique into the north-east on farmers in the Centenary and Mount Darwin areas, a mass exodus of farmers and their families from these regions was predicted. Today the same 'experts' say the farmers in the south-east and eastern regions will depart in the not-too-distant future.

They couldn't be more wrong. In few places in the world are farmers more determined to stay and 'make a go of it' than in the operational areas of Rhodesia.

While a few farmers around Chipinga and Nuanetsi have departed for safer climes, the majority are unanimous in their determination to sit out the war 'no matter what.' Backing their arguments are huge new security installations around every farm homestead and some of the most elaborate defence and radio-electronic installations yet seen in southern Africa.

It is significant that not a single occupied farm in the operational areas has yet been overrun by terrorists and its inhabitants slaughtered. The majority of farmers are adamant that, when attacked, they give as good as they get. The majority of farms attacked in the north-east were only hit when the farmer and his family were away from home.

In spite of this, many visitors to Rhodesia in recent months have expected the end of the war to be imminent. A number of foreign correspondents arriving in Salisbury, prohibited from entering the operational areas by the authorities, have gone to elaborate lengths to concoct stories of their own on the war.

A German television team which visited the country the same time I did, spent a weekend in Umtali and filed a grotesque story on the collapse of the Smith regime. Pictures of the Umtali Tattersalls showing Africans looking at a notice board which listed all the runners for the afternoon were referred to as 'Africans looking at war casualties'.

Another photograph was taken of the centre of the city on a quiet Sunday afternoon. The sequence depicted a deserted town

Rhodesian Light Infantry Colonel Dave 'The King' Parker being airlifted back to his temporary HQ at Mount Darwin during the author's time spent with the unit in the north-east. He was killed in a helicopter crash weeks later.

and the commentator said that Umtali had been abandoned by all its white residents.

Another foreign television team showed the departure of the nightly Salisbury-Bulawayo train from Salisbury's railway station, explaining that whites were departing in droves for South Africa.

Other sequences shown on overseas television screens included shots of Russian tanks rolling down Jameson Avenue in Salisbury! Closer inspection of the location revealed some distinctive Luanda landmarks.

Yet another film showed demolition taking place at the famous Meikles Hotel in the Rhodesian capital to make way for a new and more modern construction. This devastation was depicted as the result of a mortar attack on the establishment.

Perhaps the most astonishing fabrication of all, which was fairly widely used in Europe showed Africans asleep in Salisbury's Cecil Square. These, the commentator said, had been shot dead by security forces.

And yet, with all its contradictions, the Rhodesian War goes on. Clearly the end is nowhere in sight.

THE WHIRLING WINGS OF MERCY SWING INTO ACTION

A young Rhodesian soldier is wounded by rocket fire in an encounter with terrorists in Rhodesia's south-east battle zone. Yet only 34 minutes later he is being lifted into an ambulance many miles away at a remote airstrip.

Guided in by a smoke grenade the helicopter arrives to evacuate a wounded Security Force member while two fellow soldiers administer first aid.

There was a note of urgency in the voice that crackled over the radio.

'Hullo Four. Hullo Four. This is Four One Delta. Do you read?'

The man in the radio shack at operational headquarters answered quickly: 'Four. I read you threes. Go.'

The reply came back immediately. 'This is Four One Delta. Fetch Sunray'

'Wait,' answered headquarters again. There was a brief

delay before 'Sunray,' the commander of the unit, came to the set. 'Hullo Four One Delta. This is Sunray. Go.'

The voice at the other end was tense as the message was relayed.

'Four One Delta. We've had a contact. Repeat contact. Spotted three terrs and opened fire at short range. Terrs replied by firing rocket. Terr casualties unknown but we have one man with shrapnel wounds in back and arm. Condition not too serious but has lost blood. Can arrange casevac [casualty evacuation] soonest? Our position is Alpha three ...'

In the military tradition typical of the Rhodesian Army, a prearranged set of instructions was relayed both by radio and over the loudspeaker at operational headquarters. Within four minutes a Rhodesian Air Force helicopter was circling the base and heading southwards towards the reported position.

On another radio set regional headquarters was advised of the contact and what had transpired. A request went through to notify the nearest base hospital. Three minutes later it was confirmed that an ambulance would be waiting for the arrival of the chopper with the casualty.

The condition of the wounded man was no real cause for worry. The unit's medic had already stemmed the flow of blood and connected an intravenous drip to counter the effects of shock. The casualty was then moved to an open stretch of ground at the base of some hills to await the arrival of the chopper that would airlift him to hospital.

Three members of the patrol took up position in the bush around the improvised landing pad. Another man sat at the radio. The medic, together with an African member of the patrol, tended to the wounded man.

The Africans heard the chopper approaching over the low bush long before their white compatriots. They pointed towards the approaching sound and, sure enough, a minute or so later the helicopter circled and prepared for landing, led in during the final approach by the orange billows of a smoke grenade.

The wheels had hardly touched ground when the engineer had loosened the casevac stretcher and was sprinting across to where the wounded soldier lay, a youngster barely 20 years old and clearly in a lot of pain.

Two minutes later, with the casualty securely strapped across the rear seat of the cab, the helicopter rose into the early morning sky and set a course for the base hospital. Only 14 minutes later he was transferred to a waiting ambulance at the Rhodesian Air Force base. The entire operation, from the time the man had been wounded to the moment he was lifted into the ambulance, had taken 34 minutes.

To those involved in the brief drama it was just another incident in Rhodesia's continuing war against terrorism.

A TERRORIST LEADER SPEAKS

When Joshua was fired from his job as a waiter for 'unspecified reasons' he became a bitter man – ideal prey for terrorist recruiting agents in Rhodesia's north east. Fifteen months later he returned to his homeland trained to kill and armed with automatic weapons and high explosives.

Joshua G. makes no bones about the fact that until he was captured by the Rhodesian Security Forces, he was a terrorist.

Trying to recover one of the vehicles that had 'turned turtle' during a particularly hazardous phase in an external operation into Mozambique. (Photo: Author's collection)

Rhodesian African Rifle troops were a tough, aggressive bunch of fighters and got on well with their officers and NCOs, many of whom were white. (Photo: Sarah Web Barrell)

Originally from Mount Darwin in Rhodesia's north-east, this 28-year-old terrorist who rose to the rank of group or section leader – roughly equivalent to sergeant in our army – makes one other claim; that had he not been deliberately shot in the leg by his own men and left to the Rhodesian Army, he would probably still be a free man.

I met Joshua at Joint Operations Centre in Umtali. It was the first time he had seen the outside of the hospital since he had been apprehended in February this year.

Once he started speaking he spared no detail in relating his story; sometimes through an interpreter, but mostly in English.

Until July 1974 Joshua had worked for a number of companies in and around Salisbury. His last position, until he was fired for what he termed 'unspecified reasons,' had been as a waiter at a drive-in restaurant in Salisbury.

Joshua G. takes up his story: 'When I left Salisbury that July, I went home to Rusambo in the north-east. I was bitter at those who had fired me. So when someone came to me and asked me whether I would like to fight the white men, I accepted.'

With a small group of others the new recruit was taken on foot down the escarpment into the Zambezi Valley and from there into the Tete Province of Mozambique. His escort was a group of armed terrorists who were returning to base for a period of rest and recreation.

'We were taken to a place called Chifumbo, a camp run by Frelimo. There, with many other young Rhodesians we waited three days before moving on, this time into Zambia. We departed by truck in two groups of almost 50 in each party.

'At that stage we were not told where we were going but once we were headed for Lusaka the rumour got about that our final destination was Tanzania.'

From Lusaka, the groups continued their journey northwards. They passed into Tanzania at the Tunduma border post but did not stop until they had reached the main ZANU training camp in the Tanzanian Great Rift Valley. Joshua's group of 119 swelled the ranks at the terror training camp to almost 600. Joshua was to stay at the Tanzanian training base for 15 months.

'We started our day at 5:30 each morning with one hour of

physical training. We were then allowed to go to the washrooms for half an hour before breakfast, which consisted of tea and bread.

'The day really started at eight with weapons training. We were trained to use the Kalashnikov AK-47, the SKS carbine, the RPD machine gun, and other communist weapons.

'On average, we spent about a fortnight on each gun learning how to fire them, maintain and clean them and various other factors which would help us in our war with the Rhodesians. This routine usually took us until lunch.'

The noon break lasted an hour after which the men were marshalled again for drill on the parade ground. They were dismissed at four and dinner followed an hour later, with political indoctrination lectures for some hours after dark.

Known as 'group therapy', this phase was usually conducted by members of the Tanzanian Peoples Defence Force and whichever Chinese instructors were at the camp.

Joshua said that at various stages the men were also put through their paces in the handling and planting of landmines, rocket firing and anti-aircraft procedures, as well as industrial sabotage. This became an important aspect of their training towards the end of the course.

Only after the first month was any liquor allowed to the men, usually in the form of *pombe*, an East African beer.

The only other 'entertainment' provided at the camp was a series of Chinese produced films on the Sino-Japanese war as well as regular Chinese operas, which according to Joshua were tedious, because none of the men could understand Chinese.

On 24 January 1976, Joshua and his associates were finally gathered together and moved south. In several groups they were flown to Tete in Mozambique by a commercial Boeing 737 of DETA, the Mozambique airline. There they remained a day before being shifted to a Frelimo base near the Rhodesian frontier.

'Here we stayed two days after which 66 of us moved further south towards Vila Gouviea. From there we were taken to one of the principal staging posts for the Rhodesian War.

'We entered Rhodesia in armed groups on January 29,' said Joshua with a smile.

Just prior to infiltrating Rhodesia there was considerable

dissension between the ZANU and ZAPU members of his corps.

'I was a ZANU member and had been instructed that if there was any sign of wavering on the part of ZAPU members of the contingent, we were to shoot them out of hand.'

Dead terrorists are put on display at a village in the northeast to demonstrate to local tribesmen what happens to terrorist infiltrators.

According to Joshua, it was clear that the only reason ZANU tolerated the presence of ZAPU members at the Tanzanian camp was because they had been instructed to do so by the Tanzanian government, on behalf of the ANC military high command.

From the moment Joshua entered Rhodesian territory there were problems. His large group had been split into sections of eight men each, with himself as deputy head of one of the sections.

One of the first complaints from a number of the Matabele men who had originally come from the north-west was that they would have preferred to fight in the north-west among people they knew. 'This was not our country. We did not know the mountains and all that rain and forest. It was like fighting in a foreign country. Also, we could not go back because we

RLI troopies hit an insurgent base in 'Injun country'. (Photo courtesy of Chris Cocks)

had been warned that if we crossed back into Mozambique, for whatever reason, we would be shot by Frelimo soldiers.'

According to Joshua, the attitude of the leaders, who had little or no contact with the realities of the campaign, were harsh and uncompromising, and resulted in a surprising development the first day they crossed the frontier. Joshua's section commander deserted his men and disappeared into the bush.

'I had to take over command of the section and we set to work immediately. Within a day we had attacked a store and a farmhouse, militant members of the group became aggressive and some of them, quite openly, suggested they kill the newly appointed section leader and 'get on with the job'.

Several of his colleagues settled on a compromise. Training their guns on Joshua, they ordered him to give them his weapon. Two or three of the others protested, but they too were warned that if they did not comply, they would be shot.

The leader of the hostile group then walked calmly over to Joshua, placed the barrel of his Kalashnikov AK-47 against the

A member of the famed Selous Scouts is decorated for bravery under fire at a military parade in Salisbury. Rob Reid-Daly's scouts achieved an inordinate number of decorations for valour considering the unit's limited numbers. (Photo: Hannes Wessels collection)

Chapter 7
Rhodesia's War – Al Venter Looks Back

disarmed man's knees and pulled the trigger. He then called the rest of the men together and set off for the farmhouse. Barely 15 minutes later a rocket blast rocked the quiet morning.

Security forces arrived on the scene barely 10 minutes later but found no real damage or injuries to the occupants of the farmhouse. They set off in pursuit of the band of rebels, following a broad line of tracks that led back to the mountains.

Another smaller group followed the tracks that led to the farmhouse and found the wounded Joshua and one other man, the unit's medic, who had stayed behind to try to stem the flow of blood from the wound.

In the brief action that followed, the medic was wounded in the shoulder and his weapon damaged, but he managed to escape into thick bush. Joshua G. was taken captive by the Rhodesian Army.

'I thought I would be killed immediately if they found me,'

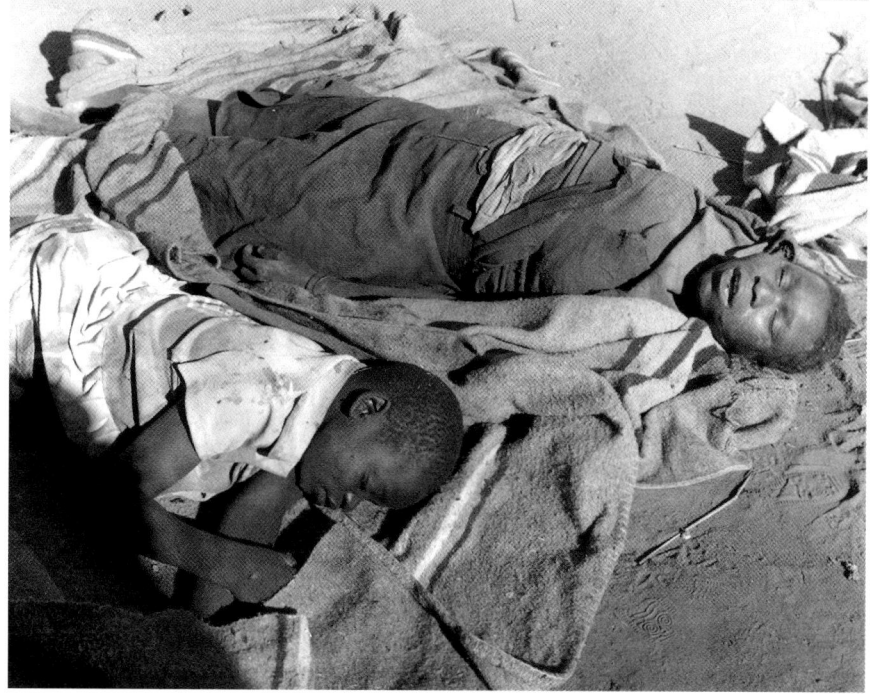

Civilians killed in a raid on a village in the east of the country. These murders were fairly commonplace and part of the process of 'bringing non-participants in the guerrilla war into the ambit of the struggle', as one observer phrased it. (Photo: Hannes Wessels collection)

Joshua recounted. 'I was sure of it. But instead they carried me to a Land Rover and took me to hospital.'

Joshua G. is being held until he has recovered from his wounds and will then stand trial in the Rhodesian Supreme Court.

A FORMIDABLE BATTLE ZONE WITH ENOUGH BLACK MAMBAS TO POPULATE EVERY ZOO IN THE WORLD.

In the Eastern Highlands Rhodesian Security Forces have more than just terrorists to cope with. They constantly wage a battle against the hostile country and continual rain. It is a grim and hard terrain of jungle creepers and deadly snakes.

All vehicles in the operational areas travel in convoy to discourage ambushes. Sometimes it never seems to stop raining. But the war against terror must go on, through rain, hail and slush.

The war in Rhodesia's Eastern Highlands is totally different from any anti-insurgent campaign the country has experienced

Chapter 7
Rhodesia's War – Al Venter Looks Back

in the past decade. Conditions are harsh in the mountains; nights are cold and often wet and the forests and ravines are unfriendly to both attacker and defender.

These are the mountains – the Chimanimani range, and Inyanga to the north – that the terrorists have to cross in order to subvert the interior. The security forces must try to stop them before they penetrate too far. Sometimes they are successful; sometimes not.

The problem is further complicated because there are many farms in the eastern region border on Mozambique and it is easy for the insurgents to cross early in the evening, lay their landmines or attack a settlement and return to their camps before dawn. Terrorists are also known to have intimidated farm labourers in the region against working for their white employers.

Because the majority of the itinerant labour force has Mozambique origins, threats of action against those who do not obey the insurgents are not easily disregarded. In April coffee farmers in the Chipinga area were hard-pressed to find sufficient labour to reap the coffee crop; one farmer near the

Left: One of the Rhodesian Air Force Alouette 'K-Cars' with twin machine guns mounted. (Photo courtesy of Chris Cocks)
Below: A combat 'stick' of four men waiting to be uplifted into action at one of the forward operating bases or JOCs. (Photo courtesy of Chris Cocks)

Chinyadima Purchase Land was losing R2,000 a day while his crop rotted on the stalks. All his labour had disappeared across the Mozambique frontier.

It is the weather, though, that plays havoc with most operations in the mountains. I accompanied a unit operating south of Chipinga in a region dotted with white farmlands.

This was a harsh land. Roads were bad and communications inferior. In parts the forest encroached to within a metre or two of the muddy track that took us across the mountains. It was ideal country for ambush. The fact that terrorist landmines were responsible for blowing up at least one vehicle a day did not make matters any easier. Nor did the rain.

It rained six inches the first night the unit arrived at its camp near one of the large coffee estates in the area. During the following two weeks another 20 inches of rain fell. Troops who came back from patrol with sodden clothes remained drenched until they could dry off in one of the sheds on the farm.

'The only consoling factor was that while conditions were tough for us, it must have been much worse for the terrorists in the area for they had to stick to the mountains and when it rains there is no shelter there,' said Major John Pile, Officer

A number of unusual anti-landmine hybrids appeared in the Rhodesian War. These were all closely studied by South African specialists and played a role in developing subsequent SADF vehicles such as the troop-carrying Buffel as well as the Casspir, which became the mainstay of Koevoet operations in the Border War. (Photo: Hannes Wessels collection)

Commanding, A Company, 4th Battalion Rhodesia Regiment.

He felt that these conditions had to a large extent contributed to several enemy units defecting and a number of terrorists fighting among themselves. 'They become disillusioned. Many of them hadn't the stomach for this kind of hardship. They were told it would be a walkover. Now they find they're up against some pretty stiff resistance,' he said.

Another officer pointed out that while security force successes were minimal at present, operations in other areas had proved in the past that if the Rhodesian Army kept at it long enough, the back of resistance must eventually be broken. 'They intimidate the locals through force of arms, brutality and murder. We ultimately intimidate the terrorists by our forceful and persevering methods. It's the only way,' the officer said.

Compared with the already well-publicised campaign in the north-east of Rhodesia, around Mount Darwin and the Zambezi Valley, the mountains of the east are another proposition altogether. In many ways, with its thickets, jungle creepers, lantana vines and enough black mambas and gaboon vipers to populate every zoo in the world, the eastern region presents formidable problems.

Patrols are restricted to paths which already exist in most of the more remote corners of the area.

If they wish to make their own way through forests of pig-horn creepers and *wag-'n-bietjie* thorn bushes they have to cut their way through with machetes. They are consoled by the fact that insurgents crossing from Mozambique cannot do likewise, for this kind of activity would disclose their position to any nearby patrol.

Probably the biggest problem facing the Rhodesian Security Forces in the east is the climate. Tracks are soon obliterated in the heavy downpours and follow-up operations after any terrorist activity are hampered.

'But with winter and the dry season here, things should be a little easier. At least now we'll be able to get to grips with them,' Major Pile said. He explained that during the rainy season there was no shortage of fruit in the valleys. 'Mangoes, guavas and bananas grow wild in the bush. On top of that every little valley has its mealie (maize or corn) crop. It's all there for the taking – for us or for them. That's why conditions here are so different from the area around Mount Darwin; there you have to grow things in order to survive.'

There is another influential factor in the east, around Chipinga, but this time of a political nature.

It is not generally realised that the mountain area where security forces are most active is also the region which once provided succour for the Reverend Ndabaningi Sithole, one of the leaders of the external faction of the African National Council. Together with Bishop Abel Muzorewa, Sithole today sits in self-imposed exile in Mozambique from where he conducts his war against Ian Smith's government.

'All roads lead to Chikore Mission,' I was told at Joint Operations Centre headquarters in Chipinga. It was there that Sithole taught for some years before turning to nationalist politics. Strategists who have visited the region have noted that much terrorist support – including several hundred schoolchildren who were abducted into Mozambique to eventually return as fully fledged terrorists – has come from the Chikore region.

An array of Rhodesian political and military dignitaries at a tribal meeting in the interior. General Peter Walls, the country's military 'Supremo' (second left) is seated alongside the head of the Rhodesian Air Force, to his right.

'Naturally Sithole would like to establish a strong point for his forces around Chikore. The trouble is that we know this is one of his aims. So we counter it and we've probably been a little more successful in our aims than he has,' said a territorial force officer who farms in the vicinity.

It is almost certain that if Sithole does not achieve quick success in the area, some of his strongest supporters may lose faith in the cause that has already resulted in so much bloodshed. And the Rhodesian Army has no intention of letting up their efforts.

RHODESIA'S GUN-TOTING GIRLS

Bella Forsythe, all of 18 years old and still sporting her schoolgirl pigtails, is not the sort of girl you would expect to find in camouflage fatigues. But Bella wears – and fills – her army uniform beautifully when she mans the guard-post desk at Rhodesia's new Joint Operations Centre headquarters in Umtali in the Eastern Highlands.

Rarely without a smile, Bella, a former commercial artist, has learnt to deal as easily with brigadiers and other senior officers as with the tough-talking members of the small corps of military policemen. Her task is to process the enquiries of anyone entering the headquarters.

There are other women in uniform in the old hotel which has been taken over by Security Forces as the operational centre. Cary Odendaal (her sister serves at Army Headquarters in Salisbury) does duties at one of the radio listening posts. In its day this was one of the most elegant rooms in colonial Africa; now the rich velvet trappings have gone and been replaced by rows of prefabricated offices, each with a security classification prominently displayed on the door.

Upstairs, Gwen Archer, mother of three almost adult children and originally from Durban, does her thing in what was once a regal antechamber. Gwen, who came to the country when the Central African Federation was still a shining hope for this part of the continent, does not talk much about what she does except that she fills an important role that would otherwise have kept a man out of the field.

Why have these girls joined Rhodesia's Defence Force? One

and all invariably answer something along the lines of their country needing them. And they mean it, for most times the conversation swings to the fact that every woman in uniform behind the lines releases a man for active military service.

Gwen Archer goes a step further. 'I love this life. I wouldn't change it for anything. Even though the money is not the best and the hours are often hard and long I feel I'm achieving something. I'm a contributor to the society I'm living in,' she says.

There are several hundred women of all ages serving in the Rhodesian Army and Air Force. Quite a few have requested to do operational duties with their men, either guarding establishments or doing routine work at the 'sharp end'. So far these requests have been refused, 'mainly,' said one senior officer, 'because this is essentially a man's war. It has its brutal moments.'

The Rhodesian Women's Services are deployed in a variety of tasks throughout the country.

Apart from the Umtali contingent, females are employed on aerial photographic and reconnaissance work. Others pack parachutes. A few of the brighter ones are engaged in crypto offices coding and decoding the huge flow of messages which must emanate from a war this size. Still more work as ground staff and on movement control at any one of a dozen Rhodesian Air Force bases throughout the country.

These regular servicewomen are supplementary to almost 1,000 female civilian volunteers who contribute much of their time doing such duties as radio watches, manning operations rooms and driving military vehicles.

The Rhodesian Women's Services are very much a part of a modern and sophisticated army and their initial training is based largely on that provided for women recruits in the British Army.

The two-week course of basic training includes a fair deal of square bashing, pistol firing and weapon maintenance, military law and regulations, organisation and, for those who want it, accounting.

Bella, Gwen, Cary and their colleagues represent a complete cross-section of Rhodesian womanhood. Half of them are, or

Chapter 7
Rhodesia's War – Al Venter Looks Back

American mercenary Dave McGrady – today living in Montenegro – was blooded as a mercenary in Rhodesia where he spent a lot of time bounty hunting. He took all his own weapons to Africa. (Photo: Author)

were, married. Some, like Mrs Anne Flatman-Brown, are recent immigrants, but most were born south of the Zambezi, either in Rhodesia or South Africa.

One of the recent volunteers is in a good position to make comparisons with other feminine military organisations elsewhere in the world. Pauline Triggol used to be a military policewoman in Singapore. Originally a native of Devon, Pauline and her husband came to Rhodesia a year ago; he serves part time with a police anti-terrorist unit.

Most of them are from average homes, and, like Caroline Odendaal, all have their tales to tell. Cary Odendaal joined the services immediately on returning from a three-month holiday in Europe. Initially she signed for a year, but on completion of her present contract, Cary hopes to sign up for three more.

A third-generation Rhodesian, Caroline left school and qualified as a state-enrolled nurse. The radio and map work she does today at JOC Headquarters, Umtali, is a far cry from lifting bed pans and she is frank about the way she feels: 'I like it. I liked the basic training and I like the routine and discipline.'

According to Cary, the girls earn up to about R250 a month, with regular issues of free uniforms. The army also supplies regulation-style handbags and shoes, which fit in well with the attractive uniform. In addition, the girls are eligible for free medical and dental care, and on completion of the contract period, they receive a gratuity 'for services rendered'.

'What else do I need? I love the life and I adore the guys I work with. I think the woman's touch was all that was needed in this campaign,' she says seriously, admitting at the same time that it is only natural that her current beau is in the army.

'In a way, I suppose you could regard us girls as morale boosters in a man's world,' Cary concluded.

CHAPTER EIGHT

QUESTIONS AND ANSWERS WITH ADAM BUSKE – A PROFESSIONAL HUNTER IN AFRICA

Forty-two-year-old Adam Buske, originally from Zimbabwe and currently working in Zambia, is not the archetypal 'White Hunter' that Ernest Hemingway wrote about in his epochal *The Snows of Kilimanjaro.* **But he does represent a tiny band of professionals that hunt animals in Africa.**

Adam makes an unusual comment about hunting Central Africa's rare bongo antelope. These days, he says, they use dogs to chase these animals. The objective, as he puts it, is not actually 'to chase them down', but rather, because the bush is so thick, to conserve them. A contradiction in terms, but he explains it as follows:

'It is a good option because it saves a lot of females from getting shot,' he declares. 'The bongo is a spiral-horned animal and the females as well as the males have horns, which is odd. What happens with the dogs is that they go in and actually bay the bongo so that we can get a good look at it. Once you have it in sight, you can see immediately whether it's a good bull or not. If it's a female, you just pull away and do nothing because you shoot males and not breeding females.'

During the past two decades or so since Buske went professional, he has hunted in most of the African countries popular with the international hunting community. That includes the Central African Republic, Zambia, Tanzania, Ethiopia, the Congo (Brazzaville), the Cameroons as well as several stints elsewhere in southern Africa. In that time he has managed to establish a significant client list, among them Americans, a number from France, Italy, Russia and Germany,

Hunting in remote African reaches no longer means the kind of isolation experienced by adventurers of an earlier epoch. These days you take your comforts with you, like American big game hunter Doug Scandril who went into the bush with Adam Buske and took his laptop with him. (Photo: Adam Buske)

some Japanese and, more recently, a bunch of wealthy Chinese.

He is discreet about names. Some trophy hunters, being in the public eye in their own countries, are not keen on this kind of publicity. They fear that the 'Green Gang' – as he calls overnight conservationists – might use the fact that they hunt animals against them, even though this activity is strictly controlled.

One American not shy to talk was Bob Gallagher, who invented the rubber worm, which has been a boon to the fishing community for decades. Another was Ron Showers, who gave the world the floppy disc for computers as well as Phil Nesnic, the man who developed sophisticated space-age filters for America's NASA space programme.

'And we shouldn't forget my old friend Dan Duncan, a true gentleman in the tradition of yesterday and who is also the thirteenth richest man in America,' Adam declares. But there are no heads of state, famous politicians or astronauts on his public list, he concedes.

As Adam likes to explain, Africa is divided into quadrants and there are different animals in separate geographical areas. He points

Chapter 8
Questions and Answers with Adam Buske – a Professional Hunter in Africa

The man himself – Adam Buske at his home on the great Kafue River in Zambia. (Photo: Caroline Castell)

out the obvious: elephants are more common further south, but then he admits, he has hunted these beasts in Tanzania, where some of his clients 'bagged' elephants with fairly good tusks.

'Hovewer,' he warns, 'there is a legal limit on the tusks you are allowed to hunt 'and also, because all the old animals in Tanzania have so consistently come under fire – from poachers especially – the ivory in this East African state is a good deal thinner than before.

'In Ethiopia we hunted mountain nyala, which, as the name indicates, are found in the higher reaches towards the north-east of the country. They tend to move all over the place, largely to avoid an increased human presence.

'Another time we headed for Dumicle and the arid north-west. There, in a region that is well below sea level and extremely hot almost all year round, we went after Sumerinks gazelle, as well as the Besa oryx, and, of course, dik-diks, which are everywhere. There are three or four dik-dik species, really beautiful little creatures. Elsewhere we'd go after lesser kudu as well as the Abyssinian bush buck.'

Hunting in the Congo, in contrast, he said, is totally different. There, everything takes place in a tropical arena that can sometimes stretch from one horizon to another and often consists almost solely of jungle overhang, forest, big rivers and swamps. 'Even moving about in that environment is almost always difficult and, naturally, there is the human element with which to contend, and that's not always easy.'

According to Adam, you are never certain what kind of reception you are likely to encounter when you move into a new hunting area. The *Daily Telegraph*'s correspondent Tim Butcher went through the Congo not long ago and had hired a reliable man who was not only familiar with the area and the people, but spoke their languages. They would arrive at some villages and his guide would be asked by some of the locals why he hadn't long ago slit the throat of this *mazungu* (white man) in his party. He would protest, Butcher recalled, because his guide, solid individual that he was, would confide in him and tell him what was said.

But then some of the people they encountered would suggest that the guide tell him where they were going to camp that night. They would come and do the job for him, they would whisper, intimating that they were quite happy to split any money recovered as a consequence down the middle. Africa is full of such surprises,

Adam Buske with a group of pygmies after a bongo hunt in the jungles of Congo (Brazzaville).

Chapter 8
Questions and Answers with Adam Buske – a Professional Hunter in Africa

Adam concedes, and the outcome of chance meetings can sometimes be unpredictable.

Most hunting in these tropical regions is usually well away from settled areas which, Adam admits, rarely present that kind of problem.

'The animals we're usually after are the bongo and the Mount Derby eland.' He reckons that he might have been instrumental in shooting about 20 bongos in his day which, he concedes, is a lot.

Adam makes short shrift of reports that maintain that the bongo is a threatened species. It is not, he declares: 'The jungle is full of them ... but in that kind of terrain where it is extremely difficult for man to penetrate, very few of these antelope are actually encountered. So people say they are rare. In fact, with us moving through the bush, they hear us coming ... it cannot be avoided when you're using a panga or a machete to chop undergrowth in order to move ahead. Obviously, when the animals hear you approach, they take the gap ... it is to be expected.

'Now the many species of duiker that you encounter in those forests are in a different category. There are almost 30 variations of these tiny antelope and you find them all the way up to the rain forest in the Cameroons. By law, you may only shoot three of the species and it is fairly strictly controlled.

'In the Central African Republic we would go after western dwarf buffalo, the yellow backed duiker and western cobb, which is a variation of the hartebeest, but that area is now seriously affected by poachers who come across from Chad with their heavy automatic weapons, and, of course, the Congo. They've made serious inroads into the CAR's elephant population and we have to face it, the situation is getting worse.'

The Cameroons and its rainforest is also different to other hunting locations, he reckons, with bongo in the south and eland and oryx in the north. These are all tough hunting expeditions because so much of it takes place on foot.

'You simply cannot drive off-road there because the tracks are atrocious. So from something like six in the morning you simply walk and hope you will eventually cut a track. In fact, you end up walking big circles ... and when you eventually do find tracks, you follow them and pray that they're not going to lead you over the horizon because at some stage you're going to have to head back again.

'On one of the hunts I did in the Northern Cameroons, it was like 24 kilometres in one direction, which made for a round trip of almost 50 clicks ... and that in a single day is really hard even for trained soldiers. But I loved it and in the end, it turned into a very successful hunt.

'Obviously, we have to be sure that the client can take this kind of punishment and also that he or she is fit enough to withstand conditions where the temperature can move up to 40 degrees Celsius in the middle of the day.

'Most of my clients who hunted there have been American, and what is pleasing is that the Yanks generally do their homework. They'll know ahead of time how tough it is when they go there, so they put a lot of effort into getting into shape ... they walk, they run, they do an enormous amount of work before getting anywhere near the place, because they know it's going to be a really tough hunt.

'Also, they are almost all familiar with their firearms and know exactly what gun they should use for what species. And when it's all over, they like to keep in touch with you, so you not only have a client, you end up with a good friend too.'

Asked what calibres he would use to shoot a bongo, Adam was specific: 'Your shots are usually at a distance of about 20 metres, and because it's a fairly big animal, I find that we do best with a .300. The bongo is built almost like a nyala, but it's a much tougher, more "boxy" creature.'

For elephants Adam reckons you need to use at least .375 and above. Anything less is illegal anyway, because it hasn't got penetration. 'Also .416s are a successful calibre ... but with the big stuff, you really cannot go less than a .375 Magnum.'

'My personal gun is a .500 nitro double-barrel, but with plains game, I prefer a .300 bolt action safari grade, preferably pre-64, because it fires a slower bullet with adequate weight.'

As a professional hunter, Adam Buske experiences much during the course of his safari duties that is disturbing. Like the oryx in the Chad Republic and Sudan that the rebels like to run down with their Land Cruisers.

'We see quite a lot of it and it is difficult to stop because of the human element, and there are just so many more people than before, when my Dad was doing this sort of thing. In fact, you are never really going to stop that kind of activity in Africa ... the more people there are, the more they're going to eat and anyway, they take it for granted that the wildlife is their heritage, so they can do what they like. In reality, it's not like that at all and in the end, much of this so-called "wildlife heritage" is going to disappear.'

Chapter 8
Questions and Answers with Adam Buske – a Professional Hunter in Africa

Civilisation has brought many other issues in its dubious wake, he reckons. Adam recalls driving a vehicle from Douala – the largest port in the Cameroons and not far from the Nigerian border – all the way to Bangui in the Central African Republic.

'It was a tough journey, halfway across an almost totally undeveloped corner of Central Africa. I must also mention that it was probably one of the most frightening experiences I've had. The people we encountered along the way – and almost all the officials – spoke only French and frankly, I can't even string two sentences together in that language. They actually gave me a really rough time of it.

'Every single town we went through had roadblocks, usually manned by soldiers. There would be barriers just before you got to the town and another as you left: same rigmarole each time. They all wanted to see our papers – identity, passport, licences, vehicle documents, carnets and the rest – not that many of them could read or write anyway. Obviously, I'd made pretty damn sure that everything was in order before I set out, but the bastards seriously harassed me.

'It was my money they were after, of course, together with anything else they could cadge, like cigarettes and liquor. But I'd run out of both after the first day on the road … you get the gist …'

By the time he reached Bangui and the Congo River, Adam believes that bribes and 'incentives' must have cost him something like US$2,000, most times because these 'trumped-up little shits' thought they could get away with it. 'And they did …' he declared with a wry smile.

'The guy would say that my papers were not in order – and he hadn't even glanced at them, mind you. I would reply that they were. Stalemate! It would stay that way until I forked up some cash.

'The other interesting thing was that I would go through this beautiful rainforest, and I'd find little pygmies standing on the side of the road selling meat, quite often duiker – all of them completely intact, skin, horns and all. I saw some species of antelope that I'd never seen before, so obviously, there is a lot more hidden in the African bush than we realise.

Born and bred in South Africa, Adam Buske had a chequered career before he turned to professional hunting, at one stage even joining the South African Army. He parted company with the military on rather acrimonious terms, something he doesn't like to talk about.

'So I went to Rhodesia, entered agricultural college, after which I thought I'd like to try my hand at some kind of engineering. I ended up installing blast freezers on tuna boats in Cape Town harbour where I worked for about eight months.

'As a kid I'd always hunted a lot, quite often with my dad and later with my buddies. That meant spending a lot of time in the bush and I loved it. I must have been about 18 or 19 years old at the time that I shook the dust of Cape Town off my boots and headed back towards Central Africa.

'You need to understand that the lifestyle I finally chose had been an essential part of me from a very young age. I think I must have been about eight when I shot my first big buck – an impala, I think it was, with a .222 rifle. It was actually quite an event for a youngster, no matter where you are.

'Finally, I got into hunting proper, but even then it was a fairly lengthy and difficult process because you had to do your time under solid supervision ... it was a kind of apprenticeship. In my day we were under the supervision of quite a few of the old hands in the business, first P.J. Forshay, then Reg Taylor, and then Pieter Swanepoel.

'They were all either in Zimbabwe or Zambia when I'd move about the various camps, giving a hand and trying to make myself useful. If it wasn't croc in Luangwa, it would be something else along the Zambezi somewhere ... there was really no shortage of opportunity.

'Each time the professional hunter – PH in the lingo – would sign my log book, he'd comment on my performance and that was there for all to read, saying that I was good with this or perhaps needed a bit more experience with that. Eventually, you get to sit your PH exams, which I did at the Zambian Wildlife Authority (ZAWA) head offices in Lusaka.

'It's a written exam – all of two hours – and can be quite tough. You can sometimes get asked questions that can be totally illogical, like naming ten clients with whom I have worked. I could have put down anybody's names, fictitious or otherwise, and nobody would have been any the wiser. But there was much more on bush skills, tracking craft, skinning and so on. There is also a lot on the legal side and that can sometimes be difficult if you haven't studied your subjects properly.

'Finally, it all comes down to the people with whom you associate professionally, and there I learned the basics from my father and from Darrell Watt, two of the best people in the business. They gave me the finest wildlife education any person could hope to achieve

Chapter 8
Questions and Answers with Adam Buske – a Professional Hunter in Africa

A Congolese pygmy carries the horns and skin of a freshly shot antelope in a sling around his head. It looks complicated but it is not, because it leaves his hands free to deal with the forest he has to pass through in order to get back to base. (Photo: Adam Buske)

and frankly, were it not for them, I wouldn't be here today.

'So I would go into the bush for, say, two or three weeks before the client arrived in the country we were going to be working in and I'd link up with some of the local Africans to get the feel of conditions there. And each time, even today, you learn something new. I would say the best trackers that I have ever worked with are those in the north of the Cameroons, as well as the pygmies in the rainforests further towards the south. You really couldn't compare them with our guys here.

'In that kind of environment, it is a completely different ball game. In the deepest, most remote jungle these little guys would know exactly what to look for. One time I was able to work with old Felix Botha, and I was following this little pygmy and a lot of what he did didn't initially make sense: he was just jogging along at a steady pace and it didn't seem like we were following anything. So I stopped him and asked him through our interpreter what it was that he was actually looking at?

Constructing a shooting hide near the Kafue River in the Mushingashi Wildlife Conservancy in Zambia with South African professional hunter Bernard Troskie. A limited quota of animals is allowed to the company for commercial hunting by ZAWA – the Zambian Wildlife Authority. This helps to cover costs in administrating the venture and its 40-something game guards. (Photo: Caroline Castell)

'He looked up at me, kind of surprised, like I was some dumb idiot questioning his ability. Then he explained that the elephant that had traversed this route before us had left mud on the leaves, because it was always wet and we consequently ended up with mud all over us. It was as plain as day and I hadn't even noticed. The same with bongo: those animals prefer a soggy environment, so when you hunt them you're most times working in the rain, which is also quite fun.

Adam explained that hunting in places like the CAR and the Cameroons, the community involved in such business was almost totally dependent on a professional operator, or whoever runs the hunting concession.

'We go in, having earlier made contact with an outfitter with whom the client and I are going to be working, for example Ndok

Safaris in Cameroon which is run by Felix Barada. He owns and runs that concession, but he doesn't have his own clients; so we take ours along and end up hunting that area for him.'

And then there is the money, Adam stated, 'because it can be an extremely expensive game.'

As he explained, an American or European hunting client won't get away with less than US$35,000 or $40,000 for a two-week safari. 'If he brings his wife along, it is another $150 or $200 a day, and that is before you have even shot a single animal, because there are trophy fees on top of that. Those can easily top $5,000.'

One of the requisites of hunting today is to show a face at the annual hunting jamborees in the United States. Adam would get to Reno or Las Vegas regularly each year, but since working in Zambia, he has an established client list and is not looking for any more business, which, he admits, is an enviable situation for any professional.

'We used to do those Chapter Shows, where Safari Club International people would all come together and each date has a chapter. So we'd go around and chat to people who would come there from all over America. It's actually all by word-of-mouth, so to speak, and this way you'd meet their friends, or friends of friends and they might end up as your clients. At these conventions we'd have our booths and anybody could walk in, which was when they'd view your references. Perhaps a letter would follow and they'd network among themselves about this 'Buske guy'. And that's basically how it goes.

As with all professions, one starts at a certain point and works up the ladder; and, as Adam likes to tell you, it can be a slow and sometimes tedious process.

'Some of the first hunts in which I was involved took place in Tanzania and that was in 1993 and 1994 when I was still a miserable "appie". I'd hear great stories like those about 44-inch buffalo and that there were herds of thousands and thousands of them. So the first opportunity I got, I went and I lived there for two years and yes, it was all true – the herds were fantastic, some of them easily a thousand-plus.

'But then, when you're actually living there, you don't pick up on the changes that are taking place. So after I left and went back a couple of years later, I discovered that the place was really getting hammered. Real changes were taking place, and some areas were really getting thumped.

'I'd get up to Dar es Salaam and Arusha and just about every person I'd meet had something to do with the hunting industry, a PH or a photographic guide. I think Tanzania ended up with about 800 companies at that time and, of course, there's a limit because it all has an effect, both on the ecology and the animals. I would find a company that might run two or three hunting areas – or what we term hunting blocks – and they would just form another company and get even more concessions. Obviously, the competition was stiff and the people involved came from just about everywhere.

'There were lots of Portuguese, Greeks, Spanish, South Africans, Zimbabweans ... just about every nation you could think of, even Americans.

'Obviously there was still government control, but then money talks a language of its own. Some of these people found out soon enough that there were ways to circumvent the controls.

That said, the PH still had to write his exams and you still had to obtain reference letters from a professional that declared that you knew the business and were competent. Also, the exams were mandatory, even for the older guys, and it never used to be like that.

'For all that, there are still a few good areas in Tanzania today, mostly run by outfitters like Robin Hurt and Tanzanian Game Trackers, and there is no question that they are efficient, well run and have the right connections. More to the point, they like to look after their areas, stick to their quotas and not overshoot.

'These were the firms that were able to make good money because they'd submit tenders to hunt over longer periods of time, which meant that they'd actually invest in their areas, developing roads, putting in anti-poaching teams, provide proper staff quarters and stuff like that.

Many other firms were transients, fly-by-night companies and they wouldn't put in anything. So, of course the areas just got mercilessly overexploited. All they looked at were bed nights and they couldn't care a damn about quotas. Their money came from fast turnabouts, which meant that if they had an empty bed they had to fill it.

Ethiopia followed soon afterwards and it didn't exactly help that for many years, decades even, the country had been ravaged by conflict, most times with guerrilla groups from across the borders. Eritrea was – and still is – especially active in these illegal activities which have left hundreds of thousands dead in the past decade or two.

Chapter 8
Questions and Answers with Adam Buske – a Professional Hunter in Africa

'Once again, in Ethiopia you had your outfitters, guides, some of whom had got their own specialists for specific areas. Basically, we'd take our clients in and because it was my show, I'd be the professional hunter in charge, which meant that their people were more like chauffeurs.

'They'd take you around, because with hunting in the Horn of Africa, you hunt just about everywhere you can. But there are certain prerequisites. When we decide to hunt oryx in the Danakil Desert, an extremely difficult hot and arid region near the coast, the concession obviously belonged to somebody. Also, Ethiopia is one of the toughest game-control areas in Africa and you've got to have a government scout with you at all times.

'When you finally get to the hunting area, the law says that you need three additional scouts, if only because in some of the places we go into, the locals will just shoot you if they don't know who you are or why you're there. An additional prospect is that, traditionally, Danakil tribal fighters emasculate their victims...

That said, most of Ethiopia's wildlife is likely to be found towards the west or south-west of the country near Lake Turkana, which fringes on Kenya. And this is also an arid region that can be incredibly hot and dry.

'Other times we'd go into the Ogaden, towards Somalia, and

The Ethiopian giant forest hog is the largest in an extensive range of *suidae*, otherwise known as the pig family, and these creatures can sometimes top 300 kilograms. Regarded as a rare but potentially dangerous species, hunting these animals is severely restricted. (Photo: Adam Buske)

look for the Abyssinian reed buck or the Abyssinian rohar buck or giant forest hogs. But there was no lion, and that wasn't easy either. The entire Ogaden is populated by people who sport Kalashnikov automatic rifles, even youngsters who are perhaps ten or twelve years old … It's the sort of thing that keeps you awake at night.'

'Perhaps the most amazing thing about hunting in Ethiopia is some of the camps in the mountains, which can reach up to 11,000 feet. That was where, in search of the nyala that lived in this rarefied atmosphere, we had our spike or main camp on one such venture.

'On the hunt itself, we'd go on upwards towards the peaks which were a series of really steep climbs, all heading towards the summit at about 17,000 feet. And once up there – with the spike camp only a tiny dot in the distance below us – the chef would arrive from nowhere with his pots and pans of hot food and he'd serve us lunch.

'He'd walk upwards several kilometres, almost sprinting all the way and by the time he reached us, the grub would still be piping hot. It was never anything but totally delicious. How he did it is anybody's guess because we lesser creatures could only manage about 60 metres at a time before we'd had to stop and catch our breath, which, as anybody who has climbed Kilimanjaro will tell you, is what happens.

'There were five of us on these hunts: me, my client and some local guys, all heading up cliffs that were more like walking along precipices, invariably with sheer drops on either side. It was all very interesting actually, but pretty dodgy as well.'

Hunting in Africa, or anywhere else for that matter, has its pitfalls, says Adam Buske. As he recollects, you sometimes can end up with some truly anal clients.

'You might have a two-on-two situation; so in the camp you have two buddies who have come from Italy, Brazil or America and who are hunting with you. Each has his or her own professional hunter, and it is obviously costing a tidy amount of cash.

'Then one member of the group shoots a bigger trophy than the other, and you end up with a series of attitude problems.

'Or the one guy is screwing the other guy's wife. Generally it doesn't happen like the movies say it does because the average professional hunter is obliged to maintain proper ethics and in any event, he is totally focused on hunting. Also, it wouldn't be good for your reputation, because the major hunting conventions would have something like 40,000 people coming through the door and any number of booths. People get to know each other and, naturally, they talk. Step out of line and very soon you'd be on the outside when it comes to new business.' As Adam explained, a single safari gone wrong can foster a bad reputation – 'and it can happen in a heartbeat.'

On a more personal basis, professional hunters, many of them away from home for long stretches, sometimes find it difficult to maintain close relationships. Quite often, their marriages suffer.

'As for your wife, she either has to be a very tough individual who is willing and able to get on with things on her own or simply accept the nature of the lifestyle you've offered her. Also, I personally do not believe a professional hunter from Africa should marry anyone who is not from the same kind of background.'

He explains that kind of rationale by mentioning some of his friends who married European women. As he says, it was fine to start with, all very glamorous and exciting. But then reality starts to kick in because you are never there and 'on your own', in the wilds, things can easily go wrong. You're out in the bush bringing in the butter...

'Also, it is not nearly as glamorous as some people like to think. Professional hunting involves total commitment and that can be hard work. And the money, though not to be sneezed at, isn't exactly brilliant either. A good professional today would probably take home something between US$50,000 and $70,000 annually, which is really not a lot when you look at the kind of money involved in an actual safari which can easily top $100,000 for two or three luxurious weeks in the bush.

'Which brings me to one of the traditional stories about hunters, the kind of thing we talk about when we're sitting around the campfire nursing our gin and tonics.

'It involves a young man with great aspirations, who starts off with a new gun and a fine pair of trackers. Well, it might take quite a few years, but he eventually ends up with an old gun, broken legs, old trackers, but goodness, what wonderful stories they can share ... and that's basically how it goes...

'There are many such stories, some real and others apocryphal. While hunting in the Cameroons, we found a baby elephant. The mother had been shot and the poachers had tried to kill the baby as well, but all they'd succeeded in doing was to blow a hole in the bottom of its jaw. I'm not sure how they managed it, but the little jumbo seemed to take a fancy to us and it followed the car one day.

'I then decided that we would grab it and take it back to camp with us ... kind of giving it a home. We started feeding it, washed it and made it comfortable in an elephant sort of way – it was an incredibly cute little thing, full of life.

'The little fellow hung around the camp for a week or so and then it wandered off. The next thing we heard was that it got hit by a logging truck. Sad story, but it was still pretty weak and the truth is that we wouldn't have been around forever to care for it.

'And my most dangerous experience? No question about that: driving anywhere in Africa at night ...'

In this modern age, electricity in the bush is no longer restricted to the few. Solar panels are an everyday sight throughout remote regions of the African continent. (Photo: Caroline Castell)

CHAPTER NINE

BY PUMA HELICOPTER ACROSS THE AFRICAN CONTINENT

Ferrying helicopters all the way across Africa is nothing new. Former South African Air Force Brigadier-General Peter 'Monster' Wilkins does it all the time – to East Africa, the Sudan, as well as to several West African countries.

'**M**onster' – a modest, quiet-spoken individual – is not sure why he acquired that rather inappropriate appellation. He suspects that it stemmed from the time that he was on a course as a pupil pilot and threw somebody who had been making life difficult for his pal Scully Levine into a cupboard. As a consequence, several more cupboards went down, almost like dominoes. Once dubbed, the appellation stuck.

Wilkins was one of the first SAAF pilots to convert to Alouette helicopters in the 1970s, after these seemingly frail choppers had been delivered from France. Almost immediately he was initiated into the wiles of the Border War, a series of experiences that were to last more than two decades. During this time he also spent time countering insurgency with the Portuguese Air Force in Angola. He eventually ended up as Air Force attaché at the South African Embassy in Washington DC.

One of the more recent forays of this illustrious aviator, still flying his beloved choppers in his mid-sixties – was delivering Puma helicopter ZS-RWO (painted white all over, so that it wouldn't be mistaken for a military aircraft) from Heidelberg in what was once the old Transvaal to Sierra Leone on the west coast of Africa. The helicopter had been chartered by a European company to fly technicians and other oil workers from Lungi International Airport across the lagoon from Freetown to the *Bedford Dolphin*. An oil exploratory vessel, the ship was lying about 70 minutes' flying time

The Starlite Aviation group, originally established in Durban in 1999, operates almost worldwide through offices in South Africa, the US and Ireland. The company works in remote places like Afghanistan, Kosovo and the Sudan and shown here is one of its Pumas in an earlier version of its livery, working off the African coast. (Photo: Peter Wilkins)

from Freetown's Lungi International Airport while working off Sherbro Island.

Getting the helicopter to the West African destination – a distance of almost 4,000 nautical miles (7,200 kilometres and 32,5 hours' flying time) was a tough option. It was also hazardous and eventful.

With stopovers and delays along the way, the journey took a week and involved transiting several countries that had been vociferously opposed to the old apartheid regime. Indeed, in the initial stages, Wilkins had to traverse the entire length of Angola – from north to south – the same country he had so bitterly opposed and fought against while still flying helicopter gunships in the South African Air Force.

Other jobs handled by Starlite Aviation in recent years have been equally hairy: there was a lengthy period in the Sudan while operating in the distant interior with Helog, a German firm. Like Starlite, that company was assisting a United Nations peacekeeping operation in Darfur, an isolated region then going through (and still experiencing) an extended period of hostilities.

This was an extremely difficult venture because, as the saying goes, in order to keep the peace you first have to establish it. The reality is that the Khartoum government has been at war with one faction or another for almost half a century.

At one stage, the country's Islamic leaders brought in fighter pilots from Syria and Iraq to bomb Christian southerners with nerve gas, something about which the international community said absolutely nothing, even though some of the victims were taken to Europe for treatment. At another time it was South Africans – all former Special Forces people who had served with the mercenary company Executive Outcomes – that were hired to train Sudanese 'Special Forces' hit squads.

This was no vague assertion. I got chapter and verse from Duncan Rykaart, a former SADF officer with the Reconnaissance Regiment who was also my escort officer when I twice went into Angola with EO. While in the Sudan, Rykaart ran his South African team from Khartoum and he died not long afterwards in a still unexplained aircraft crash involving a plane that was flying from Entebbe to Somalia. The aircraft nose-dived into Lake Victoria shortly after take-off, killing everybody on board.

The Sudan has always been an extremely difficult place in which to work. At one stage, in an extremely remote area south-east of Palogue in Southern Sudan, the choppers operated in a marshland the size of Belgium. Another project included a contract off the Sudanese coast and it also involved flying helicopters all the way from South Africa.

As to whether West Africa is preferable to conditions in East Africa, Wilkins invariably opts for the latter choice. 'West Africa is largely alien within the international community,' he confides, adding that it's the political instability and underhand methods that are responsible for much of it.

'There is much less corruption in East Africa,' he avers, coupled to the fact that there is a distinct willingness to help when problems arise. 'That is especially evident at higher levels in countries like Kenya and Tanzania,' he believes.

Wilkins: 'In West Africa, I have to prefer Ghana to the others. It is a country where I find the people more approachable and much more sociable than places like Nigeria or Guinea … and the folks are really switched on. Also, Ghanaians are generally quite helpful folk … always quick to respond when there are problems.

'One of the worst experiences the crew had was in Douala, the biggest port in the Cameroons, where we were forced to have a night stop. It took us about five hours to get through a bunch of routine things like landing charges, navigation fees (which is a cheek, because nothing works properly) and overnight parking fees which are horrific. 'It was all pretty awful,' he recalls. 'The officials with whom we dealt were only after what they could score from us ... kind of corruption gone berserk.'

Though the company did end up paying, almost nothing functioned properly, 'not to mention a repetitive fee that was surreptitiously labelled *une petite cadeau* – or "a little something for me" ...' Worse, he confided, they were quite blatant about it, 'and, if we didn't oblige, well, we'd wait some more ...'

The ultimate prize for the worst place in Africa, reckons 'Monster' Wilkins, would almost certainly be awarded to Equatorial Guinea. As he explains, that means either the derelict town of Bata on the mainland part of this utterly failed, oil-rich country or its so-called island capital, which is called Malabo and is little more than a cesspit.

'You can take your pick between those two places because, believe me, they are both awful.' Black Beach Prison on the island was where some of the mercenaries who had planned to take over the country more than a decade ago were incarcerated, including Nick du Toit: some of those freebooters died while in detention.

The most famous Black Beach inmate of them all, Simon Mann – a business partner of fellow-conspirator Mark Thatcher, son of former British Prime Minister Margaret Thatcher – was held prisoner in Equatorial Guinea for several years, though it has since emerged that the conditions under which he was held were very different to those endured by people like Nick du Toit who regards himself quite lucky to be alive. As they say, money counts and the Mann family, of brewery fame in Britain, has a lot of it.

'Libreville, the Gabonese capital city, and Pointe Noire in Congo (Brazza) follow closely, but there is little to beat Nigeria where Lagos is the ultimate hellhole for aviators not familiar with an astonishing level of graft and inefficiency.'

Prior to setting out on this transcontinental expedition with a select crew from his Durban and Irish-based firm Starlite Aviation, 'Monster' Wilkins – as company chief pilot for the group – recalled some of the torments experienced by some of his erstwhile SAAF buddies when they had to ferry helicopters halfway across Africa almost two decades ago.

One experience stands out sharply in his mind. Executive Outcomes, the South African mercenary group that turned the war around in Angola, needed a pair of rotor wings to counter the rebels in Sierra Leone. Consequently, a pair of Soviet-built Mi-17s that had been used by EO in the Angolan war, and had seen extensive service

A herd of Topi antelope in a remote area halfway between Juba and Palogue in Southern Sudan. From the air these animals with their curved horns look a little like Tsessebe. The bottom picture was taken at an airport in a rain-drenched Mozambique. (Photos: Peter Wilkins)

Photo: Peter Wilkins

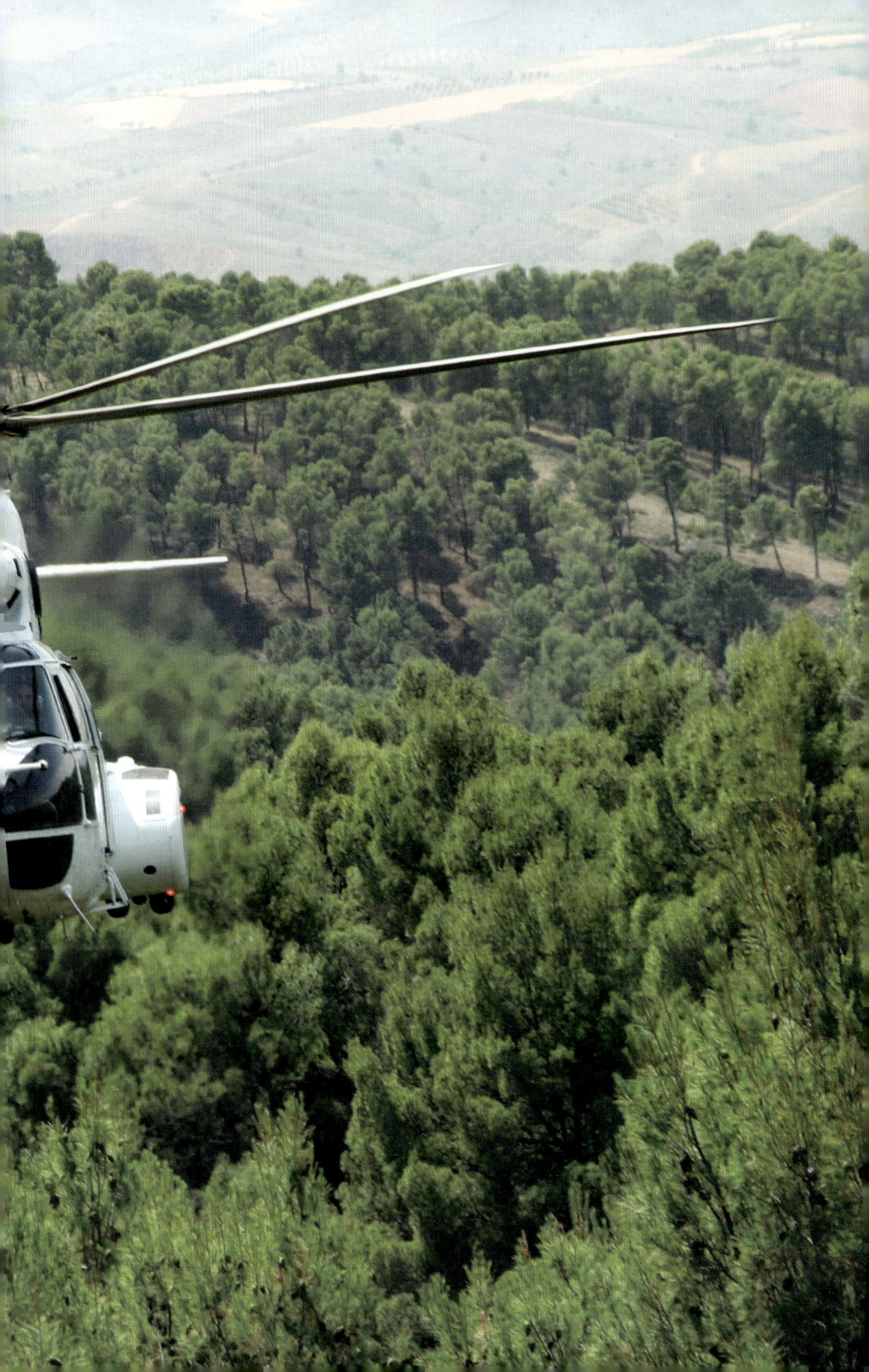

Top: Durban's Starlite Aviation Puma ZS-RWO on the hardstand in Libreville, the Gabonese capital. Middle: Sierra Leone with the surrounding hills taken from the lagoon on which this West African city lies. Bottom: Jungles of Gabon, with a very low cloud base and rising mist. The visibility as a consequence, was exceptionally poor. Also, because of unseen mobile phone and communication towers, which were anywhere, it made for hazardous flying. (Photos: Peter Wilkins)

A Lesotho Defence Force Bell-412 flown in the mountains by Dave Atkinson and below, Sonair Super Pumas in Luanda. (Photos: Peter Wilkins)

Above, cloudburst about 64 kilometres south of Lilongwe, Malawi juxtaposed with a nondescript African city, almost all of which look the same from the air. (Photos: Peter Wilkins)

A conglomeration of whirlybirds, including a Puma and a giant Russian-built Mi-26 – capable of carrying 100 fully armed troops – at Juba, Southern Sudan (top). The middle photo, above, is another Mi-26 at the airfield in Monrovia, Liberia, and below, Puma ZS-RKC at Lilongwe International Airport in Malawi. (Photos: Peter Wilkins)

Puma ZS-RVO on the banks of the Save River in Mozambique, after a (spurious) landing to check on a gearbox cooler fan belt light. The middle photo shows the military (western end) apron at Luanda International Airport and below Takoradi Airport and an airfield on the coast in the Congo. (Photos: Peter Wilkins)

Water cascading into the ocean in northern Gabon, near the Equatorial Guinea border, and below, Cape Coast Castle in Ghana from where it is said a quarter million slaves were shipped to the New World. (Photos: Peter Wilkins)

Top, a Kenyan Police Mi-8 at Wilson Airport, Nairobi, juxtaposed with an Antonov at Palogue Airport in Southern Sudan. This plane has been standing there for years after its Russian crew broke its nose wheel on the first test flight after maintenance. Middle: Starlite's Puma ZS-RKC at Lokichoggio, Kenya, and below, a sandy village in north-west Gabon. (Photos: Peter Wilkins)

Top, one of dozens of football stadiums being built by the Chinese in Africa, this one in northern Angola, with Kees Kieser map-reading in the Niger Delta (right). Below that is the final approach to Lokichoggio Airport in northern Kenya, with its aircraft 'graveyard' on the side of the runway and at the bottom, a hugely intimidating tropical storm approaching, taken south of Lilongwe. (Photos: Peter Wilkins)

Top, taken at Lungi International Airport in Sierra Leone is this photo showing flight engineer Gladwyn Rautenbach, pilots Ryan Hogan, 'Monster' Wilkins and Kees Kieser, as well as one of the local assistants. Below that, left, is Bata, Equatorial Guinea, and right, one of the small ports in West Africa. The bottom photos show a game lodge in the Kenyan highlands west of Mount Kenya and on the right, a village somewhere in Nigeria. (Photos: Peter Wilkins)

against the UNITA leader Dr Jonas Savimbi, were regarded as ideal for the task.

Both helicopters came equipped with the usual hard points for weapons under their winglets, but they still had to be wired up so the machines could be fitted with side door-mounted automatic weapons built into harnesses. It was agreed by EO directors that this would be done after they arrived in Sierra Leone, hurriedly fabricated at workshops in Freetown.

At the time, everybody accepted that to fly the two choppers across Africa was a bind, especially since most African states – even today – are nervous about people ferrying war planes through their air space. As EO quickly discovered, this applied especially to white mercenaries. Still, there was no other option short of dismantling both birds and having them shipped first to Europe, and then dog-legged all the way back to Africa. It was a hideously expensive alternative.

So fly halfway across Africa the EO air crews did. Internal ferry tanks were fitted and the boys set off from Luanda to Nigeria. Then fairly quickly, things went completely nuts.

On touchdown in Lagos, the authorities seized both aircraft and the pilots were accused – as one Nigerian newspaper labelled them – of being 'racist warmongers'. That came after someone had discovered that the entire crew had served in the South African Air Force, irrespective of the fact that conflict had ended some years before.

As a consequence, there were those in the port city of Lagos – and in the capital at Abuja – who wanted to know why these former military aviators had come to Nigeria.

For its dubious part, the Nigerian press had its day. Newspapers throughout the country carried headline banners such as: 'South African mercenaries held captive at Murtala Mohammed Airport', the country's biggest international air terminal. There were also veiled suggestions that the South Africans might be linked to subversives within Nigeria and were eager to foment revolt. Insurgency remains a recurring theme in Nigerian politics, even today.

It was of no consequence to Nigeria's military rulers that Nelson Mandela had recently been elected president of South Africa, or that the Hip helicopters were being taken to Sierra Leone to provide support to Nigerian soldiers, who, together with Executive Outcomes mercenaries, were fighting a war against a common enemy, much of which I'd detailed in *War Dog*, my first book, published in the United States, on South African mercenaries.

One of Starlite's Pumas on a cross-continent delivery trip stops for fuel at Mozambique's Pemba Airport in the extreme north of that country. (Photo: Peter Wilkins)

Chapter 9
By Puma Helicopter across the African Continent

For almost a week the helicopters remained impounded. The crews were forced, literally, to camp out under the rotors of their machines that were parked alongside the runway of the busiest airport in West Africa. Meanwhile, one of the South Africans commented: 'A cocky bunch of pie-eyed goons guarded us ... automatic weapons were regularly shoved in our faces and we were warned that if we wandered more than a few yards, we would be shot.'

That they were dealing with an obnoxious bunch of bastards was a given, one of the pilots admitted afterwards, adding that 'it came as no real surprise because that's about par for the course with so many Nigerians in uniform: they transmogrify into "Little Hitlers" the moment they set eyes on you.'

The palaver that followed became acrimonious and went on for days: in the meantime, appeals went out for help.

One of the pilots, 'Juba' Joubert told me afterwards that he'd never counted Nigerians among his favourite folk. 'It has absolutely nothing to do with race because I also look down my nose at Americans. But the fact was that while we were at Lagos, these shits actually made us beg for water ... food wasn't even a consideration,' he stated.

'We were treated like animals. And let's face it; they were really after our money. But we were damned if we were going to give them anything.'

Finally, following several appeals made by the Sierra Leone High Commissioner in Nigeria – as well as a direct approach from the Sierra Leone leader, Chairman Valentine Strasser to the Nigerian president – the helicopters were released.

Ultimately, it was cash and coercion that carried the day...

The SA 330 'J' model that 'Monster' Wilkins and his crew were required to ferry to Sierra Leone more recently is hardly a small machine.

Civilian-registered, and configured for medical evacuation operations (Medevac), the manual describes it as a 'medium-class passenger/freight helicopter operated by two pilots and an Aircraft Maintenance Engineer,' or AME.

It is an extremely versatile helicopter, to the extent that while Neall Ellis was using his old Mi-17 – nicknamed 'Bokkie' – to move about in Sierra Leone, then also in the throes of a civil war, he repeatedly tried to get the Freetown government to acquire a Puma. But there was simply no money at the time to do so.

With a service ceiling of 16,000 feet and an average empty weight of almost five tons, the Aérospatiale SA 330 Puma which was first produced in 1968, is equipped for round-the-clock flight operations using VFR, IFR and night-vision goggles or NVGs. The machine is powered by twin Turbomeca turbine engines that allows it an average cruise speed for planning purposes of 120 knots. Additionally, for long-range operations, such as the lengthy trip across Africa on which Wilkins and crew embarked, the helicopter can be fitted with external sponson fuel tanks of half-an-hour's endurance each. Removable internal ferry tanks will extend the range even further.

Interestingly, the helicopter was also selected by the Royal Air Force and given the designation Puma HC MK 1. As a result of this decision, the SA 330 was included in a joint production agreement between Aerospatiale and Westland Helicopters of the UK.

In Wilken's words, the Puma is a remarkable helicopter. But, as he says, it is also an exceptionally thirsty machine and burns fuel at a rate of 1,200 pounds/650 litres an hour. That means that on any trans-African journey, meticulous planning needs to go into every single stop en route. If there is no fuel at any one of the stops, everything comes to a halt.

In one trip to the Sudan way back in December 2010, fuel became a serious matter after the Starlite crew had left Nairobi's Wilson Airport on their way north. At Lokichoggio, last stop before the

A pair of Pumas deployed in the Sudan are corralled behind raised earth berms at the temporary base from which they operated. (Photo: Peter Wilkins)

Sudanese border was reached, a substantial fuel supply had to be arranged several days beforehand. Also, it had to be used on that specific day even though it had been paid for by electronic transfer well in advance.

The alternative, he recalls, was less forgiving: a crew member would have to go into town and pay the full amount into a Total account, return to the airport with the receipt and only then would the fuel be pumped.

The real crunch came at Juba, in Southern Sudan. Apart from an extremely expensive landing fee of more than US$200, the UN had no fuel for the chopper because this was not a United Nations operation.

Nor was there any at Malakal, the next Sudanese town along the way.

Notes made by 'Monster' Wilkins about the lengthy journey to the west coast of Africa can read like an adventure story. I quote from his logbook:

'The aircraft was readied and due to the delay in contract start time, there was time for required maintenance. However, the function check done on 20 July showed a number of problems.' This included unserviceable Instrument Landing System or ILS and VOR (Omni directional radio-range) as well as DME or Distance Measuring Equipment.

'The Marine Band radio needed to be fitted and this was done on the last night before departure. Due to the urgency of the situation, RWO was flown to Denel where it was discovered that the Mode C of the transponder was not working.' This was a serious issue because it automatically signalled the aircraft's altitude to air traffic control (radar) with TCAS (Traffic Collision Avoidance System).

'Following the use of sophisticated Denel equipment, the navigation instrumentation was declared serviceable. However, it was later discovered that the VOR – though giving off an aural identity – was not transmitting to the OBS or Horizontal Position Indicator' (on the flight panel in front of the captain and which, in turn, meant that there was no real indication of direction).

As 'Monster' recalled, there were an awful lot of things that went wrong with the machine on the eve of departure, but as with most such things in South Africa, pilots are an innovative bunch.

Apart from connections coming adrift on the Marine Band, there was suddenly no power apparent on the headsets. And the autopilot had to be worked on, 'which though improved, there was still a slight rocking from side to side in roll.'

And then, 'for day one and two, the right-hand hydraulic system seemed to be emptying into the left-hand system ... even though no leaks were evident. It was also noticed that emergency hydraulic pressure was too high, so it was suggested to switch off the pump once the pressure was up. This seemed to sort out the problem and the fluid levels now stayed stable ...'

As he says, 'there were problems all round and every one of them had to be remedied prior to departure.' He makes the point that if a vital piece of equipment fails in the depths of Africa, who knows how long it would take to fly in a new part, 'apart from the kind of unseemly hassles these tasks always become in Third World countries.'

Day One

Flew from Lanseria, halfway across the Kalahari to Maun in Botswana, a comparatively easy stop and without any hassles. Botswana officials were friendly and helpful, together with a very significant plus – they were *efficient*.

Approaching high ground in the Cameroons on a delivery trip across West Africa.
(Photo: Peter Wilkins)

Chapter 9
By Puma Helicopter across the African Continent

We continued across the Okavango Swamps – always a magnificent spectacle from the air – and landed at Ondangua in northern Namibia, where we spent the night. Fuel and landing fees were both easy and we paid by credit card. During the Border War 'Ondangs' – as it was called by the flying community – was the biggest SAAF air base in the country.

However, immigration soon became a problem. According to 'The Act' aviators are required to give prior warning to the Namibian immigration if they intend to land outside normal working hours, in this case, eight to five. We landed after hours and although the immigration official saw us touch down, he went home anyway before we could get to his office. At seven the following morning he insisted that I accompany him to his office where he showed me the dreaded 'Act'. Moreover, he said, we were in very serious trouble and that the fine was R20,000 per person, roughly $3,000.

But, he intimated, there was a way out of this conundrum. He could 'help us out' if we departed before any of the other immigration officials arrived. If we didn't depart immediately, he insisted, it would be too late and we would have to be arrested. I thanked him and gave him $30 which he said he needed to get his car out of the garage.

Moments later he said that the money I had given was not enough and that he usually asked for and got $100 in such cases. I reminded him that we had actually spoken to the tower before five the previous evening and he had seen us land. I asked whether he would like to talk to the tower? The official declined and within minutes, we were on our way.

Day Two

We landed at Lubango – Sa de Bandeira in Portuguese colonial times – for fuel. There were no problems either with landing fees or fuel, but cash was required. Within the hour we were headed north again – all the way to Luanda, the Angolan capital.

This big coastal city offered few surprises, because most of the guys had been through there before. Nonetheless, the night stop was a nightmare for Flight Engineer Gladwin.

His biggest problem was security, which one experiences in most African cities. The difference is that Luanda is the only place in West Africa where one feels unsafe or, more accurately, insecure, more often than you would like. The authorities need very little reason to put anybody in a prison cell for real or imagined transgressions.

Conditions in some African states can be primitive. This is the 'Airport Health Office' at Lokichogio in Turkana country in northern Kenya. It is an obligatory refuelling stop if you are heading north into the Sudan and you need to order your fuel several days ahead of arriving there. (Photo: Peter Wilkins)

Worse, there is no arguing and it takes an enormous amount of time, effort and cash across palms to extricate the unfortunate victims.

Prior to our departure, promises were made about fixing overdue visas during a previous stint in the country when we worked with three Pumas and a Bell 407 during the 2008/9 elections, which was only eight months before. This time our flight engineer Gladwin Rautenbach was jailed for a previously expired visa. It took until well after midnight to extricate him from that palaver and none of us was amused. Because we were in transit, he believed his expired visa would do the trick – but it did not. He had been through there for the elections and his visa had overrun, so although he didn't need one for being in transit for the ferry, his passport flagged the system. The game was on…

Meantime, fuel, landing fees and immigration needs were handled by the local representative and even that took three hours.

In many stopover points north of the Limpopo, helicopter crews have to fend for themselves fuel-wise, which often means using elbow grease to tap into the helicopter tanks, usually from drums. (Photo: Peter Wilkins)

Day Three

After further delays, which necessitated Gladwin waiting at an extremely costly hotel (Luanda is rated by the London *Financial Times* as one of the three most expensive cities in the world, in large part because of oil) we managed to take off for Pointe Noire, across the Congo River, to our next fuel stop. As the major port for Congo (Brazzaville) and not to be confused with the Democratic Republic of the Congo (Kinshasa), the procedures were painless. There was one 'official-looking' fellow who offered to help but demanded $50 upfront. We graciously declined and did everything ourselves.

Our night stop was at Libreville, the Gabonese capital. This was also fairly painless, though there was an awful lot of walking involved. A security guard said he would do everything for us – also for $50 – but we did not pay him up front, so he didn't reappear and we did everything ourselves there as well.

Day Four

It was while traversing this stretch of coast that we were reminded of our biggest potential problem of all: the weather. In the wrong season, it can become an enemy within minutes. When your machine is fitted with weather radar, most of these problems are taken care of, or at least they should be.

On a ferry flight, which involves delivering a helicopter to some distant destination, things are very different. You need to get from 'A' to 'B', usually in a straight line, because of fuel considerations. But then, as we'd discovered on previous trips, West Africa's rainforests can be dicey because of mist or cloud that sometimes appears to

Much of the terrain covered by these aircrews is Africa at its most primitive. Aircraft have gone down in these primeval forests and were never found again. (Photo: Peter Wilkins)

drop down to 200 feet. Or the jungle below might be shrouded in fog or mist – and the very large forest giants growing there are often barely visible against a white background.

To cap it, there are sometimes steel towers (cellphones?) out in the middle of nowhere. Most at eight or ten metres are fairly modest, but others can be as high as 200 metres. So you don't want to run into one of those monstrosities when you are ambling along at 150 feet.

One way of overcoming the problem is to stick to the coast and fly along the beach, just beyond the breaker line, because it is unlikely that there will be any towers or masts. Nor any oil rigs either.

The nasty part is when you have to head towards the airfield (in our case Douala, in the Cameroons) in such conditions as you simply know that there are masts aplenty around all the airfields and along our flight path. And you can't simply do a let-down, as you are on a VFR flight plan and the instruments are dicey. That means a visual approach from below minimum at 150 feet (and maybe just a few metres above the surrounding trees).

When this happens and it is raining – in the tropics it only pours waters from the heavens – you have to slow down, fly a little cross controls so you can see through the open window and get soaking wet in the process. Then you thank your guardian angels for GPS and you lie to the tower that you have things under control.

There are other hazards, such as other helicopters, particularly in West Africa's Gulf of Benin – all the way from the oil-rich Cameroon to the recently oil-rich Ghana – where choppers are the preferred medium of transport because it is convenient. There seemed to be no 'set' frequency for VFR traffic, so we had to keep a constant sharp vigil, especially in foul weather.

Douala was our night stop, but because the cloud base was down to 200 feet and some of the steel towers on our approach route were two or three times as high, it became an extremely difficult obstacle course, with even the larger trees seemingly emitting steam-like vapour.

A local CAA representative at Douala was helpful. He smoothed the way for us, even obtaining the necessary transit visas from the police chief which put us back $100 for his able assistance. However, the paper trail at this Cameroonian port is difficult, extremely tedious and involved.

After refuelling, it took us another two hours to obtain the promised visa. Meantime, the CAA representative insisted that he personally inspect the Puma, probably to establish that we weren't hauling contraband or weapons.

Along the west coast of Africa aircrews constantly find evidence of illegal logging, especially in equatorial regions. Logs become separated from the pens holding them and often float off towards the ocean to later wash up along the coastline. (Photo: Peter Wilkins)

Day Five

The next morning came and we filed a flight plan at 06:00Z for 07:00Z, but only got airborne two hours later because of the rigmarole. It took an age to settle navigation and parking fees (more than $330) and that accomplished, we had to pay landing fees but at another office.

Then, on departure, we'd been warned that the area to the immediate west was a restricted zone, which meant that we were unable to fly around the coast from Douala to Port Harcourt in Nigeria – ostensibly because of the big 'hill' in the middle. Mount Cameroon, at more than 14,000 feet is also routinely covered in mist or rain and is partially obscured for much of the year.

That meant setting a course for Nigeria that took us way out to sea again, but not too close to Malabo, which plays host to another great prehistoric volcanic structure. It was right-hand down a bit for Port Harcourt, a few miles inland and once again, completely surrounded by water and palm trees. Throughout this leg, visibility was putrid: it didn't help that there were more helicopters in the air than buzzards.

Because we weren't sure that we'd have enough fuel to get us all the way to Accra – bad weather, lots of rain and alternating ground speeds were to hamper us throughout – we went into Port Harcourt to top up the tanks.

Thanks to communications from Durban Ops, we were met by Captain Lewis, a Port Harcourt expatriate who handles these formalities. However, immediately afterwards an extremely uptight representative from the base arrived with a bunch of paperwork for our Puma. There were more Africa-style hassles which took a couple of hours to sort out, but eventually we were on our way, this time headed for Accra, the capital of Ghana.

The 428 nautical mile flight from Port Harcourt to Accra included roughly 331 nautical miles over the ocean. Fuel was carefully monitored, along with ground speed, and a point-of-no-return (PNR) established 70 nautical miles off Lagos.

The decision was made to proceed after careful consultation and we landed in Accra without utilising the reserve 600 pounds of fuel that remained.

Of all the stops on the long journey across Africa, Accra was the easiest. A helpful airports company worker took us to the flight planning centre where we paid our landing fees – a magnificent $20!

Also, the official in charge said we were VFR and we didn't have to pay any approach fees. He was very helpful with our flight plan, printing an extra copy and giving us all the reporting points. He had a full set of Jespersen manuals available and this remarkable 'one-man-band' was done with all our requirements within 20 minutes.

Additionally, the Ghanaian official said, we were in transit, and that meant that there was no need for immigration procedures. What a change after the rubbish we experienced in the Cameroons and some of the other places along the way. The crew was able to take off again, in time to make Abidjan in the Ivory Coast later the same day.

Rest Day

Abidjan, the Ivoirian capital city – once a delightful Francophonic African cultural centre, but since sullied by revolt and fratricidal divide – was reached by flying along the coast, the last hour in the dark specifically to avoid towers and aerials. There were no problems encountered.

I decided to give Gladwin a day for going over the chopper before proceeding, and he admitted that it was needed. One of the tasks facing him was cleaning up the helicopter prior to us arriving at the final destination and presenting ourselves to the client.

There should have been two Pumas in the air on the final leg, the other owned by the German company Helog, and our own. But there were problems. The first was that while they had had a floatation device fitted the day before we arrived, they were without a Marine Band Radio. They were also short of one of their ferry tanks, but they solved that issue by 'borrowing' one from the French Military at Abidjan after we told them we could not help.

Their biggest obstacle was acquiring transit permits for Liberia, which had only been a day or two before we arrived and the requisite authority still had to come through. The result was that we scrapped plans for a coupled flight to Sierra Leone and went off into the depths of 'Darkest Africa' on our own.

Final Day

The original intention had been to make an early start out of Abidjan, but because the fuel bowser had run dry, we only got airborne at 11 am. Because of poor weather (again), coupled to incomplete mapping coverage of the direct route, we set out westwards along the coast. Then, suddenly, we were faced with communication problems: the one working VHF set stopped transmitting. Radio selectors were changed, but to no avail.

We noticed that the other set on board seemed to be transmitting because its transmission light lit up when we attempted to send messages, but nothing could be heard in reply. As a result we made blind transmissions on the tower frequency, which seemed to work.

Freetown's Lungi International Airport and end of the line for one of Starlite's delivery trips. Little more than a decade ago, this was a heavily-disputed war zone where more than a thousand British troops were deployed while countering rebel forces intent on taking the capital of Sierra Leone. (Photo: Peter Wilkins)

Once in the Liberian capital, we put down safely and were met by the handler's representative. He told us that the tower had been receiving our transmissions but it was us that weren't receiving. We spoke to the chief air traffic control officer (CATCO) and explained the position, at the same time requesting permission to leave with the problem still unresolved after we'd refuelled. Interestingly, he agreed, but only if we could get away before the Presidential jet departed and the next inbound flight landed.

So we got our instructions prior to start, with the promise of a green light for take-off. We couldn't see any green light, so we took off from the taxiway and avoided crossing the runway until we were about 10 kilometres from the airfield.

Freetown at last, but even getting there on this final leg we had more communications problems. We eventually established a system that seemed to work and in the end we were given clearance to land. Quintin, our man in Freetown, showed us where to park and with plenty of help from some of the security guys, we pushed our Puma into the hangar.

To protect our asset from robbers and thieves, we had a great alarm device installed in the hanger. Each time someone approached the helicopter when they were not supposed to, the system sounded an original blood-curdling high-pitched scream. Placed under the machine, so that it covered all approaches, it had both movement-sensing and infrared ability.

However, since Africa enjoys the kind of problems not always found on other continents, we took some other precautions as well. They included applying tamper tape to check whether cowlings had been surreptiously opened during the dark hours. Part of our daily routine was thoroughly checking our fuel prior to take-off. There are many stories doing the rounds of fuel being siphoned off aircraft and replaced with water.

Neall Ellis, currently flying support missions in Somalia, subsequently added his two bits' worth by saying that it was fairly common practice in Africa and recalls events that took place while he was flying Mi-24 helicopter gunships during their West African civil war.

He explained: 'One morning in Sierra Leone, we arrived at the helicopter parked at the Cockerill barracks for a flight, and found that 900 litres of fuel had been siphoned from the chopper during the night. Fortunately, those responsible for the theft were brazen enough not to replace it with water. Another time, we did have fuel

Wherever you fly in Africa these days you are greeted by the detritus of the events of yesterday, such as the remains of this Soviet Mi-17 helicopter in the bush in Sierra Leone (top) and bits and pieces of other aircraft further south. (Photo: Peter Wilkins)

Chapter 9
By Puma Helicopter across the African Continent

Several Mozambique airports are littered with aircraft wrecks, some dating from the Portuguese colonial period. But it does not compare with the wrecks of hundreds of war planes seen here in the insert lying alongside the runway in Mogadishu. (Photo: Peter Wilkins)

stolen from the tanks and replaced with water, but fortunately, we picked that little aberration up during my pre-flight inspection. On that occasion we only lost 100 litres of fuel.'

I mentioned this to South African commercial pilot Jeff McKay, who once worked for the Natal Sharks Board, and is today flying wide-bodies out of Australia to the US and beyond. He said that the same thing had happened to him, twice actually, while flying around Africa commercially.

I quote: 'I had an incident at Nacala in Mozambique and also in Kinshasa, the Zairean capital in the 1990s with that same bullshit. Fortunately, I was operating a Beech King Air and picked it up during my flight checks.

'Operators in Africa have to take precautions, as if it is always a war zone (which, of course, so much of it is).

Then I heard something similar from Leif Hellström, a Swedish friend and fellow-author. One of his countrymen who worked in Zaire, said he happened to wander into the air force hangar at N'Djili International Airport, Kinshasa one night. There he found a C-130 military transport plane with long lengths of hose fitted into every drain valve under the wings. There were people scurrying around siphoning fuel into jerry cans, obviously for private sale. It was apparently a regular thing, he reckoned.

He goes on: 'While the Zaire Air Force had Mirage jets, these would be towed over to a petrol company terminal at N'Djili once a week for filling up, naturally at air force expense. All aircraft were fitted with maximum long-range tanks and even engineless hulks were towed across for the illicit fuelling process.

'Once they had been taken back to their original holding areas, the fuel was quickly pumped out by air force personnel and sold on the black market in the city.'

Makes you think...

CHAPTER TEN

THE UNANSWERED 'HIT' ON PELINDABA IN NOVEMBER 2007

South Africa's Pelindaba Nuclear Research Facility – the primary nuclear establishment on the continent of Africa that produced enough weapons-grade uranium to fuel six atom bombs in the 1970s and 1980s – was the setting for an armed raid in 2007 that involved two groups of insurgents armed with automatic weapons. The implications remain serious because nobody has come up with any answers yet.

For its part, the South African government has been obscurantist throughout, dismissing the incident as little more than minor. Its spokespeople maintain that the incident involved criminals. The facts suggest otherwise.

Picture the scenario. One of the biggest nuclear establishments in the Third World comes under a concerted attack by unknown elements that had gone to great lengths to plan the strike. What emerged afterwards was that the onslaught was mounted not only with clear-cut military precision, but that the evidence of inside collusion is overwhelming.

Had there been a powerful, coordinated attack by persons unknown on an American nuclear facility such as the one at Los Alamos, a defence nuclear weapons laboratory in New Mexico or possibly a highly enriched uranium production facility at Oak Ridge Tennessee, the fallout would have reverberated around the world. In the United States the media reaction might almost have been on par with 9/11. Any military strike on a high-security nuclear installation raises flags, no less so in the Third World where there are powerful revolutionary forces at work, among them al-Qaeda.

The media would have been inundated with news reports, comment and conjecture. The issue would unquestionably have been raised in Congress. Additionally, security measures would have been increased: possibly tripled or quadrupled, as has taken place with an aviation industry labouring under threats of international terrorism. The same situation would have held had the target been a nuclear establishment in Britain, France or Germany. Or, for that matter Japan. More to the point, barely a day goes by without something appearing in the news about Pakistan's nuclear assets, regarded by those familiar with the industry to be under serious Islamic fundamentalist threat.

Which begs the question: since there was a large quantity of weapons-grade uranium at risk during the armed attack on Pelindaba – enough to manufacture half-a-dozen A-bombs – why has the international community remained all but mute? More salient, what makes South Africa's nuclear facilities different from the rest? Could it be that Africa and Africans are immune from criticism? Or, as suggested by WABC radio host John Batchelor in one of his intrusive New York-based talk shows: Is it wise for the international community to ignore the kind of lax security measures that might conceivably result in a terrorist group acquiring enough highly enriched uranium (HEU) to make nuclear weapons?

What is interesting is that in response to fears that a terrorist organisation might launch an operation to 'liberate' Pelindaba's stock of fissile material (which would conservatively be worth hundreds of millions of dollars on the international black market), the South African government has repeatedly assured Vienna's International Atomic Energy Agency – as well as all the major nuclear powers – that Pelindaba, very literally, is a 'fortress'.

Of critical significance, maintains Idaho's Dan Yurman, is that the reality of the attack shows undeniable evidence of military experience and planning: a composite 'signature'. The entire process reflects a professional military presence behind its planning, he suggests.[1]

Throughout, Pretoria has maintained that the facility is 'powerfully guarded against any form of outside attack', a comment endorsed by a South African cabinet minister, though he spoke on condition of anonymity (hardly important, because there are only so many cabinet ministers involved with nuclear issues in South Africa). What he did stress was that the principal role of South Africa's Atomic Energy Corporation was to manufacture nuclear fuel for the reactor at the Koeberg Power Station, to participate in the decommissioning of the discontinued nuclear weapons programme and to perform research to support all these functions.

Facilities at the nuclear establishment include, among others, the Safari-1 research reactor (a 20MW swimming pool-sized research reactor which has been under IAEA safeguards since its commissioning in 1965), a hot cell complex, a waste disposal site as well as conversion and fuel fabrication facilities.

For all that, Pretoria's immediate reaction to the onslaught on Pelindaba from Day One was, if anything, duplicitous. The responsible ministry actually denied that the attack had anything to do with nuclear materials. Indeed, it told *60 Minutes* 'the intruders wanted to steal laptops or other commercial products at the facility,' and that, frankly, is absurd.

Look at the facts: There were at least two groups of attackers – all armed with AK-47 Kalashnikov automatic weapons, who had managed to slice their way through a de-energized 10,000 Volt electrified fence and in the process, evaded banks of security cameras. All this was achieved without them being noticed. That complicated procedure must have taken the best part of half an hour, yet nobody was made aware that an attack was taking place. Pelindaba security officials later said that guards maintaining the site's closed-circuit-video-television (CCTV) system were asleep and that they had subsequently been either disciplined or sacked.

Meantime, two squads of intruders had penetrated undetected three quarters of a mile to a control room that monitors such emergencies.

What followed was a fight between the attackers and Anton Gerber – a member of the Pelindaba staff in charge of the control room. Gerber was seriously wounded by gunfire, but in the confusion the attackers withdrew. Yet for all that activity – the rumpus included shots, alarms, an alerted reaction force and the rest – it took 24 minutes for the first security unit to arrive where all this was taking place: the same squad, incidentally, that had been

South Africa's nuclear facility at Pelindaba, on the outskirts of Pretoria. This picture was taken from the main road that runs past its main entrance. (Photo: Pierre Lowe Victor)

specifically delegated to protect Pelindaba from just such an attack. Officially, the response time that would follow break-in is listed as four minutes...'

It also emerged afterwards that at one point, a second team of four intruders were detected by a security patrol inside the site perimeter. The guards opened fire on them, but nobody was reported wounded in the exchange. This intervention may have been crucial in thwarting the intended theft of HEU. The first team, clearly, had the mission of disabling the security centre; the second was to gain access to the storage area and hijack the weapons-grade material.

Anton Gerber's heroic battle with the first team prevented them from spiking the security systems for the HEU storage area. Even if the second group of intruders had reached their intended objective, they would have remained locked out.

Considering the nature of the attack and a succession of security lapses that followed, the single conjecture most often raised by those who have been sceptical of the answers provided by the South African government, is that the hit was what some security cognoscenti might refer to as 'an inside job.'

As CBS *60 Minutes* concluded in its investigation, 'while the camera operators who missed the gunmen were fired, the investigation is stalled, leaving no clue as to who was behind the assault on Pelindaba or whether their intent was to supply uranium for a nuclear bomb...'

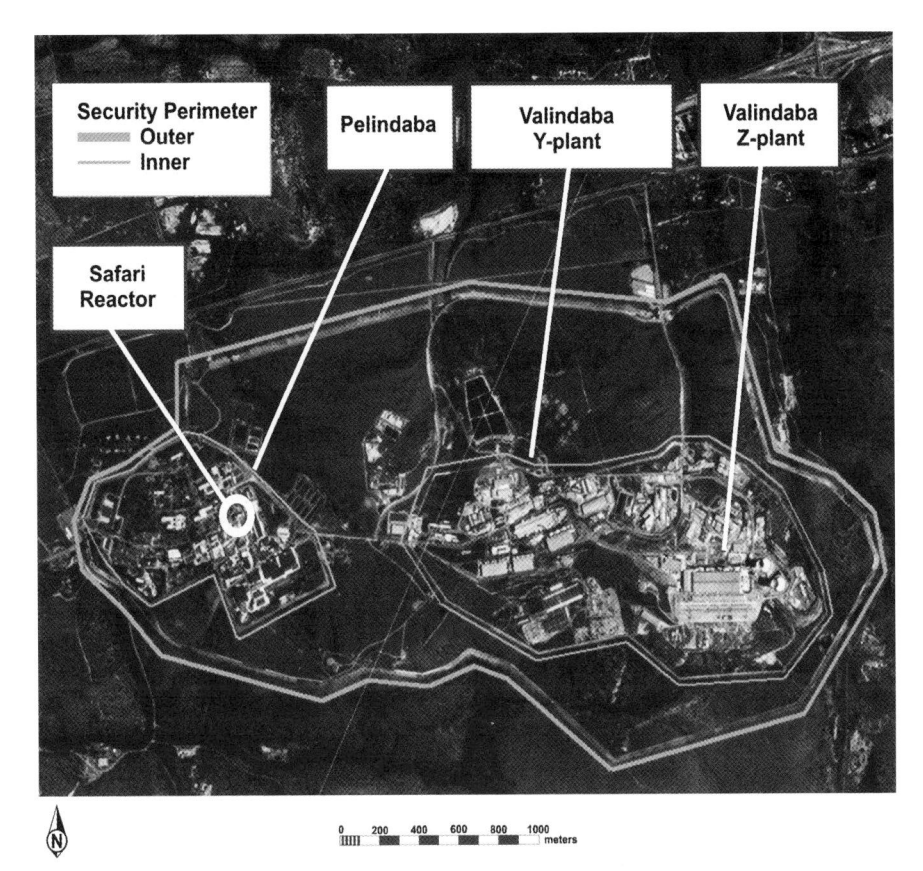

Chapter 10
The Unanswered 'Hit' on Pelindaba in November 2007

Valindaba nuclear research centre and the adjoining Valindaba uranium enrichment plants in the early 1990s. Text indicators are from the Federation of American Scientists.
(Image: TerraServer.com)

The incident took place on a November evening in 2007. Yet, apart from a handful of cursory notices in some American newspapers, including a report in the *New York Times* posted from South Africa, nobody took much notice.

The *Washington Post*'s reporter in South Africa, possibly under pressure from the South African government, declined to submit a file to his editors even after the *New York Times* published its story on the incident. It wasn't until almost a year later, that *60 Minutes* devoted a segment to an attack that remains vague and unexplained. This lapse in reporting a critical issue that has immense international ramifications is all but culpable considering the security implications.

Dan Yurman, an Idaho-based nuclear blogger with his own website, provided a timeline to this development.

It makes for disturbing comment:
- 9 November 2007 – Pelindaba break-in reported by the South African press, later censored, but not soon enough. Some of the newspapers suggest early government efforts at disinformation. For instance, one of them says that Gerber is reported to be delusional.
- *Pretoria News* reported it was phoned by a man identifying himself as a National Energy Corporation of South Africa (NECSA) legal adviser, saying the newspaper will be breaching the National Keypoints Act by publishing the story. He reportedly claimed that the interview with Gerber was 'unethical' as 'he was under sedation and thus incoherent' when it was conducted.
- Yurman sees their web pages and reports on the basic facts and event on his blog.
- 13 November 2007 – South African security forces admit there were two teams that broke into the facility. The first was to disable the security systems and the second to steal HEU. Note: Both teams were likely 'expendable' due to possible extended exposure and/or inhalation in powder form, of 90 per cent highly enriched uranium. The South African bomb programme reportedly produced enough HEU for six to seven weapons, which, at a minimum would be 25–30 kg per bomb or 150–180 kg (330–400 pounds in total). Four men could carry that weight, but not the lead shielding that stored it to prevent criticality. Some of the apparent logistical requirements for the theft remain a mystery. For instance, he asks, if the intruders were to remove the shielding to lighten the load for transport, do they then set up conditions for a criticality incident in the confines of a truck?
- 14 November 2007 – *New York Times* publishes a report from South Africa which gets some of the details wrong, but which brings the essential fact about the break-in to the world's attention. The *Washington Post* correspondent in South Africa, contacted by e-mail, declined to cover the story.
- 20 December 2007 – Miach Zenko, a graduate student at the Belfer Center, Harvard University, publishes a detailed Op Ed in the *Washington Post*. He gets all the facts right. In Yurman's subsequent telephone interview with Zenko, he expressed impatience with any theory about the break-in that would discount the coordinated nature of the attack, an inside job

or the objective, which was the theft of HEU. He does not speculate on who it was that might have been after the fissile material.

- 2 February 2008 – The International Atomic Energy Agency reviews security measures at Pelindaba and pronounces them to be in order.
- A year after the attack, on 23 November 2008, CBS's *60 Minutes* broadcasts a report on the Pelindaba break-in. They get all the facts right but make no progress in identifying who ordered the attack. Pelindaba officials talk with CBS on camera and visit the 10,000 Volt security fence, but decline to respond to questions about whether the attack was an inside job.
- Note that the incident comes four months after NECSA's newly appointed services general manager, Eric Lerata, was gunned down in front of his home after returning from a business trip in France. It is believed he was followed from Johannesburg's Oliver Tambo International Airport. Two men were subsequently arrested for stealing his car: they were reportedly driving it at the time of the arrest. Is there a connection between the compromised security systems the night of the attack and his death? With most such incidents in present-day South Africa, the country with the highest murder rate in the world, nothing ever came of the case.

The international reaction to an attempt to penetrate the security of the largest single nuclear facility in Africa and the Southern Hemisphere remains stultifying. The matter becomes more complex when it is appreciated that almost without exception, every terrorist or insurgent movement eager to acquire nuclear expertise – al-Qaeda included – is vehemently anti-American and anti-West.

Since the Pelindaba 'break-in', there has been a lot of speculation about what actually took place there on the night of 8 November 2008. While much has been published, a good deal of information linked to the attack has been kept secret. Immediately afterwards, Pretoria implemented a legal gagging order which prevented local media from following up on some of the more controversial issues under review.

What we do know is that Anton Gerber, the Pelindaba emergency control room station commander, was shot by the intruders after they had entered the facility. His fiancée, Ria Meiring, an operator at the facility, was assaulted by the four men who had managed to

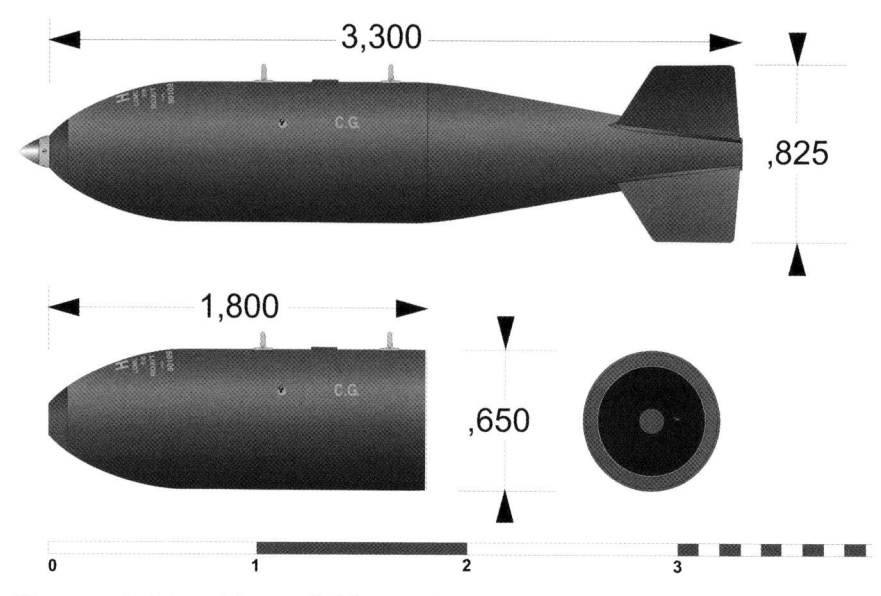

Diagrammatical view of the so-called 'business' section of the six atom bombs that South African scientists constructed in the final stages of the apartheid era (designated Hento H-2). The nuclear programme was dismantled by British, American and International Atomic Energy Agency officials prior to the handover of power to Nelson Mandela's ANC. (Image: Washington DC's Institute for Science and International Security)

penetrate the secure area. Apparently Gerber should not have been there that night, but he went anyway 'to keep my fiancée company'. There is some evidence to suggest that the attackers were as surprised to find him on duty as he was to discover their presence.

Since Gerber was armed, he was able to retaliate, but then handguns are never a match for automatic weapons. Indeed, as he himself admits, he is extremely lucky to be alive.

Meanwhile, Rob Adam, the chief executive of NECSA, confirmed immediately afterwards that 'four armed, *technically sophisticated* criminals' had entered the nuclear site by cutting the outside fence and slipping through the electric fence. This comment is disingenuous. They could not have cut through the fence unless they knew it was already de-energised. A breach of an electrified fence would have immediately set off security alarms.

He also said that the attackers had roamed the premises for about an hour, during which they stole a ladder from a fire engine to gain access to the first floor of the emergency control centre through a window, during which time a computer was stolen and placed on a balcony. Then the men moved to the control room where they attacked Gerber and Meiring before fleeing, leaving the computer behind as they fled the facility.

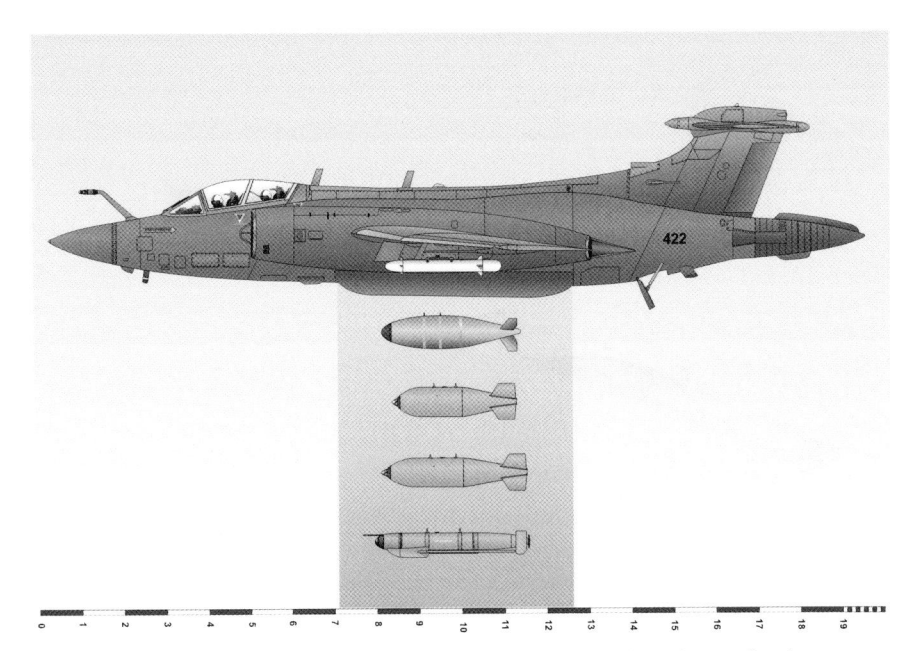

Chapter 10
The Unanswered 'Hit' on Pelindaba in November 2007

South African Air Force Buccaneer bomber which was intended to deliver the atom bombs to targets were they ever to be used operationally, with several configurations of the weapon, including two types of free-fall bombs. (Image: Pierre Lowe Victor)

Adam emphasised at the time that it was evident the criminals had prior knowledge of the electronic security systems and while there are some timing inconsistencies in what Adam said, his gist is more or less correct with what had happened.

In an earlier report, NECSA disclosed that 'these activities were captured on surveillance cameras, but unfortunately, they were not detected by the operators on duty'. After which Rob Adam muddied the water still further by adding a post-script and stating that 'at no time were the emergency control room systems compromised'.

He did, however, confirm that after the control room area had been penetrated, a breach on the opposite boundary fence was discovered by a security guard. Immediately afterwards a second group of men were spotted and all fled in the ensuing shootout.

Meanwhile, Anton Gerber and his fiancée, Ria Meiring, took legal action against their former employers and sued NECSA for damages and loss of income following their ordeal. Papers filed in the Pretoria High Court show that Gerber was claiming for about US$110,000 (at ruling foreign currency exchange rates), while Meiring was demanding a bit less.

Summonses were issued against NECSA and a security services manager, security shift supervisor as well as the two camera-room operators who were on duty and the fact that it took them an inordinately long time to come to their aid.

Interviewed by *60 Minutes*, Gerber disclosed that it took the South African Police 10 months to interview him.

When the *New York Times* finally got into the story a week after the event, Michael Wines confirmed that after the attack, 'the most serious on a nuclear installation in recent memory', the South African government was reticent to provide specifics about the attack.[2]

'Already, the attack is raising questions among advocates and analysts about the wisdom of plans by South Africa and other African states to embrace nuclear energy as a solution to chronic power shortages and the looming problems of climate change,' wrote Wines.

'The assault on the Pelindaba nuclear reactor and research centre, one of South Africa's most zealously guarded properties, is a severe embarrassment to the government. The eight gunmen escaped cleanly, neither caught by guards nor identified on surveillance cameras.'

Subsequently, after an internal investigation, about which nothing has been made public, the three security guards responsible for monitoring the process at Pelindaba on the night of the entry were fired. They had been asleep in front of the monitors when the two groups broke into Pelindaba and were found to be negligent. More to the point, were they asleep or were they paid to look away?

Since then, the Pelindaba attack had become something of an item of discussion in the security industry abroad, so much so that Mike Kantey, the chairperson of the Coalition Against Nuclear Energy in South Africa (CANE), said that it had been developed into a defence safety analysis case study. That was almost followed by Matthew Bunn of Harvard's Kennedy School of Government, who told *60 Minutes* that if terrorists got hold of the uranium, 'it would not be hard to build a crude atomic bomb'.

Meanwhile, Pretoria has consistently remained on the defensive. Arie van der Bijl, general manager of NECSA, denied in the same programme that the two attacks on the same night were linked. He was supported by Adam who believed it was a random criminal act and that if these were 'sophisticated terrorists', Gerber would not be alive. Abdul Minty, South Africa's one-time nomination for director-general of the International Atomic Energy Agency (IAEA), reached the same conclusion after a senior South African Police official declared that the case was being investigated by the Serious and Violent Crimes Unit. There was a clear indication that what took place at Pelindaba was more than a 'mere break-in', said the police officer.

Which leads one to speculate how a similar event, had it taken place on American soil, would have turned out…

Since Nelson Mandela's African National Congress took power in South Africa, there have been a number of incidents related either to the country's nuclear facility or to the country's weapons industry.

In 1997 for instance, there was an unscheduled visit to Pelindaba, on instructions from the Office of the President in Cape Town, by Reza Amrollahi, Iran's Deputy Minister of Atomic Affairs, who presented the then incumbent head at South Africa's nuclear programme, Dr Waldo Stumpf, with what he referred to as 'a nuclear shopping list'.

Specifically, what Amrollahi was asking for was material with which to build an A-bomb – and this was in the presence of Pik Botha, for a brief time Minister of Mineral and Energy Affairs in Mandela's cabinet. Of course, recounts Stumpf, the Iranian was politely rebuffed: the two South Africans took the defensive line that the provisions of the Nonproliferation Treaty simply did not allow either Stumpf or any other member of his staff to comply with such extraordinary demands.

Dr Stumpf told me subsequently that his riposte was along the lines of South Africa having recently signed the NPT and that Pretoria's entire nuclear arsenal had been demolished by the IAEA in concert with Washington and London.[3]

This episode was dealt with at length in the September 1997 edition of *Jane's Intelligence Review*. But that did not prevent this author from coming under critical attack at ministerial level by members of the Pretoria government, even though Pik Botha admitted to South Africa's *Mail and Guardian* that he was actually in the office at Pelindaba when the initial Iranian request was made. Notably, the government version was supported by Stumpf, who denied that he had ever discussed such matters with Al J. Venter. What is significant is that Dr Stumpf has since recanted: he has admitted that the meetings with both the Iranian Minister Reza Amrollahi and this correspondent took place, though it took him years to do so. His initial duplicity exposed me to serious credibility problems with Britain's Jane's Information Group at the time because the South African protest was made at the topmost diplomatic level.

Another event which hardly warranted comment in South Africa's media at the time was the disappearance of drums of fissile waste material from Pelindaba after a winding down of the country's nuclear weapons programme. According to Dr Ben Sanders of the Programme for Promoting Nuclear Nonproliferation, this was a serious matter, but no satisfactory answers were ever forthcoming about the issue from Pretoria.

That was followed by the shipment from Pelindaba of a complete zirconium tube factory to China, also during 1997.

Zirconium is a greyish-white lustrous metal commonly used in an alloy form (i.e. Zircalloy) to encase fuel rods in nuclear reactors – and here too there is a Tehran connection – though zirconium tubes can be used with equal efficiency to hold fuel in reactors for commercial as well as military uses.

With Iran striving for self-sufficiency in all aspects of its domestic

Steel casings for the South African atom bombs prior to assembly. (Photo: Pierre Lowe Victor)

nuclear programme, it would ultimately be in need of zirconium tubes, great numbers of them. However, under restrictions imposed by the international NSG, Tehran is forbidden from acquiring them from any supplier in the West.

As Tehran was to discover, there was an easy way to overcome this imbroglio. While the Iranians might have taken advantage of their close ties to Moscow and possibly bought such a plant from them, they sought another route. The same year that Dr Waldo Stumpf recanted on his original story, strong evidence was to emerge that the Iranian government – in complicity with Beijing – tried to secure a surplus zirconium tube factory in South Africa. Moreover, it was to have been accomplished without any of the customary nuclear checks and balances in place.

What we do know is that the packing up and dispatch of a disused zirconium plant at Pelindaba had progressed to the point where it was about to be shipped out of the country without mandatory end-user certificates. Then somebody blew the whistle. The publication *NuclearFuel* is on record as stating in its 19 December 1997 issue that Washington feared the plant might end up in Iran, and for good reason. China had apparently contracted with Tehran to build a zirconium plant at one of its nuclear facilities a short while before and the Pelindaba plant would have been an ideal stop gap.

The story emerged after a group of about 40 Chinese technicians entered South Africa on 'business' visas in August 1997. They spent months at the nuclear establishment preparing the plant for shipment. In fact, it was already packed into a number of reinforced cases when an alert journalist doing a routine story on Pelindaba tipped-off the South African Police that something illicit was taking place there. Only after details surfaced in a South African newspaper file did the police raid the place and promptly arrest all these foreigners for what was termed on the charge sheets as 'illegally working in the country'.

Business visas, the police said, did not permit aliens to work in South Africa and certainly, not a large number of mainland Chinese.

Then followed the first surprise: on the authority of a South African cabinet minister, the Chinese contingent was released from custody, even though the Ministry of Home Affairs was explicit that the activity of the group had violated the terms of their stay. The second surprise came when another minister interceded and prevented the Chinese group from being deported.

An observation made by a Western diplomat at the time was that the Chinese had gained regular and routine access to an extremely high-security nuclear establishment. Moreover, while this went on for months, nobody questioned their presence. Another source claimed that the group put in ten and twelve-hour shifts, six days a week. Somebody was in a desperate hurry.

What was of concern to those familiar with NPT Accords was that while the original contract for the sale was concluded between South Africa and China in the summer of 1997, almost nothing was made public about the deal. It hadn't even gone through Parliament, a pre-requisite for state-owned enterprises. In fact, it only became newsworthy when the so-called 'Chinese illegals' were arrested.

Had this event not caught the eye of the individual who tipped off the authorities, there might have been nothing to prevent the entire plant from leaving the country. And that would have taken place even though South Africa is a signatory to the Nuclear Suppliers Group, or NSG.

According to David Albright, the president of Washington's Institute for Science and International Security (ISIS), NSG provides clear dual-use guidelines for the export of such equipment.

'It would appear that these were not observed,' he stated. This is pertinent because under SA government regulations, the Council for Nonproliferation of Weapons of Mass Destruction of the Department of Trade and Industry – an interdepartmental export control body headed by the same Mr Abdul Minty, who for a time, sat on the IAEA Board of Governors in Vienna – should have been informed as a simple matter of procedure.

Since Pelindaba was then and still is a high-security government installation, the people in charge of the installation were obviously aware of what was taking place in their own backyard. But nothing was said and one must ask why this was allowed to happen and more salient, *on whose authority.*

Also, such shipments require end-user certificates since a zirconium tube plant is classified as dual-use or nuclear-related equipment. The South African government has always been aware that such transfers cannot take place without official sanction.

At issue here, said *NuclearFuel*, was a facility that had been in use until 1993 to make zirconium tubing for fuel loaded at the two Koeberg nuclear reactors just north of Cape Town. The sequence of events went something like this:

Early 1997, South Africa's Atomic Energy Commission requested tenders for the sale of the zirconium facility. Brokered in the Channel Islands by a firm calling itself Pacific Development Services, a

Chapter 10
The Unanswered 'Hit' on Pelindaba in November 2007

Multi-level underground nuclear storage vaults at a facility near Pretoria known as 'The Circle' where the assembled bombs were housed. (Photo: Institute for Science and International Security, Washington DC)

deal was concluded with the China National Nonferrous Industry Corporation at Shaanzi in north-central China. The price, quoted by Dr Stumpf, was $4,6 million.

Still more peculiar was that subsequent attempts by the media to make contact either with the broker or the listed company, failed. This raises another issue: if the deal between the governments of China and South Africa was legitimate, why would anyone have involved an obscure middleman who is not only untraceable, but has yet to come forward to clarify some of the more sensitive issues? Clearly, something is seriously amiss.

Dr Stumpf has said in a public statement afterwards: 'We will get an end-user statement from China before the plant leaves South Africa.'

The background to the zirconium plant is interesting. Originally it had been part of a nuclear fuel production complex for the Cape Town nuclear power plant at Koeberg and cost US$42 million to build. Since final qualification of the plant for nuclear-grade zirconium alloy cladding was achieved in 1988, it had produced 75,000 tubes for the Cape's reactors. The plant was shut down in 1993 after international sanctions against South Africa were lifted and cheaper tubes became available from France.

The AEC has since stated that it had tried to convert the zirconium factory to non-nuclear use but failed because of 'the very specialised nature of the installation'.

According to a statement issued at the time by the South African Ministry of Foreign Affairs, 'there are three pieces of equipment in the zirconium plant which require official authorisation under the Nuclear Suppliers' Group dual-use guidelines'. Stumpf described these as CNC machine tools used to make complex moulds.

Washington's comments on the subject included a statement that, independent of a pledge provided by China to cease nuclear trade with Iran (in exchange for nonproliferation certification by the Americans), it was not impossible that Beijing could still go through with the export to Tehran.

Questioned about the Iranian link, Stumpf said that the sale to China was limited only to equipment in the plant.

'China won't get any transfer of technology,' he added.

The Iranian connection with South Africa did not end there. Following the appearance of an article about the sale of the tube factory in *Pointer*, another Jane's publication, ('Is Iran in RSA-China Zirconium Deal?') South African Minister Abdul Minty wrote a letter of protest to Jane's Information Group in Britain.

Dated 9 March 1998, it states: '... the article is filled with half truths and innuendo and the author's investigation uses as a basis another inaccurate report appearing in *NuclearFuel*' (published in Washington DC 12 January 1998). Minty also made the point that South Africa's relations with the United States in regard to nuclear matters were exemplary.

The thrust of the article is inaccurate, he goes on. 'It indicates incorrectly that the whole contract was done under cover of darkness and even with the hope that the zirconium tube plant could leave (the country) without anyone knowing that South Africa had not complied with all the requirements of the Nuclear Suppliers Group (NSG).'

That is 'clearly not part of this government's policy ... nor it's style,' Minister Abdul Minty declared.

Chapter 10
The Unanswered 'Hit' on Pelindaba in November 2007

So what are the facts with this disturbing event that clearly attempted to elude government oversight?

- Details of the contract came to light after police, acting on a tip-off, raided Pelindaba because the Chinese group involved had originally entered South Africa on business visas. On prima facie evidence, they had no right to be in the country for any other purpose, never mind have access to and work in a nuclear-sensitive installation.
- As a result of that action, a journalist with the *Independent* newspaper group broke the story.
- The application to export the equipment on the Nuclear Suppliers' Group dual-use equipment list was made five days *after* the paper first reported the account of the planned sale to China. This was confirmed in a letter from Stumpf, to the editor of *NuclearFuel* dated 13 January 1998.
- According to a subsequent report in *NuclearFuel* (9 March); only after the story appeared in the press, was it disclosed that the Chinese had been working at Pelindaba. This too, was in Dr Waldo Stumpf's letter.
- Following these developments, according to *NuclearFuel*, 'Western officials and experts raised concern that South Africa's export control regime was not functioning smoothly.'

It is significant that there have since been more nuclear-related events reported from South Africa.

There was a report by a Pretoria-based television station that a nuclear smuggling case was in the process of being handled in a South African court house. Because of security restrictions that involved 'gag orders', it was not established whether the case was related to Pelindaba.

Also, at the time of the Pelindaba attack, another nuclear-linked case emerged. This one involved the attempted smuggling of high-voltage switches used to coordinate the detonation of the explosive trigger for a uranium-fuelled atomic bomb. As Dan Yurman questioned, was it someone's plan to hijack the pieces of a nuclear weapon through different channels?

More recently, on 8 November 2009, a woman appeared in Cape Town Magistrate's Court on charges of helping to smuggle parts used in manufacturing nuclear weapons from the United States to South Africa. This woman, Marisa Sketo, aged 46, allegedly helped to export nuclear weapon parts illegally from South Africa to Pakistan and was facing charges under the Weapons of Mass Destruction Act. An unnamed American source reportedly disclosed that the parts were 'rapid high-voltage electric switches'.

A nuclear weapons expert subsequently explained that the switches 'were used in nuclear weapons'. Most likely they were Krytron detonation switches or something similar.

Nuclear weapons can't be manufactured without them, explained the expert. 'It's an essential part in making atomic bombs.'

1 Blog: Idaho Samizdat – http://djysrv.blogspot.com.
2 Michael Wines: 'Break-In at Nuclear Site Baffles South Africa', New York Times, 15 November 2007.
3 Al J. Venter: *Iran's Nuclear Option*, Casemate Publishing, Philadelphia, 2005 pp. 156–162 and by the same author, *Allah's Bomb: The Islamic Quest for Nuclear Weapons*, Lyons Press, New Haven, 2007 pp. 181–185.

Close-up view of the steel bomb casings, which at one stage towards the end of the Border War came within a whisker of being deployed after the Angolan Army had been accused of firing chemical weapons at South African troops. (Photo: Pierre Lowe Victor)

CHAPTER ELEVEN

VALENTINE STRASSER – AFRICA'S VAGABOND KING

When 25-year-old Valentine Strasser seized power in Sierra Leone in 1992, he became the world's youngest head of state. He was also responsible for bringing in the South African mercenary group Executive Outcomes in a bid to counter the rebel insurgency that had enveloped his nation. Today he lives with his mother and spends his days drinking gin by the roadside. What went wrong?

Simon Akam tells all in *The New Statesman*

There are two ways to drive inland from Freetown. The first is to go through the eastern, poorer quarters of the Sierra Leonean capital. There decrepit vehicles jam narrow streets lined with mouldering clapboard houses. With such heavy congestion, it can take many hours to make the journey. The alternative is to take the so-called mountain road. You drive up into the hills, past the camp of the British army-led training team left over from Tony Blair's little war in 2000. Soon the tarmac ends and a dirt road threads past straggling villages into the forest.

The track of reddish laterite – which bypasses the city and its traffic – is treacherous after rain, and traces a route down into a broad valley. A mile or so before it rejoins the main highway leading inland, a side road branches off to the left through a quiet village. At the far end of the settlement stands a faded sheet-metal advertisement for Goodyear tyres. And there, most afternoons, a tall man with close-cropped, greying hair sits on an open porch by the side of the road, often dressed in just a pair of shorts. If you arrive late in the day he may be drinking gin from a plastic sachet. His name is Valentine Strasser; he is 45, and was once the youngest head of state in the world.

'Bokkie' was the Soviet-era Mi-17 helicopter that Sandline brought in to cope with some of the logistical problems the country faced during the period that Strasser was in control. (Photo: Author)

It is more than a dozen years since the end of the 11-year civil war in Sierra Leone. In 2007 power changed hands at the ballot box, and yet, to the outside world, the iconography of that long war – child soldiers, violent amputations and conflict diamonds – is ineradicable.

The story of Strasser, a young man who, in 1992, seized power in a military coup at the age of 25 – and ruled for four years until he was deposed by the same method – is unusual even by the experience of West African dictatorships. His improbable rise to executive power and his precipitous fall to roadside penury is a parable of the human consequences of premature kingship.

Strasser says he was born on 15 September 1966 in Freetown. His father was a teacher, his mother a small-time businesswoman. After attending the Sierra Leone Grammar School (founded in 1845), he became an army officer, serving in neighbouring Liberia as part of a regional peacekeeping mission, the Economic Community of West African States Monitoring Group (ECOMOG). Like Sierra Leone, Liberia was established as a colony of freed slaves. Civil war had broken out there in 1989, and in 1991 ECOMOG was attempting to secure order in the capital, Monrovia. 'Fighting was going on in every corner from three factions,' Strasser told me one evening, speaking softly and with a slight lilt.

Chapter 11
Valentine Strasser – Africa's Vagabond King

After seven months in Liberia, he returned home. The war followed him. In March 1991, rebel fighters crossed over from Liberia into the remote eastern part of the country. This incursion of as many as 2,000 men, most of whom were on loan from the Liberian warlord Charles Taylor, marked the beginning of Sierra Leone's decade-long conflict.

Led by Foday Sankoh, the rebels came to be known as the Revolutionary United Front (RUF). Sankoh was a former army corporal and one-time jobbing photographer and, like others among the initial RUF leadership, he had received training at al-Mathabh al-Thauriya al-Alamiya, Muammar Gaddafi's world revolutionary headquarters in Benghazi, Libya.

By 1991, Sierra Leone was close to ruin. After independence from Britain in 1961, there had been a brief period of relatively functional democracy under the leadership of Sir Milton Margai. He died in 1964 and was succeeded by his less respected stepbrother Albert, who disbursed vital positions in government to people of the Mende tribe regardless of qualifications.

The decline accelerated under Siaka Stevens, a trade unionist who was elected in 1967 but did not become prime minister until

Freetown is not the biggest city in West Africa but it is certainly one of the most crowded. Things were worse during the civil war when a million or more refugees crowded in from the countryside because of rebel activity. Neall Ellis took this photo of the city while flying over it.

This action took place while Valentine Strasser ruled the roost – an Executive Outcomes operation in the jungle country to the east, planned and coordinated by Roelf van Heerden, still one of the best counter-insurgency commanders in the field. (Photo: Author)

the following year because of a series of coups. In 1971, Stevens declared himself president. Charming but spectacularly corrupt, he systematically degraded state institutions and operated a system of personal patronage. He plundered Sierra Leone's diamond wealth and even entered into negotiations with an American company to have toxic waste dumped in the country in exchange for a fee of $25m.

"At the age of 80, Stevens left office with an estimated fortune of $500m," says Sareta Ashraph, a London-based lawyer formerly at the UN-backed Special Court for Sierra Leone who is now working on a history of the civil war.

"The sheer corruption and violent repression of the Stevens regime extinguished the hopes of an entire generation and laid the foundation for the country's brutal civil war."

Following riots in Freetown, Stevens stepped down in 1985. Two years later, at a ceremony held in the grounds of parliament, a local preacher compared the former head of state's reign to a '17-year plague of locusts' in an address that was broadcast on national radio.

The next president was Joseph Momoh, a military officer. Despite his initial promises of reform, corruption persisted under him. He acquired the nickname Dandogo, which means 'idiot' in the language of the Limba people of northern Sierra Leone. By 1991, Momoh had been in power for six years and the nation was ripe for revolt.

Wounded in Action

On Strasser's return from Liberia, he joined a unit fighting the rebel incursion in the east. The conditions for the government troops were wretched. Logistical support was poor, supplies of weapons and ammunition were limited and there was scant medical provision. On 1 May 1991, he received a shrapnel wound to the leg while defending a bridge.

'I was inside a bunker and I got blasted,' he said. 'It was a shell that actually landed on the sandbags.' On another occasion when we spoke, he said: 'No casevac [casualty evacuation] procedures were made. In terms of helicopters or ambulances to shift the casualties … the problem was not with the level of training, but with the equipment that was available and the manpower. My disgruntlement stemmed from the fact that after I got wounded in action, I could not be evacuated, either by an ambulance or a helicopter."

Aware that they were fighting a war that their political masters would not resource properly, Strasser and other junior officers began plotting a coup. On 29 April 1992, they launched Operation Daybreak, raiding the office of the president in central Freetown as well as the lavish old presidential lodge off Spur Road in the West End of the city. They found President Momoh hiding in the bathroom of the lodge, wearing a dressing gown. He was bundled into an army helicopter and taken over the border to Guinea.

Strasser emerged as the public face of the uprising, in part because of his supposed language skills – he spoke English well enough to read out a statement on the radio. As a captain, he was also of a higher rank than his co-conspirators. Some argue, too, that Strasser got the top post because those around him felt that he could be manipulated easily. "He was chosen in spite of, not because of, his leadership capabilities," says Joe Alie, a professor of history at Fourah Bay College in Freetown and the author of a 2007 history of the country since independence.

Joseph Opala, an American historian who first came to Sierra Leone in 1974 as a Peace Corps volunteer and has spent much of his adult life in the country, witnessed the wild early days of the new regime. Avuncular and bearded, he runs a project to restore the former British slave fortress on Bunce Island, near Freetown. Shortly after the 1992 coup, Opala was rounded up by soldiers and taken to State House, the white-walled seat of power in the city centre that bears an odd resemblance to a lighthouse.

The windows in the president's office had been shot out. Momoh's staff stood erect, in abject terror. Sitting around wearing camouflage fatigues and Ray-Ban sunglasses were the young officers who had mounted the insurrection. They were cleaning their Kalashnikovs and were stoned.

Strasser turned to Opala. "A wan know if America go recognise we gobment?" he said, speaking in Krio, the Sierra Leonean lingua franca. Krio is built on an English chassis but has a distinct grammatical structure and uses borrowed words from a plethora of other sources. In response to Strasser's question ("I want to know if America will recognise our government?"), Opala asked him in turn if he had spoken to the American ambassador. The new leader replied that he had, but that he had not understood what the diplomat had told him. "En English too big," he said. "A no undastan natin way e talk."

An extraordinary scene ensued. At Strasser's direction, Opala left State House and walked through deserted streets to the US embassy, which at the time lay one block away. There he told a jumpy marine guard that he had a personal message for the ambassador from the

Chapter 11
Valentine Strasser – Africa's Vagabond King

The two Mi-24 helicopter gunships operated by Neall Ellis and his friends in Sierra Leone. In the latter stages of his campaign, the chopper spare parts had to be pirated from one machine to the other simply to keep one aloft. (Photo: Neall Ellis collection)

coup leaders. He was allowed in and explained to the head of the mission that the heads of the new government wanted to know if Washington would recognise it. The ambassador, a black American named Johnny Young, said that he had spoken at length to Strasser and had outlined the position of the US administration – that in general it did not acknowledge regimes installed by force but, in this instance, because the previous government had also not been democratically elected and considering the dire condition of the country, it was prepared to make an exception.

Ukrainian Connection

In the early days, Captain Strasser's coup was popular. There were promises of a fresh start for the country. Young people were mobilised to keep Freetown clean. Celebratory murals and other street art flourished. The new rulers of Sierra Leone called themselves the National Provisional Ruling Council (NPRC) and Strasser was the council's chairman.

For all the jubilation, there was still a war to fight. Out in the bush, the army continued fighting the rebels. The junior officers who formed the NPRC had experienced the wretched conditions of the government troops. They wanted to improve matters, so besides tripling the size of the army, they went shopping.

When the author visited Sierra Leone under the auspices of Executive Outcomes in the mid-1990s, he moved about in this Mi-17 that had been flown in from Angola. (Photo: Author)

There have been few better periods in history to buy guns than in the early 1990s. The Soviet Union had disintegrated, leaving huge arsenals in the hands of often unpaid and unsupervised officers. Dollars went a long way and official documentation was circumnavigable. Crucially, too, Sierra Leone's new leaders had a Ukrainian connection. During the cold war, the Soviet Union had funded scholarships for students from the developing world. Sierra Leoneans were among those who took up the chance to study in the USSR. One such was Steven Bio, who had studied in Kiev. A cousin of Julius Maada Bio, a member of the new junta, he had useful connections with gun runners in the Ukraine. He would be the go-between. [Maada Bio has since been elected the Sierra Leone leader.]

However, as the arms bazaar began to thrive abroad, the jubilation that had greeted Strasser's assumption of power at home began to diminish. In October 1992, the RUF took Koidu Town, capital of Kono District in the diamond-mining east. The capture of the town marked a step up in the conflict.

In Freetown, the NPRC government announced that it had uncovered an attempted coup and disarmed the instigators. Executions followed on a beach on the outskirts of the city, but the

29 people shot were considered to be innocent, and soon afterwards Strasser declared a nationwide period of mourning. 'To people who were politically savvy, what it meant was that there was no coherent government,' Opala told me. "The conclusion was obvious – no one was in charge." (Nineteen years later, the mention of the executions stirred Strasser to anger. 'Fuck off, man. In Texas they kill people every day,' he said when I pressed him on the subject.)

Power in Sierra Leone was now in the hands of a group of very young men. 'The children are running the country,' it was said. A photograph of Strasser at the 1993 Commonwealth Heads of Government meeting in Limassol, Cyprus, shows a young man in sunglasses and a T-shirt, emblazoned with the words 'Sunny Days in Cyprus'.

There were parties, too. Strasser made Valentine's Day a great national celebration, along with Bob Marley's birthday. The junta favoured pale-skinned women, creating a craze for bleaching among girls in Freetown. Women who tried to lighten their skin tone with chemicals were called 'wonchee girls'. Older Sierra Leoneans still mention that phrase readily when asked about their impressions of the NPRC. But perhaps the most telling indication of the onset of decadence in Strasser himself was his choice of accommodation.

Kabasa Lodge is in many ways the embodiment of all that is wrong with post-independence Sierra Leone. Built by the kleptocratic Siaka Stevens, it is a monumental structure the size of a missile silo or respectable late-medieval castle, and squats on a hilltop in Juba, in the West End of Freetown, with expansive views both out over the Atlantic and to the forested hills of the peninsula south of the city. It was here that Strasser chose to live.

The 1992 coup had decapitated the command structure of the army; brigadiers were expected to take their orders from captains and lieutenants. In the countryside, both rebels and the poorly trained soldiers were often more interested in looting property from civilians than in fighting each other. The line between the resistance and the rebellion became blurred, reflected in the neologism 'Sobel' – soldier by day, rebel by night.

By late 1993, though, the much-enlarged government army was close to defeating the rebels. In December Strasser called a ceasefire, but that turned out to be a mistake: the RUF regrouped and began setting up jungle bases around the country in 1994 and 1995. The rebels were a threat once more and the government was losing control.

Glittering Prizes

In the south, the RUF attacked the facilities of Sierra Rutile, a company mining titanium ore, cutting off a crucial source of state revenue. The rebels set up a base in the town of Moyamba which put them within a day's striking distance of Freetown. Vehicle ambushes left few people willing to travel upcountry.

With the security situation deteriorating, the NPRC was becoming increasingly unpopular. It was then that Strasser turned to foreign fighters. White mercenaries are a charged subject in Africa, conjuring up a host of associations, from 'Mad' Mike Hoare in the Congo of the 1960s to Richard Burton and Roger Moore in the 1978 film *The Wild Geese* and, more recently, the farce of the 2004 'wonga coup' in Equatorial Guinea. However, in Sierra Leone, shortly after South Africa's first multiracial elections in 1994, ex-apartheid enforcers re-engaged as soldiers of fortune and ended up saving huge numbers of lives. They nearly saved the country, too.

In February 1995, the NPRC engaged the services of a company called Gurkha Security Guards (GSG), which employed Nepalese ex-British-army troops led by Robert MacKenzie. This American officer had fought in Vietnam and, in spite of an arm injury sustained there, he later passed selection for the Rhodesian SAS. He also worked as a correspondent for *Soldier of Fortune* magazine. His masterminding of GSG's involvement in Sierra Leone was a debacle: he was quickly ambushed along with Strasser's aide-de-camp, Abu Tarawalli. It is still not known for sure if those responsible were the rebels, or whether he was betrayed by Sierra Leonean army soldiers he was meant to be assisting.

After MacKenzie went missing, his wife asked Al Venter, compiler of this volume of stories, with a long interest in mercenary affairs – to visit Sierra Leone to investigate what had happened. Venter discovered that a group of nuns had also been captured and taken to the camp where MacKenzie was held. The nuns were eventually released, but before then they saw the American strung up, and his heart cut out.

The next group of white mercenaries to land in Sierra Leone was Executive Outcomes, which blazed a trail for private military companies of the modern era. Composed predominantly of former South African Special Forces troops, Executive Outcomes was active in Angola during the civil war there, fighting both for and against Jonas Savimbi's South African-funded rebel army, Unita.

The brokers of the deal that brought Executive Outcomes to Sierra Leone included Simon Mann, later of the botched 'wonga

The Executive Outcomes main staging post in the Kono diamond fields was this camp overlooking the town of Koidu in the east of the country. It was supplied a couple of times a week from Freetown by one of the Hips. (Photo: Author)

coup'; Tony Buckingham, who now runs Heritage Oil, a company whose prospectus hints at the risk that the media may mention his previous mercenary adventures; and Eeben Barlow, a former South African Special Forces officer. The role of Executive Outcomes was to combat the rebels. The mercenaries would be paid in diamond concessions and cash.

They arrived in Sierra Leone in small numbers – about a hundred on the ground at any one time. Most of the operatives were black but the leadership was white. They used helicopters, they had their own logistical train and they were fearsomely competent. 'These people knew Africa,' Venter said. 'They set up their own supply units ... they brought everything with them. They drove [the rebels] well away from Freetown, then they launched an operation into Kono. They did it; they turned the war around in record time.'

Joseph Opala recalled how Executive Outcomes would give a radio to each of the paramount chiefs, the leaders originally appointed from the ranks of local kings and queens by British colonial administrators at the end of the 19th Century. 'They said: "If you call us we will be there in 15 minutes." And they were.'

The mercenaries achieved what thousands of UN peacekeepers five years later were unable to do: they stopped the war. 'At a total cost of $35m (just one-third of the government's annual defence budget), the fighting in Sierra Leone had ceased and over one million

Cobus Claassens, took this photo of a Soviet-era amphibious BMP-2 heading east towards the diamond fields with a motley crew of armed men onboard.

displaced persons returned to their homes,' wrote P.W. Singer of the Brookings Institution in his book *Corporate Warriors: the Rise of the Privatised Military Industry*.

'They did what they were here to do – that I can assure you,' Strasser told me. 'In fact, fighting stopped. It was a war machine that was capable of handling the security difficulties there at the time.'

But the mercenaries were soon forced out of Sierra Leone by other countries' disapproval. There was substantial international support for a peace accord that was negotiated in Abidjan, Côte d'Ivoire, in 1996, and the RUF made withdrawal of foreign forces a provision of signing it. Executive Outcomes left in January 1997. Without a disarmament programme in place, the Abidjan agreement proved ineffective. Clashes continued and after another military coup in May 1997, the violence escalated once more. In January 1999, the war reached its nadir when RUF fighters sacked Freetown in Operation No Living Thing.

As for Strasser, he was deposed in a palace coup on 16 January 1996. He had gone to inspect a passing-out parade at the military training academy in Benguema, less than 50 kilometres from Freetown. In the afternoon he went, without a substantial security escort, to a meeting at the defence headquarters at Cockerill, back in the capital city. There he was overpowered and bundled into a helicopter and flown to Guinea, just as had happened to Joseph

Momoh four years earlier. Strasser's successor, the leader of this second coup, was Julius Maada Bio. The new leader was still only in his early thirties.

When I asked Strasser why his reign ended as it did, he refused to accept there had been a coup. He claimed he had merely stepped down at the end of the ten years of military service for which he had signed up. That statement is fantastical, and must be discounted.

Anything for a Quiet Life

The post-deposition period is perhaps the strangest in Strasser's unusual life, taking him from West Africa to Coventry in the West Midlands, UK. When the international community had negotiated with the NPRC over the reintroduction of civilian rule, one of the incentives offered to members of the junta in return for relinquishing power was the opportunity to study in the west. And even though Strasser had eventually lost power by less graceful means, he was able to take up this chance.

Warwick University's decision to consider admitting him was controversial. 'When it became known who he was, there was a lot of disquiet in the law school and the university,' recalls Roger Leng, an expert in criminal law at Warwick who later taught Strasser. There was a fierce internal row over whether he should be allowed to enter as a student, despite assurances from reputable sources to the university that Strasser was not responsible for human rights violations.

Eventually he was accepted and took a foundation course to compensate for his lack of formal qualifications. The intention was that he would then progress to a law degree.

Leng was surprised when he met Strasser for the first time. 'He was quiet. I don't really think he was equipped to study at this level,' he said. 'I'd expected a swaggering, arrogant guy and he was quite the opposite.'

Strasser's second life as a civilian in England did not go well. His unwanted celebrity status was a problem. He took up residence in an anonymous red-brick terraced house at 47 Poplar Road in suburban Earlsdon in Coventry, the city nearest the university, but the local and national press began to take an interest in him. He claims, too, that his stipend was inadequate. It even turned out that among Strasser's fellow students in 1996 was a niece of one of the victims of the extrajudicial killings of December 1992.

According to him, the woman spoke against him on television and lobbied against him. The archives of *The Boar*, Warwick University's student newspaper, mention inquiries launched into his presence. 'The university's belief that Strasser's studies will contribute to the democratisation process has been attacked by those who consider that an individual with such a brutal background should not be afforded acceptance within wider society,' *The Boar* reported in October 1996.

Later he had an unsuccessful affair with a supermarket checkout girl. 'She knew who I was, because the papers in Coventry had things about me,' Strasser said. 'She knew I was a former dictator.'

Warwick University closed its file on Strasser in January 1998. A spokesman for the university, Peter Dunn, believes he left campus before then. 'My recollection was that he wrote to the university staff saying that he was leaving,' Dunn said. 'One of his concerns was that he was fed up with his history in Sierra Leone being constantly brought up.' Strasser corroborated that account. 'I saw front-page articles saying "former dictator" and "human rights violations",' he said. 'It was impossible.'

After dropping out of Warwick he moved to London, but there he found no peace. Albert Mahoi, a Sierra Leonean who goes by the nickname of Carlos, was running a business in south-east London that offered cosmetics, money transfers and international calls when he met Strasser. Mahoi recalled encountering him at a nightclub in Camberwell; another Sierra Leonean exile was abusing him and Mahoi felt he had to intervene.

'I said: "Don't do that – he was our president,"' Mahoi told me. 'I talked to Strasser, I told him to calm down.' He bought the former head of state a bottle of Courvoisier. 'He was stressed up; you know when someone loses everything. There was no respect for him.'

With the *Guardian* newspaper questioning why a one-time West African strongman was living in London, Strasser left the country. The Home Office would not comment on whether his visa had been revoked. In December 2000, he went briefly to the Gambia and then back to Sierra Leone. And he is still there.

Moving With the Times

The civil war finally ended in 2002 after a Blair-led British military intervention stiffened a floundering UN peacekeeping mission. The peace has held, and in November the country will hold its third multiparty election since the war's end. Large iron-ore mining projects were coming on line, and the IMF predicted massive GDP growth.

Yet Sierra Leone remains impoverished; it ranks 180th (out of 187 countries) in the UN's Human Development Index and per-capita GDP stands at just US$325 a year. The country also has a large pool of marginalised ex-combatants and other young men who continue to pose a threat to stability. Despite enormous expenditure of foreign aid, corruption remains endemic and progress on infrastructure frustratingly slow.

Desmond Luke is a former chief justice who trained at both Cambridge and Oxford. 'One of my biggest sadnesses is when I travel out of Sierra Leone and I come back,' he told me recently at his house in Freetown. 'The only change one really does see is that it seems to get dirtier.'

Some of the figures from the war years are still in politics, too. Maada Bio, who deposed Strasser and was briefly head of state, became the candidate for the main opposition party in a subsequent election.

Strasser lives quietly with his mother, Beatrice, in the house he built at Grafton, east of Freetown. The once-elegant white villa is run-down and the walls are stained. Across the potholed road stand the burnt-out ruins of another house that Strasser had built while in office, but which was bombed by Nigerian fighter jets during the civil war.

He receives a government pension of 200,000 leones (about $50) a month. That is an improvement on the 64,000 leones ($15) he used to get. He is desperately poor and does not even have a mobile phone to hand as he sits by the roadside in the afternoons. 'It's a new set of circumstances and I've got to accept them,' he said of his life with his mother.

I asked Sheka Tarawalie, Sierra Leone's Deputy Minister of Information, why the former leader received such meagre support. 'You know, Strasser was not an elected head of state,' Tarawalie said. 'That is one of the problems. He came in as a military man.'

'Bad Dictators'

One evening last summer, at the start of the rainy season, I arranged to meet Strasser for a final dinner. I went to see him with a friend and a British researcher resident in Freetown. We drove over the mountain road and picked up Strasser from his house.

He sat in the front seat of my Land Rover, wearing trainers and cut-off jeans. At his suggestion, we went to eat at a Safecon petrol station on the main road upcountry. There we sat at a table outside in the evening light.

It did not go well. He was drunk at the start of the meal and became agitated. When I mentioned his time at Warwick, he raged at me – I was his assassin, he said. I was the president of America. He became increasingly unstable and threatened to have us arrested, only to change his tone. 'I'm not going to arrest you,' he shouted. 'Otherwise you'll say I'm Idi Amin or another bad dictator like Colonel Gaddafi.'

Then he wrote this, in block capitals, in my notebook: 'Europe still continues to underdevelop Africa. Africa's raw materials are Europe's tool to keep black Africa under so that Western Europe continues to improve.'

There was something of Lear in Strasser that evening, the broken king raging at the injustices of the world. I met him again several times after that and he was always sober and lucid. Yet, that night I had seen a different Valentine Strasser and begun to understand something of the burdens he carried.

As we drove back over the hills in the tropical dark, it was clear to me what a terrible misfortune it was for him to have been crowned by accident.

James Appleton contributed additional reporting from Warwick University; article courtesy of *The New Statesman*, **2 February 2012.**

CHAPTER TWELVE

LANDMINES – HIDDEN KILLERS

A South African military-related website ran the following ad in April 2013. It read: '... reports that the United Nations has disclosed that there is an urgent need for 24 people to clear and destroy landmines in the Sudan. Salaries range from between US$5,000 and $7,000 a month.' Contact details were provided.

W ho would have believed that it was possible to use rats to detect landmines? Unlikely, but true, because exactly that has been taking place in Mozambique, in some places not far from South Africa's border with our eastern neighbour.

There is a difference though: these creatures are termed 'hero rats' and some are almost the size of cats. But they really can sniff out live ordnance. In fact, they have been doing so for years and have saved countless lives.

The Mozambique civil war ended almost 20 years ago and one of the enduring legacies is the number of landmines that were spread about the country, as well as the skeletons of mine victims, often left untouched for years because nobody was brave or stupid enough to enter the minefields to recover the dead.

Employing rats to identify landmines emerged by a rather curious process. It was common knowledge in the old days that the ancient Chinese could diagnose tuberculosis by the smell of a person's saliva on a flame or hot rock. Afrikaners use the word *tering* to describe the smell of tar, which is the same odour that TB patients exude and in Africa the disease is endemic.

Then somebody came up with the idea that if it was possible to actually smell TB with our dilapidated olfactory senses, then dogs – and possibly other animals – might be able to detect it at a much earlier stage. That was when 'hero rats' were brought in for trials.

It is significant that in Tanzania – where less than half of TB patients are diagnosed before death – these rodents detected almost a thousand cases of tuberculosis in 2008 and 2009. An NGO group in Tanzania subsequently estimated that the rats prevented at least 14,000 transmissions. Bart Weetjens, the brain behind another non-governmental organisation that calls itself APOPO – a Dutch acronym meaning Anti-Personnel Land Mines Detection Product Development – thought that it was possible that if 'hero rats' could detect disease, they might also be able to point out explosives hidden in the ground.

Previously, the Belgian-born Weetjens spent several years involved in landmine recovery in Third World countries. In the spring of 1995, he was made aware that scientists were studying the use of gerbils in bomb detection, but they were using a system involving brain electrodes which Weetjens found unsustainable. Instead, he declared, he wanted a locally based solution that might empower communities, like impoverished societies in Africa. That was when he was reminded of TB experiments involving 'hero rats'.

Soviet-era anti-tank landmines like the TM-46 and subsequently, the TM-57, with more than 6 kg of TNT, could easily blow a vehicle to scrap, which is what happened here. Both are triggered by pressure switches or tilt-rod fuses. (Photo: Author's collection)

To actually get the project going was no easy task. The International Campaign to Ban Landmines recorded that from 1999 to 2009, landmines and related devices were responsible for 73,576 casualties worldwide. Campaign data from 2007 say there were 5,426 recorded casualties, with almost a fifth in two dozen African states, among them Mozambique, Zimbabwe and Angola. In regions where resources were scarce, Weetjens felt that rats were ideal for the task, but, he admits, he first had to get past people ridiculing the concept.

Gradually, with numerous experiments, his annual report of his APOPO group disclosed certain advantages of using rats for this work.

First, he recounts, rat olfactory senses are superb. Second, 'hero rats' are native to the African continent. So, unlike sniffer dogs brought in from abroad, rodents are impervious to tropical disease. Most important though, quite large 'hero rats' are rarely heavier than the three-to-ten kilograms usually required to trip a mine.

'It also helps that mine-sniffing rats are not bonded to individual trainers or, as dogs might be, prone to ennui,' suggested another expert.

Weetjens explains: 'Cost is especially an advantage in Africa. It takes limited skill and only six to eight months to train a rat – or possibly a year for a "slow" rat, because some are smarter than others.'

Moreover, the cost to train a rat is about US$7,700, roughly a third of what it costs to train a dog to do the same work. Where dogs need expansive kennel facilities and regular veterinary care because of African climates, rats need little more than regular feeding.

Robert Bryce, in an insightful article for the *Foreign Affairs*[1] wrote that nearly a century ago, while serving as a British liaison officer to the Arab tribes during World War I, the British Arabist T.E. Lawrence developed many of the techniques of modern insurgent warfare. Lawrence's fluency in Arabic and a profound understanding of Arab culture helped him invigorate the Arab Revolt of 1916/18. His savvy military tactics certainly ensured its success against the Turks, says Bryce.

He goes on: 'In his memoir, *Seven Pillars of Wisdom*, Lawrence revealed his most effective tactic: Mines were the best weapon yet discovered to make the regular working of their trains costly and uncertain for our Turkish enemy.' He goes on to say that but for Lawrence's pioneering use of precisely placed explosives, the Arab Revolt might well have failed.

In Afghanistan today, the insurgents are using similar weapons against Coalition Forces. Instead of referring to them as landmines, they are called IEDs – for 'Improvised Explosive Devices' – and vehicles, as opposed to trains (in the TE Lawrence era) are being targeted. The effect is just as devastating.

The statistics are sobering. The number of mines being used in Asia, and the share of casualties for which they are responsible, says Bryce, dwarf anything ever seen before by the American military. 'During World War II three per cent of US combat deaths were caused by mines or booby traps. In Korea that figure was four per cent. By 1967, during the Vietnam War, it was nine per cent, and the

Pentagon began experimenting with armoured boots. From June to November of 2005, IEDs laid by insurgents in Iraq were responsible for 65 per cent of American combat deaths and roughly half of all non-fatal injuries, things are hardly any better today...

It is to be accepted that both the nature and deployment of landmines have evolved since Lawrence's day. Iraqi and Taliban insurgents are armed with a surfeit of explosives and ordnance, ranging from TNT to artillery shells. In addition, Iraqi dissidents were making bombs from some of the 380 tons of high explosives that vanished from an Iraqi bunker after the American invasion early in 2003. The missing arsenal includes truckloads of HMX and RDX, all of it military-grade explosives so powerful that they were monitored by the International Atomic Energy Agency (IAEA) before the war. Some of this ordnance has filtered to other countries, including several in Africa and here, Mali – where al-Qaeda elements, or rather AQIM (Al-Qaeda in the Maghreb), active against government forces in Mali especially – is a case in point.

He explains that detonation techniques are myriad. The insurgents have used pressure switches, infrared beams, cellphones, garage-door openers and even garden hoses (which, when run over by a vehicle, send a stream of water into a small bottle, activating a detonator).

The international community seems committed to clearing the minefields of the world, but there is trouble in the workplace.

A US State Department survey titled *Hidden Killers: The Global Problem with Uncleared Landmines*[2] identified almost 70 countries with landmine problems. It also expressed concern at the slow speed that this work was being accomplished and, more importantly, the variable degree of certainty that an area – once certified as clear – is actually completely free of explosives.

This has been a recurring problem in places such as Cambodia, Afghanistan, Angola, south Sudan and elsewhere and is invariably the consequence of ongoing conflict. Africa with its inordinate range of problems is likely to be the focus of much of the world's mine-clearing endeavours for the future.

There are almost two dozen African states that need minefields cleared and all are eager for help. Some are not averse to embellishing their problems. Egypt, for instance – in a bid to achieve a larger piece of the pie – claimed for many decades that there were still eight million mines left over from World War II. Cairo upped that figure to 24 million at an African Union conference held in South Africa;

Chapter 12
Landmines – Hidden Killers

On the left is a combination of three of the mines most commonly used in African guerrilla wars, with a box mine (so named because it is housed in a wooden box and tripped by a pressure switch), a TM-46 (top right) and an anti-personnel PMN-1 mine which is smaller than a human hand and will blow a man's foot off. On the right is another variant of this nefarious weapon. (Source: International Committee of the Red Cross)

the highest tally in the world. Of course much of it was nonsense.

Libya, too, has indicated that its 'millions of landmines' buried in the desert almost 70 years before be removed. When still in power, President Gadaffi said he wants to use land around Bengazi and Tobruk for underground water and for farming.

In Namibia, there are minefields still in place from a succession of border wars of the 1970s and 1980s. While some effort has gone towards removing them, much of this work has been piecemeal. Several areas were swept by the old SADF using rollers, but there was no physical or manual follow-up afterwards because it wasn't considered necessary at the time. The result is that casualties continue to mount.

It wasn't until after Desert Storm that the international mine-clearing community devoted real attention to standard operating procedures (SOPs) and the process continues to evolve.

Zimbabwe, too, has its problems, but not on the scale of some of the other countries, including the western Sahara, Ethiopia and Eritrea. Many of the mines still in the ground north of the Limpopo were laid in Rhodesia's 'cordon sanitaire' more than 30 years ago; mainly along its common border with Mozambique to the east. Though properly demarcated, these killing fields have proved hazardous to civilians, livestock as well as wild animals.

While the EU voted millions of dollars to clear them, there is purported to have been some unsavoury business, much of it linked to the arch tyrant Robert Mugabe and including local companies named as favourites in the tender process. Consequently, the issue is being looked at again.

In Mozambique things went a lot better. Officially, the Maputo government claims to have about a million mines along its borders. There are another 300,000 or more (mainly anti-personnel or AP in the lingo) mines that were internally laid. The UN concurs with this figure, but these have presented some serious problems because of a civil war that went on for far too long.

In Cambodia – where UNTAC[2] tended to be focused on short-term objectives – much of the work was fragmented to start with. Only when all aspects of mine-clearance work were vertically integrated into a single entity did things start moving. In retrospect, it is now accepted that not enough attention was given to post-UNTAC requirements for the continuation of the programme. This includes management skills and funding, the lack of which eventually led to complications. More serious, the reputation of the UN in mine-clearing in Cambodia took a knock. It soon became evident that the resultant lack of confidence worked against productive collaboration with NGOs, donors and sister UN agencies in other settings.[3]

This scenario was compounded in Angola, regarded by some authorities as the definitive case study how *not* to run a national mine-clearing operation.

In this huge West African country twice the size of Texas – with a population of between 11 and 15 million (a proper census has been impossible for decades) – a promising beginning soon gave way to an impasse that included the kind of bureaucratic in-fighting that, at its worst, if that be possible, started to resemble conditions in ungovernable Somalia. There were some huge differences as to how the problem should be tackled, which, in turn, resulted in bitter disputes over the assigned division of finances, labour and responsibility. There was also a significant failure to establish a clearly defined relationship between the Angolan government and the expatriate community on the ground.

As one observer who was in Angola at the time noted[4], 'Byzantine administrative and recruitment procedures caused additional grief.'

At the core of it, the UN-sponsored Central Mine Action Office (CMAO) had almost nothing to do with the government for the first year of mine-clearing. This body was originally created in 1994 to provide for the day-to-day management and coordination under the combined leadership of the Special Representative of the Secretary General and UCAH, a United Nations body responsible for humanitarian needs. Therefore, there were contrasting needs between those of 'Military UN' and 'Humanitarian UN'.

'CMAO was doomed from the start,' says a UN report.[5] 'Initially it was an ad hoc amalgam of staff and equipment from the UN Dept of Humanitarian Affairs and the Dept of Peacekeeping Operations and their respective field operations, UCAH and UNAVEM.

Externally this organisation was ignored. And while mine action plans for CMAO abound – the study team was given 11 different mine action plans written by different people over 19 months – none was ever given an operational budget. Nor is there evidence that any of the plans were approved formally within the United Nations system,' it states.

Also, it says a lot that no regular donor meetings on mine action were ever scheduled, though individuals did meet informally, usually in Luanda. Moreover, different sources of funding 'tended to foster institutional allegiances and work against a team endeavour.' In the end it was private companies that did the work under UN auspices.

This clearly untenable situation was further compounded by the government of President dos Santos hiving off on a development of its own. The minister responsible for such matters – without consulting the UN – demanded that MINARS (the Ministry for Social Reintegration and Assistance) be the leadership focus for all mine activities in Angola, naturally with appropriate 'incentives' in place, which went into his own pocket.

He then created a secondary opposition body, the National Institute for the Removal of Obstacles and Explosives (INAROE), which was totally superfluous to everything else linked to mine-clearing in the country just then.

There was a further impediment on the part of the government when vehicles and equipment intended for mine-clearing operations arrived at the ports of Luanda and Lobito Bay. All were seized and would not be released until taxes and import duties had been paid; and that in spite of the fact that until then, Luanda had not been asked to contribute a penny towards the biggest rehabilitation programme the country had experienced.

It is doubtful whether the Angolans ever paid anything towards the effort. Luanda pledged more than a million dollars in 1995; the check never arrived even though Angola is one of the major international earners of oil revenue and according to Washington, US$1 billion or more simply disappears in the accounting process *each year.*

Acrimony between the different players has resulted in further resources being wasted. Part of the UN programme[6] was geared to train Angolan nationals to lift their own mines once the United Nations had moved on. A training school was established for this purpose, manned by a full contingent of UN mine specialists. Due to government administrative, managerial and logistical obstacles (and the failure to grease the right palms), this entire crew completed a full six months in-country without instructing a single Angolan.

Governments pushed their own interests. Paris, through its own mine-clearing body, seconded an advisor to the director of the international body. This was done without consultation with anybody else. One of the results was that during the first three years of mine-clearance, less than 200 hectares of mined land were cleared.

Finally, there was Unita, the Angolan rebel group headed by Dr Jonas Savimbi. While still operational, Unita consistently tried (and succeeded) to hamper operations. As a result of one Unita delaying action on the Malange-Saurimo road in the north-east, a UN-sponsored mine-clearing team sat in the bush for 103 days (at $8,000 a day) while Savimbi prevaricated.

Significantly, once the teams did get through and started work, it was found that many of the anti-tank mines laid had been removed and stashed for possible use at some later date. The same applied to the road between Quelenges and Chongoroi in central Angola. On-site vapour samples proved that much, but more of that later. What soon became obvious to everybody involved in the UN mine-clearing effort was that Unita regarded the presence of these foreign teams with disdain; Savimbi's people had little regard for the 1994 Lusaka Protocol which should have been an instrument for peace. Meantime, Savimbi is long gone and things have improved only marginally.

What is obvious is that if the international community was better focused on removing landmines worldwide, the problem might not be insurmountable. This was the view of Dr Vernon Joynt, at that stage chief executive officer of Mechem – a South African company that had been lifting mines in Mozambique, Bosnia, Angola and elsewhere. He believed it was possible – with the technologies in hand – to solve the landmine problem in his lifetime.

Perhaps not, he added, in the 10 years envisaged by Initiative 2010 (where 20 donor countries were tasked to find a billion dollars a year for five years) but certainly within the foreseeable future.

'We simply need to get our act together,' was his view.[7]

Joynt maintained that the problem is that not all the money that has been allocated to demining was going into the job of physically lifting mines. Instead, it was being diverted to a variety of causes. Some of them, he conceded, are excellent, including the priorities of the maimed and the dispossessed. But it does detract from the

Lifting landmines in Mozambique has come a long way from the primitive and sometimes dangerous methods used in earlier years. But it is still a life-threatening process and mine-clearers are getting killed and wounded. (Source: International Committee of the Red Cross)

real problem. 'And that is getting the mines out of the ground.' He added that one of the immediate results of inaction was that while everybody kept talking, more people were getting maimed and killed.

The industry is partly to blame, Joynt believed. 'The companies that offer mine-clearing services are constantly shooting themselves in the foot by trashing their opposition. They try to push their virtues above those of others in the business and have not been averse to bad-mouthing if the occasion warrants it,' he claimed.

'The result is that donors sometimes feel that it is safer to back humanitarian issues in a particular part of the world than a demining programme that possibly has a good chance of going awry.' Angola, he pointed out, remains the prime example.

The reasons, he said, were obvious: mine-clearing is a risky business. It is difficult to get into the business and contracts themselves are often precarious in setting up. Then there is the physical side, which can become critical in the process of doing the job. Clearly, he suggested, there were hundreds of imponderables: some involve physical injury or worse. Also, places where the mines are to be found are often confined to remote and hazardous regions.

But there was another problem, he added. He called it the 'RC Factor' or, more to the point, resistance to change.

'Rather than try something new, a lot of people would prefer the familiar. Since there is much that is revolutionary coming on to the market that makes mine-clearing not only easier, but safer and cheaper too,' that is simply not good policy, Vernon Joynt averred. It was his view that the only way the problem could be overcome was the establishment of an international controlling body that would oversee all the world's landmine problems.

But that, he reckoned, would be like trying to rewrite the constitution of the United Nations…

When Mechem started with their project in Mozambique in 1994 they first had to clear a lot of bush from most of the target areas.

Also, ongoing conflict had resulted in some designated roads to be completely overgrown. In fact, some weren't even shown on modern maps and, occasionally, the company was made aware of some of them only if the oldest inhabitants in the area could remember their locations.

There were a host of other problems. A number of these 'forgotten roads' had large trees growing on them. Still, mines had originally been laid and they had to be cleared. Once started, the programme was fairly effective.

Concurrently, a UN spokesman indicated that the Mozambique programme also suffered from a lack of consensus among the

A child holds up a sign that warns of the presence of landmines in Guiné-Bissau.
(Source: Guiné-Bissau Mine Clearing Centre)

participants. This was particularly applicable among key stakeholders on the most appropriate institutional model: it needed to be developed to ensure that the national authorities were not only in charge, but able to sustain a capacity to deal with some of the more pressing long-term problems.

Again, the use of commercial companies, some pursuing their own national objectives, proved disruptive. At the time, Mozambique was rated as the third poorest nation on earth and without foreign help and aid, it would unravel totally.

A number of mine-related lessons emerged in Mozambique:
- Mine action was dominated by the institutions responsible for the peace process. This, says the UN, eroded the space needed for humanitarian mine action and tended to complicate matters;
- The UN pushed for too long for a Cambodian-style of mine action in the face of donor opposition; and
- The Maputo government never really developed an authoritative mine action mechanism which would have enabled it to coordinate all mine action activities and to determine overall policy.[8]

One of the single biggest problems encountered in Africa by the mine-clearers is that much of the information related to these dangers is hearsay. Many areas claimed to have been mined in the past were left untouched by the local population, sometimes for years. This sometimes caused serious economic dislocation. In one area near Chimoio in Mozambique, for example, there was an incident where a woman was blown up in a mango field. It was said that the whole 15-acre plantation had been mined. A dozen years later, when the sappers did eventually go in, they found only four more mines, three of which were dud.

According to one authority[9] who worked in Africa for much of the past decade, minefields in Mozambique were regarded by those lifting them as relatively uniform.

With few exceptions it was found that anti-tank (AT) mines had been laid only on the roads – and then mostly sparingly and very rarely in concert with protective anti-personnel mines. Conversely, most minefields in the countryside are limited to anti-personnel mines that were fairly easily cleared with Casspirs fitted with metal wheels.

Angola proved to be a very different proposition. United Nations mine-clearing teams in this West African country encountered problems that were sometimes regarded as insurmountable. Also, there is not a province in the country that had not seen mines laid over the past 40-something years. Some had originally been put down by machines; others were AT, each of which was surrounded by three or four APs.

There was also a lot of UXOs (unexploded ordnance) lying about. It has been estimated that for every landmine lifted, there were four or five times more unexploded ordnance.

The result, according to a Mechem spokesman, was that in order to comply with the tenets of the UN contract (of opening a seven-metre corridor) mine-clearing teams simply could not go in with any type of machine and detonate them at will.

While there are many machines capable of adequately handling the job, Angola presented a series of problems of its own. Until recently, there were almost no permanent bridges left intact in the interior. An immediate result was that it had been impossible to use equipment like the German Minebreaker 2000. In fact, the only way to get the equipment through was to fly it in and that needed special types of aircraft which were often not available.

Also, once in a specific area, the machines couldn't be transferred overland to another area because of transport problems that involved both bridges and more mines: Angola is straddled by a myriad of rivers and streams.

As the teams got busy – they were tasked to do 16 clicks of road clearance a day – they were stymied by yet another obstacle. Teams, having cleared one stretch of road, would suddenly find new mines laid behind them. This made quality assurance difficult. Gerbera, the German company responsible for such matters and who initially did not have basic African experience to run their own camps, lived with the mine-clearing team and were constantly being called on to check all phases of the work, including the end result.

Having certified a stretch of road that was later mined again, Gerbera was able to testify to subsequent subversive activity, in this case Unita. Quite often the reason for finding more mines on cleared sections was simple.

In one case, to the west of Saurimo, a Zimbabwe mine-lifting team vehicle was destroyed by a mine in an area that was declared mine-free. A subsequent investigation showed that Zimbabwean troops had been surreptitiously visiting the women of some of the local soldiers. More significant still, the transgressors had been

Chapter 12
Landmines – Hidden Killers

warned that it was going to happen if they didn't stop messing with their womenfolk.

In another case a 122 mm shell was detonated as an IED along the road. There were more injuries from Unita soldiers jumping off the speeding vehicle than from the explosion itself.

In Angola, Mechem sent in two teams and worked exclusively on the roads; one to the north (in an area adjacent to the diamond fields) and another in the south. In each case, a 35-man crew manned a dozen 12-ton mine-protected Casspirs. In some areas, anti-tank mines were laid under tar (and sometimes in tunnels under the road). It was here that the pattern differed radically from Mozambique where protective perimeter minefields were laid around every little village and dam to deny the guerrillas access to these communities.

Looking back in history almost half a century at a Portuguese soldier having exposed an anti-tank landmine that had been laid by an insurgent group in Angola. (Photo: Author's collection)

In Angola, Mechem found that just about every AT mine had three or four protecting APs, often coupled to South African-made pressure switches. They were also aware that minefields, had been laid in the standard Soviet zigzag pattern with APs about a metre apart, usually in ragged lines about 10 metres across.

Where manual clearance on unpaved roads became essential, the men would be expected to cover about five kilometres a day. Because of heavy shrapnel left over from previous battles, progress was sometimes limited to perhaps 500 metres a week: every piece of metal that sounded a signal on the detectors had to be checked for bombs.

Also, the roads in Angola were not nearly as intensively mined as the bush. The crews found roughly between 18 and 30 AT mines per 100 km stretch of road. The contract also required the clearance of bridge abutments for repair. These were calculated at the same square-metre rate of payment as for the roads: a 50 km radius from the bridgehead was specified.

Another problem encountered here was booby traps, all of which had to be manually cleared.

There were a variety of bombs encountered by the clearing

teams. Apart from a preponderance of Chinese Type-72s, there were numerous AP fragmentation PROM-1 and PP-Mi-Sr bounding mines. Also found were PMR-2As, PMA-3s, PMNs, East German PPM-2s, the full range of PMDs and just about every AT mine in the book except South African #8s.

There were also a number of South African R1M1s and R1M2s as well as a lot of improvised stuff; half-ton aircraft bombs coupled to cortex knotted to the nose cone and, again, connected to a pressure switch.

In this regard, there was an incident on the road between Huambo and Ganda in the Central Highlands where 137 artillery shells were found to be connected to two pressure switches. Detected and blown in situ it caused a crater eight metres deep and with a 20 metre diameter.

Jump-mines – the Vietnam-era 'Bouncing Betty' – were always a problem, especially in a country where the people tended to burn grass during the dry season. Or the wires might have been eroded by rain. Each one of these bombs had to be cleared manually.

Mechem's initial Angolan contract was for a six-month period and necessitated almost 8,000 kilometres of road to be cleared. Because of delays and other factors (including the abduction of a mine-clearing team in the south which needed 'negotiations' for their release) it went on intermittently for almost a year. Finally 4,800 kilometres of road in the north and south were declared cleared.

Mechem teams suffered two casualties in this time; one was a Gurkha who had an AP mine blown up in his face while he was clearing away the sand from around it. The other was a recently arrived medic who crossed a bridge to talk to some Unita soldiers. The soil on the bridge had been freshly laid. In Mozambique, Mechem had one of its operators lose an arm and a leg.

Dogs were used in Angola throughout as a clearance procedure. Afterwards, Mechem preferred to deploy dogs for area reduction around minefields when conducting level-2 (technical) surveys.

The dogs would then be deployed to establish a perimeter to the field, the dog handler operating his animal in a figure-of-eight pattern in the area ahead. Or Casspirs with metal wheels would be brought in to provide the team with safe passageway tracks along which they could safely move.

In Mozambique, in contrast, differential GPS (with real-time correction mode) would be used to measure the corner-points of the minefield. This gave accuracy to within half-a-metre. Level-3 surveys were only done after the area had been declared safely cleared.

Some mine-clearing operations take place under the most difficult conditions. Some bombs laid decades ago are today covered by heavy natural overgrowth. But the mines still have to be lifted. (Photo: Author's collection)

The use of dogs in mine-clearing operations anywhere in the world remains a controversial issue. As part of Mechem's MEDDS programme[10] in Angola, dogs were essential to the equation. Without them, one of the officials told me, it would have been a much more difficult option.

In Africa there are two possible scenarios involving canines: free-running dogs or the animals used as they were in Mechem's MEDDS programme.

Each had its own set of positives and negatives. In the use of free-running dogs in the field, issues were sometimes exacerbated by dog-handler problems which might have included a poor understanding of mine-clearing SOPs and, occasionally, a lack of understanding basic scientific parameters. At the same time, they did achieve a better than 80 per cent recovery rate regularly which was not only officially claimed in Afghanistan but was experienced with other Mechem teams working in Africa.

To achieve percentages up to the acceptable 99.9 per cent level, a minimum of three dogs have to cover every area.

Free-running dogs, wherever deployed, perform useful roles. They are ideal for use as a backup to metal detection. Also, they allow a quick search of a large area and for quality assurance on a percentage basis. Finally, free-running dogs are relatively easy to deploy and cheap, because training has been minimal.

Negatives cover a broader spectrum: The MEDDS system, it was consistently shown, could not detect concentration gradients. Nor was it subjected to a real-time system. Also, answers were limited to absolutes; a simple yes or no. Another disadvantage was that MEDDS dogs could not work in high-intensity battle zones or minefields and, finally, the cost was high.

Free-running dogs, in contrast, tended to show a low reliability factor in their performance.

According to Dr Joynt, it was seldom better than 60 per cent. Also the handler was exposed to danger and performance could sometimes be inconsistent. In the African bush, dogs are easily distracted by wildlife, like a dog will spot a hare and go after it.

They are also area and threat dependent.

Examining the broader picture, there are some interesting lessons for the future. The first is that, like biological weapons, the landmine (at about $3 for a standard AP mine) is cheap. It has become the 'weapon of choice' in many late 20th Century war zones such as the one currently being fought in the Congo and which is also ongoing in parts of the Sudan and Uganda.

An estimated 110 million landmines are scattered in 64 countries worldwide and they continue to claim new victims each day. Since every single mine costs, on average, about $1,000 to identify, remove and destroy, an estimated $33 billion is required to deal with only those existing minefields, never mind what is still to come.

Costs, says the UN[11], will inevitably increase as new minefields – which outstrip the pace of clearance – place additional people in peril.

1   Robert Bryce: 'Man Versus Mine', *Foreign Affairs*, January/February, 2006.
2   UN Transitional Authority in Cambodia.
3   Robert Eaton, Chris Horwood and Norah Niland: *Study Report: The Development of Indigenous Mine Action Capacities:* UN Dept of Humanitarian Affairs, New York, 1997: p.24.
4   *Ibid.*
5   UN Angola Verification Mission.
6   Personal interview at Mechem, a division of the South African manufacturing cartel, Denel, in Pretoria, 24 July 1998.
7   Robert Easton, Chris Horwood and Norah Niland: *Mozambique; The Development of Indigenous Mine Action Capacities*; UN Dept of Humanitarian Affairs, New York, 1997.
8   Interview with J. Van Zyl, who headed Mechem field teams in Mozambique and Angola 1992/98; Pretoria, 26 July, 1998.
9   Dr Vernon Joynt: *Mined Roads Clearance*; Pretoria, March, 1998.
10 Angola: see note #4.
11 *Ibid.*

CHAPTER THIRTEEN

FEMALE GENITAL MUTILATION IS NOW WORLDWIDE

> One of the lasting impressions of having lived and worked in West Africa was meeting the occasional women – and sometimes young girls, quite a few of them pre-pubescent – who had been subjected to female genital mutilation or FGM. In other words, vital parts of their genitals had been removed, more often than not without any kind of anaesthetic and under the most unsanitary conditions. In some cases rusty razor blades were used for the purpose.

I travelled widely while I lived in Nigeria. Several times a year, I'd get into my car and drive all the way north to the northern cities of Kano and Maiduguri, near the frontiers of the Niger Republic and Chad.

Other times I'd head out east, stopping only when I reached Calabar, then a delightful little tropical backwater not far from a border post that allowed entry to the Cameroon Republic. Since then it was used to house and 'protect' Charles Taylor, Liberia's deposed tyrant. But that was before he was handed over to the International Court of Justice to stand trial.

Obviously, you meet people when you move about and Nigeria was no different. Indeed, it is one of the most ebullient and gregarious nations on earth. Also, unlike many African states, women were already making their mark in the workplace in this West African country and I would talk to managers, receptionists, accounting and administrative staff and others in the offices I visited. There were also the women who served me dinner or breakfast in the hotels at which I stayed. And, of course, there were the bar girls, or in more discreet language, 'the ladies of the night' and there were an awful lot of them. But more about African women 'of easy virtue' a little later.

The truth is that Nigeria is probably the most diverse nation on the African continent. With all its customs and religions hurled willy-nilly into an enormous melting pot that today numbers more than 150 million people, it allows for some astonishing contradictions.

Some Nigerians follow strict Islamic Law. Others are Christians, many in name only, but there are also millions who are every bit as devout as their Muslim counterparts. In-between there are myriads of other followings, not necessarily of a religious nature. The Animists of the forests follow primitive traditions that range from appeasing jungle gods to worshipping their forefathers, and in some communities they even bury their dead right beside the homes in which they and their families live. Still more believe in primitive voodoo rites, or, as it is known locally 'Ju Ju' and its practices sometimes involve human sacrifice. The old European colonial administrations of the previous century knew about these traits, but it was something rarely commented upon.

But there is one custom found all over Nigeria and practised by all sections of society – and in many other African countries, including some Arab states – and that is the use of a primitive form of surgery to keep their women 'sexually in check'. If it sounds grim, believe me, it is.

Indeed, one report put out by the World Health Organisation (WHO) in 1997 stated that there were 135 million women and girls who had had their clitorises removed. The obvious question here is how did they reach that conclusion? It is hardly the sort of thing that people who practise such primitive customs are likely to talk about. Notably, the report also stated that not only people of African extraction believed in this practice, but that it was widespread in the Middle East as well as in parts of Southeast Asia, Indonesia especially. Another detail to emerge was that age was of no consequence. The surgery is often performed a few days after birth to the mid-teens, and occasionally in adulthood.

There is no written record about how this 'fetish'– for want of a better word – originally came about, or when it actually started.

Speak to some of the old men in their flowing robes that you encounter along the way in West Africa – the *griots* or, more appropriately, soothsayers – and they will tell you that that system has been in place since the beginning of time. What we do know is that the term 'pharaonic circumcision' stems from such practice in Ancient Egypt under the Pharaohs, and 'fibula' (as in 'infibulation') refers to the Roman practice of piercing the outer labia with a fibula, or brooch.

Chapter 13
Female Genital Mutilation is now Worldwide

The African elders, with whom I spoke about this tragic custom, would usually argue, sometimes quite vehemently, that there was absolutely nothing brutal or inhumane about it. Like male circumcision, they maintained, it had certain hygienic implications. There would be no mention of its fundamental purpose, and that is to stop females from enjoying normal climax during sex. There has also been talk of it being used to prevent female masturbation.

In Black Africa – as opposed to Arab Africa, where this aberration would never raise its head in normal discussion – you launch into the matter of female circumcision at your peril. Most times, when such things are mentioned, the barriers immediately come down, or worse.

After I had done some of my own research and felt more comfortable with the full implications of what was clearly something inordinately inhuman, I was able to become more intrusive in my questioning. At such times, when I mentioned contemporary studies that suggested that the suicide rate among women who have had a clitoridectomy – as the surgical removal of the clitoris is termed in the medical books – was two or three times as high as among women with their genitalia intact, I was invariably given the brush off. Contrary to the accepted West African wisdom, the process is rarely needed as a therapeutic medical procedure, such as when cancer has developed in or spread to the clitoris.

The truth is that most removals of the clitoris are defined by the World Health Organisation as 'procedures involving partial or total removal of the external female genitalia or other injury to the female genital organs whether for cultural, religious or other non-therapeutic reasons.'

The WHO goes further, and offers several classifications of FGM. The main three are Type I which involves the removal of the clitoral hood, almost invariably accompanied by cutting out the clitoris itself (clitoridectomy); Type II removes the clitoris and inner labia and Type III (infibulation) is an incision that takes out all or part of the inner and outer labia, and usually the clitoris as well.

In plain language, this is the most extreme form of FGM, because the entire external genitals are cut away. The wound left will be sewn up, with only a tiny hole left for menstrual blood and urine. Around the time of her wedding, a young woman will be cut open, just enough for penetrative sex. She is also further cut to give birth and then re-sewn: harsh words, indeed, because the procedures involved can hardly be described as anything but punitive.

The report goes on: 'Around 85 per cent of women who undergo

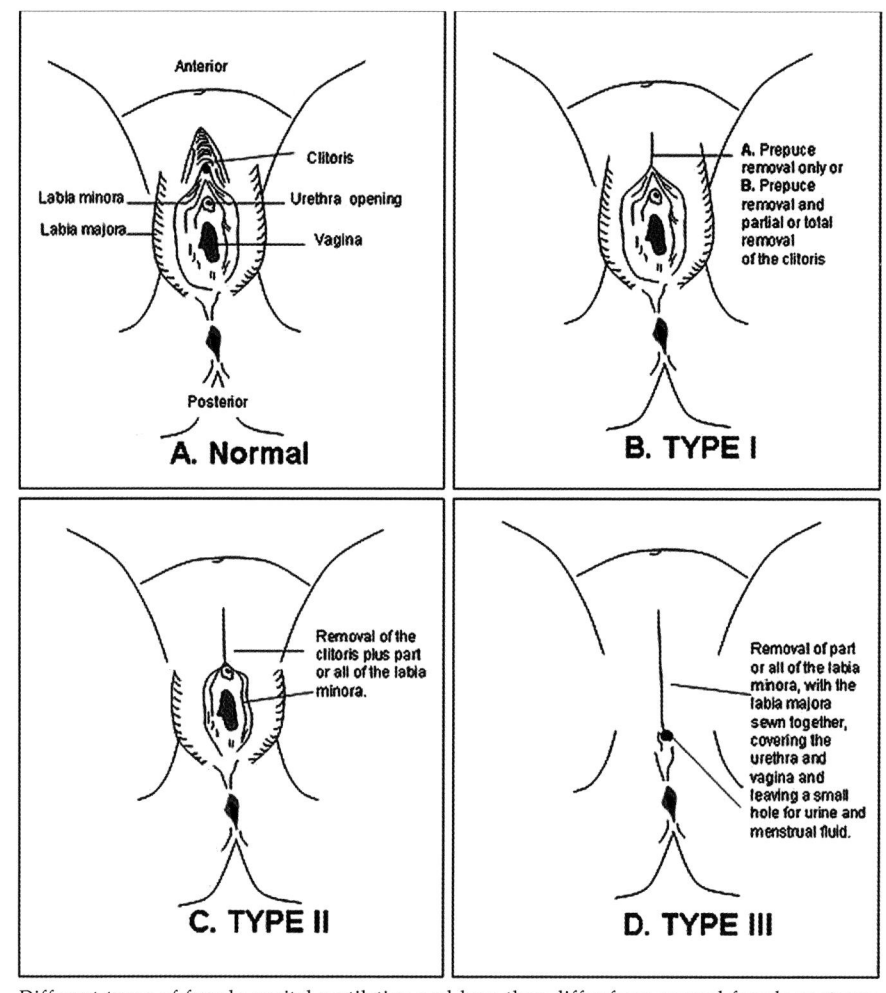

Different types of female genital mutilation and how they differ from normal female anatomy.
(Source: USAID Policy on Female Genital Mutilation/Cutting etc)

FGM experience Types I and II, and 15 per cent Type III, though Type III is the most common procedure in several countries, including Sudan and Somalia' – both countries in the Horn of Africa, which, possibly by coincidence, are rated among the most violent countries in the international community and where there have been killings going on for decades.

'Several miscellaneous acts are categorised as Type IV. These range from a symbolic pricking or piercing of the clitoris or labia, to cauterisation of the clitoris, cutting into the vagina to widen it (*gishiri* cutting), and introducing corrosive substances to tighten it.' In some areas this is referred to the 'Gaza cut'.

A recent London report stated that one of the disturbing developments in recent years was that immigrants from some Third World countries often take their customs with them when moving to Europe or the Americas. Obviously, some are good, but there are others that are questionable and the United States has increasingly become part of the equation.

At present, it declared, there are estimated to be between five and eight million African and Arab immigrants living in the West. Many of these communities practise female genital mutilation. A court in France, in February 2011, sentenced a woman from Mali to eight years in prison for the ritual mutilation of 48 young girls – all between the ages of one and ten years. Currently, there are several FGM trials pending in some European countries and in North America. There are also reports of similar incidents among immigrant communities in Australia.

The United Nations estimates that about 130 million African women have had their genitals removed. While filming in Uganda during the 1990s where I made a film on AIDS, I watched one traditional medicine man 'circumcise' about a dozen girls standing in a row before him. For that purpose he employed razor blades and from where I stood, I could see that none had been disinfected. Nor, in all probability, had they ever...

He moved from one victim to another, not even bothering to wipe the last girl's blood off the blade before starting with the next victim. It gets worse, because others involved in this kind of savagery have been known to use a jagged piece of tin can that had been sharpened on a stone.

One doesn't need any kind of medical training to be aware that such procedures are dangerous. In Africa – and in Arab countries such as Egypt and Tunisia – about a quarter of the victims become infected. Medical authorities that have studied the wider implications of female genital mutilation reckon that a single-digit percentage die because of inadequate medical treatment.

The report mentions a 13-year old Cairo girl who lapsed into a coma three days after having had her clitoris cut out. She died shortly afterwards. The event, widely covered by the media, caused a furore in the Egyptian press.

'Several Western governments are now working on laws that forbid these acts. New measures will also include the prosecution of parents who allow it to take place. Following the sentencing of the Malian woman in France, more than 20 parents who had allowed their daughters to be circumcised were given suspended sentences.

Sign on the side of the main road between Kampala and the west of the country in Uganda.

'Then, the BBC reported that newspapers in Bamako had complained that the incident had been highlighted by European media "for political reasons to portray Africans as savages." Indeed, initial reports indicated a certain element of racial bias that had little to do with the actual case.

'Meanwhile, several United Nations experts have warned that punishing those who carry out female genital mutilation might be counterproductive. Two UN special *rapporteurs* went on record recently and suggested that education and the promotion of alternative rites of passage were possibly the best ways to end the practice. That was followed by a statement by the Congolese health minister, Mashako Mamba, who some months ago condemned the practice. He declared that it not only increased the death rate among women but also helped to spread disease, especially sexually transmitted ones. He added that 'the practice was also a hindrance to child bearing.'

A report from Tanzania claims that female circumcision, in spite of having been banned by the government, is on the increase. Helen Kidjo, a spokeswoman for the Tanzanian Centre for Human Rights, told Oregon's *Daily Astorian* that her group had discovered that the rite was being secretly practised in areas like Kilimanjaro

Chapter 13
Female Genital Mutilation is now Worldwide

Sheelan Anwar Omer, 7, continues to cry after genital cutting was performed on her. More than 60 per cent of women in Kurdish areas of northern Iraq have been circumcised, according to a study conducted in 2010. (Andrea Bruce/*The Washington Post* via Getty)

and nearby coastal regions. Other Tanzanian children, like those from the Kuria tribe, were being taken across the border into Kenya where the practice had not yet been banned and was widespread.

It has been estimated that about 60 per cent of all Kenyan females have been genitally mutilated.

One of the more serious problems faced by those trying to abolish FGM in primitive societies is that traditionally, an uncut girl is considered unsuitable for marriage and might be rejected by her community.

In Numbers:

62%: Percentage of 15- to 19-year-olds subjected to FGM in Ethiopia, compared to an 81% among 35- to 39-year-olds.

140 million: Estimated number of women globally subjected to FGM.

5,315: The number of villages in Senegal that were known to use FGM that have signed public declarations abandoning it.

Less than 20: African countries to pass laws banning this process.

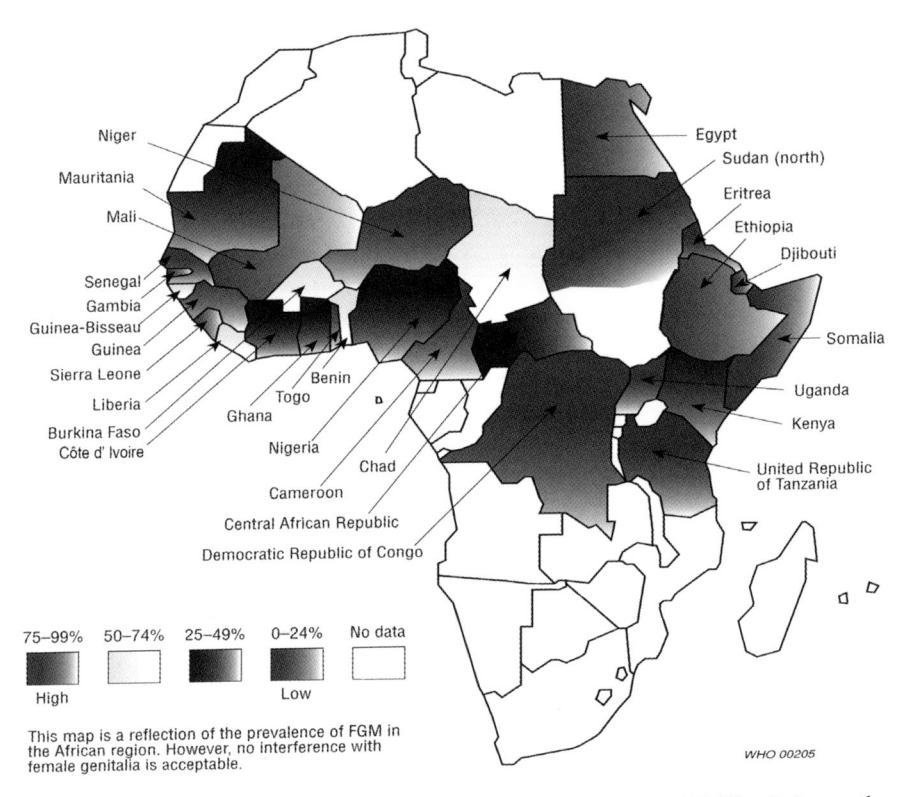

International Red Cross map showing the prevalence and intensity of FMG activity on the African continent.

CHAPTER FOURTEEN

THE ENIGMATIC SARAH BARRELL

Sarah Webb Fairbanks Barrell was blonde, long-legged and lovely. As veteran foreign correspondent Peter Younghusband described her in his book Every Meal and Banquet, Every Night a Honeymoon[1]*, she also had intelligence and courage. Not surprisingly, she was highly successful in her career as a photojournalist.*

Sarah Barrell spoke in a low-pitched voice at all times, because otherwise it became kind of squeaky. If you wanted to analyse her meticulously – as men sometimes tend to do when they put a beautiful woman under a microscope – you might say that she had everything going for her except for the sometimes squeaky voice.

But Sarah had so much going for her that her voice didn't really matter. In fact, had she contrived to find a way of going through life without uttering a word, it would hardly have been noticed.

She was six feet tall and lissom and walked with the sexy lioness-like tread of the ramp model she once was, all of which, of course, dramatised her beauty. When she entered a restaurant, men stirred like startled gazelle.

She was tough. Very tough. She had to be. She was competing in one of the world's hardest professions and had got there by a bruising, knockabout route.

In the small American town in which she was born and bred she had been seduced by a teacher at the age of 14 and became pregnant, which had required an abortion.

She ran away from home to become a model, at which she did remarkably well, until led into vice by the chief executive of her agency who hired her to become a plaything at parties for his friends in the advertising industry.

This led her to become a highly paid callgirl, working a beat around New York's top nightclubs and five-star hotels.

She once asked me: 'You ever hear this shit about me once having been a whore?'

I was silent as I fumbled for an answer. She laughed and said: 'Yeah, well mostly it's just gossip or nastiness, like when I scoop someone or won't sleep with someone. But as a matter of fact, it's true.'

And she went on to tell me, in her soft Southern drawl, about her three years as a high-class hooker, sometimes laughing as she worked through the anecdotes.

'It wasn't all bad,' she said. 'I actually remember times that were fun. And I met a lot of interesting people – and some famous people. And the money was good. Some girls I knew in the business made enough bucks to invest and retire on. The trick was to know when to stop. I think I got that right. I began studying photography in my spare time and I quit when I had enough saved to buy cameras and an air ticket to Rome and to give me a lifestyle there while I took a course in fashion photography.'

An affair in Rome with an Italian news photographer took her to Vietnam where she accompanied him on an assignment. That was the beginning of her career as a foreign correspondent, as a writer who illustrated her dispatches with her own photography. Soon photo features by Sarah Barrell, distributed to major newspapers and magazines through a leading photo agency, became a known product in international journalism. In career terms, she had arrived.

When her Italian boyfriend returned to Italy, she stayed in Vietnam and commenced a relationship with a well-known television correspondent reporting the Vietnam saga for a major American network. It was in Saigon that I met her, briefly, for the first time.

Sarah moved onto the Cambodia story with her new guy, but broke up with him in Phnom Penh during a row in the Inter Continental Hotel that became legendary in international press corps recall. She threw his typewriter, electronic equipment and clothes out of an upper window of the hotel and he responded by, in turn, throwing out her cameras and clothing. Colleagues and other hotel residents sunbathing beside the swimming pool below had to take cover as the sky rained cameras, tape recorders, jeans, T-shirts, jockey underwear, panties and brassieres.

Sarah left on an assignment to Cairo after that and from there moved down to Johannesburg, which was where we met again. She moved busily around southern Africa and began to focus on the then Rhodesia, the lead story in the region at that time. She became fascinated by Africa, as so many first-time visitors do. 'I love this

Chapter 14
The Enigmatic Sarah Barrell

RAR Major Andre Dennison preparing to jump; he was an enthusiastic skydiver. (Photo: Sarah Web Barrell).

place,' she told me once. 'I feel my destiny is here.' She was not wrong about that.

Her visits to Rhodesia became increasingly frequent until she finally moved her base from Johannesburg to Salisbury, as Harare was then known. The attraction of the place for her was understandable. It had some of the familiar elements of Vietnam: an ongoing war being fought by an army of big, suntanned, attractive men; a resident press corps covering a permanently high-profile story, with the added excitement of other correspondents, cameramen and photographers coming and going. Lots of action, lots of news, lots of parties, lots of fun. All the things, in fact, that Sarah was good at and loved.

There were some problems. Sarah, as I have already indicated, was no ordinary woman. Inasmuch as her extraordinary good looks proved a valuable asset in some aspects of her work, in other ways her attractiveness was a distraction and even caused offence.

War is a serious business and military commanders don't like having their troops distracted in combat situation by the presence of film-star-quality blondes.

In Vietnam – in fact in any American war theatre – tolerance of female war correspondents was about as broad as you could get. Officers in the field cursed at their arrival but none would dare go so far as to object, as long as they didn't do anything silly and as long as they didn't insist on separate latrines in situations where it was difficult to provide them.

I can recall an intense, dark-haired girl in Vietnam representing a Greek ethnic publication in the United States who went to pieces in a nasty situation and insisted on tearfully cradling the heads of wounded marines. She was quickly flown out.

In truth, though, most of the women correspondents I have worked alongside have been highly professional people, in some instances outpacing some of us males in performance and sheer courage.

Sarah Barrell was certainly in this upper echelon. Well established as a war correspondent, she also knew the score on the finer points and she worked hard at keeping a low profile: she wore no make-up on military assignments and did her best to keep her blonde tresses unobtrusive under whatever headgear the army provided.

But she just couldn't hide her femininity. Even in camouflage fatigues, flak jacket, steel helmet and paratroopers' boots, she looked like she was modelling military wear for *Vogue* magazine.

Major Andre Dennison (second from left) at one of the bases in the interior with his men. (Photo: Sarah Web Barrell)

Chapter 14
The Enigmatic Sarah Barrell

It was more of a problem in Rhodesia where, to begin with, the military didn't want any truck with journalists, and access to the combat zones was strictly limited. It was a smaller but no less vicious war than Vietnam's – whites were fighting for their very survival. It took me six years to breach the protocols and get an assignment to a combat situation – after which I was deported because it was felt I had written about it in too light a vein.

Sarah was taking pictures and reporting from the front line within weeks, to the fury of the long-established resident press corps – and of course the inevitable conclusions were drawn. It could only be because she was trading sexual favours.

'Yeah, yeah, I know,' Sarah sighed when she heard the gossip. 'I've heard it all before. Why don't these creeps learn that you don't have to sleep with the general to get a good army assignment? You only have to be nice to him.'

Not, she would remark in an aside, that she was above using the ultimate feminine strategy to achieve a really worthwhile objective. 'After all,' she would reason, 'if you've got it, why not use it?'

Her arrival in Salisbury certainly disturbed many of the regular news gatherers.

The Rhodesian War had been going on for more than ten years and the Salisbury reporters had become an insular and clubbish little community. It had entered that stale phase that afflicts all press corps when a story becomes old. The coverage had become lethargic and had reached the point where correspondents tended to help rather than compete with each other. Recognised old hands who came and went were welcomed, but newcomers tended to be excluded from the inner circle of shared information.

This was always a dangerous policy because every now and then a feisty new arrival would feel snubbed and adopt the 'Screw you bastards, I'll show you!' attitude, work hard at finding an exclusive angle and scoop everyone to smithereens. There would follow cries of dismay from wounded hacks as they rushed from bars, leaped out of swimming pools or extricated themselves from between the moist thighs of women and rolled out of bed to respond to angry call-backs from irate editors. It was certainly the quickest way for a newcomer to be invited onto the circuit.

Sarah Barrell didn't want to be on the circuit. She was a loner who had never cared for pack journalism. 'You run with the crowd, you might never get scooped, but you might also never get a scoop,' she used to say. Which was true enough.

Thus, she was destined to become unpopular among most of her colleagues in Rhodesia.

It wasn't just her work style. It was also her appearance. One would expect that a tall, beautiful blonde would enjoy instant popularity. This is not necessarily so.

Women hated her from the start. Female colleagues felt outgunned and, in general, women didn't like the way their menfolk looked at her.

Male colleagues tended to be intimidated by her. For one thing, she spoke their language, even down to the usual much-used four-letter words, and she was inside their heads, knowing what they were thinking when they looked at her, cynically aware of what they were saying about her behind her back. It wasn't that she had second sight. It was just that in her short life – she was 31 years old when she came to Africa – she had done more and seen more than most men twice her age, and she had become wise beyond her years.

It disconcerted most men that her approach to them was very similar to their own approach to women. She would stand a round of drinks at a bar and, if she wished to, she would set out to seduce a man of her choice for a one-night stand with the self-assurance of a practised philanderer.

Major Andre Dennison at a medal parade in Salisbury where he was decorated for bravery in action. (Photo: Sarah Web Barrell)

Chapter 14
The Enigmatic Sarah Barrell

I always had the impression that Sarah shuffled men like cards. She would cast aside those who bored her or who did not attract her and focus her interest on those who appealed to her. She seemed to have a liking for two types: dark, intense men and those who were big and rugged. She liked men in uniform and she preferred tall men, an understandable preference of most tall women.

She did not care for frivolous advances and she hated being touched if she did not want to be touched. Her reaction to being imposed upon could be devastating.

One of her first affairs in Rhodesia was with a captain of the Selous Scouts (the Rhodesian Special Forces) called Mike Donnelly. She was sitting in a lounge at the Meikles Hotel when a slightly inebriated member of the press corps placed a friendly hand on her knee.

'Please don't do that,' said Sarah, coolly. 'Otherwise I'll have to ask Mike here to hit you with his cock.'

One of Africa's more distinguished correspondents, a physically small man, also made the cardinal error of fondling her publicly during the cocktail hour at the Salisbury Press Club. She looked down at him almost sympathetically and said: 'Aw gee, Chris, you'd just like to go up on me, wouldn't you?' Turning to her companion she said: 'I can't stand horny little people, can you? Let's get outta here.'

Physical demonstrations of affection are part of southern Africa's way of life, and it could be said that Sarah was being overreactive. But it probably had a lot to do with a part of her life she wanted to forget.

Whatever the case, it added to her growing unpopularity among the hacks on the Rhodesia story. She began socialising less with the press corps and more with the military and the robust farmers who comprised the irregular forces of the army. In this way she also gathered information and opportunities that enabled her to scoop her colleagues quite frequently, which eroded her popularity still further.

There is nothing bitchier than a bunch of aggrieved journalists – and I'm referring here to bitches of both sexes. References to Sarah Barrell became coloured by comments on her origins, her past history and the alleged ways in which she acquired her exclusive stories.

They nicknamed her Sarah Dum-Dum, derived from the worn-out cliché that because she was a blonde she must be dumb. But dumb she certainly was not. The army and police, as it turned out, thought she was a lot brighter than the rest of us.

A PATU (Police Anti-Terrorist Unit) commander told me: 'She showed us she could strip and reassemble an AD-47 rifle as well as an American M-16. By the time she left us she could also strip and assemble an FN. She could even do it blindfolded. She also knew how to operate an RPG. I've never met another journalist who could do all those things. Write about it, maybe. Do it, no.'

Rhodesia may have ended up as just another war assignment in Sarah's eventful life, had she not fallen in love.

'This is it!' she wrote to me in a long letter. 'I have never loved like this before. It makes me realise that all the other times may have been a preparation for this, to help me know the value of what I have now.'

The focus of her new passion was Major Andre Dennison, a company commander in the Rhodesian African Rifles, well known in Salisbury journalistic circles, who had proved himself in many combat situations to be a fine soldier and an outstanding officer.

It was an affair that could have emerged from the pages of a romance novel: she the tough, worldly-wise blonde war photo-journalist and he the dashing soldier whom she had accompanied professionally on several of his combat missions until he was wounded, after which she helped to nurse him back to health. On assignment she carried a .38 pistol given to her by Dennison for her protection.

Rhodesians were a small community thrown together and tightly knit by their tribulations and war of survival where most people knew or knew of everybody else, and their affair became much talked about. It broke up Dennison's marriage and quite naturally people took sides, not least of all among the more garrulous members of the press corps.

I received one more ecstatic letter from Sarah. She and Andre had taken an apartment in Salisbury and were living together. After the war they would get married and buy a farm. Rhodesia was to become the end of the rough and wild road through life, and would become her home.

I had come to know Sarah Barrell well enough to know that there was a side to her that was seldom revealed to the very tough and cynical world in which she moved. She revelled in her experiences, her success in journalism and the excitement of it. She drank deep of the action and the romance. She was rightfully proud of the international reputation she had carved out for herself in what was still, essentially, a male-dominated profession.

But there was a soft core to her that was very carefully guarded

Chapter 14
The Enigmatic Sarah Barrell

by an exterior that allowed close friendship or intimacy only on her terms. It was the inner essence of womanhood that persists in most ambitious and career-motivated women no matter how much obscured or relegated. In Sarah's case it did not lurk even close to the surface, but glimpses of it sometimes showed in contact with children or animals.

I recall an occasion when we were seated beside a swimming pool, and a little girl from a nearby group toddled up to her and stood before her, sucking a thumb and gazing at her with the wide-eyed look with which very small children sometimes appraise strangers. Sarah, who was reading, lowered her book a fraction to meet the stare. After a few seconds, intrigued, she removed her sunglasses, whereupon the child leaped straight into her lap. Curiously, neither of them had spoken a word.

I think Sarah was driven by certain events in her childhood, and undoubtedly her subsequent life and her work satisfied a hunger for adventure and for life itself. I believe that in Andre Dennison she had truly found the way to her secret goal: marriage and much else that women hold dear.

But it was not to be. Once again Africa took its toll. Dennison was killed in a shoot-out with guerrillas near Fort Victoria. It had been a

Sarah Barrel took this photo of the coffin that held the body of her lover Andre Dennison, as it was being ceremoniously carried into church by some of his men. It was probably one of the last pictures she ever took, because after the service she returned to her apartment and shot herself with the pistol he had given her for her protection.

271

Major Dennison prior to a parachute jump before taking off from Salisbury's Sarum airbase. (Photo: Sarah Web Barrell)

night operation and, tragically, in the darkness, he had been shot by one of his own men.

The incident left Sarah grief-stricken, isolated and lonely. She attended Andre's funeral, but family members and friends formed a protective circle around his wife and excluded her from the graveside.

Her life had become centred on Andre Dennison and, once he had gone, she had few people she could turn to for support or consolation. Rhodesia, her home-to-be, had again become just another foreign country in her tumultuous life.

She telephoned me in Cape Town a few days after the event. She was alone in her apartment. She sounded subdued and shattered in spirit, but spoke calmly.

I tried to console her as best I could, speaking on a long-distance line from 2,000 miles away.

Had I known that hours earlier she had visited a local attorney where she had made a will directing the sale of her cameras and leaving the proceeds and all else she owned to Andre Dennison's regiment, I might have realised what she had in mind and been able to do something to stop it.

A few hours after she telephoned me – it could have been the last call she made – she shot herself with the pistol Dennison had given her. She was 33 years old. What a waste.

1 Peter Younghusband; *Every Meal and Banquet, Every Night a Honeymoon*, Jonathan Ball Publishers, Cape Town, 2003.

CHAPTER FIFTEEN

PORTUGAL IN AFRICA – GOOD TIMES FOR SOME

In Africa's so-called 'Colonial Era', Luanda and Mozambique's Lourenço Marques – Maputo today – were regarded by many who travelled extensively to be among the most progressive cities on the continent. The most striking of all was Luanda, inappropriately, perhaps, called the 'Paris in Africa'. By any standards, the Angolan capital was a beautiful and innovative city.

The first time I sailed into Luanda harbour was on a bright tropical day in 1959. I was a lowly crew member on board the South African navy frigate SAS *Vrystaat*, 'showing the flag' in the Portuguese overseas 'province' as Lisbon liked to call it. Thereafter, we would visit Matadi, the Congo's largest port, then still under the Belgian colonial administration.

The visit to a West African destination was a revelation for most of us who had never been further north than Salisbury or Lourenço Marques.

In Luanda, we were to discover a bustling, prosperous cosmopolitan city with all the trappings of a European capital, including modern buildings, restaurants well beyond our meagre earnings and suburbs that vied with anything that Cape Town or Johannesburg had to offer. That and the craziest traffic south of Marseilles where, to our astonishment, the locals drove on the wrong side of the road…

The entire city fringed an enormous lagoon, overlooked by the impeccably kept Fortress of São Miguel that was built almost a century before the Dutch first settled at the Cape of Good Hope. That massive structure with its unusual polygonal-shape and numerous bastions overlooked the favourite hangout of the crew during our brief visit, the Ilha, or island, connected to the mainland by a bridge

Bartolomeu Dias was the first European to sail around the Cape in 1488 and, as a consequence, opened up the sea route to India. That had a secondary influence of Lisbon setting up 'refreshment stations' along the coast of Africa, in Angola, Mozambique and elsewhere. This monument to the great navigator was pulled from its plinth after independence in Bissau. (Photo: Author)

Chapter 15
Portugal in Africa – Good Times for Some

and with more restaurants, clubs, jazz joints and whorehouses than any other city on the continent of Africa.

The intention was for the ship to stay a week. But after a first night of cheap booze and licentious broads in town, coupled to the kind of sometimes-violent dislocation that ended up making the newspapers back home, our rather ostentatious state visit was abruptly cut short.

Much of the drama was centred on the plunder of a number of thousand-litre wooden wine barrels that were standing on the quay alongside the frigate. There were no barriers around them, or, for that matter, any guards. As the Luanda police remarked afterwards, who in his right mind would take the trouble to steal something as mundane as wine anyway? There was so much of it all over the place and not even the locals bothered to take it without paying.

My shipmates didn't share that view. Those crew members who were required to remain on the ship, used chisels and hammers to broach several of the wooden wine vats and helped themselves and, as we were to discover the next day, the alcoholic-inspired melee that followed resulted in the arrest of several South African sailors, with the rest of us remanded to remain on board, or as they say, even in the navy, 'confined to barracks'.

The bottom line was that the *Vrystaat* – to the exasperation of Captain Terry-Lloyd, our captain, and an officer who was always a stickler for discipline – as well as the South African consul ashore had been utterly disgraced. So the skipper called it a day, let go fore and aft and we continued on our journey up the coast towards the Congo and our final port of call.

In Matadi none of the ship's company was allowed ashore even though we were there for days: the reason given was that they feared we would turn that harbour upside down as well.

I returned to Luanda not many years later. I'd left the navy, qualified professionally in London, returned to South Africa and, in 1965, I decided to head back to Britain. That was the four-month overland journey that took me up the west coast of Africa, through Lambaréné and Albert Schweitzer's famous jungle hospital.

In the process I entered Nigeria by dugout canoe from Victoria in West Cameroon, spent time in Ghana, from where I had to make a run for it because somebody in Accra got wind of my South African origins, travelled the length of the Côte d'Ivoire by bush taxi and continued overland through Sierra Leone, Gambia and Senegal.

It was a tough, rigorous journey that included my going down with

Ancient cannons guard the ramparts of Luanda's Fortaleza de São Miguel, built in 1634, half a century after the city was founded by the Portuguese explorer Paulo Dias de Novais. It houses many of the weapons and some of the war planes and other weapons used against the Angolans during the war with South Africa. (Photo: Author)

malaria in Lagos, a lonely trudge through Liberia and a nightmarish visit to Guinea, then in the throes of its own Marxist revolution under the dictator Sekou Toure. Soon to become a ruthless tyrant, who murdered his political opponents, Toure – and his modern harbour at Conakry, a great city on the Atlantic Ocean and, until then, a virtual NATO preserve – had been embraced by the Soviets.

Moscow flooded Guinea with all sorts of gifts that included a shipload of snowploughs and another of cement. The first ended up rusting on a quay in the harbour – nobody knew what the machines were for – while the cement was delivered in the rainy season in paper bags, which means that Conakry still has the largest rock-hard mountain of concrete in any port in Africa. Clearly, there was somebody in the old Soviet Union who hadn't paid attention to African geography, or its climatic conditions, while still at university.

I reached Luanda the second time round on a fairly long haul north from Angola's port city of Lobito where I had been arrested by the local military because foreigners travelling overland were not only a rarity, but suspect as well. The guerrilla war which the

Chapter 15
Portugal in Africa – Good Times for Some

Portuguese Army was trying to contain in the north of the country was on the upswing and somebody concluded that because I was hitchhiking, I could only have been a foreign spy. Though I spent the night in the cells devoured by mosquitoes, my South African passport and valid visa got me released the following morning.

I reached the outskirts of Luanda late the following day. It was rush hour and the truck driver who had given me a lift was in a hurry and sped through the outskirts into the centre of town, dropping me off adjacent to the city's famous lagoonside Marginal.

From the moment I arrived, I was awed at the astonishing pace of a great city in the process of closing shop for the night. This time, I had no ship to report back to and, in any event, not enough money to think about making a habit of getting drunk. At something like a dollar or two for a good bottle Douro *vinho tinto*, I was easily tempted, though.

The Luanda of the mid-1960s was a somewhat different place from what I'd experienced five or six years before, while still in the navy. For a start, with an ongoing war in the Dembos – the jungles to the north of the port city, there were people in uniform everywhere. These included soldiers, sailors and airmen. In the bars and restaurants that I frequented, I observed that the military component appeared to mix easily with the civilian population, both black and white. In fact, the informality of interracial association astonished this newcomer from a South African society just then in the process of shoring up its racial barriers.

Part of the reason was that Lisbon, a decade or two before, had changed its citizenship laws in a bid to encourage those Africans and people of mixed blood in the colonies – the *mulattos* – by granting them what could best be deemed 'honorary Portuguese' status. They were officially referred to as *assimilados*, or people that had been assimilated by the mother country, and though it was a shrewd political move to get more support from the locals, it actually worked. More to the point, as mentioned by somebody who had been born and bred in colonial Angola, an *assimilado* was someone who had assimilated the Portuguese language and customs, had a formal education, would adopt European names and, of course, eat with a knife and fork…

Looking in from the outside, it was obvious that this form of inverse racial classification in Portugal's African possessions was both demeaning and about as insulting as it gets, but it was certainly an enormous step and streets ahead of anything going on in apartheid-obsessed South Africa at the time.

Obviously there were many people in Angola, Mozambique and in Portuguese Guinea who seized the opportunity to improve their station and, with time, *assimilados* became a significant bridge between the cultures of Africa and the Metrópole. These 'chosen few', in theory, were able to be elected to public office (and indeed, some were), work in jobs of their choice, travel without permits and see their children enjoy higher education. More salient, with the war gathering strength, they could aspire to commissioned rank in the military.

One of Lisbon's most famous 'sons' was a young officer then fighting in Portuguese Guinea. Declared an *assimilado* some years before, Captain João Bacar became one of the most celebrated and highly decorated men serving in the Portuguese Armed Forces. Shortly before I spent time with him at his base in Tite (not to be confused with Tete, in Mozambique) he had been awarded the coveted Gold Order of the Tower and the Sword, Lisbon's rough equivalent of the Victoria Cross. A week after I'd gone on a patrol with Captain Bacar and his seasoned squad of *Commandos Africanos* in a swampy area to the south of the capital, he was killed in an ambush. The entire Portuguese nation mourned his death.

Very much the same situation held for Angola, where I was to meet still more African war heroes and even travelled to Cabinda with a distinguished young combatant who had taken on a group of guerrillas on his own and saved the day for his company. Yet, in other respects, Angola was very different from Mozambique and Portuguese Guinea.

In the East African Lusitanian colony that fringed the Indian Ocean for its entire 1,400 kilometres, those with money tended to congregate towards Lourenço Marques and the south; they left the rest of the country to a rugged bunch of more adventurous farmers, settlers and entrepreneurs. It was also a reality that, unlike Angola where farming had always been intense and foreigners were encouraged to buy land in the interior, three quarters of Mozambique had never been developed or exploited, which meant that it was Portuguese in name only.

Also, the average white Mozambican in Lourenço Marques had little time for those members of the military who had arrived from Europe to fight guerrilla insurrection from Tanzania and the north. They made few attempts to support them, and unlike Angola – where the army was embraced by the settlers – it was uncommon for the average white resident of Lourenço Marques to invite military personnel into their homes for a meal or a chat.

Chapter 15
Portugal in Africa – Good Times for Some

In fact, this kind of hospitality was something of a two-edged sword because there were several incidents in which Portuguese soldiers 'misbehaved' in the homes to which they were invited, making passes at the wives of their hosts and things of that sort, in part because the majority of young conscripts in the Portuguese Army were rural, or of the *fadista* type from Lisbon.

In Portuguese Guinea conditions were even more severe. An unhealthy, low-lying country with mangrove swamps stretching deep into the interior, the tropical climate was too severe to foster any kind of permanent residence by the majority of Europeans who were sent there on government business or to trade. Consequently, the military personnel deployed in that country were very much on their own.

For their part, the Angolans took the initiative in most things that affected their ultimate destiny, and for very good reason. The first Portuguese had originally landed near the mouth of the Congo River in 1482, which meant that by the time I got there, the country had been either sporadically settled or colonised by Lisbon for more than five centuries. More to the point, there were Portuguese families of all races in Angola who had been there for centuries and they were proud of their Angolan heritage and willing to fight for it.

The author was in Luanda covering Lisbon's war in the interior when he took this photo of the largest military parade of the year, in which all three arms of the military were involved. The men towards the front left, are airborne-trained soldiers, while the barrels of some Portuguese Army Panhard VCRs (light armoured personnel carriers) are protruding to the right.

Indeed, Angolan whites, and those locals who supported them, believed that they had become an inviolable part of Africa. There was even surreptitious talk at one stage to launch the same kind of unilateral declaration of independence or UDI, as Rhodesia had done a short while before. In the end, nothing came of it, which was probably just as well because the Angolans would truly have been on their own in the face of an encroaching insurgency that claimed more lives each year.

Instead, these white, *mulatto* and black nationalistic elements, with strong government support, would loudly proclaim that the country was theirs, to the point where radio stations throughout Angola would routinely broadcast the slogan *Angola é Nossa* – 'Angola is ours' and they did so dozens of times each day. They really believed it.

Though the *assimilado* concept had its uses, partially by marshalling the aspirations of some of the more politically astute African citizens towards the interests of President Salazar's *Estado Novo* regime, it also resulted in the alienation of some of the more politically seasoned dissidents; those people who refused to be categorised as 'second-

Other ancient monuments are found along the West African coast, including this religious statue sitting on a high point south of Luanda. (Photo: Peter Wilkins)

class citizens', as one youthful firebrand at a Luanda university viewed it. I only remember him by his first name, which was Saraiva, but this was a bright young man who had had a tough time of it because he totally disagreed with his white classmates about the future of what he referred to as *my* country, and, by inference, not theirs...

A true *mestizo* – his father was a white trader and his mother was black – he deeply resented the prospect of having to serve as a conscript in the Portuguese Army in a conflict that he unswervingly believed was totally unjustified. He'd been called up and was due to join the army within months.

The Portuguese must all go back to Portugal from where they originally came, he would tell me, and then he'd wait for a reaction. But I wasn't prepared to argue politics on his patch. It did surprise me that he would pour out his soul to me, an *estrangeiro* (his word, not mine) in a way that he would never have done with one of his own white countrymen. Frankly, his views were sobering for somebody who had never experienced 'somebody of colour' with such strong views.

'Africa is for the African', Saraiva would state emphatically, and the more Cuca beers he drank, the more outspoken he would become.

He clearly had had a tough time at school, not necessarily because of the colour of his skin, but because he would tell everybody who was prepared to listen that there were other forces active that would eventually change the status quo in Angola. These, he intimated, were to be found in Angola and abroad, and offered him something better than the role as a minor functionary in the local administration when he eventually got out of uniform.

His hero, he made clear, was Agostinho Neto, somebody whom I'd never heard of before. But I would come to recognise that name often enough in the future, after I'd started covering those African guerrilla struggles for the various publications for which I wrote.

Like Saraiva, Neto came from an *assimilado* background. His father was a Methodist pastor in Luanda and, having finished school, the younger Neto left Angola for Portugal and studied medicine at the universities of Coimbra and Lisbon. He combined his academic life with covert political activity of a revolutionary sort, was arrested by PIDE (the Portuguese secret police) for his separatist activism in 1951 and spent seven years in prison. On release, he finished his studies and, on the same day that he finally graduated, Neto married a white, 23-year-old Portuguese woman.

Two years later this youthful revolutionary was back in Angola where he helped put the MPLA on the map, the same political party that has ruled Angola since the mid-1970s and is better known internationally as the *Movimento Popular de Libertação de Angola*.

I stayed in Luanda on that visit for almost two weeks and it was a charm.

It wasn't long before I'd joined a small circle of student friends and after hours, we'd move about the city from one night spot or restaurant to another. In the process I discovered a vital, dynamic and charming conurbation, the likes of which I had never dreamed possible on the continent of my birth.

Very much like South Africa, the European settler community in Angola was forthright and uncompromising in its views, whether about food, entertainment, politics or sport. This was also a much healthier outdoor community than that of their relatives in the Metropolis. Army instructors in Lisbon would complain that new conscripts were often below par physically when they arrived for their basic military training, but that was a rare event in Angola. In this African colony people were accustomed to lengthy sporting sessions while still at school or perhaps heading out into the bush with their families or fishing down the coast, for no other reason than that they liked doing so. Also, just about everybody and his uncle was a hunter of sorts and in this regard, Angola's resources were endless.

In Luanda, Lobito and Nova Lisboa – which, after independence was to change its name to Huambo – the emphasis among the youth was on education, sport and culture: just about every youngster whose parents could afford it aspired to a university degree. In Luanda there were academic clubs that catered for these needs with mathematics and science clubs and even a privately owned observatory in one of the suburbs.

Traditional and classical concerts were regular, with chamber groups and even a small national orchestra. Overseas artists performed routinely in all major centres and the lovely Amália Rodrigues, with her distinctive *fado* following, was almost regarded by locals as a regular. While musical fare was largely European or American, one of Luanda's most elite clubs, Xavarotti, sometimes hosted prominent artists from Brazil.

For the majority who had almost nothing, their music was traditional, African and enjoyable, with the *kissange*, a primitive thumb piano typically constructed with metal strips on a wooden

Chapter 15
Portugal in Africa – Good Times for Some

Luanda today – formerly named São Paulo da Assunção de Loanda – is an enormous African conurbation of 5 million people, though with its extensive, often overwhelming slum sub-settlements, some say the real figure is closer to 8 million. (Photo: Peter Wilkins)

base, predominating. It is called the *mbira* in Rhodesia.

Things were cheap in Angola in those days, in part because prices hadn't been bumped up by tourists, because there were hardly any. Portugal was coping with its conflicts and anybody who wished to visit the country had to have a very good reason for doing so before they were issued a visa. That category obviously excluded the American and European hunting fraternities, because Angola boasted some of the best safaris on the continent. But that, as the saying goes, was strictly 'big bucks'.

Ensconced as I soon was, in Luanda, I had a clean room in one of the local hotels for about US$10 a night and I could eat an excellent seafood dinner for about half that. After I emerged in the mornings, I would saunter down to a huge open coffee house near the harbour with windows as big as doors and get myself a jug of *café com leite* with enough bread to carry me through to lunch. The place was the haunt of many of the white Portuguese dock workers, taxi drivers or tradesfolk who would noisily start their day very much as I did.

There was an excellent public transport system in Luanda in those days and it was possible to move about the city for a pittance. Like today, the city was divided into two parts, the Baixa de Luanda (lower Luanda, the old city) and the Cidade Alta (upper city, or the new part). The Baixa with its narrow streets and old colonial buildings was situated next to the port, and it was there that my friends and I would spend most of our nights on the town. And, if the mood took me, I could get a day job on one of the boats that plied the coast and accept my wages in fish once we got back to port, which would provide me and my student friends with dinner: Angola was that kind of place in the old days.

It was an idyllic life, obviously, and I would have liked to stay. But the rest of Africa, and, at the end of it, London called.

Interestingly, I had a contact in Luanda that I was urged to visit by a friend back home and his name was Jannie Geldenhuys, then recently appointed vice consul at the South African diplomatic establishment in the city.

'Unofficially' as Jannie told me over dinner on my second night there, he was a major in the South African Army. But Angola, being a province of Portugal, didn't have full diplomatic status and military attachés were restricted to Lisbon. Since the war had become a reality and Angola fringed on South West Africa's northern border, somebody in Pretoria thought it a good idea to get somebody into the consulate who could keep tabs on the war.

A stretch of bush country with a river running through it in Angola's underpopulated south. (Photo: Peter Wilkins)

Chapter 15
Portugal in Africa – Good Times for Some

Vice Consul Geldenhuys had a good life in Luanda. He and his wife had a growing circle of friends, diplomatic and otherwise, and a delightful home in the main part of the city. He was to stay at his post for four more years, and another South African military man, Major 'Kaas' van der Waals – today retired Brigadier General Van der Waals – was appointed in his place.

'Kaas' went on to write the definitive book on the guerrilla struggle, then steadily edging closer to Luanda; *Portugal's War in Angola: 1961–1974*.[1]

Indeed, when I returned three years after my first meeting with the future General Jannie Geldenhuys – specifically to cover that war and write a book about it, I was taken on a Portuguese Air Force supply mission to one of the beleaguered military posts immediately north of Luanda. We went up in a creaking old French-built Noratlas transport plane and I was surprised that the actual drop – by parachute, physically hurled out of an open hatch by the loadmaster as we circled some granite hills completely surrounded by jungle – took place barely 30 minutes' flying time out of Luanda's international airport. Things were obviously getting tough…

Even with the war going on, life in Angola continued much as before. Conflict was restricted to the jungle regions adjoining the Congo and to the east, out of the Congo's Katanga and Zambia. None of these regions were economically viable, though the north had been the source of much of Lisbon's hardwood as well as some of its tropical produce. The coffee industry, the diamonds, gold, the oil and a lot else besides were totally unaffected by ongoing hostilities.

During my initial visit, you couldn't miss the cut and thrust of many of the trading companies active in the interior that made millions for their owners back in Portugal. The name of the game was exports – commodities like palm oils, cotton, cocoa, timber, tobacco and some of the best coffee to be found anywhere. The Angolan bourgeoisie was born trading in rubber and ivory, in the same way that earlier generations had made their fortunes in the slave trade.

I spent quite a bit of time in a huge metal structure in the city that is still known by its original name, the Palácio de Ferro, or, in English, the Iron Palace. It was originally built by the French engineer Gustave Eiffel, who gave his name to the most famous tower in Paris, and in Luanda his confounded structure eventually became a kind of home away from home to many of the city's artists. The origins of the place remain shrouded, because it was originally intended for

Madagascar, but the ship taking it there sank off Angola's Skeleton Coast, from where its modular sections were salvaged and hauled to Luanda.

Much has changed in Luanda since the Portuguese scarpered back to Europe almost 40 years ago. Its population has burgeoned, in large measure because of the 27-year civil war and Luanda is now the third biggest Portuguese-speaking city in the world, after Santos and Rio de Janeiro in Brazil and is about twice the size of Lisbon.

Just about everything in the country today centres on the oil industry, with Angola having become the second largest producer of crude in sub-Saharan Africa after Nigeria. The downside is that in 2012, Luanda was declared the most expensive capital in the world, having donned the dubious mantle that Tokyo claimed for decades. There are no more hotel rooms for $10 a throw: these days prices range from $400 upwards, with the run in from the airport likely to cost you $50 or more.

A simple hamburger at one of the fast-food joints will put you back $15 or more and 100 grams of spaghetti costs $8. As in the old days, tourism is not encouraged and, once again, anyone intending to visit the country needs a jolly good reason for doing so.

The wheel, indeed, has turned almost its complete cycle…

1 W.S. van der Waals; *Portugal's War in Angola*, 1961–1974, Protea Book House, Pretoria, 2011.

CHAPTER SIXTEEN

BIAFRA'S AERIAL WAR OF ATTRITION

Considering that Nigeria is again – almost determinedly – sliding into another self-perpetuating civil war, it is perhaps appropriate to look back at the Biafran conflict of the late 1960s. A million people died in that tribal conflagration – a very large proportion of them children. Sadly, history seems to be repeating itself in this corner of West Africa.

The introduction that I did for my final article on the Biafran War, shortly after I'd emerged from the fighting there late in 1969, just about says it all: 'It was only a jungle airstrip in the heart of tropical West Africa, but Uli Airport – codename Annabelle – became a legend among the airline pilots of the world.'

What I didn't say, was that after weeks in that embattled enclave in which we were rocketed, machine-gunned and bombed every day, I was not only starving – there was no food in an enclave completely surrounded by Nigerian troops – but I was fairly seriously shell-shocked. Once I got back to Nairobi, my base at the time, I ate solidly for a week. My problems were compounded by the fact that each time a car backfired or somebody slammed a door, I would hurl myself to the ground. Those Nigerian experiences left their mark and the truth is, I still cannot handle noise...

Like most things in that dreadful conflict, everything that went on at Uli, the hub of the Nigerian civil war for three years in the late 1960s, was improvised: Uli's 'airport' runway – lined on both sides by primeval jungle – had once been a stretch of main road between the towns of Aba and Onitcha in Eastern Nigeria.

When the electrics blew, which happened almost every night – usually as the first of the relief planes arrived overhead – ground crews would use cans of palm oil with lighted wicks to show the pilots where to bring their planes down. It was typically West African Heath Robinson, especially whenever the wind blew, but it worked. And things went on that way for two years.

Frederick Forsyth said it best in his introduction to one of the finest books to come out of the war[1], Mike Draper's *Shadows: Airlift and Airwar in Biafra and Nigeria*':

'It was crazy, it was hairy, it was impossibly dangerous; it should never have worked. But somehow it did, night after night. When the planes landed and taxied into the welcome darkness by the side of the motorway-turned-landing-strip, willing hands hauled sacks of milk powder and bundles of stockfish out of the fuselages and away into the feeding centers. That done, the pilots taxied back to the take-off point, the lights flickered on for a few seconds and they were gone ...'

Forsyth, who was down with malaria when I got there, recalls that this was the story of the strangest air bridge the world has ever seen.

The airplanes used by the aid people were a ramshackle collection of time-expired or phased-out workhorses of the skies, culled from boneyards all over the globe. Had it not happened, he reckoned there would have been another million Biafran children starved into oblivion because the rebel state was blockaded by land, sea and air.

A group of mercenary and Biafran pilots with their tiny Swedish-built Malmö MFI-9Bs Minicon warplanes at Libreville Airport in Gabon, prior to flying into an increasingly beleaguered Biafra.
(Photo courtesy of Michael Draper)

Chapter 16
Biafra's Aerial War of Attrition

For their part, the Nigerians were just as active. Apart from shooting down an International Red Cross DC-7B relief plane loaded with baby food, South African, British, Egyptian and other mercenaries flew hundreds of MiG-17 missions for the Nigerian Air Force (NAF) against Biafran ground targets.

Interestingly, Moscow sold the MiGs to Nigeria with the proviso that no Western pilots were to get anywhere near them, though with the vicissitudes of war that quickly changed, Ares Klootwyk from Cape Town, an RAF-trained, South African mercenary pilot, became the first Westerner to take one of these Russian MiGs into combat.

Almost all these freebooters were recruited through a single company in Switzerland. The Egyptians, in contrast, who flew Nigerian Air Force Ilyushin IL-28 bombers were notable for their inability to achieve anything spectacular. They would rarely drop below 10,000 ft for fear of ground fire which, at best, was pretty marginal because there was so little AAA ammunition being airlifted into the country.

In a sense, the single common denominator in this bloodletting was similar to what we see in Israel today: both sides hated each other with a religious-driven fury that even today defies description.

The Biafrans weren't altogether inactive in countering the Nigerian air offensive, though the rebels were able to offer only limited resistance with a tiny air force called 'Biafran Babies' that had been put together at the behest of a swashbuckling Swedish philanthropist, Count Carl Gustaf Ericsson von Rosen, who had a rather persistent delusion that he could 'change' Africa. It was Africa that killed him in the end and he died in a guerrilla attack in Somalia's Ogaden war in 1977.

He clandestinely brought five Swedish-built Malmö MFI-9Bs to the breakaway Nigerian state and created the Biafran Air Force. Initially the planes were ferried into Biafra from Libreville, the capital of Gabon. Because of losses, American intelligence sources disclosed that these were supplemented by several more, totalling eight Minicons by the time the war ended.

As 'fighters' go, the 'Minicons' were among the smallest modern combat aircraft ever built. 'Von Rosen's Vengeance' – as the little prop-driven planes were called by the media – proved astonishingly effective.

One blogger, who calls himself 'Srbin' (all we know about him is that he was born in 1986) commented that 'even the Skyraider was like an SR-71 compared to the little putt-putt plane around which

Von Rosen built his force: the tiny Swedish trainer looked like those ultra-lights that people build in their garages. This plane could park in sub-compact spaces at one of Stockholm's shopping malls ... it had a maximum payload of 500 pounds; or, as he said: 'me plus a couple of medium-sized dogs'. Lucky those Swedes are so skinny...

'... in Gabon, Von Rosen slapped on a coat of green VW paint to make them look military and on each aircraft, he installed twin wing pods for French-built Matra 68 mm unguided rockets. Then he and his pilots – three Swedish volunteers who took time off from their civilian jobs, together with three Nigerian Ibos – flew them back to Biafra and this unlikely septet went into combat.

'They blew the hell out of the Nigerian Air Force as well as the Nigerian Army. These little fleas were impossible to bring down. Not a single one was knocked out of the sky, although they'd buzz home, sometimes riddled with holes ... they flew three missions a day and their list of targets destroyed included Nigerian airfields, power plants, and troop concentrations.

'Caught napping on the ground, they also knocked out three Soviet MiG-17 jet fighters (and damaged two); one Ilyushin-28; one British-built Canberra bomber (as well as another damaged); the 'Intruder' (a twin-engine DC-3 transport plane used to bomb civilian aid aircraft as they landed in the dark), as well as two helicopters, with another damaged. That was not a bad tally for a rebel air force that the Lagos government, throughout the three years of hostilities, routinely declared 'did not exist'.

At one stage, to supplement the Minicons, the Biafran leader General Odumegwu Ojukwu bought a dozen T-6 Harvards, but they were in a poor condition because only four were airworthy. During their transit flight from Gabon to Biafra, two were lost. The remaining pair was used in strikes, usually in conjunction with the MFI-9s, nine of which were then still in service. During the latter part of the war, two MFI-9s were destroyed, presumably to ground action, which could sometimes be intense.

Interestingly, Artur Alves Pereira, a Portuguese mercenary pilot (and at one stage, a squadron leader who flew T-6's as well as Minicons) left Biafra's last remaining airport at Uga on 9 January 1970 and flew to Gabon. From there, he headed home to Lisbon and although the war was over and all rebel offices in Portugal were closed, the now non-existent Biafran government sent him a cheque which covered all the war missions he had flown, as he told friends, 'down to the last penny'.

He commented afterwards that this small example showed how

Chapter 16
Biafra's Aerial War of Attrition

South African mercenary pilot Ares Klootwyk stands in the cockpit of one of Moscow's MiG-17s, recently delivered to Nigeria from the Soviet Union. Klootwyk was the first Western pilot to have flown these still top-secret warplanes, very much against the wishes of the Kremlin. His subsequent disclosures to Western intelligence agencies was of immense value in understanding the fighting capabilities of these jets. (Photo: courtesy of Leif Hellström)

special a people the Igbo [Ibos] are. 'Which country in the world, let alone in Africa, would bother to fulfil its commitments to this extent? Which messenger wouldn't feel tempted to keep part, or even all of the money?' Which, he admits, was quite a lot at that time, especially when the future seemed so uncertain to everybody involved.' Obviously, he concluded, there would have been no court to which to complain.

Another significant comment was that with experience gathered over time at the 'Sharp End', the tiny Minicons, in true guerrilla style, turned their weaknesses – small size and low speed – to their own advantage.

They were so slow that they *had* to fly real low – which made them almost impossible to hit in the jungle, since you never saw them until they were almost on top of you. The modest speed made for better aim: almost half of the four hundred 68 mm rockets they fired hit their targets, which is an amazing score for unguided aircraft munitions. (There used to be a joke in the United States Air

Rolf Steiner was given the rank of Lieutenant Commander and served in Biafra's 4th Commando Brigade during the Nigerian Civil War. Unlike most other mercenaries, he stayed in the country almost until the end and asked no money for his services because, he told his detractors, Nigeria's southern Ibo people were being massacred. After fighting in the Sudan, he eventually retired to Germany where he wrote his memoirs *The Last Adventurer*.

Chapter 16
Biafra's Aerial War of Attrition

One of more than 20 civilian aircraft that either crashed at Uli Airport on landing or takeoff, or were bombed by Nigerian planes while trying to deliver food and war material to Biafra. (Photo courtesy of Leif Hellström)

Force during World War II and Korea, that if it wasn't for the law of gravity, unguided rockets fired from aircraft couldn't even hit the ground.)

Clearly, the little Swedish MF-19Bs packed a decisive punch. Apart from the Harvards, there was also a surplus World War II American-built B-26 bomber which had mixed fortunes before it crashed on a bombing raid over Lagos, while the author was resident there.

For much of the war, Uli remained the tenuous lifeline between Biafra and the world outside in this grim, internecine war.

The 'miracle of Uli' as the hacks referred to it, hosted about 20 flights a night – though sometimes there were as few as five and, occasionally, as many as 40 aircraft – often loaded well beyond accepted international safety limits with tons of food and weapons and ammunition. All ran the Federal Nigerian blockade, crossing the coast near Port Harcourt where Soviet anti-aircraft guns were positioned.

The relief planes took numerous losses, some were hit while taxiing, while others were bombed by the so-called 'Intruder', an antiquated Nigerian Air Force C-47 that had been adapted to carry

A sidelong view of the Soviet MiG-17, with one of the British mercenary pilots who flew it with Nigerian ground crew. (Photo courtesy of Michael Draper)

the 50-pound as well as 100-pound canisters of explosives that were manually hurled out of the aircraft's open side door. Later the Nigerians bought some surplus B-25s.

Several of the civilian planes involved in the airlift were also accidentally shot down by Biafran ground fire, though the rebels denied it. They said it couldn't happen, though on my own flight into the country, our DC-6 was nearly hit by heavy machine-gun fire from the ground as we came in.

It certainly wasn't Nigerian fire coming up at us because their lines were many kilometres away.

With time, the Biafran conflict devolved into a series of holding actions, with the majority of the population doing their best simply to stay alive. In reality, though, after the first year of the war, the food situation in Biafra had become so critical that the entire nation was starving.

The only way to get food in was by an air bridge operated either from the Portuguese island of Sao Tomé or from Libreville, the Gabonese capital. The International Red Cross flew some flights from the former Spanish island of Fernando Po (Equatorial Guinea today) and from Cotonou in what was then still Dahomey, but that wasn't a regular event and halted in June 1969 when one of its planes was shot down by a mercenary pilot flying a Nigerian MiG-17.

By mid-1968 international relief organisations were carrying out flights on a limited scale, often using the American airlines that ferried weapons from Europe to Port Harcourt and later to Uli, that airstrip then still in Biafran hands.

Chapter 16
Biafra's Aerial War of Attrition

When the Americans later refused to go in because of risk, Swedish Count Von Rosen, made a flight for the German Caritas welfare group in August that year. The air connection from Sao Tomé was organised by a Scandinavian group called Nordchurchaid and by January 1970, a total of 61,000 tons had been ferried across to Biafra in more than 5,000 flights. The International Red Cross, sometimes operating from Fernando Po and Cotonou, had taken in 20,290 tons by June 1969, when flights were finally suspended.

Once in Biafran air space, always after dark, following the first few months of hostilities, things often got hectic, extremely so at times.

The following is an extract from a flight report from one of the aid pilots, dated May 1969:

> '... spent one hour and four minutes waiting in the air over the Uli field ... made five aborted approaches. Nigerian bombers were harassing as usual, the landing lights came on too late or were turned off on final approach. The Intruder, i.e. the bomber, released his first bomb when we were at the end of our final approach.
>
> 'When we first got clearance from the ground to approach at an altitude of 2,500 feet – from the east and towards the airport – we got instructions to return to the beacon we came from, EZ. An aircraft was being observed between us and the ground. The plane flew south.
>
> From Uli airfield we were told that this plane probably was GJE (New Zealand DC-6 from Cotonou). What he was doing there and who gave him clearance to go there I do not know.'

Uli airfield was bombed incessantly during some periods, but the damage was quickly repaired. A total of 11 aircraft were destroyed and 21 members of aircrew killed. That figure included 9 aircraft and 13 pilots belonging to church groups.

In November 1968 a Joint Church Aid DC-6 was damaged by a 20 kilogram shrapnel bomb that exploded alongside the aircraft. Five people were killed and many injured, including the co-pilot Jan Erik Ohlsen and the pilot Captain Kjell Bäckström. Ohlsen was flown out by a Red Cross plane, but Bäckström decided to try and do the impossible and take his damaged aircraft out. It had 50 shrapnel holes along one side and two of its engines were leaking oil. Despite his injuries, Bäckström succeeded in getting himself and his aircraft

Swedish pioneer aviator, mercenary and humanitarian Count Carl Gustaf von Rosen flew relief missions with cargoes of baby food into Biafra before he bought five – later increased to eight – MFI-9Bs Minicon warplanes in Sweden and had them secretly flown into the rebel enclave. A remarkable man, he was killed in Ethiopia's Ogaden War. (Photo courtesy of Leif Hellström)

to Sao Tomé, where he was operated on at the local hospital by Portuguese surgeons. Three pieces of shrapnel were removed from his body.

Eight crew members of the Red Cross were killed in a crash in May 1969 and in an aircraft shot down by Nigerian Forces in June 1969. Joint Church Aid lost a total of 13 crew members. Four men died when a German aircraft crashed in July 1968, but that was before Joint Church Aid was formed. On 7 December 1968, a German DC-7 crash-landed at Uli, killing four.

Then, on 4 August 1969, a Canadian Canairelief Super Constellation crashed, killing its crew of four. Five Americans died in an air crash on 26 September 1969. Thereafter, four additional aircraft were totally destroyed without loss of life and two more damaged beyond repair, all at Uli.

In spite of these losses in crews and machines, the air relief programme was an enormous success. One needs to look at the figures to appreciate this.

In church relief flights alone (never mind arms-runs which were

Chapter 16
Biafra's Aerial War of Attrition

A collection of images from the three-year war in Biafra which eventually ended with the death of more than a million civilians. The Nigerian leader Colonel Yakubu Gowon is in the middle row on the right, while Ron Archer, one of the pilots flying relief missions into the beleaguered little country is in the bottom row, right. Bottom left is one of the improvised Biafran tanks.

a sizeable tally each night) there were 7,350 freight flights into Biafra in the three years that war ravaged eastern Nigeria. In this time almost a million tons of supplies, including arms, were taken into the beleaguered territory.

During the course of all operations into Biafra there were 15 aircraft lost and 25 aircrew killed, the majority buried in a small cemetery adjacent to Uli Airport. The Nigerian Army bulldozed their graves when it was over: they didn't need any 'martyrs' in the aftermath, the military declared.

Early in the war Egypt sent 15 MiG fighters to the Nigerian Air Force. Cairo was then supporting a host of revolutionary groups, including a huge effort to overrun Yemen in the southern Arabian Peninsula. And which, for several years was countered by Britain's Special Air Service, with the help of mercenaries, including the French freebooter Bob Denard.[2]

Later, helped by Algeria, Cairo assisted again with six Ilyushin-28s. In addition, twelve L-29 Delphins came from Czechoslovakia, two Jet Provosts from Sudan, two Westland Whirlwinds from Austria and a pair of Gnome Whirlwinds and an FH-1100 from Britain.

While I worked for John Holt Shipping Services in Nigeria, the Delphins were parked on the runway outside my office and since the second Nigerian Army mutiny took place while I was living in Lagos, I deal with these episodes in considerable detail in one of my books, *Barrel of a Gun*, which was published by Casemate Publishers in America and Britain in 2010.[3]

Shortly after hostilities started, the Nigerian government decided to recruit mercenary aircrews, largely because Nigerian pilots were unable to manage the intricacies of modern fighters and bombers. These 'guns for hire' came from a dozen countries.

What followed, starting in 1967, were a huge number of attacks by the Nigerian Air Force on schools, hospitals and marketplaces. Though there were sporadic halts, the aerial strikes continued until the end of hostilities. Virtually every hospital in Biafra was attacked at some stage or another, sometimes many times over, underscoring observations made by independent observers – including members of the church who worked in the enclave – that these were 'terror' bombings and had absolutely no military value. Indeed, it was confirmed long afterwards by others who put pen to paper that the attacks served only to strengthen Biafran resolve to resist.

During the first few months of the war, Biafra had certain advantages in the air war, especially since they had pilots who were better trained and fought with greater motivation, if only because their survival was at stake.

Most Biafran Air Force (BAF) pilots and mechanics had previously served with Nigerian Airways or the fledgling Nigerian Air Force and, obviously, though Scandinavians and European mercenaries were hired by the rebels, they all played significant roles.

An important contribution was also made by Friedrich 'Freddy' Herz, an old friend of most of the Biafran pilots trained in Germany. On the outbreak of this West African struggle, Herz was living in West Germany. He received letters from his Biafran friends, asking him to come over and lend a hand. After some deliberation, he went to Cameroon, got permission to enter Biafra, where he was taken to Enugu, the newly created Biafran capital, by his friends.

Since this was his first visit to Biafra, he was carefully vetted. Only after a few weeks did he get to meet the BAF Commander, Colonel Zoki, who believed his explanation that he wanted to help

Chapter 16
Biafra's Aerial War of Attrition

World War II vintage B-25 bombers – some of which had seen action against Japanese forces in the Pacific War – were also used in the Biafran War by both sides. (Photo courtesy of Michael Draper)

the Biafrans with no other compensation than free food and board.

At this time, the situation at Enugu was critical. The Nigerians were pushing in hard from the north and were close to the town. At Enugu airport, the Biafrans had two B-25 Mitchells and one B-26 which was christened 'The Marauder'. All three aircraft had to be flown out of Enugu to prevent their being captured by the approaching Federal Forces. Freddy had never flown these types before, but together with Colonel Ezilo, he managed to fly the first B-25 to Port Harcourt, return to Enugu by road and later saved the remaining B-25.

The B-26 caused more problems; its wheel brakes were faulty and the Biafrans didn't want to allow it to take off. And because both the airfield and Enugu were taken by Nigerian troops soon afterwards, that bomber was lost in the fighting that followed.

A few weeks later the Air Force Commander, Colonel Zoki, was killed. During this critical phase of the war, Freddy also participated

Nigerian Air Force jets were often just parked at the end of jungle strips and left there for the night, without any protection from the elements. The same situation could be seen outside the author's office at Lagos's Ikeja Airport, with new Delphin jet trainers bought from Czechoslovakia that were often left with their cockpits open to the rain. (Photo courtesy of Leif Hellström)

in a ground operation at Onitsha, on the Niger River, where he helped Biafran soldiers erect rocket launchers.

Freddy later arrived at Port Harcourt, where the two B-25s were now stationed. Together with the Biafrans and a Cuban pilot, Freddy checked the aircraft carefully and then did test runs on both. Shortly afterwards he carried out a number of raids in the two B-25s as well as a DC-3 Dakota converted to a bomber. The targets were enemy positions and formations, primarily in south-eastern Biafra and in the mid-west region. This was done in cooperation with the army, and the BAF activity delayed the Nigerian advance on the southern front considerably.

Late in 1967 a night raid was carried out against the Nigerian port city of Calabar, adjacent to the border with the Cameroun Republic. The city was then in the hands of Nigerian troops. As detailed in Gunnar Haglund's book published in Swedish and titled *Gerillapilot i Biafra* (Guerrilla Pilot in Biafra) the raid was to be carried out with the DC-3, one of the 'liberated' B-25s and a newly delivered B-26, said to have been flown to Biafra directly from South America.

After dark, the three crews prepared for takeoff. The DC-3 and B-26 had already been refuelled and loaded up with incendiary bombs, many of them home-made. Orders were that the DC-3 and the B-26 bomber would depart first, find their targets (which were designated Calabar's industrial area and airfield) and they would drop their incendiaries. In the light of this intended carnage, the idea was for Freddy to arrive over the target area in his B-25 and drop conventional high-explosive bombs on factory buildings and hangars in the vicinity.

The three aircraft took off and formed up over the airfield before setting out for Calabar at relatively low level. The crews were tense, since Calabar was known to be ringed by heavy anti-aircraft emplacements.

Just before arriving over an astonishingly well-lit Calabar, the DC-3 and B-26 climbed to a little over 3,000 feet and then dived and dropped their loads, resulting in a number of blazes. Parts of the area was 'lit up almost like day', Freddy recalled afterwards and he could easily make out the factory buildings they were after. He came in low at a couple of hundred metres and dropped his HE bombs, but was greeted from the ground by intense AAA ground fire.

The aircraft involved in the strike took a number of hits, but as he admitted afterwards, the plane emerged reasonably intact and none of the four men on board were injured.

Freddy made a steep turn with his B-25 and headed back towards Port Harcourt at low altitude, in part to avoid any Nigerian Air Force MiGs that might be circling the region. It wasn't long before his instruments told him that his fuel tanks were leaking. Their aircraft had taken a good deal more damage than he first realised.

Freddy said afterwards that they finally managed to make contact with air traffic control at Port Harcourt and given clearance to land after one of the aircraft immediately ahead of them. By now, he recalled, the fuel gauge was registering almost zero, and from experience, he was aware that he had perhaps only a dozen or so litres of fuel left in the tank.

At that point they were very close to the airport, the runway lights stretching out ahead of them, which was when air traffic control gave them clearance to go in directly rather than complete the usual circuit. Freddy reduced power and that, in itself, was a huge relief.

Haglund records events as follows: 'Their old B-25 made a short turn in towards the runway and descended a bit more. Flaps were extended to reduce speed, then the landing gear. The other aircraft, which had been just in front of them all the way, had reached the point where it was in the process of landing and Freddy's aircraft had only a few hundred metres left to touchdown.

'Suddenly the traffic controller called over the radio: "Abort landing! Immediately!" Apparently a plane just ahead had crashed on the runway!

As Freddy recalled, everything happened very quickly. 'They had to interrupt their landing and climb again, raise their landing gear, pull up flaps and moderate the throttle to avoid wasting what little fuel remained. The cockpit crew feared the worst.

Freddy prayed that it might just be possible to go around the field, just a small circuit, so that ground crews could get the crashed aircraft off the runway. But then, not entirely unexpected after half a circuit, one of the engines coughed ... then the other ...

'Both engines stuttered again in unison for a few seconds and then fell silent. Freddy and Ezilo prepared for a make-or-break emergency landing in the dark, turning on their landing lights in the process while sinking fast towards the ground.

Freddy spotted a clearing in the bush diagonally in front of them. The bomber was just above the ground when one of its wings hit a tree. A moment later the aircraft ploughed into the ground, bounced a few times and slid along the ground into a clearing. Freddy remembers the thuds, the screech of metal-on-metal, together with scrapes and creaking noises everywhere. 'Finally, there was a terrible bang and everything went quiet.'

Freddy and his co-pilot woke to find themselves in the Port Harcourt hospital. Sammy, their navigator, had been killed instantly. The rear gunner was a lot more fortunate because he had fallen out of the aircraft on impact and came away from it all with an injured leg.

Despite this, the records tell us today, the raid on Calabar had been an unmitigated success. Numerous targets had been destroyed, the airport, the city's factory area as well as a fuel depot – all in the same vicinity – had been devastated, largely having been set alight by incendiaries.

According to Haglund, Freddy's nerves had taken a pounding and he wanted to get away from the war. After almost three weeks in hospital, and with his leg mending, he returned to Europe.

But like most veterans bored with domesticity at home, it seems that this aviator couldn't keep away from where everything was happening and by January 1968 he was back in Biafra. By then, Nigerian forces had taken Port Harcourt, as well as the two surplus American bombers which were left standing at the airport, and there was nothing for him to fly.

The year 1968 passed without Biafra acquiring any new aircraft. Several times there were attempts to buy old surplus planes from different sources, both jet and propeller aircraft. Most deals came close to being closed with the aircraft prepared for delivery, but each

Chapter 16
Biafra's Aerial War of Attrition

time the transactions failed. Those deals ended costing the Biafrans bucket-loads of precious foreign currency, but they still did not get the aircraft they so desperately needed.

Enter Count Von Rosen and his Swedish Minicons, which warrants a few words about this remarkable aviator.

During the Italian invasion of Abyssinia in 1935–1936, the Count flew a Heinkel HD-21 and later a Fokker F VII that had been equipped as ambulance aircraft. Then, following the Russian invasion of Finland in 1939, he donated a DC-2 and two Koolhoven FK-52s to the Finnish AF. The DC-2 was rebuilt as an ad hoc bomber by SAAB in Trollhättan in Sweden with a dorsal-gunner's position and external bomb racks. Apparently, the DC-2 was considered for a bombing sortie on the Kremlin! During the war, Von Rosen flew several sorties in Blenheims as well as the DC-2.

Getting to Biafra from São Tomé or Libreville was an event: the Nigerians were waiting for us. My own arrival was no different.

As soon as we crossed the coastline somewhere near Port Harcourt, I spotted flashes of artillery fire on the ground that quickly became brilliant orange balls of flak as they exploded a few thousand feet

Nigerian Air Force personnel, with Cape Town's Ares Klootwyk (in combat gear, second from the right) alongside one of that country's fighter aircraft. (Photo courtesy of Leif Hellström)

Crashed Soviet MiG-17 that came down in the jungle near Port Harcourt. Apparently the pilot did not pay attention to his fuel levels. (Photo courtesy of Leif Hellström)

below us. I watched the panoply through the porthole nearest to me, transfixed by the sheer terror of it. It was a bit like being at the movies.

Only after the war did it emerge that the nightly shuttle of aircraft was part of a giant charade – a chess game of sorts that the superpowers tended to indulge in from time to time. Nigerian anti-aircraft guns and their crews were Russian and somehow, those who made these nightly flights into Biafra were aware that their fuses had been set at 14,000 ft. Meanwhile, we crossed the coast at 18,000 ft. They could have shot us down any time they chose.

Our approach to Uli Airport was made in the black. Once we crossed the coast, there wasn't a light to be seen anywhere on the ground, apart from some heavy calibers shooting at us from what I worked out were the front lines of the war. What compounded matters, I was soon to discover, was that none of the aircraft approaching Uli used navigation lights, even though there were sometimes eight or ten aircraft stacked above and below us.

Getting on to the ground at Uli was a mammoth nightly operation that seemed to work but, considering the impediments, shouldn't have.

Chapter 16
Biafra's Aerial War of Attrition

There was a joke among relief crews: that if they were all to switch on their lights while circling Uli simultaneously, half the pilots would have died of heart attacks. They were flying that dangerously close to each other.

The actual landing process too, was dicey. With time, a succession of routines was developed with the result that our descent was ultra-steep. Pilots would manoeuvre their aircraft into position before sets of improvised runway lights were switched on for about five or six seconds. That was all the time they had to get their bearings. Meanwhile, our man was talking with ground control.

Though the world was black outside, most of the pilots would have some idea of where they were while circling because landing lights flashed irregularly before touchdown. Once into short finals, another few seconds of lights were allowed and that was that. It was a pretty precise operation and spoke volumes for the skill of the old timers flying these ageing hulks: many of the pilots were retired airline veterans.

More mercenaries flew a Nigerian Air Force bomber that had been dubbed 'Intruder' by the civilian flight crews. It usually hovered at about 18,000 ft and would wait for things to develop. Its pilot would try to drop his HE canisters just as an approaching aircraft came into finals, the hope being that the explosives would go off immediately before touchdown.

As Forsyth recalls, 'anyone listening in on the same wavelength could hear merc pilots flying the Nigerian bombers jeering at them, daring them to land when the lights flashed those few elusive seconds.'

The bombers rarely succeeded in causing serious damage. But when they did, the Nigerian propaganda machine would spin into action and Lagos newspapers would crow that Uli Airport had been crippled. It sometimes took a week to put things right again and often the Biafrans would find alternate stretches of road. Then the process would begin all over again.

A notable sidelight to these events is that in their final approach to Uli Airport, many pilots would come in so low that their fuselage would sometimes clip the tops of palms. Later, back at base, aircrews would compare notes about 'green props'. Just about everybody experienced them from time to time. There was also the occasional 'red props'. Since most loading teams were made up of tribesmen who knew little about the dangers of modern aircraft, there were instances of them walking into propellers while the planes were being offloaded.

Out of Libreville, our own flight had its moments. As the only passenger on board, I was relegated to the back. Between the flight deck and me was a mountain of babyfood.

From where I sat, I had a grand portside view of what was happening. It wasn't much, but a full moon allowed me to see a few of the contours of a black and rather ominous African continent below. Diminutive flashes peppered us once we crossed the coast, not far from Port Harcourt, and exploded harmlessly below where we were flying. Things became tenser once we approached Uli. What I wasn't to know until after it happened was that the 'Intruder' had dropped his load while our L-1049H Super Constellation – in concert with half a dozen other freighters – were brought into finals. Our wheels were already down.

Then came a brilliant flash, quickly answered by some heavy stuff from clusters of Biafran Bofors anti-aircraft guns on the periphery. A line of tracers cut across our nose. Our pilot pulled back sharply on the throttle. The old four-engined bird lumbered slowly towards starboard and an excuse for cloud that passed for cover. We circled for another hour before we tried again and this time were able to get down.

It is perhaps appropriate to look at the causes of this African civil war in which a million people died. At the time, it was the biggest military conflict the continent had experienced since the end of World War II.

What happened in the earlier phases was that with independence from Britain in 1960, Nigeria was divided into three distinct regions: the two in the south were largely Christian/animist while the northern half of the country was both bigger and more populous than the other two together. Also, it was thoroughly Islamic.

The Muslim heart of the upper half was centred on the ancient trading city of Kano. It also had control of Nigeria's government and its army and therein, sadly, lays the seeds of a bitter, bloody internecine war that was to last three years.

The flashpoint that led to this carnage came in 1966 when a group of young Eastern (Christian) officers launched a military coup d'etat against the central government in Lagos which, in their wisdom, they believed was utterly corrupt and being run by zealots. Almost as an afterthought, they murdered some of the most respected northern political/religious leaders including the venerable Sir Abubakar Tafawa Balewa, honoured by the Queen on Nigeria's independence in 1960, as a Knight Commander of the Order of the British Empire.

Chapter 16
Biafra's Aerial War of Attrition

Three images from the Biafran civil war that ended early in 1970. In the middle is a photo of Colonel Odumegwu Ojukwu, one of the most unlikely guerrilla leaders to emerge in Africa in recent decades. The son of a Nigerian millionaire, he had attended a British military college before returning home and becoming embroiled in the aftermath of a southern military putsch. He died in his bed, at home in Nigeria, in 2012.

In the time-honoured tradition of Islamic retribution, this act demanded more than a simple riposte.

Seven months later, a group of northern army officers, most regarding themselves as 'Sons of the Prophet', struck back with a countercoup. They ousted the Ibo leader, General Ironsi, who had taken over government and with that act, launched a vicious pogrom that resulted in the deaths of tens of thousands of easterners who had settled in the north, some of them generations ago.

Multitudes of Ibos fled back to the protection of their self-appointed leader, Lt Col Odumegwu Ojukwu. Already the Eastern Region was referring to itself as Biafra. At the same time, confident that the vast oil resources of his region could support him, Ojukwu refused to accept any kind of military authority that Lagos wished to impose on the country. If the violence against his people continued, he warned, he and his tribal people would go at it alone and Biafra would secede from the Nigerian Federation.

This was the last thing that Britain and the US needed at the height of the Cold War. Vietnam was still a strategic factor and if Nigeria were to fragment, the domino effect could affect Africa as well. They were also alarmed because overnight, a young Nigerian Army upstart that nobody had heard of before was threatening their oil investments.

Acknowledging they were powerless to stop a situation which, because of the slaughter of the innocents was being termed 'barbarous' by the international media, Biafra declared itself independent. By this time Ojukwu had secretly launched a massive build-up of arms involving people like the American arms dealer Hank Warton and Rhodesia's illustrious Jack Malloch.

Both men, together with arms merchants from France, Holland, Germany and China worked hand-in-glove with several European governments including France, Portugal and Spain to take in weapons to the rebel state that was recognised by four African countries: Tanzania, Gabon, the Ivory Coast and Mauritania.

South Africa, too, eventually got sucked into this morass with Special Forces Colonel Jan Breytenbach and several others involved in Biafran operations, training and tactical issues. It suited Pretoria to get clandestinely involved because it took the focus of attention off their problems back home.

In the end, there were mercenaries from a variety of nations in Biafra. For several reasons, which included isolation, lack of communications, an extremely harsh tropical climate in an area that us hacks had dubbed 'the armpit of Africa', these 'Dogs of War' had little impact on the eventual outcome of the war.

They very quickly ran up against an entrenched level of bias from Biafra's officer corps who believed that they could do better than a rag-tag bunch of hired guns. The fact that almost all of the mercenaries were white didn't help.

Hostilities ended abruptly in January 1970 after the Biafran people, simply put, had been starved into submission. It is notable that the slaughter of Ibos – which was to be expected after Federal forces had overrun the rebel territory – never happened.

Today, well into the new millennium, history seems to be repeating itself in Africa's most populous nation.

1 Michael Draper: *Shadows: Airlift and Airwar in Biafra and Nigeria*, 1967-1970: a delightful work detailing the exploits of former Biafran relief pilot Michael I. Draper, with an introduction by Frederick Forsyth (who had been in Biafra for more than a year by the time that the author arrived in the enclave).
2 Duff Hart-Davis: *The War That Never Was: The True Story of the Men who Fought Britain's Most Secret Battle*, Century, a division of Random House, London, 2011.
3 Al J. Venter, *Barrel of a Gun: A War Correspondent's Misspent Moments in Combat*, Casemate US and UK, 2010.

CHAPTER SEVENTEEN

GHANA: CONTRADICTORY WEST AFRICA

Once I had crossed the border into Ghana, a delightfully buxom woman who said her name was Mama Makola walked slowly across the busy road and took my hand. I had come from Lome, capital of Togo, I told her. Bouncy and effervescent, she had sparkling eyes that laughed and a smile that might once have belonged to the original African queen.

Mama led me to her stall, a ramshackle affair that stood open to the weather on three sides of four. A rusty tin roof suggested more: it might be modest, but it's mine!

'You must be hungry,' she insisted. She thrust into my hands a plate lined with banana leaves and a cup. Who was I to argue? That, briefly, was my initiation to Ghana; the Aflao frontier post, a doughy fufu stew that was so hot it could curdle the brain and my new friend Mama Makola. The palm wine she shoved across the table was optional.

Arriving in Accra for the first time can be a bit like being abruptly thrust into an unending African Mardi Gras. The noise and the bustle, together with traffic of an Asian intensity, can stultify. And, of course, there is the humidity which in the past has caused many people of European or American origin to cancel their contracts halfway through.

Hardly anybody in those days had air conditioning. Fetid and intrusive, this is the kind of climate that can nurture mushrooms on the carpet of your hotel room and turn leather green in a week. But then, as we used to say, 'that's the coast,' and those who could stay the distance were referred to as 'coasters'.

Not as big as Abidjan or Lagos, the Ghanaian capital, like all the cities between Dakar and Douala, is boisterously busy. One observer referred to it as 'a savoury blend of many African cultures', and of course he was right. The frontiers were man-made in an age when people knew only tribal boundaries and, for the rest, moved freely up and down the coast as the mood took them.

'While first impressions are of raucous dislocation, Accra – even in those days – worked. While there was very little money about, most folk seemed to manage.'

I wrote those words the first time I visited Accra in 1965. It was a couple of days after Mama Makola had fed me and some months before Winston Churchill died. To get there I'd paid the driver of a mammy wagon enough to let me sit up front.

Above my head, brilliantly emblazoned in Day-Glo paint on the cab was the inscription: 'Beware: He Go For Die'.

I had been travelling overland through Africa and it had already taken me several months from the Cape to London on a mainly land-bound expedition that tended to hug the coast. Ghana, following eight weeks on the road, was a diversion and after the equally enervating Lagos, I found this place exhilarating, enough to ask for a job back there when I eventually got to the UK. But it was not to be, because I was sent to Nigeria instead.

First impressions of Ghana remain indelible. Some of it reflected

Accra's Kotoka International Airport, named after Lieutenant General Emmanuel Kotoka who, as a lieutenant colonel, ousted Ghana's first president *Osajyefo* (Redeemer) Kwame Nkrumah in a coup d'etat in 1966. Kotoka was himself killed in an aborted countercoup a year later. (Photo: Peter Wilkins)

what those Americans I met along the way liked to term 'culture shock'. I'd been spared that in Lagos because the malaria had got me after I left Onitcha and I was bedridden for most of the time that I spent in the ersatz Nigerian capital. Anyway, I quickly discovered Accra was another sort of place and it sometimes defied description.

Though I've been back many times since, very little changed over the years. The people, the looks they gave us occasional whites moving about at their impecunious level, the smells (which could vary somewhere between the infusive pong of a rugby club change room and the fragrance of an upmarket curry den) were enchanting but sometimes stifling and repugnant, the open drains especially. Other sensations were timeless, especially the music – mainly Hi-Life. Even scavenging vultures over garbage pits on the edge of town could make for something new, and so too the medicine men and their stalls where all manner of potions were sold.

In a sense, Accra today is the same rambling, accessible, rambunctious friendly place it has always been, probably because it's the Ghanaians and not a bunch of expatriates who run the city. Their pride shows. For a start, Accra has never had that emaciated, scoured look that you find in some of the new, high-falutin capitals like Abuja, Yaoundé or Lilongwe in Malawi, and, I suppose, it's a plus that you don't trip over Americans and Japanese wherever you move, as in the Nairobi or Cairo of yesterday.

A Peace Corps volunteer I met on my first day there told me that in order to really see and understand what Ghana was about, I should get down to the bus station off central Accra's Barnes Road. It's a dirty, dusty stretch of real estate, she warned, though today it has a French hotel overlooking one end of it. In those days Novotel didn't exist.

'Look for a *tro-tro* heading down the coast towards Winneba, pay your cedis and sit tight!' she reckoned. Once clear of the city, another world would emerge and, of course, she was right.

Once on the road, the pandemonium of city life retreated on the great road west and quickly gave way to clusters of stalls and chop bars where the home-made kenkey and fish and goat's meat soup were a delight. As if by demand, social obligation seemed to dictate the pace, but most striking was the fact that just about everybody seemed if not happy, then at least content.

The clothes of many of these folk were threadbare and only the mammies carried weight, but life seemed to be good. Beyond the bright lights, it was also more relaxed.

There were other variances, like the costumes of some of the locals and the complicated regalia of elders, or the occasional cane rat – some as big as cats (they call them 'grasscutters' here) – strung up on bamboo stakes and for sale along the entire length of the road. Though they are rodents, cane rats are much prized for providing a distinctive flavour to gari stews, and they are also dished up in Benin, Togo, Nigeria and the Cameroons further east.

Sometimes, as we sped past, I would spot the tiny charred, black, almost human carcass of a vervet monkey strung tight over a charcoal fire.

But, of course, it was the people that made the place and it says a lot when a publication as widely known as the *Lonely Planet* handbook on Africa reckons that if an award were to be given for the friendliest nation on the continent, Ghana would be a powerful contender. 'Especially if budget travellers are doing the voting,' it declared in a fairly recent edition, and for good reason.

Part of the country's charm lies with the reality that this most modest little West African state – it is almost the same size as Britain – is not yet part of the full-blown international tourist circuit. Also, compared to more familiar haunts, the place is cheap. Stall meals at the side of the road start at a dollar, though that's pushing it and you'd be wise to give them a miss because who knows how long that meal has been lying exposed to the elements and some of the largest green flies on any continent.

Accra is different, but in terms of hygiene, only marginally so. A reasonable dinner in the Ghanaian capital – in a local, as opposed to a Western restaurant – shouldn't cost you more than US$20 and if it does, you've been had. Depending on where you are, the main dish might include lobster caught earlier in the day, brought ashore by one of the Kru boat crews.

It's almost the same with lodgings. Outside Accra you can sometimes get a tiny budget room for as little as $5. But if you prefer your comforts and can't live without air conditioning, one of the better hotels might ask $40 and in the capital, a lot more.

Lonely Planet suggests that if you work carefully with your money, you could manage Ghana on as little as $20 or $25 a day, but those days have changed and $50 might just cover bare essentials. A moderate hike in standards could up the total to double that, including clean and comfortable bedding, running water and regular restaurant meals. And don't forget departure tax at Accra's Kotoka International Airport which is also paid in American dollars.

Chapter 17
Ghana: Contradictory West Africa

Ghana these days is not a very different proposition from the place that I discovered more than half a century ago when I hitchhiked up the west coast of Africa the first time. For a start, it is pure African. More important, Ghanaians always like to make time for strangers.

While there is no country without crime, you can still walk about Accra, Kumasi, Takoradi or Tamale at all hours without fear, something I'd never try in any city in southern Africa. And please don't try that in Lagos or around Treichville in the Ivory Coast!

While the French seem to have a hand in just about everything that happens in their old dominions – and you see a lot of that among Ghana's Francophonic neighbours – that is not the case here. With some notable exceptions, it was Ghanaians, led by *Osagyefo* Kwame Nkrumah, who took power in 1957 when Britain acceded to independence under an elected majority. And though there have been hiccups since, the country manages very nicely today, thank you.

This is a society that presents a pretty unique face to the world. For a start, its roots are diverse, which is why so many of the old colonial traditions prevail. Ask any Ghanaian where else in the world he would rather live if he were forced to move and the answer would invariably be London. Ghanaian pride and initiative is evident everywhere, even if it's not yet catering to Nairobi-style, safari-hatted tourists or Western expatriates.

On my first visit, after a hectic week in Accra, I finally made my way towards the west and the ubiquitous mammy wagon was my vehicle of choice. They were cheap, reliable and, most important, bulky: if we hit *anything*, we had a chance.

Along the way I stopped over in Winneba, spent a couple of nights in Cape Coast looking at the great and beautiful Elmina Castle – where the slaves were dungeon-quartered in chains before being shipped out to the New World – examined the twin cities of Sekondi and Takoradi from up close, and for once, splurged on a night in the Atlantic Hotel where they had air conditioning. I also went and 'lived bush' for a day or two in a coconut plantation near Axim, a coastal settlement that has one of the saddest slave castles anywhere. History will chasten some of these old fortifications, but they are an unusual experience found almost nowhere else. All are worth a visit.

Finally, I reached Half Assini, a coastal village about 20 minutes' drive from the lagoon that separates Ghana from the Ivory Coast.

Quaintly named, modest and impoverished, like the rest, Half Assini must be one of the most colourful villages along this stretch

Fishing village to the west of Accra. The entire southern region is largely dependent on its small-boat fishing industry – and the country's gold mines – for its survival. (Photo: Peter Wilkins)

of coast. When I first got there, it lay at the end of a strip of tar that suddenly disappeared by the sea, and though things might have changed since, the place offered little but bare essentials. In those days Half Assini had no proper hotel, few restaurants that might have qualified for the appellation and more bars than I care to remember. One of them, where I spent most of my time once the sun had dipped towards the west, doubled as the town's social club.

What Half Assini did boast was a splendid Roman Catholic school where Kwame Nkrumah spent nine years of his early life. His egalitarianism probably stemmed from what the Jesuits taught him, though I doubt whether any other lasting impression remained. Nkrumah, it was said, was agnostic, which was why he was able to flirt with 'Consciencism' for as long as he did. Though that didn't stop him from adopting the title *Osagyefo*, which, loosely translated, means 'Redeemer'. Nkrumah's problem, once the British had handed over power to this emerging West African nation, was that he saw himself as having been anointed by a God he didn't believe in.

The people of Half Assini saw a lot of me. At my favourite watering hole the old scoundrel who ran the place sometimes charged me more than he should have, probably because I was the only white man there. But I never complained because they looked after me in other ways. It was that sort of place.

I lived frugally in a shack just off the beach, close enough to dip

Chapter 17
Ghana: Contradictory West Africa

into the surf when I needed to and get a shout when the boats went into the surf, usually pretty early. I'd head out in the Kru boats and, on returning to shore an hour or so later, help the guys haul in their nets – tough work when there was a swell running or more fish than usual were snagged. Whatever the outcome, I always got my share of the catch and though it wasn't much, it did make life a little more comfortable. Also, I could swap barracuda for a couple of bottles of Star beer.

And a month or so later, when the time came to move on, I asked the local headman for advice. After a bit of a palaver and an exchange of the necessary, they piled my things aboard a rusty old truck that was probably used for smuggling contraband and drove me a dozen miles along a great totally deserted beach to an equally remote lagoon.

There I was given a paddle and a seat in a 12-man *pirogue* and we headed north across an inland sea to the just recently independent Côte d'Ivoire. It took us five hard hours of work and halfway across, we almost lost sight of land. My arms ached for a week.

For all that, in Ghana, everything starts and ends in Accra. Unlike Europe and the Middle East, you need to create your own pleasures, though you're never short of advice.

The day usually starts at Accra's markets. A good place to begin is at the Arts Centre in the heart of the city: you walk down High Street towards Independence Square. This is where the artisans gather in stalls to sell their wares and a variety of entertainers will hassle you for a clutch of cedis to buy food. Count on catching some type of singing, dancing, jamming or just plain fun and don't be shy to join in.

Look carefully and these days, with the Ivory Coast verging on civil war, you might find some good examples of African art there. As in the Cameroons, metal works are in the vogue. On a recent visit, I bought two fine Benin bronzes: a large, erect Oba and his smaller Bini queen. What you need to watch for are distinguishing (and disfiguring) marks made by machine tools, so avoid them. Obviously the handmade items are also more valuable, and since the average Ghanaian is nobody's fool, he knows it too. Prices for such works can be high.

Search, too, for Foumban metal art from further towards the east. These pieces are most often cast, using raw aluminium and many are sand-sprayed to provide a rough patina to the work. Another time I bought a selection of one- and two-ounce polished traditional

African heads that are sometimes used for key rings. Originally used for fetish, most are cast in bronze in the 'lost-wax' method, which means that every one of them is an original. Some have the signature of fine craftsmanship.

There are several 'lost wax' workshops along the coast where artists produce remarkable items, many of which find their way abroad.

What happens in this process is that each work is first fashioned of wax. It's a difficult medium to work with if the design is intricate: you need good eyes and a steady hand to achieve results. The worked wax is then completely enclosed by wet clay that is allowed to harden. That achieved, the combination is heated: the wax melts, is poured away and the exposed hollow is filled with molten bronze heated to about 1,000 degrees Celsius in a home-made furnace, sometimes with bellows made of goat skin. Once it has cooled, you knock away the clay and *voila!*

West African artisans have been working this way for a thousand years and the results can be enchanting.

And then there is the gold, which gave the country its original name: the Gold Coast. Even today, much of the regalia used by the Ashanti Asantehene is pure gold, some of it dating back centuries. The British seized a lot of this national heritage when they sacked Kumasi during the Ashanti Wars of the 19th Century.

Like Lord Elgin's marbles, some of these treasures are still in the British Museum, while the two governments continue to argue about it being returned.

Accra is distinctive in that it has more goldsmiths than any other African city. At last count, there were about two hundred and, as I have seen often enough, their creations can be stunning.

Not far from the Arts Centre is the Makola Market, which brims with a diversity of glass-bead and batik sellers. Many foreign curio dealers come here to stock up on supplies and buy wholesale. The range is good and prices competitive.

You need to choose carefully because there is a lot of trash about. And don't pay the first price asked: the visitor is expected to haggle. As one tour operator told his group: 'Be reasonable. Don't knock these people.' To which he added: 'Remember, most of them are poor and what they offer is sometimes all they have. They, too, need to put bread on the table.'

Other places of interest in the capital are Kaneshie Market on the western side of the city with its displays of foods and African spices. Beware of red chili fufu because it can leave you breathless.

Another tip for Westerners: Ghana is a tropical country and, with time, the hardy metabolism of the locals has become resilient to what we in the developed world refer to as 'bugs'. As with Asia and the Middle East, you should not even try to eat everything you see. With alfresco culinary delights, I have a single guideline: if it's on the road and you can't peel it, don't eat it! You aren't going to go hungry: in Ghana there is fruit galore.

Another place of note is the Du Bois Memorial Centre for Pan-African Culture. With its gallery of manuscripts and research library the place has become an inspiration to many Africanists. The grave of this famous African-American scholar (and that of his wife) are also here. Similarly, the George Padmore Research Library of African Affairs is in Accra.

Of course, none of this would have happened had there not been a Kwame Nkrumah. What he left behind is worth a visit because the man did succeed in leaving his mark on Africa, tarnished though it might have been because he fostered revolution rather than progress. When he was ousted in a military coup, Ghana was bankrupt.

While Pan Africanism wasn't exactly the brainchild of *Osagyefo*, it was he, by practical example, who led the way. Nkrumah's perception was of a continent-wide 'flame of freedom' that would ultimately fan its way across Africa. And though he wasn't around to see it, the culmination of his efforts was President Nelson Mandela taking over the former all-white South African government from President F.W. de Klerk. While many of his critics have forgotten what Nkrumah stood for, most of his ideals came to fruition in the more than quarter-century since his death.

Although some African museums are a bore, Ghana's National Museum is an exception. It stands three blocks east of where Kwame Nkrumah Avenue intersects with Castle Road and its displays of drums, chiefs' chairs, Ashanti cloths, stools, swords and old photographs are interesting. All this stuff provides an insight into how it was on the west coast not all that long ago.

There are also records of more recent wars in which Gold Coast troops fought this century. Some of them – such as in helping to drive Mussolini's fascists out of Abyssinia – are quite illustrious. But the history of Ghana goes back well before that.

What we do know, is that the country was originally comprised of a large part of the Dogomba and Mamprussi kingdoms that flourished in the 12th and 13th Centuries. At about that time, groups of Akan speakers – among them the Ashanti and the Fanti – migrated from the savannah grasslands and established a series

The majestic old slave castle at Cape Coast on the main road west towards the Ivory Coast was originally built by Swedish traders for the Gold Coast's timber, ivory and gold. Only afterwards did it become the fulcrum of the Trans-Atlantic slave trade along this stretch of the West African coast.
(Photo: Peter Wilkins)

of predominant cultures below the forest line. Initially they formed a succession of small states. Within two or three centuries, these people carried on a lively trade with their sub-Saharan neighbours to the north.

The country itself is named after the old Ghana Kingdom whose heroes are still commemorated today in the country's folklore, and Basil Davidson recorded much of it.

The first whites to arrive – they got there in 1482 – were the Portuguese who built much of the Elmina Castle you see today. The British expanded it and then came Lisbon, followed by just about every country in Europe – Dutch, British, Danes, French, Germans and others. All of them, at one time or another, or sometimes conjointly, plundered this vast stretch of coast, starting in Senegal and moving south and east.

First it was gold that they sought. Later came the demand for slaves, or as these hapless souls were known in the argot, 'black gold'.

For Britain 'the Coast' represented opportunity – a national gamble always there to be taken up by the spirited, the misfits or the unwanted. Locals would sometimes refer to them as 'white trash' and in some respects they were right: many European layabouts

Chapter 17
Ghana: Contradictory West Africa

One of the ancient British mortars – short, stocky and on the face of it, quite ungainly as antiquated cannons go – which were used to defend Cape Coast Castle from attack, together with a healthy supply of cannon balls. (Photo: Author)

ended up in parts of Africa because they couldn't make a go of it back home.

But there was a difference with other British possessions. Unlike India or the New World, few people of accomplishment saw much in making lives for themselves in the tropical regions of what became known as the 'Dark Continent'. If they could stay the pace with their rotgut rum and keep the fever at bay, those that could, had it made: the poor indigenes simply had no idea what was being done to them.

There is many a story of traders setting up business in out-of-the-way places along the coast and offering beads and other trivia for precious metals. Truth be told, some dubious fortunes were made because so many of these newcomers offered little else but avarice. More positive aspects like communications, a judiciary and a competent administration came only much later.

As someone commented: how many notable British families had their fortunes embedded in the shady African ventures of a century or two ago will never be known. And while the history of South Africa's Randlords has been well documented, this aspect of the West African legacy must still be exposed.

You get a glimpse of it in the graveyards of Accra, Elmina and elsewhere. Whenever I visit West Africa, I make a point of spending a bit of time in the old cemeteries that you find on the verge of most settlements. The Imperialists – British and French alike – like their nabobs and box-wallah counterparts of India, were involuntary patrons, obviously of necessity. Wandering about, reading inscriptions on carved-granite headstones, it always astonished me that so many of them died so young. A good number of Britons buried in the old Gold Coast were teenagers or barely in their twenties.

Their women are also there. The majority were the wives of company or government officials or some avaricious trader. So many of them died within months of taking passage that, in retrospect, it is surprising the government didn't prohibit them from going to what was later termed the Fever Coast. You had a less than 50 per cent chance of surviving once you got on land. About two-thirds of those who spent time in places like Ghana and Sierra Leone succumbed to malaria or yellow fever in less than a year. Some died within days of getting there. I recall seeing headstones that would state that the afflicted took ill in the morning and was dead before dark.

Also, hygiene wasn't what it is today. Diseases were constantly ravaging settlements. If it wasn't the plague, it might have been cholera or typhoid, only they didn't then know them as such. The cause of so many of these ailments was never properly recorded, except that they were fatal.

What we do know, is that smallpox – also brought to Africa by the white man – sometimes wiped out entire communities, never mind the STDs.

CHAPTER EIGHTEEN

UGANDA'S INVASION BY THE TANZANIAN ARMY AND THE END OF IDI AMIN

Covering the civil war in Uganda in the mid-1980s was a bit like walking backwards down a dark tunnel. You never knew who was coming at you from the other end, or who would jump at you out of the gloom. No question, it was scary.

It didn't help that there were government spooks just about everywhere, goons in grey suits with non-reflective eyeshades, the characteristic African equivalent of Hollywood's answer to the spy game, even if the temperature was a stifling 40 degrees in the shade and humidity hovered somewhere around 99 per cent.

After the Tanzanian Army had sent in their invasion army from the south – they first took Entebbe and then moved cautiously north, pulverising areas ahead with heavy artillery, a tactic they used throughout the war – it gradually came clear that Idi Amin's days were numbered. 'Idi Amin Land' – as the hacks would sometimes call it – suddenly looked vulnerable. The fat tyrant always said that the Tanzanians were a bunch of hopeless hooligans and he ended up believing his own propaganda.

I had arrived in Kampala from Nairobi, taking a more circuitous route from Jinja to avoid a Tanzanian immigration check, and befriended a youthful American. By the time the Tanzanian Army dominated just about everything in the Ugandan capital we spent our time hanging around what was left of the old Intercontinental Hotel. It was called the Obote something-or-other at one stage, but with each change of government these glass-and-marble edifices tended to alter their names, almost with the regularity as some people change their underpants.

There were pitfalls aplenty. We'd head back to the hotel after dark and as you approached the tallest structure in town, you had to be circumspect about your approach because there were things going on above your head. The reason was simple: Idi Amin – courtesy of his paymaster, Libya's Muammar Gadaffi – had embraced Islam. That meant that hundreds of thousands of copies of the Islamic holy book were flown to Uganda and passed around as the new 'Doctrine of No Choice at All' and this is a nation that had always been staunchly Christian.

What had happened was that Idi Amin had stuffed all of Uganda's hotels with Qurans, including the Kampala Intercontinental. That meant that each time a Tanzanian officer booked into a room, the first thing that would disappear over the balcony would be that book, all three kilos of it and beautifully bound in red. Get that on your head from a hundred metres up and you're going to be looking for a hospital, only there were none worth the name in the Ugandan capital just then because Tanzanian War wounded came first. Ugandan troops no longer had that consideration – those found still alive after a battle were hauled into the nearby bush and shot, simple as that!

The Geneva Convention in many of these African conflicts might have been a computer game...

My young American friend was clearly disturbed, and frankly, very much out of his depth. He claimed to be a journalist, but the only writing he did was signing wads of blank traveller's cheques, of which he had quite a pile. Also, some of Idi Amin's security people were taking an unhealthy interest in this guy.

I knew some of the Tanzanian officers who had come up from Dar es Salaam and would strike up a conversation whenever the opportunity allowed. Because the American was in my company quite a bit, conversation eventually turned to him. I asked a few non-intrusive questions and eventually got a pretty straight answer: my American friend was a CIA agent, which frankly, was nonsense. First, he was far too young and, more to the point, Langley's people were distinctive in that they always operated in 'them foreign parts' in pairs. It was a characteristic trait that still tends to persist to this day, which makes them so easy to spot. Also, my pal was far too immature to be versed in the esoterics of espionage and, more to the point, totally inexperienced in the machinations of modern African politics.

Still, even I was puzzled because he never directly answered me whenever I asked him what he was doing in Kampala.

Life for us in a city caught in a cross-fire was pretty straightforward. The high-rise skyscraper in which we had hired rooms had balconies and each evening we would sit out there and watch the tracers curling up into the night sky like a firework display. And when some of the bangs got too close, we would go inside, but usually not before we had had a few toots. While I enjoyed traditional golf tangos, newspaperman's speak for gin and tonics, the Yank preferred his waragi – a pretty potent local spirit made of triple-distilled banana leaves – straight!

It was a heady concoction that would probably curl hair, but he loved it.

The end of the Cold War had brought severe tensions to this part of Central Africa towards the end of the 1970s. The reasons were varied.

Superpower money had dried up: The Soviet Union was gone, and the United States had new global priorities. Further, radical Islamic fundamentalism had begun to flex its muscles, and, as always, Central Africa was vulnerable to natural disasters, anarchy, and tropical diseases.

Also, Uganda, the Sudan, and Zaire were faced with an increase in cross-border raids and domestic insurrection. Civil war threatened to envelop the region. European and South African mercenaries were active in small numbers in all three countries.

Entered the buffoon Idi Amin whose eight-year dictatorship established new, 20th-century standards for barbarism and governmental corruption. He was forced into exile in 1979 following his war with Tanzania.

Relations between Tanzania and Uganda had been strained for some years before the war started. After Amin seized power in a military coup in 1971, the Tanzanian leader Julius Nyerere offered sanctuary to Uganda's ousted president, Milton Obote. He was joined by 20,000 refugees fleeing Amin's attempts to wipe out opposition. It was a story repeated often enough in Africa over the decades, and in some parts, continues to this day: insurrection followed.

A year after Obote fled, a group of exiles based in Tanzania attempted – unsuccessfully, as it happened – to invade Uganda and remove the dreaded ogre. Amin blamed Nyerere for backing and arming his enemies.

Things remained static for several years. In October 1978, dissident troops ambushed Amin at his presidential lodge in Kampala, but he escaped with his family in a helicopter. This was during a period when the number of Amin's close associates had shrunk significantly, and he faced increasing dissent from within Uganda. When General Mustafa Adrisi, Amin's Vice President, was injured in a suspicious car accident, troops loyal to Adrisi (and soldiers who were disgruntled for other reasons) mutinied. Amin sent troops against the dissidents (which included members of the elite Simba Battalion), some of whom had fled across the Tanzanian border.

Amin ended up declaring war against his hated enemy Nyerere and sent troops to invade and annex part of the Kagera region of Tanzania, which Amin claimed belonged to Uganda. The Tanzanians retaliated and the rest is history, except that Tanzania was broke when it sent its troops north and ended up bankrupt by the time they all headed home again. The country never really recovered economically even though the Tanzanian Army methodically stripped Uganda of every single piece of machinery, equipment and furniture that hadn't been bolted down. If it could be pillaged, it was. The booty was then hauled back to Tanzania, as it was euphemistically phrased in local papers, 'to help pay for the war'.

Only massive efforts on the part of the West got the Ugandan economy on its feet again, this time with a new man at the helm, former guerrilla leader, Yoweri Museveni.

One of Idi Amin's biggest blunders early on in the war was to invite almost 3,000 Libyan troops to Uganda to beef up his army. It was also a move that facilitated an unexpected national switch towards Islam. At the same time, he dispatched his rag-tag army on raids into Tanzania.

When it became clear that the Tanzanians were gaining ground, the Libyans, instead of getting on the first planes out, hung around until the end. And when they finally did make their move, it was too late.

In that final stage in and around Kampala they'd head down that same airport road that I'd used earlier and run straight into Tanzanian Army units that would be waiting for them near Entebbe. Ambushes would be set at several likely spots and once in the killing zone, the Soviet armoured personnel carriers the Arabs used would be the first to be destroyed. Those Libyans that managed to survive these initial onslaughts would rush into the jungle.

At that point, local people – civilians, one and all – would go into action. With their long machetes, they'd slaughter any Libyan they found hiding in the banana plantations or in the long grass. Each time somebody reported an Arab presence, the old, the young

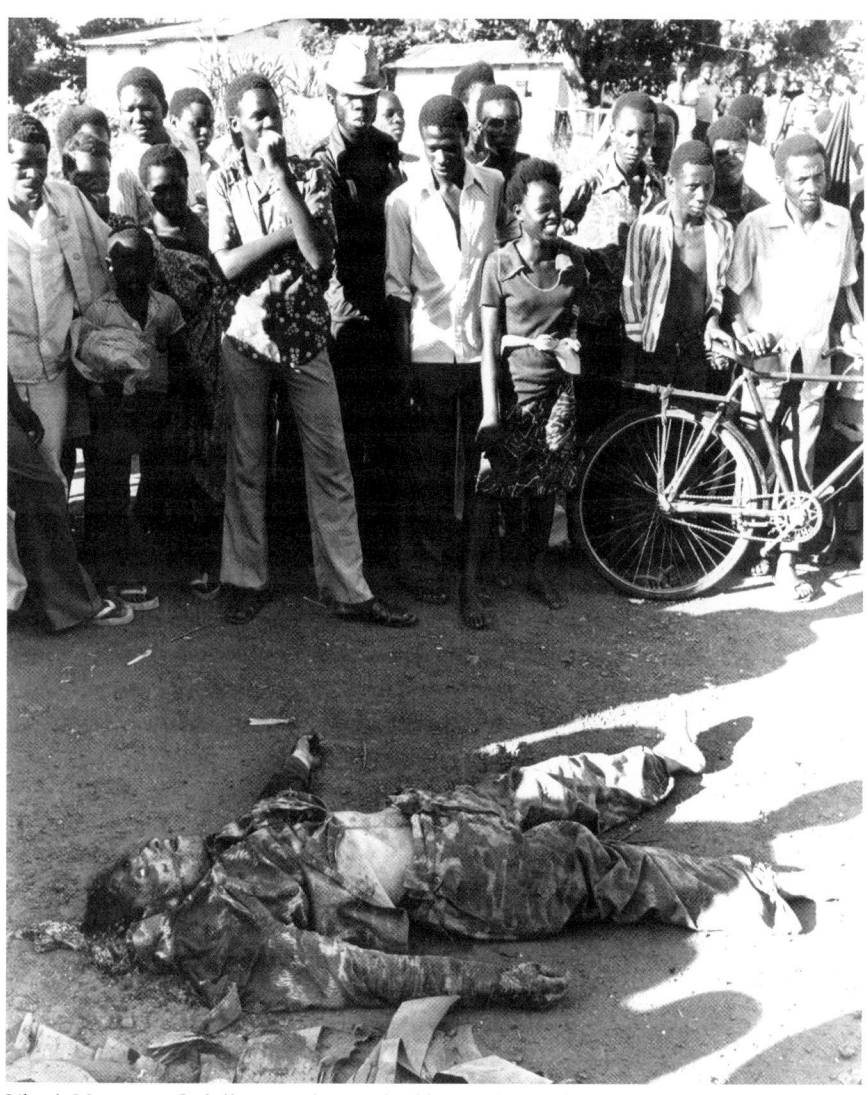

Chapter 18
Uganda's Invasion by the Tanzanian Army and the End of Idi Amin

Libya's Muammar Gadaffi sent a thousand soldiers to boost Idi Amin's disjointed defences, but they didn't last long after the brutal dictator had fled. Several hundred Libyan troops that weren't able to fly home from Uganda were hunted down by civilians on the main road between Kampala and Entebbe with long knives and machetes. (Photo courtesy of the late Mohammed Amin of CameraPix, Nairobi)

– male and female – would pile into Land Rovers, buses, trucks or even tractors and hunt them down. It tells you a lot that not a single Libyan prisoner was taken.

I watched one such hunt from a taxi on the main road to Entebbe out of Kampala. Word had it that there was a fair bunch of Libyans holed up in a building just off the main road. Eventually a group

After Idi Amin had been forced to flee, following the Tanzanian Army's invasion of Uganda, we discovered scores of massacre sites around Kampala where his opponents had been executed. At this farm there were dozens of bodies left to rot, many of them children whose hands and feet had been bound with wire before they were killed. (Photo: Author)

of local 'head-hunters' arrived, eager for battle. They all had long knives and were shouting, whistling and chortling, with the women around the periphery ululating as if there was no tomorrow. It was enormously intimidating, even though I wasn't the subject of their ire.

Gradually the crowd got bigger and whoever was cornered in the building did the obvious and stuck a white cloth out of a window. With that, the crowd went berserk and surged forward. There was no stopping them and while some of the youngsters tried to break through windows, the bunch of attackers out front managed to batter down the door.

Moments later three or four camouflage-clad figures were hauled out, to whoops of undisguised joy from the crowd. Everybody who was able to laid into the hated Arabs with their blades. The entire Libyan contingent was dead within minutes. They laid the corpses out alongside the main road and though I moved on, I heard later that they remained there for days – untouched, except by large flocks of vultures and forest animals that emerged to feast on the bodies at night.

For these Arab soldiers, a large part of the problem was that while Uganda was an African nation, Gadaffi's troops weren't black.

Chapter 18
Uganda's Invasion by the Tanzanian Army and the End of Idi Amin

Nor could many of them speak English. And even though some of these poor souls tried to worm their way into the woodwork, so to speak, they were very easily spotted, especially in the kind of underpopulated bush country that makes up so much of Uganda's interior.

Consequently, their fate was sealed. The few that did get away, managed early on to board the last flights back to Libya. Or a few of the more enterprising fugitives stole a boat or two and slipped away across Lake Victoria to Kenya.

The Libyans weren't the only Arabs with whom Idi Amin worked clandestinely. He had close links with a large Palestinian group linked to Yasser Arafat's al-Fatah terror movement, and the first we knew of it was the morning that the Tanzanian Army took over his official residence on Nakasero Hill, within walking distance of our hotel.

I was fortunate to get a tip-off that I could get into the building unimpeded and was able to spend an hour walking about all the rooms, including his bedroom where I found a box that had contained a new Smith and Wesson revolver in .44 Magnum calibre. The box and the guarantee lay next to the bed, but the gun itself was gone, as were probably a score more.

What wasn't missing was a large safe against one of the bedroom walls that somebody had blasted open, spewing hundreds of gold coins onto the floor, each one of them emblazoned with the dictator's face. In fact, they weren't solid gold but only plated, and I grabbed a couple of pockets-full, one of which eventually went to Elize Botha, wife of the South African president at the time. It was given to her by my old friend Professor Willie Breytenbach of Stellenbosch University who kept one for his missus after I'd given him a bunch.

Then somebody came up the stairs and said that there were some interesting things discovered in an adjoining building and we went down there together. The house in question had a direct link through the garden to State House and was a large old colonial structure that had been the Popular Front for the Liberation of Palestine (PLO) headquarters in Kampala. All the occupants had fled, but because they had obviously made a hasty and unexpected exit, they left behind an assortment of explosives and bomb-making equipment. This included a couple of letter bombs, made ready for dropping into the mail but not yet addressed.

By then we had been joined by several other 'journalists' each one of them intent on scratching about in the affairs of what was then

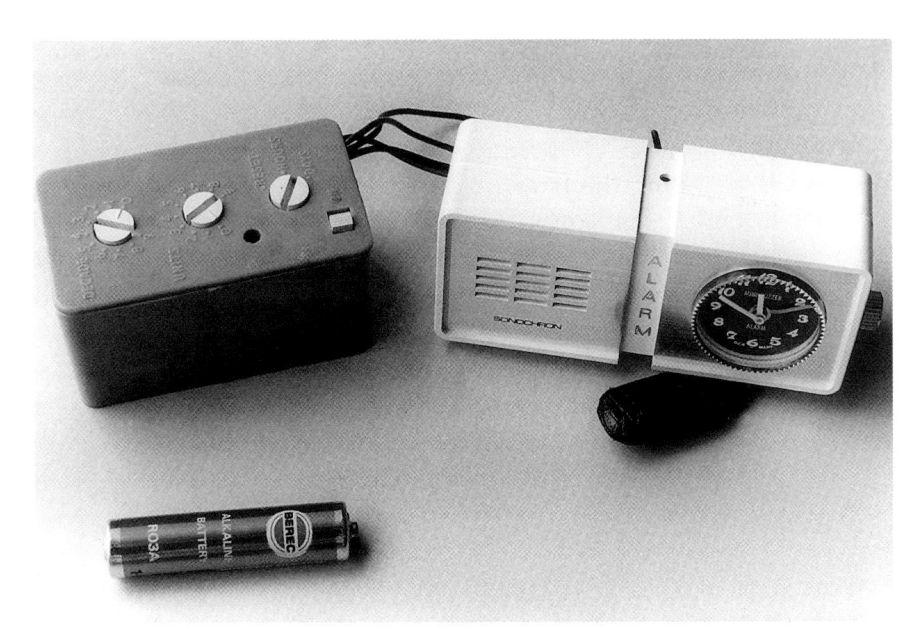

This tiny clock, with a penlight battery alongside, formed the basis of many of the bombs that were manufactured on a property run by Palestinian al-Fatah terrorists: it shared a fence with Idi Amin's presidential home on Nakasero Hill in Kampala. We also uncovered a stack of explosive letter bombs of the type that had been posted to prominent people in Europe and the Middle East.
(Photo: Author)

the leading terror group in the world. Curiously, by the time I was ready to leave, the two letter bombs had been filched from a position near one of the windows where somebody had placed them.

There were several rooms towards the back of the building that had large drums of what was clearly some kind of liquid explosive or possibly a precursor for the stuff because it oozed fumes that gave us all headaches. Elsewhere there were piles of small detonators like those used for blasting explosives on South African gold mines. Adjacent there were timing devices, which I photographed and are reproduced here. There were also some pipe fittings lying around, clearly intended for making pipe bombs.

It was all very compact, though there was no thought given to safety because the explosives, detonators and other bomb-making material lay around all over the place. I was glad to get out of there after I'd taken my photos. And though I mixed with the international press corps pretty freely while I remained in Kampala, I was never to see any of those individuals who had gone over the PLO building again. Almost a man, they must have all been spooks...

What we know today is that one of the pipe bombs that was manufactured at that building that housed the PLO bomb-making squad, almost certainly killed Bruce McKenzie, Kenya's Minister for Agriculture and close advisor to President Jomo Kenyatta, on the afternoon of 24 May 1978.

Relations between Kenya and Uganda had taken a serious downturn following the Israeli rescue of hostages when a group of German terrorist hijacked an Air France passenger jet and took the aircraft and its 248 passengers to Entebbe Airport where they were held hostage 26 months before.

Idi Amin and his backers were severely embarrassed by the Israeli rescue and, as I was to discover over the years, memories in East Africa die hard.

Eager to try to patch things up with his western neighbour, Kenyatta sent Bruce McKenzie on a fence-building mission to Kampala, having carefully cleared the minister's path through diplomatic channels beforehand. The message that came back to State House in Nairobi was that Idi Amin would be happy to receive Jomo Kenyatta's emissary.

McKenzie flew to Entebbe in a light aircraft piloted by Paul Lennox. He was driven to State House in Kampala, had an amicable lunch with President Amin, and as a gesture of goodwill, was given the gift of a lion's head carving, which McKenzie took on board the aircraft with him. The plane blew up in the air 17 minutes before it reached Nairobi's Wilson Airport.

There was the usual investigation that followed and though positive proof emerged of a bomb explosion, it stayed under wraps until international pressure forced Kenya to admit that it had been a pipe bomb that had been responsible for the death of Bruce McKenzie.

What was notable was something the hack community had always been aware of: that McKenzie, though of Scottish ancestry, had a Jewish mother, something the PLO must have picked up along the way. What also emerged very much later was that the only white minister in Kenyatta's cabinet was also a British intelligence operative, with a history of association with the SIS that went back to World War II.

What made conditions in Uganda different from the rest of Africa was that Amin was one of the first post-colonial dictators in Africa to unleash mass killings as a response to internal opposition.

During his eight years as president, beginning in 1971, his government was responsible for the deaths of as many as half a million of his countrymen. Another 100,000 fled into exile while

WARNING!

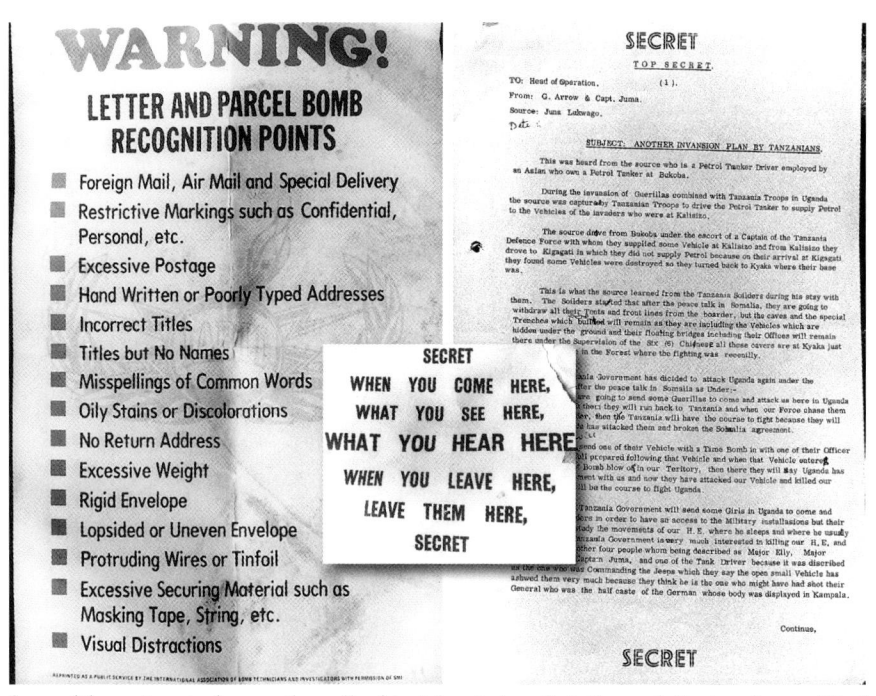

LETTER AND PARCEL BOMB RECOGNITION POINTS

- Foreign Mail, Air Mail and Special Delivery
- Restrictive Markings such as Confidential, Personal, etc.
- Excessive Postage
- Hand Written or Poorly Typed Addresses
- Incorrect Titles
- Titles but No Names
- Misspellings of Common Words
- Oily Stains or Discolorations
- No Return Address
- Excessive Weight
- Rigid Envelope
- Lopsided or Uneven Envelope
- Protruding Wires or Tinfoil
- Excessive Securing Material such as Masking Tape, String, etc.
- Visual Distractions

SECRET
WHEN YOU COME HERE,
WHAT YOU SEE HERE,
WHAT YOU HEAR HERE
WHEN YOU LEAVE HERE,
LEAVE THEM HERE,
SECRET

Some of the posters stuck up on the walls of Amin's notorious State Research Centre where political prisoners were interrogated, tortured and, almost unfailingly, killed. (Photo: Author)

thousands languished in prisons and underground torture chambers. Before Amin, we were all aware that Uganda's economy was regarded as one of the healthiest in East Africa. Like Zimbabwe today, it ended in utter shambles.

There is no question that Amin, who won the Uganda heavyweight boxing championship in 1951 while serving as an NCO in the then still British-dominated East African army, was a certifiable madcap. It was also one of the reasons why those of us who reported from Uganda at the time believed he was suffering from an advanced form of syphilis. What made it that much more astonishing was that he would never have achieved power had his British mentors, of all people, not encouraged him to oust his equally demented predecessor, Milton Obote.

That contemptible monster, it should be noted, ended his years in exile in Zimbabwe and enjoyed both the protection and the patronage of his host, Robert Mugabe. It says much that Westminster was also responsible for bringing Mugabe to power.

Of all of Africa's dictators, Idi Amin was arguably the most unhinged, though the absurdly racist antics of the Zimbabwe dictator make him a close second. While in power, 'Idi the Conqueror'

Top: The author with Cobus Claassens during the time he spent with the Executive Outcomes mercenary group in Sierra Leone. The photo was taken after the South Africans had overrun the Biama rebel camp near the Kono diamond fields. Below, a Ugandan Army Soviet-built tank knocked out by the rebels and abandoned on the road north of Kampala to Gulu. (Both photos from author's collection)

A diverse collection of photos from Fiona Capstick and Manuel Ferreira from the period when the Comores was under the control of French mercenary Colonel Bob Denard. The island was Grand Comores and the deck scene, top right on the opposite page, was taken on board the ship that the French commander used to invade the island group.

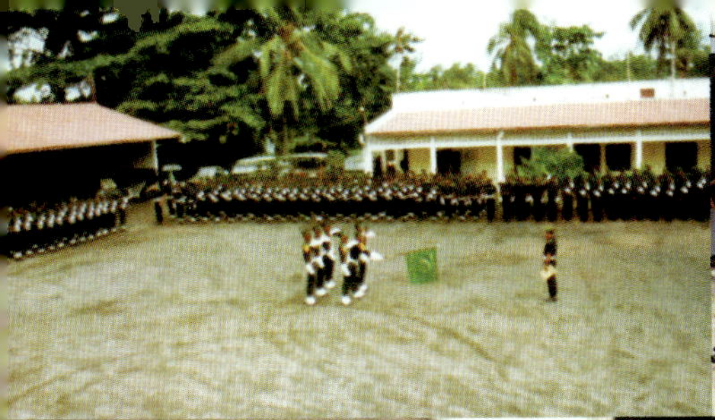

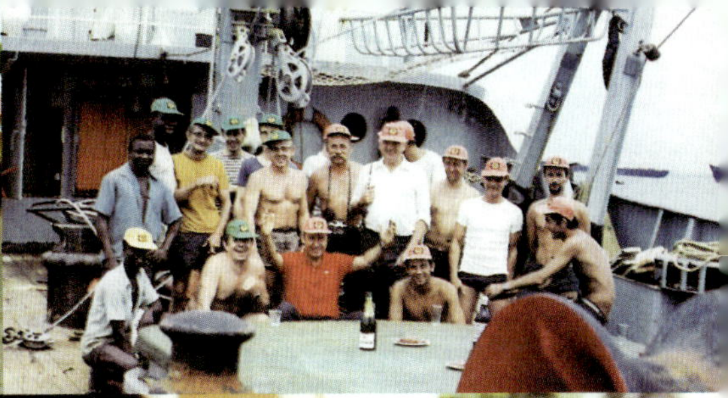

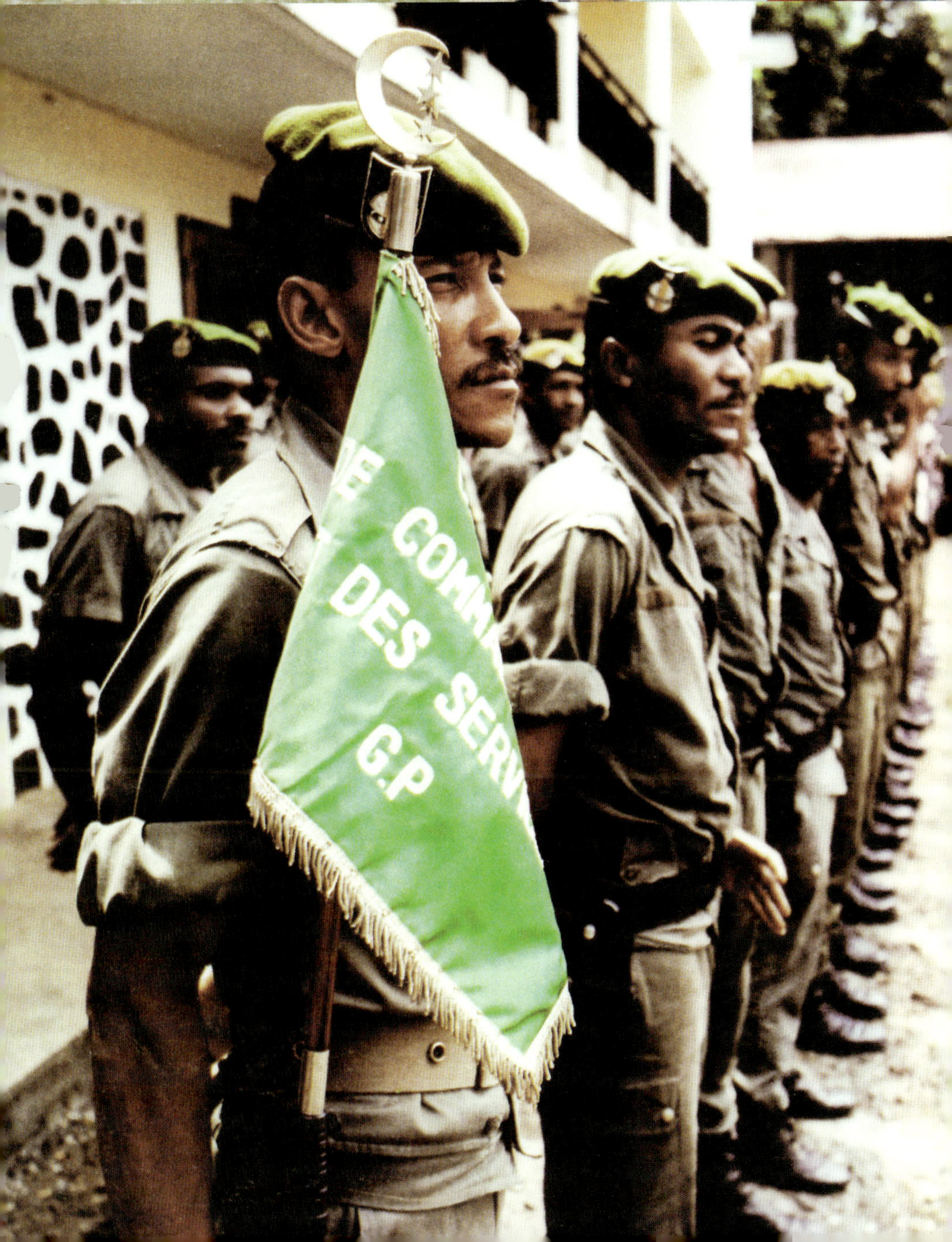
DE
COMM
DES SERV
G.P

A squad of Rhodesian soldiers, the majority not yet out of their teens, on patrol among the coffee plantations in the east of the country. (Photo: Author) The three inserts were drawn by the historian Dr Richard Wood and show the fundamentals of an airborne fire-force attack involving mainly Alouette helicopters.

A Fire Force Action of the Phase One 1974-1976

A Fire Force Action
of the Phase Two
1977-1979

A Fire Force Action
of the Phase Three,
The Jumbo Fire Force
of 1979

A selection of photos provided by Chris Cocks and former Rhodesian-SAS operative Darrel Watt of anti-guerrilla operations in the bush.

The Biafran War was the biggest military confrontation that Africa had seen since the end of World War II. The rebel state battled bravely for several years – including producing its own banknotes – but it simply could not match the military aid and hardware that the Nigerian government received from Moscow and London. (Photo: Author) Bottom right shows one of the irregular diamond pits mined by the locals in Sierra Leone, some of them full of rainwater. (Photo: Author, taken from Neall Ellis's Mi-24 gunship)

The grim jungle terrain of Sierra Leone, much of it controlled by the rebels while the war lasted. It was an extremely difficult country in which to fight a guerrilla war, but in the end, South African mercenaries showed the world how it was done. Bottom: The author on his way north in Uganda with a French television crew. In the end they had to run for their lives. (Photos: Author's collection)

The atrocities committed by the Ugandan tyrant Idi Amin Dada against tens of thousands of civilians, many of whom were killed by his security goons, was unconscionable. Many were tortured in this primitive 'electric chair' using open wires attached to body parts, including genitals (bottom left). Only after he had fled were we to see the extent of the slaughter with mass graves outside all the cities and towns and skulls left as a warning, displayed on stakes on the side of many of the country's roads. (Photos: Author's collection)

More images from the CIA-sponsored anti-guerrilla war in the Congo of the 1960s which involved large numbers of mercenaries. The photo top left shows a rocket strike on enemy boats that had been using Lake Tanganyika as a supply conduit, while opposite, unloading from a US Air Force transporter one of the Swift boats that the Americans deployed in Vietnam. These craft were used against the insurgents on some of Africa's great lakes. (Photos courtesy of the Leif Hellström collection)

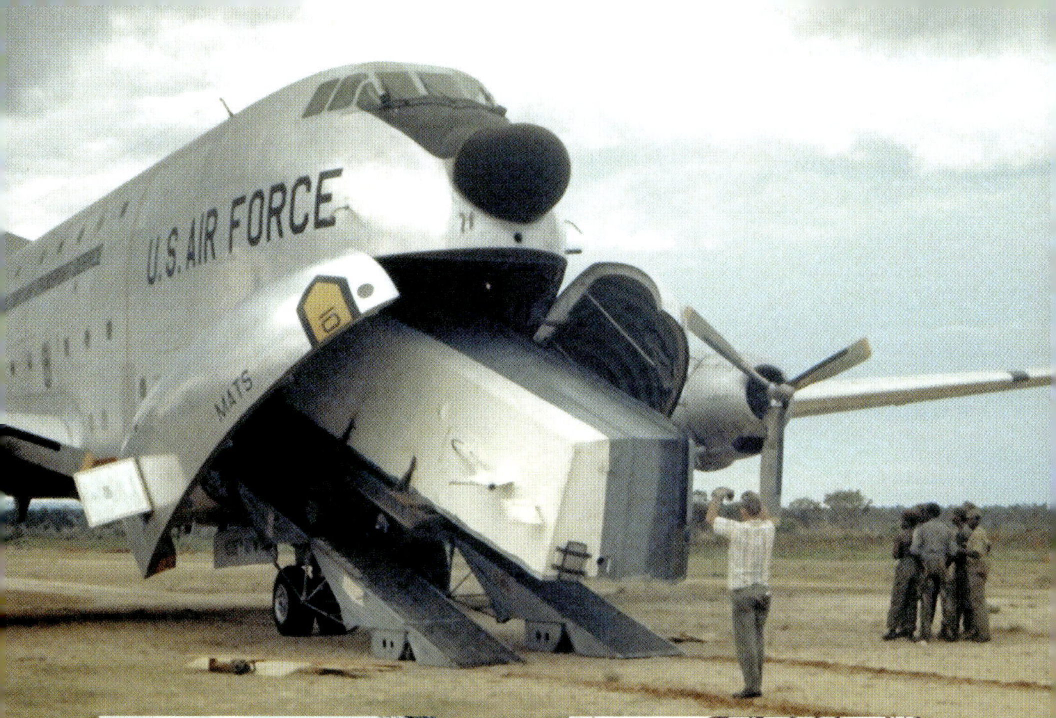
U.S. AIR FORCE
MATS

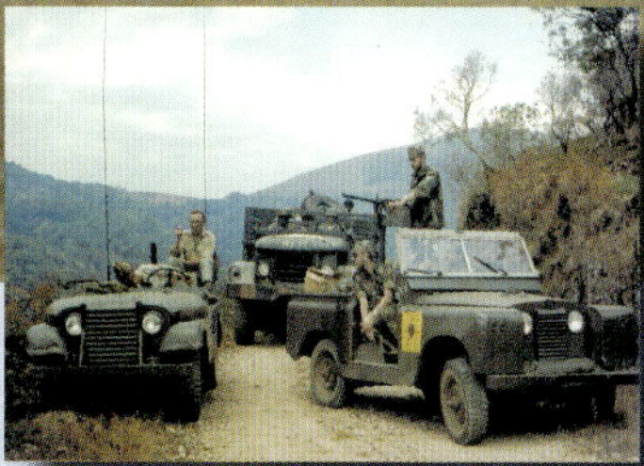

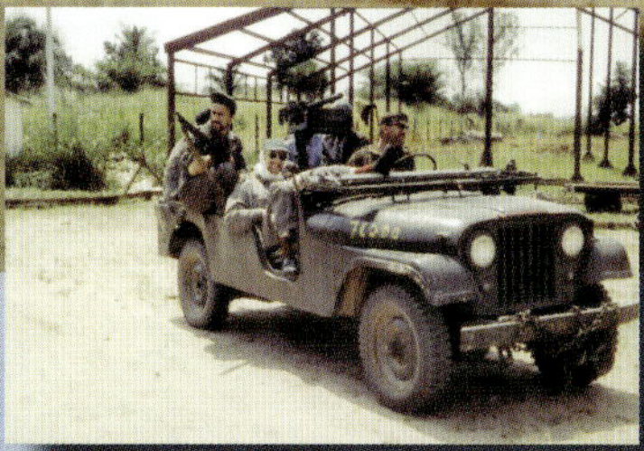

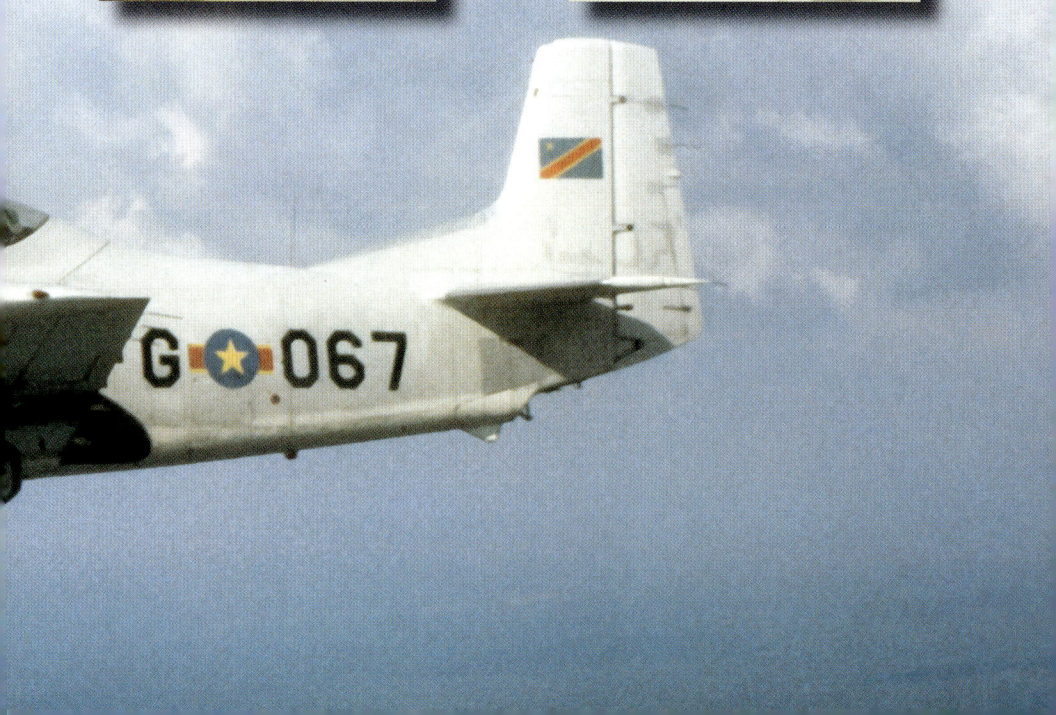
G 067

Images of the Border War, with 'Oom Willie se Pad' – it ran west to east through Caprivi, never very far from the Angolan border and that meant that landmines were commonplace. The other photos show the mounted and the motorcycle units, both attached to SWA Special Operations while the war lasted. (Photos: Author)

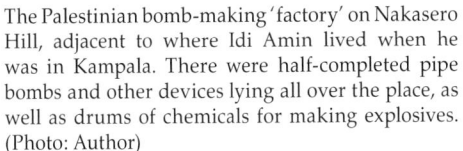

Chapter 18
Uganda's Invasion by the Tanzanian Army and the End of Idi Amin

The Palestinian bomb-making 'factory' on Nakasero Hill, adjacent to where Idi Amin lived when he was in Kampala. There were half-completed pipe bombs and other devices lying all over the place, as well as drums of chemicals for making explosives. (Photo: Author)

awarded himself the Victoria Cross and announced that he was adding to his list of titles – which included Lord of All the Beasts of the Earth and Fishes of the Sea – that of Conqueror of the British Empire. Perhaps then, and not altogether surprisingly, it was Amin the buffoon, not Amin the butcher, who first caught the world's attention.

He raced around Kampala in a red sports car, watched Tom and Jerry cartoons, plunged into swimming pools in full military uniform during diplomatic functions and boasted that he had fathered 35 children.

A cruel, ruthless man, Amin presented himself to the world as a ridiculously absurd figure. He volunteered himself as King of Scotland, so that the Scots, as he liked to say 'could be free of British rule' – a theme which resulted in a brilliant film that went on to win an Oscar. Then he would send telegrams to the Queen of England, insulting and taunting her. He once challenged the president of Tanzania to a boxing match.

When the capital of Kampala fell on 10 April 1979, Amin, along with his wives, mistresses and a very substantial quota of children had already boarded a plane for Libya. From there the entourage was quickly dispatched to Saudi Arabia where he eventually died. Muammar Gadaffi, another African delinquent then very much in the spotlight, did not need the presence of this buffoon to further tarnish his already dubious reputation.

Uganda was an interesting place to visit in the old days and, as others discovered, it could also be perilous.

The main entrance of Idi Amin's notorious State Research Centre in Kampala. Curiously, it was Milton Obote, his predecessor and the man whom Amin had ousted as president, who founded this wicked establishment. Obote ended up as Mugabe's 'guest of state' after he had been thrown out of office a second time. (Photo: Author)

My old *rafiki* Mohammed Amin – Idi's namesake, and certainly no relative – ran his illustrious news agency that he called CameraPix out of Nairobi and he would regularly tell me that his latest source of news or photos in Kampala had 'copped it'. There were six or eight of these stringers murdered by the general's goons. Several disappeared without trace.

As a journalist, Uganda was part of my unofficial news-gathering brief, which suited me because you never came away from Kampala without something either interesting or ridiculous to write about. I went there with my wife once and we were among the score of tourists to have booked a visit to the Murchison National Park that year. Despite the risks, it was a memorable trip, boating on the Upper Nile and taking pictures of some of the biggest crocodiles on the planet. Amin, we were to learn later, fed many of his victims to these beasts.

What disturbed me most was that we were under surveillance by the Uganda secret police from the moment we stepped off the plane at Entebbe. Even at Murchison, where we slept in a tented camp – and there were obviously no doors to lock – I was aware that Amin's agents were always on the periphery. My wife was the

Chapter 18
Uganda's Invasion by the Tanzanian Army and the End of Idi Amin

THE PRESIDENT

Khartoum, 12th. July 1976

Dear Excellency,

Please accept my personal greetings and fra ternal wishes for your goodself, Government and people.

I feel it my duty to acquaint your Excellency through this personal message, with the details of an act of external aggression to which the Sudan has been subjected. Through a handful of dissident elements headed by Sudanese ex-politicians, the Libyan Arab Republic has brought about havoc , bloodshed and destruction into our country.

The members of acertain religious sect have tried to challenge the authority of May Revolution by taking up arms against the Government of the Land. That uprising had to be quelled, but a few of its followers took harbour in neighbouring Ethiopia claiming refugee status.

My Government had, through the good offices of H.R.H. Prince Saddrudin Khan, tried to persuade those so-called refugees to return home where stability, law and security had prevailed. Mis-guided by religious fanatacism, a few thousands were determined to stay abroad. It was then, in 1970, that the seeds for this armed aggression began to germinate, with the active encouragement of the ruling clique in Libya.

They have, over the last few years, failed to appreciate our views on how a unified Arab programme of action can best be implemented. These differences were fully exploited by those Sudanese dissident elements whose followers started to migrate to Libya in small groups. Intensive military training on modern arms started in the Libyan region of Kafra and Jebal Omoweinat.

This letter was one of a bunch that the author grabbed when he went through Idi Amin's house after he had fled. He also left with a pocketful of gold-plated medals bearing Amin's head and which were never issued. (Photo: Author)

One of many roadblocks on the road north to Gulu photographed by the author while travelling with a French television crew at Murchison. Some of these militants were barely into their teens. (Photo: Author)

proverbial innocent in paradise, so I said nothing, though obviously, I got very little sleep.

It was during this time that Amin murdered two journalists, an event that caused us all to take heed.

Then his 'killer squads' murdered two Americans, Nicholas Stroh, a journalist and heir to the Stroh Brewery in Detroit and Robert Siedle, a sociologist who had been studying the care of the elderly in Africa while teaching at Makerere University in Kampala. Years later, Siedle's son – who was 16 when Amin came to power – reported that he had been living with his father in Uganda at the time. He also disclosed that his dad had come to know Amin before the general took control of the country and was initially impressed with him.

Everything that happened to young Siedle appears in his book, *A Tree Has Fallen In Africa*.

As Siedle tells it, unspeakable cruelty such as murder, torture and rape committed by Amin and his poorly disciplined army began to circulate in the months that followed the madman's putsch. About then his father and Stroh became suspicious of the thunderingly gregarious general.

'When rumours that hundreds of soldiers at the army's Mbarara Barracks, some 250 kilometres outside of Kampala, had been

Chapter 18
Uganda's Invasion by the Tanzanian Army and the End of Idi Amin

slaughtered on 22 June 1971, filtered through to Kampala [they] set out into the African bush to seek confirmation of the atrocity.

'So, on 7 July 1971, the two men cranked up a battered old pale-blue Volkswagen station wagon with a handwritten 'Press' sign attached to the windshield and drove off into the tangled heartland of Uganda, never to be seen again.

'Their disappearance alerted the world for the first time of the policy of mass murder of the Amin government that came to be referred to by the International Commission of Jurists as Amin's "reign of terror."

'Only weeks before, I had celebrated my 17th birthday in Africa with my father. A few days later, I returned to the United States alone. Neither my father's body nor Stroh's was ever found. Pleas by the US State Department to the Ugandan government to have my father declared dead so his estate could be settled and life-insurance benefits paid were met with denials by Idi Amin.

'My father and Stroh, the hefty general said, had simply left the country, gone on holiday, the American Embassy in Kampala was told.

'Twenty-six years later, in May 1997, I returned to Uganda as a guest of General Muntu, commanding officer of the Ugandan Peoples Armed Forces. The intention was to interview the soldiers who murdered my father and dig for my father's body …'

Using Nairobi as a base, I went back to Uganda repeatedly over the years, both before and after Idi's rule. Sometimes we scribblers would score pay dirt, perhaps by being invited to State House where we were expected to grovel before this uncouth idiot. Most of the European scribes would cower and smile, usually sublimating their fears in booze, of which there was always more than enough. I never did, in part because I thought it wise to stay sober if I was to keep my head, which might have been why Amin remained reasonably civil towards me during the few times we did make contact, once at his home on Nakasero Hill which overlooks some of the better parts of Kampala, including the diplomatic quarter.

Towards the end, he even sent me the Muslim equivalent of a Christmas card during the Eid.

Getting into Uganda during Amin's rule was, at best, problematic. Everybody who arrived from abroad – and even from Nairobi – was watched. That meant that I preferred using alternative routes, like overland through Rwanda several times, or ferry across Lake Victoria.

Going in by lake steamer was always a delightful voyage, but only if you travelled first class. I'd customarily board at Kisumu in Kenya – usually at the end of Kendu Road, in a harbour affectionately named Port Florence in the colonial epoch. Flying boats en route to Europe and back to South Africa would overnight there in those heady colonial times before World War II.

During the boat trip that took us across Lake Victoria, there were stops a-plenty en route, some in Tanzania further south. Throughout, we'd keep a sharp eye for lake flies that could descend on the ship in dark, noxious clouds, often half a kilometre wide. People are known to have been suffocated by those dense, slow-moving swarms.

Once berthed at Entebbe, I'd join the rabble and try to get through customs and immigration without fuss. Usually I'd latch onto some backpackers who were always around and most times I'd succeed. Then I'd take what might have passed for a cab along one of the most dangerous roads on the continent of Africa to Kampala, though that would usually begin with a 10-minute haggle over fares and my checking the vehicle.

Whenever I used local transport in East Africa, there was always a strict routine that needed to be observed, like holding onto my baggage and first checking both wheels and brakes. Quite often the intended car would be faulted on both counts: the treads on an astonishing number of vehicles on Uganda's roads were down to their canvas underlays and blow-outs were as commonplace as fuel stops.

Of the dozens of times that I made this hazardous journey, there were almost always accidents along the way. The bodies of victims would be carefully laid out on the verge for the families to collect and, if there was none, or the word hadn't yet got out, the cadavers would be buried somewhere nearby a day or so later. Because putrefaction sets in within hours in that heat, it was the sensible thing to do, not that anybody concerned themselves unduly with graveyards...

What eventually caused Idi Amin's crunch was his murder in February 1977 of Uganda's Anglican Archbishop Janani Luwum, together with two senior cabinet ministers. They all died in what was described as a car accident, but there was evidence that the archbishop was clinically butchered. In fact, I was subsequently told by several former members of his cabinet that parts of this eminent ecclesiastic were later fed to guests at a banquet held for members of the diplomatic corps in Kampala.

By then, world opinion had turned against this lunatic and for the first time, several African nations broke their silence about the excesses of a fellow African leader. In fact, they were far more outspoken about Idi Amin then than they've subsequently been about Zimbabwe's Robert Mugabe.

Moving around Kampala during that uncertain time of transition had its moments. There was nothing to stop us going into what was then still innocuously referred to as the Ugandan State Research Centre, the ultimate misnomer, because it was Idi Amin's torture chamber.

In reality, this relatively modern cluster of buildings, that had several deep dungeons and was surrounded by a tall concrete and razor-wire fence, was equated by many Ugandans to Moscow's old Lubiyanka Prison. It was a grim, austere sort of place; anybody taken through those iron gates on Nakasero Hill while the tyrant ruled, very rarely emerged alive.

With Idi Amin out of the way, the security system so assiduously cultivated over the years fell apart. Those who had previously been in charge became the hunted and families settled old scores with a vengeance that almost equated some of the earlier violence.

An immediate consequence was that there was nobody around either willing or able to shred many of the documents that implicated thousands.

There were piles of files and papers lying scattered about on the floor of every room in the State Research Centre, some half a metre deep. Many were marked 'Top Secret' and I grabbed those that looked interesting.

Early on, I was able to make my way through several dark corridors to the dungeons in the basement and it was an appalling experience. They were still removing the dead from those cells

Thousands of human skulls were scattered about the countryside by the time that Idi Amin was deposed. This tragic bunch lay on the ground alongside the main road out of Kampala to the north.
(Photo: Author)

during my first visit and the stench was almost overwhelming. It took me a while to do the rounds and it was obvious that there wasn't a cell where there hadn't been inmates shackled to the walls, many naked, every one of them emaciated.

While males predominated, there were also women inmates. Who will ever know to what abuses those poor creatures were subjected; the walls of almost all the chambers were caked in dried blood. We didn't need to be told what it was because a water main had broken somewhere in the building and the lower floors were lightly flooded. Where the water reached up onto the walls, the black mucous that was scattered in irregular patches everywhere reverted to its original crimson.

What came next surprised even a few of the hardened newsmen that had observed human rights excesses in other parts of the world. There was a large room at the far end of the deepest concrete tunnel that had obviously been used for torture. What appeared to be a home-made wooden chair stood in a corner, complete with canvas buckles on the armrests and still more to clamp the feet of the victim. All around wires protruded both from the walls and from a device that looked like a small generator.

We were already aware that Amin liked to be present when some of his victims had electrodes clamped onto their heads, ears, nose and testicles. Whether they talked or not was irrelevant because within days, all were dead.

Long before he had been deposed by the Tanzanians, we were aware that Idi Amin had taken over the day-to-day procedures involved with running his government, much like Zimbabwe's Robert Mugabe of more recent times. This monster consolidated his power under three security groups, the military police, his so-called Public Safety Unit as well as the dreaded State Research Centre. All enforced his decisions with the kind of terror that, had Amin still been alive, would have probably led to him standing trial at the International Court of Justice at The Hague.

Indeed, the State Research Centre conducted some of its 'public executions' at its headquarters, in the heart of the capital.

There is no question that the diplomatic corps in Kampala was not aware of what was going on. Nakasero Hill was the suburb of choice of many diplomats, as well as some of the well-heeled businessmen who had decided to stay. In fact, at that stage, the residence of the French Ambassador was only across the way and the screams of prisoners were so bad that his wife had to be flown out for treatment at a clinic in France.

Chapter 18
Uganda's Invasion by the Tanzanian Army and the End of Idi Amin

But this, it was argued at the time, was Africa. The country was newly independent and in the main, Europe and America, much to their discredit, tended to turn a blind eye to such excesses. While South Africa was being castigated about its apartheid policies, hardly a word about Uganda was whispered in the corridors of power at UN Headquarters in New York.

Black people, the apologists would say, didn't do such things. In fact, they were only emulating some of the excesses that Europe had experienced in its recent past at the hands of an Austrian political upstart who had made corporal in World War I.

History then went on to repeat itself in the Congo, Equatorial Guinea, Liberia and more recently, in Zimbabwe.

Things have improved a lot in Uganda in recent years, but there are still serious problems, many of them symptomatic of Third World conditions.

Kampala is still as it ever was, a crossroads of sorts in a difficult corner of the world. A Kenyan writer described it as follows in his book[1] *One Day I Will Write About this Place*: Kampala, he tells us, 'seems disorganised, full of potholes, bad management and haphazardness. It is the kind of Africa that so horrifies the West in all of us. The truth is that it is a city overwhelmed by enterprise. I see smiles, the shine of healthy skin and teeth; no layabouts lounging and plotting at every street corner. People do not walk about with walls around themselves as they do in Nairobbery.'

The city has its downside, many, in fact. On my last visit to this Central African region, I met three German businessmen who had attempted to set up a trading business – a simple trade: shipments of raw coffee, which Uganda has in abundance, for planeloads of cattle. It was a reciprocal venture, subsidised in part by a government agency in Kampala: the cattle were being channelled through from Egypt on charter planes.

The three men were quite dismal about the venture by the time I made contact with them at our hotel. Even though the deal had started out well enough – there were to be 15 shipments in both directions altogether, with the coffee ending up in Europe – things had gradually gone 'toes up', as one of those who was involved explained.

Dieter G, the man who ran the show, was an old Africa hand, had spent many years in southern Africa and admitted over a few beers that he should have known better because it was all a scam.

'The first two shipments went well,' he explained; cattle flown in and bags of coffee – tons of it at a time – going out. 'Then, with the third shipment, we were told that the coffee hadn't yet come through from the interior.'

Never mind, the German said, the plane would go back and fetch more cattle and though it would cost a bit more, the European consortium accepted that it was Africa and this sort of thing sometimes happened.

'Trouble was, it happened again after the fourth load of cattle arrived and we accepted that as well. But by the time it came to the fifth shipment and there was still no coffee to show for our efforts, we knew we'd been had: they had four lots of our cattle and in exchange, we'd been given two shipments of coffee ... which was when we pulled the plug,' Dieter G explained.

It was all pretty short-sighted, he said. This sort of sharp practice might make a bit of money to start with and some Ugandans might be laughing up their sleeves, but the word does get out.

'Kampala will have difficulty finding the next chump willing to be taken for a ride,' were his words. 'And we also know that this will affect the next German aid tranche,' he added.

More recently there have been problems of a different nature. In July 2012 there was a major outbreak of ebola in western Uganda that almost overnight left more than a dozen people dead.

This was a serious problem because the disease manifests itself as a haemorrhagic fever, is extremely infectious and kills quickly. According to Atlanta's Center for Disease Control and Prevention, it was first reported in 1976 in the Congo and named after the river where it was recognised. There is no cure or vaccine for ebola, a dreadful disease which results in blood pouring from every orifice in the body, including the pores of the hand and the soles of the feet; the last Ugandan outbreak killed 224 people.

Clearly, stated one report, its resurgence this time round resurrected terrible memories. In fact, it caused such panic that, when it was first reported, all the hospital patients in the area fled.

They were terrified of being infected by contagion.

1 Binyavanga Wainaina; *One Day I will Write About this Place – A Memoir*; Granta, London.

CHAPTER NINETEEN

OPERATION PALLISER – AN UNUSUAL BRITISH DEPLOYMENT TO WEST AFRICA

Britain's decision to take control of Sierra Leone's Lungi Airport and deploy a large number of troops around its periphery and along its approaches was a bold action taken by Whitehall. British Paratroopers and the Royal Air Force were put on standby on 3 May 2000 for what was termed 'a potential non-combatant evacuation'. As the situation unravelled and the rebels went on to the offensive, conditions quickly changed and a very different scenario emerged:

The Joint Rapid Reaction Forces (JRRF) operation launched in May 2000 to bring Sierra Leone – as British newspapers of the day phrased it – 'back from the brink' was one of the most successful limited operations launched by London in decades. That was the view of Lieutenant Commander Tony Cramp, Operational Liaison Reconnaissance Team (OLRT) and media officer at a briefing held at the High Commission in Freetown shortly before British forces headed home.

While he was not prepared to comment whether this was likely to be a pattern that might be followed elsewhere in Africa in the future, this Royal Navy officer did confirm that it was the largest and most complex British defence deployment in Africa since the Suez debacle in 1956. This West African operation was headed by Brigadier David Richards, today Britain's Chief of the Defence Staff, General Sir David Richards.

What was clear prior to dispatching a military force to Sierra Leone was that this was a most unusual deployment. Britain could certainly not send a carrier force (even if it still had one) – together

A pair of British Chinook helicopters – with a Royal Navy chopper in the background – lined up on the tarmac in Freetown. (Photo: Author)

with the task force that such an exercise would demand – a quarter of the way around the world each time the natives were restless. 'But it's good to know that we did when the occasion demanded make some pretty stiff decisions,' Commander Cramp commented.

Whitehall was pleased with the outcome, he declared. 'Obviously what we achieved with Operation Palliser once, we will be able to do again, but that is beyond the scope of this discussion. Those decisions are made in London.'

This time, when push became shove, he added, 'it was to prove a severe test' for a number of British military combinations. Operation Palliser included the staggered dispatch of two pairs of C-47 Chinook helicopters plus 85 aircrew and ground support staff from RAF Odiham on 5 May. It was a remarkable effort, and typified the rapid response from all three services. One of the Chinooks was actually in the middle of a special exercise in Scotland when the warning order came through.

The first pair took just 60 hours to make the journey and the second, an incredible 37 hours, routing to Lungi via Portugal, Gibraltar, Tenerife and Senegal. Internal long-range tanks were used for the journey, with one leg being more than 1,200 kilometres over water. Both pairs arrived in time to play a vital role in the subsequent Non-combatant Evacuation (NEO) Operation.

When British forces first arrived at Lungi Airport they were met by a sense of catastrophe, in the view of at least one of the remaining

Chapter 19
Operation Palliser – An Unusual British Deployment to West Africa

British correspondents, 'that was almost palpable'. The Freetown government, or what was left of it, was on the point of collapse, accentuated by the all-but-imminent departure of the country's president. The presidential helicopter was already parked, on stand-by, in the grounds of State House.

As Commander Cramp recalls, movement in and out of the country had been frozen. All international flights were suspended and the only way for non-military travellers to get in or out of the country was by a single commercial Mi-8 helicopter. There were also a few intermittent flights by an Antonov-26 abetted by an antiquated Czech Turbolet, both aircraft flying between Lungi International Airport and Conakry. The same applied to any kind of air-traffic control, which was virtually at a standstill until a British UKMAMS team was brought in to supplement what remained of the domestic complement.

What concerned Brigadier David Richards just then was that Foday Sankoh's RUF rebels were known to have acquired SAM-7s from Libya. Intelligence and radio intercepts had indicated earlier that these had been brought across the border into Sierra Leone from Liberia. It was also one of the reasons why British Paras quickly set about extending their field of operations into the interior, pushing the limits as far up the road towards Port Loko and Rogberi Junction as logistics and rapid reaction permitted.

By now there were RAF and United Nations C-130s arriving by the hour, supplemented by RAF Tristar flights out of Brize Norton, bringing in more troops and equipment. Heavy-lift Antonov AN124-100s had also been chartered from Air Foyle, bringing in more hardware for the UN.

Three Indian Air Force Mi-24s came disassembled in one of them and work was quickly started at the far end of the airport apron in putting them together again. They were soon used in a succession of attacks on rebel positions, including a daring combined RAF and Indian Air Force rescue of the last 223 hostages held by the RUF from Kailahun in the eastern extreme of the country, adjacent to the Liberian border.

A pair of Chinooks – with guns mounted at side ports and at the rear – was deployed in tandem with the IAF Hinds. The helicopters inflicted heavy damage on the rebels. At one stage, an RUF brigade HQ was captured at Pendembu, for long regarded as the rebel 'nerve centre' in their war. That followed the destruction of a rebel radio complex at Kailahun. Also killed was one of the senior RUF commanders.

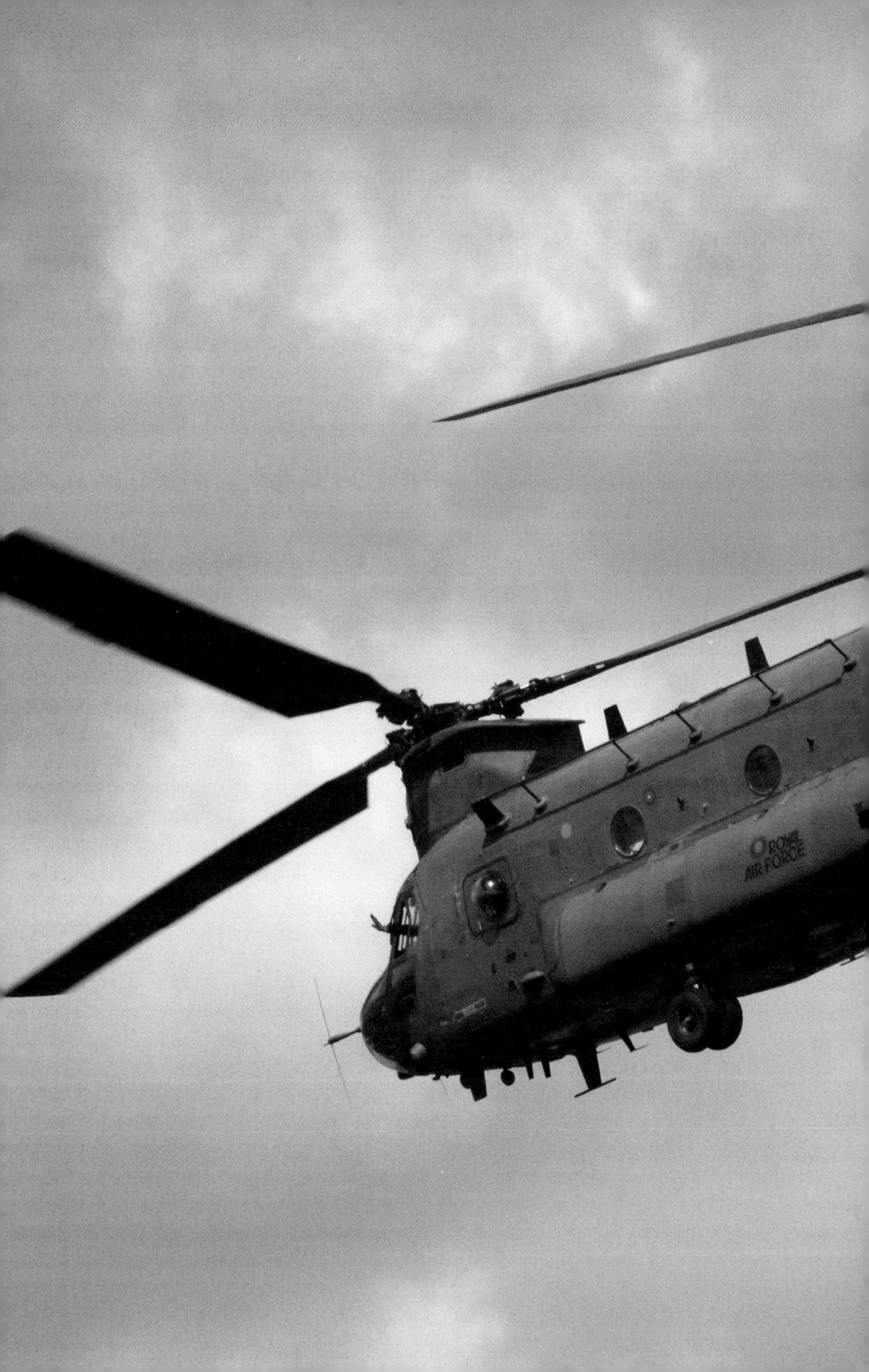
ROYAL
AIR FORCE

Royal Air Force Chinook helicopter in flight at an annual Farnborough Air Show.
(Photo: Peter Felstead, Editor, IHS/Jane's Defence Weekly)

Meanwhile, the airport and its environs were being patrolled by Paras in three-man Land Rovers fitted with the new Weapons Mount Installation Kit (WMIK) which includes GPMGs and a .50 Cal Browning on each. These versatile medium-sized fighting vehicles stayed until the end and were eventually replaced by Indian and Nigerian armoured personnel carriers.

It was the Parachute Regiment that created the real turnabout in the battle for Lungi Airport. As the press were told shortly afterwards, a Para pathfinder platoon was ambushed by rebels at Lungi Lol on the approach road to the airport about ten days after they arrived. Officially it was 'a minor scrap' involving about 40 rebels of whom it was said, 'four died with no Para losses.'

In reality, it was a very different affair. It was also indicative of the resolute approach Britain had towards the expanding crisis, which their presence managed to curtail.

What happened was that a Para battle group had been dug-in along a forward position on the road north, when intelligence indicated a large rebel force heading towards them. A break came when one of the rebels defected. He told the local commander that his force would be attacked that night. The Paras took the bait and the trap was set.

At about three the next morning, the Paras were called to stand-to. They always did so, just before dawn, but this was different. By then a force of 'about 200 RUF' was creeping stealthily – some of them on their stomachs – towards them. Their officers waited until, as one of them recounted afterwards, 'they got close enough, almost to smell them.' The contact was initiated with flares immediately afterwards.

What had happened was that the main body of the attacking rebels was caught in their surreptitious advance, plum in the middle of open ground. The Paras did the rest.

While little has been said – either in London or Sierra Leone – about the actual numbers killed, I was able to glean that the body count was somewhere 'between 40 and 60', more probably the latter, as one of those who was involved, was prepared to intimate.

What was not disclosed to the media was that once the rebels withdrew, several squads of Paras went after them, hitting them several times again. That was the last time that the RUF ever came anywhere close to any position held by British troops during Operation Palliser.

Chapter 19
Operation Palliser – An Unusual British Deployment to West Africa

Having received the order to deploy at mid-morning on Friday 5 May, Commander Cramp's 10-man Operational Liaison Reconnaissance Team (OLRT) led by Brigadier David Richards, head of Britain's deployable Joint Force Headquarters – left Northolt RAF base in Britain towards evening the same day. They were settled in the British High Commission in Freetown just before noon the following morning.

By then, Commander Cramp disclosed, the main body of the RUF rebels was advancing on two fronts towards Freetown, the closest barely 40 kilometres east of the capital. Others were at Rogberi Junction, further north where two international journalists, an American with Reuters and a Spanish cameraman with the Associated Press, were killed in a road ambush only weeks later.

'We could see immediately that the situation had become critical: the word in Freetown was that the RUF headed by Foday Sankoh was preparing for its final push on the city.' Later reports indicated that the threat caused a succession of ripples of panic among some of the city's two million residents – which, by now, included a million refugees.

'We were aware that if something wasn't done quickly, matters could get out of hand,' the commander added.

He explained that the population knew very well what the rebels had done to innocents in the past: the maiming, the dismemberment of children, rapes, amputations, looting – the list is endless, all of it mindlessly barbaric. As he said, the entire city was aghast. 'They were fearful that it might happen again.'

But since all roads stopped at the sea in Freetown, there was nowhere else for this surge of humanity to go, even if they were able to. 'Also, with 500 of its troops held captive, the UN wasn't of much use to anybody,' he intimated.

What eventually persuaded the British government to give the nod to Operation Palliser was based strictly on a succession of security considerations.

That, in turn was coupled to a variety of international implications. It included the reasoning that if a group of rebels – based in a neighbouring state, fuelled and supplied by the Libyan tyrant Muammar Gadaffi – was allowed to dictate events in any country that was not able to protect itself, the effects, ultimately, on the rest of Africa could be cataclysmic. Looking back, another of the team OLRT told this writer, the gesture might ultimately have changed the pattern for the future in all of Africa.

'For a start, it showed that the West is simply not prepared to

Chinook helicopters have been deployed in all major wars for decades, playing crucial support roles, just as they did in Sierra Leone when the British came to the rescue. This one, with United States Army markings, was recently active in Afghanistan's war against the Taliban. (Photo: Neall Ellis)

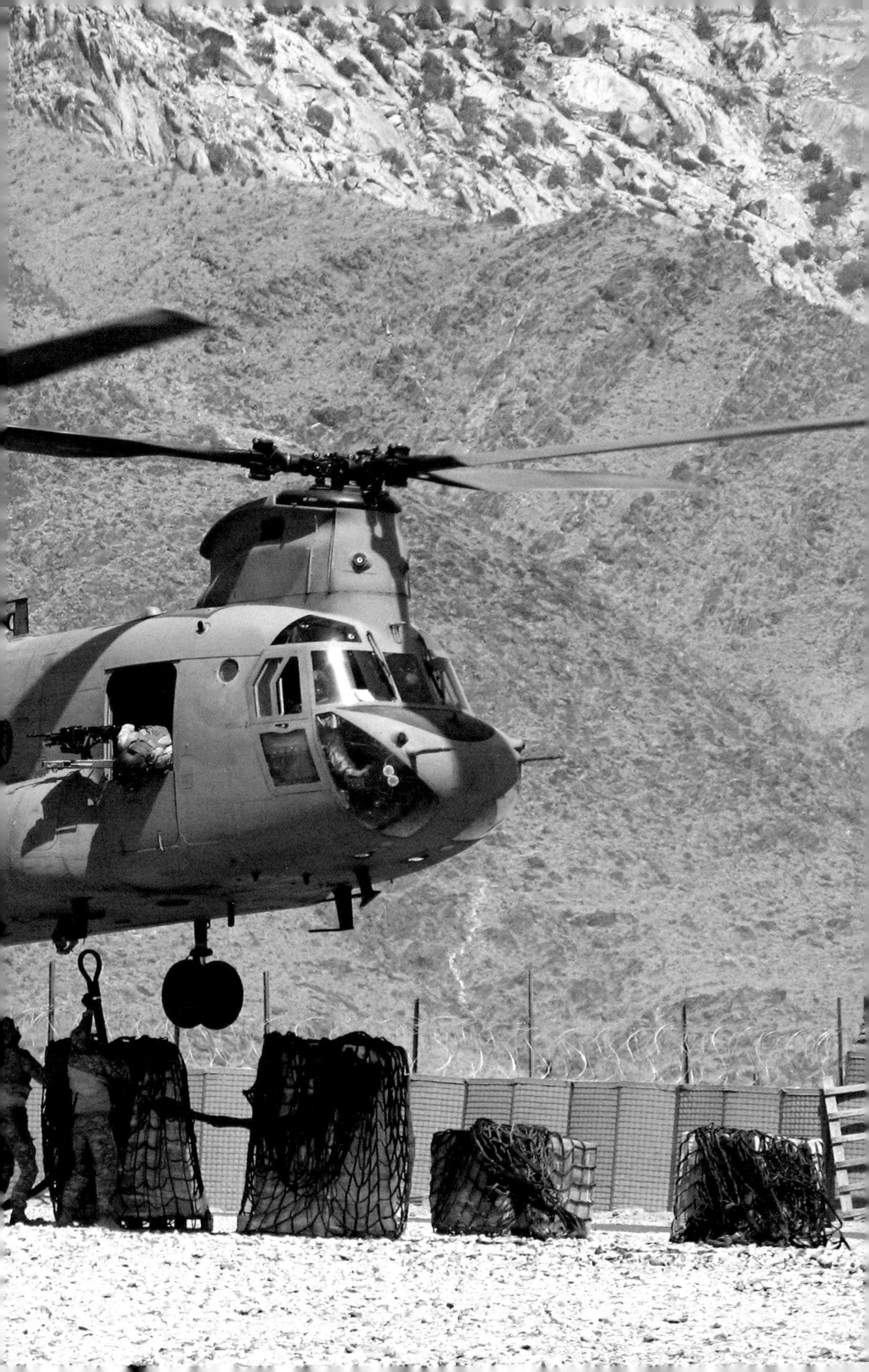

tolerate the kind of terror that was being advocated by the RUF. Also, the rebels had invaded Sierra Leone from Liberia, which had itself just emerged from a civil war, he stated. What had gone unsaid, was that there was no doubt that Britain would not have stepped into the breach had Whitehall not received the nod from Washington. For their part, the Americans were making demands on Taylor to stop giving succour to the rebels.

On the British side, a request for the Lead Company of the Spearhead Land Element to deploy to West Africa was made by Brigadier Richards, Chief of Joint Operations at the Northwood HQ, on May 7th. The first of 800 members of 1 Parachute Battalion touched down at Lungi in RAF C-130s the following morning. It was the start of an air bridge to Africa. According to Commander Cramp, the entire force was complete, deployed, supplied and in-theatre a day later, some of them 50 kilometres into the interior. Meanwhile, a Forward Mounting Base (FMB) – a Joint Task Force HQ (Rear) supported by five C-130s – had been established at Dakar.

The authority to use Dakar as a forward staging post had been negotiated with the Senegalese government only a day before the helicopters were due to arrive. A request was made to Guinea to also allow the use of Conakry Airport, should that be necessary. UN flights were already moving freely between Guinea and Sierra Leone, underscoring the Republic of Guinea's commitment to prevent a rebel success in the neighbouring state.

A linked development shortly afterwards was the departure of a large force of well-armed and equipped Liberian dissidents that crossed the border from Guinea late July. Their objective, it was subsequently established, was to initiate insurgent activity against the government of President Charles Taylor and so bring pressure to stop him from supporting the RUF.

What is significant about the British force airlift from Britain was that this was only the third time in modern times that an air bridge had been established to Africa. Both previous occasions involved the Soviets: Moscow rushed military aid to Angola in October 1975 to counter the advance of South African forces on Luanda. Three years later – in the successful bid to stem a Somali invasion of the Ogaden – scores of Soviet transport planes ferried tens of thousands of tons of military equipment to Ethiopia.

In Sierra Leone, meanwhile, the Main JTFHQ – including a Special Forces (SF) detachment – was set up at the High Commission. The

Chapter 19
Operation Palliser – An Unusual British Deployment to West Africa

balance was deployed at Lungi across the bay and included two C-130s designated specifically for SF use. An Amphibious Ready Group (ARG) based around the helicopter-carrier HMS *Ocean*, was by now also steaming south, as was the just fractionally smaller HMS *Illustrious* which arrived with its additional air assets which included Royal Navy FA2 Sea Harriers and RAF Harrier GR7 jets on 12 May. Until then, the Army and the RAF, principally, had driven Operation Palliser.

When the call came, 42 Royal Marine Commando (embarked in HMS *Ocean* in the Mediterranean) was actually on a live-fire exercise in the south of France.

The nature and extent of this British military operation is significant for several reasons.

While Whitehall is reluctant to discuss the possibility that events in Sierra Leone during May and June 2000 might point to further involvement in Third World countries in the future, the consensus is that that might well be the case should a specific similar situation warrant it. It is necessary therefore to understand the machinations of a rapid reaction force.

The extent and nature of the Sierra Leone military operation was directed by Britain's Permanent Joint Headquarters (established in 1996 to enhance operational effectiveness and efficiency) as part of the Defence Crisis Management Organisation (DCMO).

In an exclusive briefing that this author received in Freetown that July – where he was covering the war while flying regularly with mercenary helicopter gunship pilot Neall Ellis – it was explained that the primary role of the Permanent Joint Headquarters (PJHQ) commanded by the Chief of Joint Operations (CJO), 'is to be responsible – when directed by the Chief of Defence Staff – for the planning and execution of UK-led joint or multinational operations.' This included directing, deploying, sustaining and recovering the military forces involved. In contrast, at the operational level, the Joint Task Force HQ (in Sierra Leone) was responsible for these duties.

The logic that dictated this rationale was that the nature and frequency of UK military operations since the end of the Cold War, 'made a revision of command structures to provide highly responsive military and political command and control in a rapidly changing world a priority,' the source disclosed.

Across the UK's three military services, units are held at one of five levels of readiness. The Spearhead elements and others, classified Level R1 are on permanent 48-hour standby: their members include the Joint Force HQ (JFHQ) a permanent standing HQ of 53 specialist officers, elements of which are on less than 24 hours readiness. In Sierra Leone's case, some of the participants were in the air eight hours after being told to muster and it was these people that came into play in the West African operation. Level R2 components are on a five-day standby, R3 on eight days and so on.

Therefore, explained Cramp – who was among the initial OLRT group to arrive in Sierra Leone – Operation Palliser might be regarded as the first fighting force since the end of World War II to be deployed as a consequence of the establishment of a command of expeditionary and joint operations within the British Defence structure.

These ranged from fighting wars (as in the Balkans), peace support (Sierra Leone) or in the provision of disaster relief and humanitarian aid (such as was provided earlier that year after the floods in Mozambique and Operation Tellar in Honduras, 1998).

One negative consequence of maintaining genuinely high readiness forces is that full protection against malaria cannot be achieved by the leading elements. However, success can rarely be achieved without some element of risk and with all personnel trained to recognise symptoms and with additional physical protection, less than 100 of the 4,500 deployed on the operation contracted the disease.

Based at Northwood in north-west London, the PJHQ is co-located within the headquarters of Commander-in-Chief Fleet, NATO's Eastern Atlantic Command and the maritime element of 11/18 Group Royal Air Force. The United States had clearly been in on it from the start.

A point made subsequently by Lieutenant Colonel Tim Chicken of 42 Royal Marine Command in Freetown, was that the Sierra Leone operation was not simply a collection of British military air, sea and land assets that had been dispatched abroad. His Amphibious Ready Group (ARG) provided what he termed 'a tactically configurationally entity that is available for immediate use, anywhere we choose to send it.'

There were roughly 2,500 servicemen and women on permanent standby for any eventuality, he disclosed. Their role might include force protection, air defence (anti-surface and anti-submarine) 'and brought with it 30 days of sustained operational capability'.

In Sierra Leone, for instance, the group's immediate firepower included fixed-wing aircraft from the carrier, rotary assets (armed Lynx helicopters), indirect fire support batteries of 105 mm guns as

Chapter 19
Operation Palliser – An Unusual British Deployment to West Africa

well as nine 81 mm mortars, some of them mounted.

'Because we are mobile and with our own air, land and maritime elements, it was not necessary to develop a beachhead ... we can – within certain parameters – go in just about where we like,' he said.

By the time that the full force had arrived in Freetown – one of the largest natural harbours in the world and a gathering point for Allied convoys during Hitler's War and for the Falklands 40 years later – it comprised 4,500 personnel (1,350 ashore). A classified number of aircraft, as well as seven Royal Navy ships and Royal Fleet Auxiliaries were lying off Freetown at one stage.

What was interesting about the entire venture was the narrow timeframe in which it was executive: literally a couple of days.

The British Chief of Joint Operations was aware that because of the chronic political situation in the country, the JTFHQ had a window of about 24 hours – at the outset 48 hours – to get in, grab a foothold and consolidate the situation militarily before the rebels arrived. Without Lungi Airport, overlooking the main harbour, Sierra Leone would have been lost. Then the RUF would have had a gateway to the world.

As Liberia proved in the mid-nineties, the rebels would have been very difficult to dislodge once they were ensconced in a strongpoint that provided adequate air access. This was one of the reasons why the rebels had been making such a determined bid to move south from Rogberi. Their prime target, then, and subsequently, was Lungi.

The situation in Freetown when the first British troops arrived was frantic. In one of his last interviews before returning to Britain, Brigadier David Richards explained:

'When we got here, the UN presence was in a state of collapse. After assessing the situation for a day, I warned the UN Force Commander, Indian Army General Jetley, that if he didn't do something positive and quickly to revitalise the situation, the population could well turn on his blue berets. I actually feared for their safety. Many of the locals felt the UN had betrayed them,' he declared.

The situation was deteriorating by the hour, he said, and went on: 'Already there were some rebel units deployed at Newton, not far from the capital. Meanwhile, completely demoralised by the turnabout – coupled to the inability of the UN to react – Sierra Leone government forces had given up just about everything except their weapons: many had gone so far as to hide their uniforms.'

Worse, Richards intimated afterwards, the government was at the point of capitulating. The President had ordered a chartered helicopter be parked at his lodge for the previous six days. It was clear that he intended getting away if he had to, though he was probably thinking like one of his predecessors, President Momoh, who did just that when he was deposed by a squad of junior officers.

About all that was working by the time that Richards and his team arrived, was a lone government Mi-24 Hind helicopter gunship flown by the former South African mercenary Neall Ellis. 'Very effectively it kept the rebels from taking the city,' he said.

Five weeks later, a British military presence in Sierra Leone had stabilised the situation enough for it to withdraw.

A sidelight to these developments was Washington's sudden involvement in West African politics, obviously at the behest of Tony Blair's government.

On 16 July, Thomas Pickering, US Undersecretary of State for Political Affairs, told Liberia's President Charles Taylor while on a visit to Monrovia that he was to stop messing about in Sierra Leone. Either that or face the consequences, he said.

'Liberia has become the primary patron and benefactor of the Revolutionary United Front rebels,' said Pickering. He warned bluntly, and almost in as many words, that if immediate steps were not taken, his government would do what has to be done.

'There will be consequences very severe for our bilateral relationship,' he cautioned.

A source in Washington meanwhile intimated that one of the first steps being mooted, was the suspension of the registration of American (and all allied) ships on the Liberian register. That precedent was already in place elsewhere: similar restrictions were imposed on Panama when that country's President Norreiga's government became a target.

'It would be a relative simple matter to do it again,' he reckoned.

CHAPTER TWENTY

LION ATTACK

Civilisation suggests progress, but in some parts of southern and eastern Africa, an astonishing number of lion attacks still take place. Scour the web and barely a month goes by without reports appearing of incidents that involve these predators.

There was a time, a few short years ago, when thousands of Mozambican nationals attempted to cross illegally into South Africa. Civil war had ravaged their country and with no work and few prospects back home, conditions in the former Portuguese colony were hopeless.

Desperate for improvement, many of these people crossed the South African border on foot, their paths meandering through the Kruger National Park. Though South African newspapers were wary of being too graphic about what was taking place, there was no question that many of these poor souls died while trying to flee. Four-footed predators took a dreadful toll.

In the three or four days that it took to traverse the park, the illegal entrants were forced to avoid established tourist camps like Pafuri, Letaba or Skukuza. There were fairly intense security patrols, many of them involving the military. As a result, most of these people lived 'raw' in the bush and many of them – because they came from Mozambican cities and towns – found themselves in a totally primitive environment. The majority had nothing but knives or machetes for protection, and unless they slept in trees, they were easily targeted.

While the illegals have since found other ways to enter South Africa, lions are still killing people in other parts of Africa. A report in a Nairobi paper in May 2012 said that Kenyan wildlife service agents had shot and killed a lion moving around Karen, a well-to-do expatriate Nairobi suburb and the area on which Karen Blixen based her book *Out of Africa*. Only days later, three lions attacked and killed goats outside Nairobi's famed National Park. Rangers in four-wheel-drive vehicles chased the animals back to the park.

For fear of intimidating Kenya's large transient tourist community, Nairobi and Mombasa newspapers, while reporting innocuous incidents like these, rarely mention attacks on humans. These happen, and with an astonishing regularity, as might possibly be expected in an environment where the population is escalating at a heady rate. But in East Africa such things are generally left unsaid.

Others haven't been that lucky. Honeydew's Lion Park, on the outskirts of Johannesburg with its scores of 'tame' lions, has been attracting visitors for decades. There are signs posted everywhere that it is dangerous to leave your car, so most people are quite content to drive about and view these magnificent creatures, sometimes from only metres away.

But in November 1993, two groups of Chinese tourists visited the place about a month apart and both times those visitors emerged from their cars to pose for photos, almost as if they were enjoying a day in the park. Two tourists were savaged and killed the first time and three the following time around. Which begs the question: just how stupid can you get?

That these creatures can be dangerous is without question. In November 2010, a tourist was killed by lions in a Zimbabwe safari camp. Peter Evershed, a 59-year-old businessman, was mauled by five lions while showering under a tree at the Chitake Springs bush camp in the magnificent Mana Pools Nature Reserve.

Evershed was the last of his family and friends to take a shower that evening as darkness fell. What he didn't know was that there were lions in the long grass, probably watching his every move. When he emerged from the shower, they attacked. His friends heard him scream and ran to the showers, but he was already dead from a gash to the throat.

I've had my share of run-ins with lions over the years. As a youngster, having completed three years' naval service, I decided to hitchhike to Kenya from Johannesburg, something you could do quite safely in those days because much of Africa was being very efficiently administered by a minor army of British colonial officials. In a word, the continent in 1960 was safe, certainly a lot more secure than today. I would sleep on the side of the road in Bechuanaland and both Rhodesias, usually near a convenient service station and think nothing of it.

Chapter 20
Lion Attack

It was not an easy trip. For long stretches, particularly north of the Zambezi, it was slow going and could sometimes be quite rough. The route followed the so-called Great North Road, 'great' only in the enormous clouds of dust that passing vehicles generated, and the many potholes that destroyed legions of heavy-duty axles because the road was not yet tarred.

There were other problems, and malaria was only one of them. By the time I reached Lusaka, my groin was covered in ticks. I'd had tick-bite fever before, so it didn't reoccur: the problem was solved with a razor and some foul-smelling liniment. Consequently, one tended to do the trip in stages.

On one of my last nights in Northern Rhodesia – soon to become independent and renamed Zambia – I was obliged to overnight on the verandah of Mpika's Crested Crane Hotel, then the only hostelry worth the name on the highway between Kapiri Mposhi and the frontier with Tanganyika at Tunduma. The owner, a choleric British expatriate, was quite happy to serve his food and have me enjoy his drinks at double the going rate for his occasional regulars, but his attitude changed sharply when I asked whether I could sleep on the floor of his public lounge. He made it quite clear that it wasn't on.

The man had other problems. He was totally racist where people of colour were concerned. A British government group – the Monkton Commission – had passed through Mpika a few months

Photo: Darrell Watt

before, charged with trying to establish whether Northern Rhodesia was ready for independence or not. Of course the country was not, he would loudly proclaim at the bar, making some derogatory remark about locals being inferior to primates. Worse, he said, some members of the dreaded commission were African and he was forced to actually allow them to sleep in *his* hotel...

'Never had that before,' he grimaced, adding that if he had anything to do with it, never again either.

Having turned me out for the night, the silly little man from Surrey locked all the doors and I had to make the best of it on a stretch of concrete on his porch. The trouble was – and he'd actually taken the trouble to warn me – that there were lions about. Give him his due, he wasn't being duplicitous either.

Whether the lions were aware of my presence or not – they must have picked up my smell because I could clearly hear them snarling and growling in the nearby bush – they didn't become threatening. Only once did one of these creatures come up close, which was when it couldn't have been more than three or four metres away because I could not only hear the animal move about, but its odour – strong and pungent – was unmistakable.

Come daylight, I'm not sure who was happier: me to hear the rattle of keys in the front door, or the owner, cautiously sticking his head around the corner to check whether I was still alive.

I was certainly not going to spend another night in that Godforsaken hole, so after breakfast I set off on foot in search of a lift on a road that probably didn't boast more than a dozen vehicles a day. My path took me across a lot of the ground that had been covered by lions the previous night, but nothing untoward happened.

Nor would I have been able to do anything about it should one of them suddenly have appeared out of the bush.

Curiously, lions don't always spell trouble. My partner, Caroline, and I drove with South African professional hunter Bernard Troskie from Pretoria to Zambia in the winter of 2010. The intention was to spend some time with Darrell Watt at his Mushingashi Game Conservancy, which abuts onto the Kafue National Park. We stayed a couple of weeks along the banks of that great river and then headed home. Bernard stayed on and helped out with safaris for another six or eight weeks.

After he'd returned home he e-mailed us his own story of an encounter with a lion, or rather, a couple of them.

'It was winter in the bush and the hunting season was well into

Chapter 20
Lion Attack

its stride. Many of Darrell's clients were after big cats and because 'Mushi' was allowed only a very limited quota, his company went to considerable lengths to ensure that animals targeted were killed and not wounded. Quite often that involved setting out a bait – usually an impala or a puku – shot for the purpose and strung up on a rope well within sight of a blind or hide nearby. It was Bernard's job that day to build one.

'The previous day we'd chosen the position in an area frequented by a fairly large pride of lions and I went back there fairly early in the day, accompanied by one of Darrell's game scouts. He was an enterprising fellow by the name of Peter who knew the bush and its creatures better than most.

'I parked the Land Cruiser next to the track and together we went forward to the site, a short walk about 80 metres away. The trouble was, I made the kind of mistake that could have cost us both our lives – I left my rifle in the vehicle.

'We had barely reached the area where we were going to build the blind when Peter called me, almost in a whisper. He used the word *bwana* to draw my attention. There was something urgent in his voice and when I turned, he pointed, wide-eyed, at a pair of lions roughly halfway between us and the Land Cruiser. The animals were totally at ease, stretched out and had probably been dozing in the morning sun. Our arrival must have woken them.

'All I can say is that my heart sank. It took me a moment to assess our options, which frankly, were zero. There was no big tree near enough for us to climb, and had we tried it, the lions would almost certainly have got one of us before we were halfway up the trunk. Instead, Peter turned directly towards the predators, raised his arms high above his head and told them in a loud voice in his own language, to "shoo!".

'Then, to emphasise this unusual approach, he marched forward a few steps and repeated the process, his arms still in the air.

'We will never know what the lions made of this rigmarole, but they were obviously perplexed. They were probably weighing up their own options as to what these two crazy humans were up to. Moments later they got up off their haunches and, half alarmed, looked about the bush around them.

'When Peter took another step forward, this time screaming loudly, both animals took off and disappeared into the scrub. We didn't waste time hanging about either: I reckon we were back in our vehicle in a few dozen strides.'

Bernard admits that it was a close call, extremely so. It was also something that might have ended in tragedy had Peter not done this thing, all of which was pure gut reaction, the scout admitted afterwards. And since this sort of thing had probably never happened before to the two animals, it was a classic case of fight or flight.

'Thankfully the animals chose the latter course ...'

Zambian hunter, Shaun Reeve, chairman of the Mazabuka Farmers Association, has his own story about a lion attack. Only this was one that almost cost this 35-year-old professional his life.

Featured in the *Zambian Farmer Magazine*[1], the event was headlined 'How Reeve Survived a Lion Attack' and it epitomised some of the problems that highly experienced people who have grown up in the bush sometimes encounter.

Shaun was out hunting in the Zambian bush with a Spanish client, Juan Carlos Alonso Martinez, in June 2006. They, too, were after lion and had constructed a blind while waiting for a specific pride to arrive. It was cold and dark and the two men struggled to keep awake in the early morning pre-dawn cold.

The pressure over the previous 14 days of hunting had been tough. Shaun did his best to ensure that his client collected all the trophies he was after, but this one was taking its toll. Several times Shaun caught himself lightly dozing off. Even the heavy fetid smell of the bait – a huge chunk of rotting hippo, no longer had any effect.

Suddenly Juan shook his shoulder, 'They're here,' he hissed.

The Luangwa Valley where the two men were hunting, was not new to Shaun. Born at a Mission Hospital in Central Zambia and the son of Tom Reeve, a respected Zambian farmer and avid hunter, he had been hunting the valley since he was a boy: he'd bagged his first buffalo at the age of 16. Now 20 years on, he needed all his experience to bring this quarry to bear.

'My client had been led to believe shooting a lion in the Luangwa was going to be easy,' he recalled. 'We'd shot a big leopard earlier and the client was happy, but it was this intended lion that was his priority. Also, after two weeks in the wild, he wanted to get home, and obviously, the pressure was on me to produce the goods.

The lion that the two men were after was well known in the area. The beast had scared the living hell out of resident game scouts for a while and had eluded other hunters, which meant that the scouts were anxious that they should have a successful hunt.

'I too, had had several close encounters with him, and the animal made no secret of the fact that we were not welcome in his territory. On one occasion, sitting in a blind, the lion must have been aware

Chapter 20
Lion Attack

that we were there, because he came right up close and growled. That gave us quite a fright.'

Accompanied by a lioness, the predator pair frequented an area along the Carimberi River and most days Shaun and his tracker were able to pick up their tracks among the dense combretum thickets which made hunting in the area both difficult and dangerous.

'Not helping us was the fact that the lion was busy with his girlfriend and passion being higher on its list of priorities than eating, the animals often came close to the bait but did not feed. The decision to pass up a chance of a shot earlier in the hunt, partially due to long grass partially obscuring the cat, only added to our frustration.

'After all those disappointments, the moment that Carlos touched my shoulder, I snapped awake. Judging by the silhouettes, I knew it was them, the male hanging back while the female tucked into the hippo meat with gusto. Carlos, understandably, became very excited and I tried to get him to calm down and wait for the light to improve.

'Throughout the hunt, I had been bringing my scoped 30.06 to the blind, to supplement my .404 Jeffries as a long-range back-up option. But now of course, not having it with me on this critical morning, I cursed, leaving it behind in the camp that morning.'

Dawn was beginning to break when the lion presented the two men with a perfect side-on shot. Shaun whispered that Carlos should shoot, which he did. His .375 Magnum cracked and both men clearly heard the thud as the bullet struck. The lion cramped, then leapt into the air, landing on his head and thrashed around in a welter of dust and debris, roaring all the time.

'I hollered to Carlos to shoot again, but he fumbled and finally loosed one off as the cat left the scene. It happened so fast that it was all over in a flash. My open-sighted .404 was virtually useless in the poor light, so we sat and listened as the clearly unimpressed female growled nearby.

'Approaching the bait with some trepidation, I was pleased to spot a large pool of blood, which meant that it was badly hurt. But as it was of a dark, brownish red, I was alert to the realities and aware that I may well have a very angry, wounded lion on my hands. We decided to make a fire, Carlos having a smoke as we waited a short while. The lioness continued to be vocal and we knew that she was not far away, the dense thicket taking on a very threatening appearance.

'After 30 minutes we set off and followed the trail, hoping that if the lion was not yet dead, the wound would have had time to stiffen up. Every step we took was with great deliberation as the vegetation was dense and perfect for the lion to hide up in.

'I became concerned as the angry female kept calling her mate and snarling when we got close. That, together with the wounded male, added to our anxiety, as we very carefully followed the blood trail. After about 90 nerve-racking minutes, I noticed a clearing up ahead and bet on the pair moving through it which might give us a clear shot. So we waited again and listened carefully to the noises of the bush.

'The most prominent sound just then was guinea fowl, lots of them, and we waited for their chattering to quiet. Then we heard the lioness move out and hoped that the male would follow. Creeping forward carefully, I heard what I thought was the slightest sigh, and sensed that it might be our quarry. But our trackers, who from long experience have excellent hearing, signalled they had heard nothing.

'Unconvinced, I took several careful steps forward and then there was a beige blur as the enormous lion exploded out of some low scrub from a distance of about 10 metres. I clearly remember seeing its yellow eyes: they were fixed on me as a huge mass of muscle, hair and bone launched itself in my direction.

'Juan's rifle roared as I concentrated momentarily on trying to get in that one good shot.

'I hit the lion square in the chest but it was obviously not enough. A moment later, with teeth barred and claws outstretched, the animal was on top of me. Only afterwards did I realise that it had smashed into my torso and broke some ribs.

'Amazingly, despite its size, weight and forward momentum, I still managed to keep my footing. But then, poised on its hind legs and with my left arm enveloped by its jaws, it tore into my arm and shoulder just below my neck. There was a crunch of bone and flesh tore as I frantically tried to gorge its eyes with my free hand, but this was having absolutely no affect.

'Many thoughts go through a person's mind when faced with what might be ultimate disaster, and there was no question that I felt I was on my way to the happy hunting grounds. Then, quite unexpectedly, the lion's body sagged to the ground. The two racking shots had taken their toll, the animal loosened its grip while I rammed my injured hand into its mouth to let him gnaw, endeavouring to keep its massive teeth from my neck and head.

'Thankfully the lion was dying and I collapsed backwards with

Photo: Darrell Watt, Mushingashi Game Conservancy, Kafue, Zambia.

Photo: Caroline Castell

Photo: Manya Corbane

Sable antelope, above, are found in many Zambian game parks, especially along the great Kafue River. While wild dogs are a rarity in parts of East Africa because of rabies, the Kafue area has many packs. Both photos from Darrell Watt, Mushingashi Game Conservancy, Kafue, Zambia.

Caroline Castell took this remarkable sequence of a young elephant bull crossing the Kafue River while fishing for vundu from a boat. This beautiful tributary of the Zambezi – it links up with the 'mother lode' south of Lusaka – remains one of the most fascinating, still-unspoilt, wildlife hideaways on the continent of Africa, and former SAS-operative Darrell Watt intends to keep it so. In a dozen years he has transformed Mushingashi from a poachers' haven into a wildlife paradise that today 'exports' lion and leopard to other Central African reserves. His website is at www.mushingashi.net.

Photo: Darrell Watt, Mushingashi Game Conservancy, Kafue, Zambia.

Photo: Manya Corbane

Photo: Manya Corbane

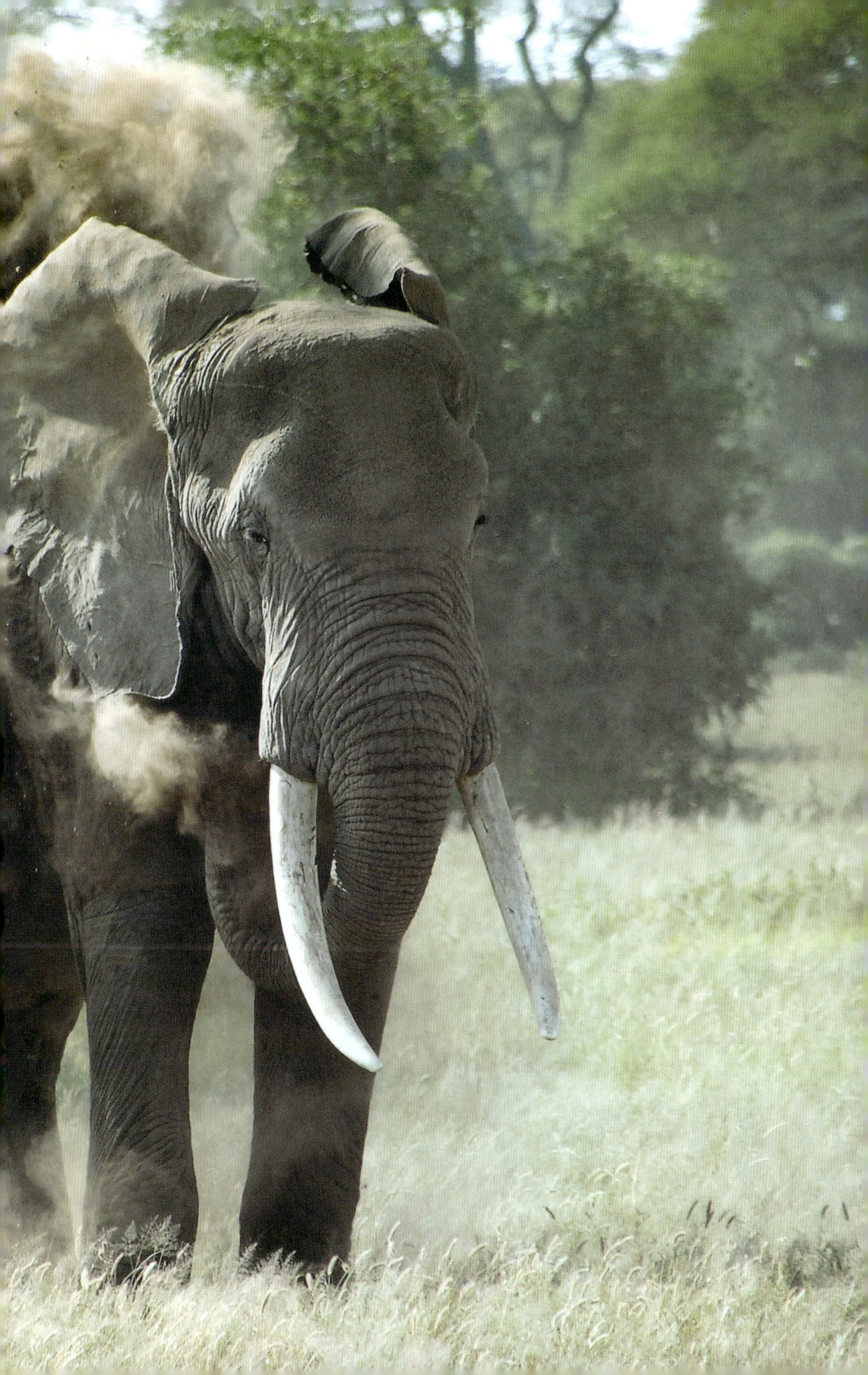

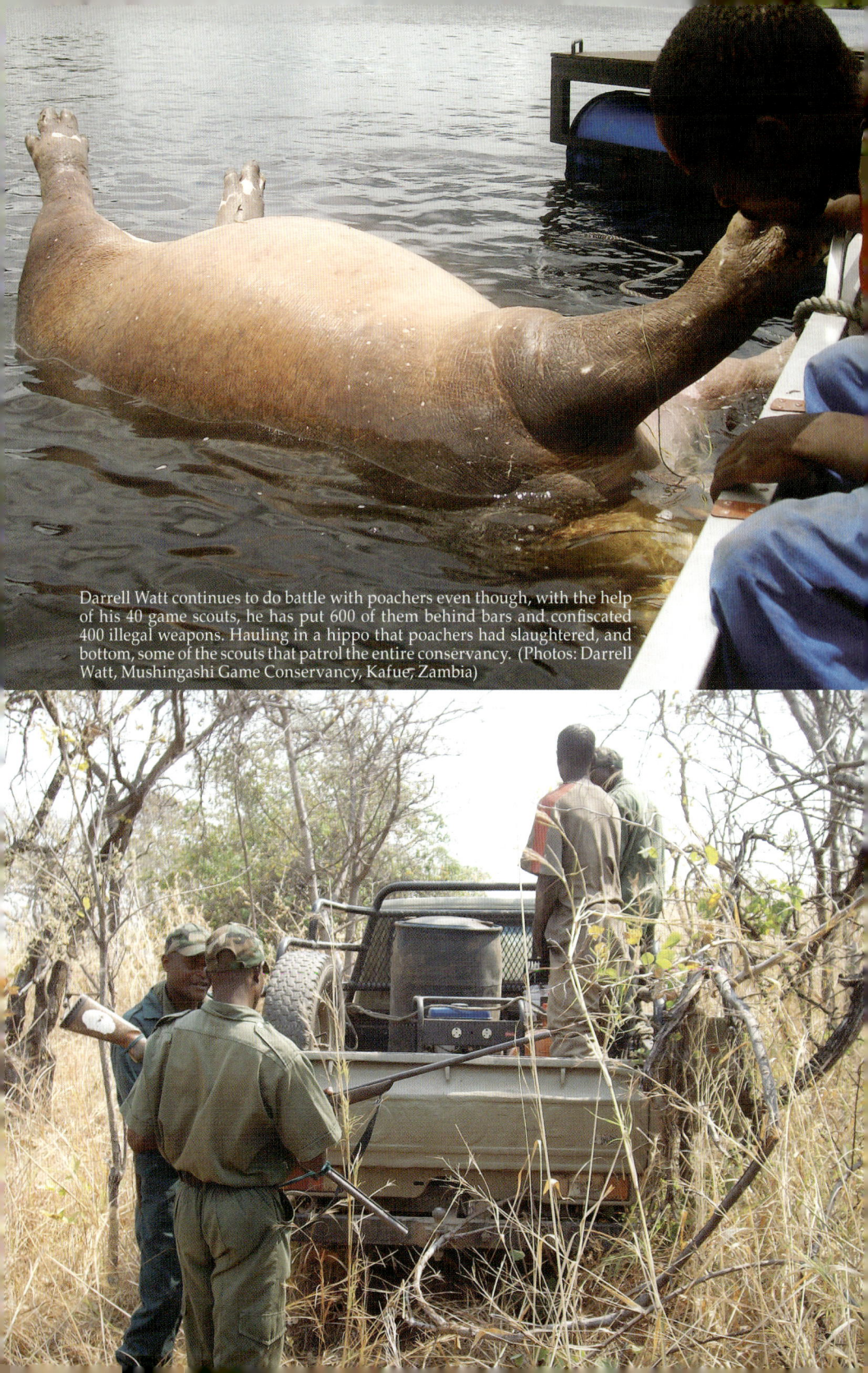

Darrell Watt continues to do battle with poachers even though, with the help of his 40 game scouts, he has put 600 of them behind bars and confiscated 400 illegal weapons. Hauling in a hippo that poachers had slaughtered, and bottom, some of the scouts that patrol the entire conservancy. (Photos: Darrell Watt, Mushingashi Game Conservancy, Kafue, Zambia)

Some of the spoils taken over the years from poachers at Mushingashi that include weapons, bikes, wire snares, hunting knives and other bush paraphernalia. The dugouts were seized from a bunch of felons who were catching fish to sell in Copperbelt markets, while the dead man, bottom right, was trampled by an elephant bull during the rutting season. (Photos: Darrell Watt, Mushingashi Game Conservancy, Kafue, Zambia and author)

The Kafue, like the Okavango Swamps further south, in Botswana boasts enormous crocs, and given the opportunity, these creatures regularly attack humans. After one of the game scouts at Mushingashi had been taken, Darrel Watt shot the creature and recovered the man's remains. The croc was then skinned and the hide treated: Today it greets visitors to the game park. (Photos: Darrell Watt, Mushingashi Game Conservancy, Kafue, Zambia)

Africa's baobab tree can grow to an enormous size, such as this one on the road west out of Lusaka to Mushingashi. Bernard Troskie from Pretoria, all of 6 ft 4 in tall, provides a measure of perspective. (Photo: Author)

Africa's Victoria Falls on the Zambezi River – more than a mile across at this point – is one of the natural wonders of the world. Caroline Castell had to pay $25 to view the facility, which many tourists regard as exploitative. (Photo: Author)

Chapter 20
Lion Attack

the beast smothering me. Carlos then shot him again, this time in its side and at point-blank range. Carlos's rifle was now empty, but undeterred, he set upon the lion with the butt of the rifle and the trackers also climbed in with their axes. As I was pulled out from under the lion, soaked in saliva and blood and trying to gather my wits, I realised that I was seriously hurt because of the amount of blood that was pumping out of my wounds. For a while I thought I would surely bleed to death.

'With my shoulder muscle slightly torn away, I could clearly observe my carotid artery pulsating. The cat's canines had missed inflicting instant death by a slither.

'Suddenly concerned about the lioness, I reached for my weapon but then I realised that I was incapacitated. I looked at my hand and was shocked to see my thumb hanging by a thread of skin, the bone sliced through as if cut by a razor. The stench from the lion's saliva was sickening.

'At this stage, Carlos tore off his shirt and tried to staunch the bleeding. We had to make urgent contact and raise the alarm, but were distressed to find that we'd left the satellite phone back at camp. I was in no condition to drive and was further distressed while considering the terrain that we needed to cover to reach my father-in-law's camp 30-something kilometres away.

'After an extremely painful walk to where we had left the vehicle I was suddenly overwhelmed by a total sense of despair, which wasn't helped when the driver, obviously worried by my condition, proceeded to hopelessly bog down the Land Cruiser in the sand while crossing one of the rivers along the route.

'Looking at the volume of blood still pumping out of my wounds, it suddenly struck me that though the lion hadn't killed me, I was almost certainly going to die from loss of blood. Momentarily I let my mind wander, giving thought to what I should do in my final moments. On reflection, I became aware that I needed to rise to the challenge, which caused me to buck myself up and give myself another 20 minutes.

'My thoughts just then went along the lines that if I managed to survive for that length of time, I would make it. Meantime, the crew heaved and pushed the vehicle while I looked on hopefully.

'Twenty minutes later I was struck with a new resolve, picked myself up and staggered forward but was only able to make little distance. Feeling faint and weak I sat down and waited. My spirits soared when I could see that the vehicle was out of the sand and coming towards me. The trackers then made an impromptu bed of grass on which I lay as they prepared for my trip to my father-in-law's camp. Mike Heath's bush camp was still some distance ahead, though.

'This would prove to be another ordeal. My driver, a new fellow on his very first bush trip was actually in a worse state of shock than me, were that at all possible. He was shaking so badly that I eventually asked Carlos to take over at the wheel. But having never driven in the African bush before, he struggled to control the vehicle and we were all over the place. The Land Cruiser careened, on and off the track, and sometimes even collided with trees and bushes. Every bump, every single jolt sent waves of pain shooting through my ribcage. In terrible agony I despaired, which was when I told my driver to take over, but he was no better.

'Suddenly, to our astonishment, we ran into my brother-in-law, Ross Heath, who was out on a buffalo hunt of his own. Having gotten over the shock of seeing me in such a state, he leapt into the driver's seat and had us in the camp in a short while.

'We immediately radioed Lusaka and an hour or so later a King Air with Early Beech, a local paramedic with Speciality Emergency Services, landed and quickly administered morphine and wasted no time at all in cleaning my wounds with the help of a saline solution from a drip.'

Specialty Emergency Services (SES) has been operating as an Advanced Life Support ambulance and evacuation service in Zambia since 1991. A locally owned operation, the company has proved itself many times in emergency situations. It did so again with Shaun Reeve because a Lear Jet arrived almost shortly after he arrived in Lusaka to take him to Johannesburg.

'I was in the theatre for a good four hours, where I underwent a thorough cleansing procedure to rid my wounds of as much bacteria as possible and for good measure, was topped up with antibiotics. A couple of days later I was back in surgery for another session, followed by a third when they cut away rotten flesh and inserted over two hundred stitches.

'Feeling human again, I was advised not to tell the nursing staff the exact nature of my business. Most of them were decidedly anti-hunting, so I told them that I had been darting lions for translocation. This seemed to be well received because there were smiles all round.'

His thumb reattached, Shaun is back on his farm in Mazabuka with almost full use of both arm and hand. One last operation, probably

Chapter 20
Lion Attack

seven months after his ordeal, still awaited him. He has now dug deep and ordered a new rifle – this time something more appropriate for angry lions in the calibre of a .500 Jefferies.

Interestingly, back in the bush, two fully expanded bullets in .400 and .375 calibre were located against the slightly damaged spine of the lion's lower back regions after the animal had been skinned.

On a more personal level as writer and observer, I was on a hunting safari near Matetsi in Zimbabwe with Italian professional hunter Giorgio Grasselli. We were out looking for buffalo with his client, a Frenchman. I'd hunted often enough with Giorgio before, though my preference was always with a camera rather than a rifle, unless there was very good reason to kill.

In time, I was to discover for myself that lions in that corner of north-west Rhodesia, which adjoins north-east Botswana, were an unusually aggressive breed of the big cats. In fact, attacks on locals were commonplace.

On the hunt, it would sometimes take a shot in the air to stop them from stalking us, which was awkward because it also frightened away other animals, and, more often than not, the potential trophies we were stalking. These predators seemed to be perpetually on the hunt.

Grasselli himself narrowly escaped being taken by a large black-maned male while we were out scouting near the Botswana border one sunny afternoon. He'd got out of his Land Rover for a pee, and in deference to his clients, did his thing a few metres to the rear of the vehicle. Without even a warning growl, a huge lion shot out of the bush about 50 metres away and headed straight at him. Swift, silent and deadly, these creatures are able to move at incredible speed.

Because the Italian didn't take his rifle with him – and firing it at such a short distance might have proved problematical anyway – he giant-strided it back to the Land Rover, opened the door and jumped in. The impact of the animal slamming into the side of the vehicle closed it for him.

Lucky man...

Another memorable event evolved while I was with Giorgio. It followed a visit to his farm at Rushoek by a group of Matabele tribal elders from a local village. They were a pretty distressed group and obviously desperate.

The leader of the group complained that a pride of eight or nine lions had been indiscriminately killing their cattle. The problem wasn't quite as simple as that because the predators wouldn't hunt down just a single animal and devour it. Instead, they would sometimes kill three or four of the poor beasts in a night, much of the flesh going to waste. And since cattle have always been a measure of status within rural African societies, they urgently needed Giorgio to do something about it. 'Protection', they called it.

With much emotion, the spokesman for these Africans explained that if things went on like that for much longer, all their cattle – their only real assets – would soon disappear and, being a temperamental sort, Grasselli couldn't resist the challenge.

The next afternoon, with his client and me in tow, we set up a hide near the previous evening's slaughter, using one of the quarter-eaten carcasses strung up as bait in a mopani tree. Just as the sun was about to disappear over the horizon, the pride returned. In about 40 seconds we'd shot dead five of the eight lions that had been terrorising the area and none too soon either; within minutes it was dark.

The three surviving members of the pride, all mature females, steered well clear of the area after that…

The trouble was, that years later, when I showed my daughter Leighla a photo of the three of us standing over the carcasses, hunting rifles in hand, her immediate reaction was that it was 'disgusting'! It took a while for her to accept that what we'd done was essential, and that such things happened in the African bush.

Even so, she wasn't totally convinced.

Though scribes generally do a lot of crazy things, lions don't usually form a part of it. That said, there were few incidents as interesting as the one that took place during one of my journeys in Central Africa when I travelled from Burundi to Kampala. It was a long, tedious haul, through Rwanda and on into Uganda, all of it overland by truck or bush taxi.

On that trip I was keen to get from Lake Tanganyika to Entebbe as quickly as possible, but I simply couldn't get onto a flight from Bujumbura. So, what the hell, I hitchhiked!

It was hard going; the roads, not entirely unexpectedly, were bad and there were few vehicles, especially at night. Because there was so much military hardware around, bandits had become a problem. Finally, a truck dropped me by the side of the road about a kilometre from the main lodge at the Kagera National Park in Rwanda, south-east of the legendary Mountains of the Moon in neighbouring Uganda: it was quite dark by the time I got there, perhaps 8 o'clock.

Chapter 20
Lion Attack

There was no moon, but I could clearly see a road leading up to the lodge where the lights were on. So I shouldered my gear and set off at a good pace.

When I finally walked through the door into the reception building about 10 minutes later, a French tourist sitting with a small group looked up at me in disbelief and dropped her glass. For a few seconds everybody in the room gaped at me. Then one of the men came forward, a Belgian who was managing the camp. They didn't know I was coming, he told me.

'We didn't hear your car, he declared, clearly puzzled.

'I have no car,' I answered.

'So how did you get here?'

'I walked. How else?

'From the road? All the way from the road?' he asked, incredulous.

'Yes, of course,' was my reply

Photo: Caroline Castell

Silence.

One of the women in the group suggested that I was kidding. 'Look outside and see where his car is, Jean,' she suggested. The Belgian did so and returned to the group.

'No car!' he said flatly. I asked what this was all about.

In the past week, he told me, a pride of lions had been terrorising the countryside around the lodge. Three of their staff had been eaten. In fact, it was serious enough, he intimated, for everybody in the area to be terrified.

'Nobody even budges at night except in a vehicle ... it is simply too dangerous,' he told me.

'So why don't you shoot the brutes?' I asked, perturbed.

'Because we haven't got a permit ... we've asked, but this is Africa ... you know the scene.'

I suppose I was just lucky that night. Or possibly the lions had already dined.

A real and ongoing tragedy is that while lions still make the news, this animal has become a seriously threatened species. In 1955 we had close to 500,000 wild lion in Africa. There are now, the pundits tell us, only an 'optimistic number' of about 25,000 of these creatures left alive in their original natural environment. Of these, barely 3,500 are rated in the 'big male trophy' category.

Look at the statistics. In the decade starting in the year 2000, hunters are recorded as having shot 6,500 of these. This is the figure listed by CITES (Convention on International Trade in Endangered Species of Wild Fauna and Flora), an agreement between governments whose aim is to ensure that international trade in specimens of wild animals and plants does not threaten their survival. CITES does not include animals killed by local tribes.

Facts speak for themselves. According to former South African Brian Gaisford, now based permanently in New York, 'a perfect storm' is developing and is likely to culminate into the extinction of the lion in the wild, possibly within our lifetime.

His warning is specific when he says he is referring to lions still in their natural environment and not the predator version that is bred and slaughtered in what is now known as the 'canned' hunting industry, which are still widespread in southern Africa until fairly recently. Most are bred in captivity and released into confined areas so that, for substantial fees, they can be targeted by trophy hunters. For so-called 'safety' reasons, some are even defanged and declawed.

Indeed, declares Gaisford, proportionate to the number of animals being killed, there is very little actual *wild lion* hunting taking place.

He goes on: 'Because we are running out of wild lion to shoot, 'canned' hunting has become a lucrative industry and, as a consequence, has spread into Zimbabwe and Zambia. I met a safari operator in Zimbabwe recently who told me that he had transferred 40 raised lions into Zimbabwe from South Africa.

The truth, says Gaisford, is that some hunters are shooting 'tame' or raised lions in Zimbabwe and don't even know it.

'Hunting outfits in Zimbabwe are even bidding on mature lions that had been rescued and placed in wildlife sanctuaries. One bid was for US$18,000 on a pet male lion but the owner refused ... he refused to sell it to be shot for sport.'

He makes the point that while there was a public outcry in South Africa over 'canned' hunting of lions (and other threatened species) and the 'sport' was banned for a short while, it is in full swing again.

'I do not approve of such unethical killing of lion, but if it is going to save a wild lion then, sadly, so be it.'

Human Conflict

Conflicts between humans and lion over territory in the wild are leading to the indiscriminate killing of wild lions.

The population explosion in Africa, and the fact that lions need huge areas in which to range, has pitted local tribal folk against wildlife, especially since some of these predators target domestic animals like cattle or sheep for no other reason than that they are accessible. Poisoning is the preferred means to stop cattle deaths. In East Africa the pesticide Furadan is used to lace baits and in South Africa Temic is used. The poison kills everything that feeds on the carcass including other big cats, hyena, jackal and even vultures. There have been instances where entire prides of lions have been wiped out.

Assisting Gaisford in his crusade is his son Tuck, as well as Kenyan national Nunu Chimblo: all three men have been involved in getting the American company FMC, makers of Furadan, to institute a buy-back programme in a last-ditch effort to halt the killings.

'We have been partially successful,' says Brian Gaisford, 'because the pesticide killed millions of American birds and was then banned. However, it is still being manufactured in the States and exported. And yes! Chemicals that are banned in the US can still be manufactured there and be exported all over the world, mostly to Third World countries. We then end up eating some of the produce from such countries, Mexico included.

'I travelled to Mali last November in a bid to track the desert elephant, reportedly the largest of all the world's elephants. That they are enormous is a given, but all their tusks are broken off due to digging in the hard mineral-rich ground and it is this factor that has saved them from ivory poachers. That said, there are only about 500 of these beautiful creatures left.

'I may have been the last white man to see these pachyderms: al-Qaeda has taken over much of the desert region in which they roamed. In fact, the next group of visitors who followed us in were geologists and they were kidnapped. However, I saw large quantities of Furadan for sale there, so presumably that will also impact on desert elephants as they are increasingly raiding the farmlands.

'Another group of conservationists, the Lion Guardians who operate largely in Kenya and Tanzania, are trying to educate, compensate, and help the Maasai to build stronger enclosures to protect their cattle from lion predation. Referred to as "Living Walls" or "Green Walls", these barriers are fast-growing thorn bush walls that keep the predators out of villages and cattle enclosures.

'Tuck worked with this group last summer, and while they are doing a great job, it's an uphill fight.'

Poaching

Because of the population explosion in Africa there is an upsurge in subsistence and commercial poaching. This is contributing to a wipe-out of the lion's food source.

Ritual Killing

Hunting of lion by the Maasai to prove their manhood has cultural, social and historical significance for this tribe. That means that the slaughter of wild lions is rampant.

'Although I applaud the courage of the Maasai, because this is *real* hunting – with only a shield and spear – it is not sustainable. There are many more warriors and sadly, a lot fewer lion. Tuck also worked on this, helping to disarm seven Maasai *moran* and save a lioness and her cubs. This lioness was subsequently poisoned with Furadan. There is no legal trophy hunting of lion in Kenya, nor has there been for decades.'

Disease

Bovine tuberculosis or BTB was originally spread to the Cape buffalo by domestic cattle in South Africa. Lion eat the buffalo and, as a result, contract a very bad form of TB that eats away at their hips and main joints. Roughly 65 per cent of all lion in South Africa's Kruger National Park are now infected and the disease is spreading into Zimbabwe and Mozambique. Most lion are also infected with feline Aids.

'Both Tuck and Nunu Chimblo were involved with this problem and we made a short video on BTB to expose the fact that the South African Parks Board were keeping the problem quiet. They felt that if the public knew that tuberculosis was rampant there tourists would no longer visit. We confronted the head of SANParks at the Explorers Club in New York City and demanded that his government acknowledge the problem.

'Subsequently we put together a meeting at the famous Onderstepoort veterinary facility in South Africa. Among those present were several medical experts, parks' officials and the lion research team headed by Dr Deevalt Keet. He furnished proof of the problem and it was agreed that our wild lions are in real danger throughout southern Africa and that the issue needs to be seriously addressed,' concludes Gaisford.

Chinese Lion Bone Trade

I regard this as a very serious and looming threat to Africa's wild lion population. Asians are now not only after elephant ivory and rhino horn for the unsubstantiated benefits these potions are supposed to give, but they have also been targeting tigers, now critically endangered. Like lions, there is a strong Asian demand for predator bones and body parts. As a result, Chinese traffickers will now pay US$15,000 for a single lion skeleton.

There is no real difference between tiger and lion bone structure, but the Asians believe that the remains of captive or raised lions are not as powerful as those in the wild. So again, the wild lion comes into devious focus.

Currently, the African lion is not listed by CITES so they have no protection under this treaty from the sale of their body parts. Which begs the question: why not?

We also need to establish whether the international hunting lobby has had an influence in this oversight. What is apparent to everybody who is involved in this critical issue is that African wild lions do need some form of protection to stop the sale of their body parts to the Asians. If this does not happen, these creatures ultimately face the same fate as the rhino.

Trophy Hunting of Wild Lion

Trophy articulates the 'largest' or the 'best' of any species, be it animal, fish or fowl. Therein lies the problem. We are losing our gene pool and disrupting the prides. Consequently, when a trophy pride lion is destroyed, we end up losing at least eight to fifteen of its potential offspring. By some estimates, the loss is much higher.

The hunter will think he has only killed one lion, which is not the case. The pride lion is now gone and one or two of the nomadic lions will take over the pride. The new alpha male is genetically wired to kill all the cubs in its new-found pride and there will also be a few females who die while trying to protect their cubs. The reason is simple: lion males kill cubs to bring the females into oestrus and allow the new pride lion to sire his own cubs and create a gene pool of his own.

The trophy hunter, by shooting one lion, has just killed off most of the pride. I was in Hwange National Park in Zimbabwe in August 2012 and a report came in from the lion research team that Oliver, a very well-known pride lion with a collar and ten cubs, had just been baited and lured out of the park to be shot by a well-known safari operator.

The hunter even brought in the collar, which had been put on Oliver only three days before.

Then, a week later, a three-year-old lion was shot. Seven or eight days later, a third three-year-old was killed by the same hunter. The shooting of a lion under seven years of age (a pride lion) must be regarded as totally unacceptable for all these reasons, apart from being disruptive and unethical.

1 *Zambia Farmer's Magazine*, February 2007.

CHAPTER TWENTY ONE

THE CENTRAL INTELLIGENCE AGENCY'S AIR WAR IN THE CONGO

There are not many people who are aware that for many years, Washington was directly involved in the Congo's civil wars. The CIA even hired a bunch of expatriate Cubans living in Miami to fight the rebels opposed to Mobuto Sese Seko's Kinshasa government. They flew them to Africa and gave them the planes with which to do the job, including a bunch of American-built Trojan trainers. Leif Hellström made an extensive study of these events and he provides the gist of it...

Above the Ituri rainforest, North-east Congo: Saturday 29 May 1965

It was an uneventful flight, until the American-built T-28 Trojan aircraft piloted by a Belgian in the employ of the CIA ran out of fuel.

Not dissimilar to the early T-6s or Harvards flown by the South African Air Force as trainers for many years, the T-28 was designed for use in counter-insurgency roles in Vietnam. Just then, this aircraft – one of two in the air over some of Africa's almost impenetrable rainforests – was on an operational mission in the Congo.

The pilot's wingman Luis de la Guardia had switched radio channels to talk to base operations at Paulis airfield (Osiro today, way east of present-day Kisangani on the road to Bunia) to tell them that his flight was in trouble. When he switched back there was no reply from his flight leader, only static.

Bracco must already have bailed out, he decided. His own fuel warning light had been on for some time and he knew the engine

Washington's Central Intelligence Agency supplied Mobutu Sese Seko with a number of World War II-vintage T-28 Trojans (similar to the Harvards flown by the SAAF) for use in ground attack roles. Bottom left shows how deeply supernatural traditions in Africa often penetrate. Following a battle in which members of Mike Hoare's 5 Commando were involved, some of his black soldiers stripped down to avoid what they believed were the influences of enemy Ju Ju curses, and right, a group of French mercenaries in the Congo. (All photos courtesy of Leif Hellström collection)

of the T-28 would quit within minutes. There was no chance of reaching any landing ground before then and no question: he was going down in the jungle.

Earlier that afternoon it had started off as a routine mission. A message had come in that a detachment of government troops was in trouble and 'Mish' Mishou, the CIA air operations officer at their field, dispatched the two T-28s to give support. He told the pilots that their underwing rockets and machine guns would give adequate support.

The lead aircraft was flown by Roger Bracco, a veteran Belgian mercenary who had served in the Katangese Air Force against the United Nations. His wingman was De la Guardia, a Cuban pilot who had recently arrived from Miami.

They had flown to Titule, a mission station some 350 kilometres north of Stanleyville – Kisangani today – where a squad of about 50 troops, led by three Belgian officers of the 6th Commando was pinned down by rebel mortar fire. The Belgian mercenaries had been hired to provide leadership and 'stiffening' to the local soldiers.

'It shouldn't have been any problem,' De la Guardia recalled. Their orders were to fly to Titule, make radio contact with their ground forces, do what was needed and return to base. It should have been a cake walk, but as it turned out, it wasn't.

As it happened, one of the officers taking fire on the ground from the rebels was a personal friend of Bracco. So they started talking and Bracco was asked to do this and then that, and so it went on.

The two aircraft fired their rockets at enemy positions pinpointed from the ground and then things would go quiet. But shortly afterwards the unit on the ground started getting mortared again, so they had to go in again and repeat the process. Clearly, the rockets weren't having the effect they'd hoped for.

The wingman did his best to give Bracco protection. In stages, he was flying low trying to pinpoint enemy positions and from where the mortars were being fired. Meantime he stayed high, cruising around at about 3,500 feet, to see whether other ground forces were shooting at the two aircraft.

'Of course the rebels knew exactly what we were doing,' he declared afterwards. They saw the other airplane loitering above and said, 'Don't make any smoke, because if you do, that guy up there is going to come right down on us!'

The two planes loitered a while longer, all the while trying to draw out the rebels. By now, De la Guardia was getting worried about fuel and told Bracco it was time to go.

'Yeah, yeah – five more minutes!' the other man replied.

'OK, five more minutes. We talked to the people on the ground and they asked us to let go everything we had and they would use that opportunity to move out ... it was about 16:30 in the afternoon with another 90 minutes or so to go before dark.

By now, De la Gaudia was worried. 'Bracco, it is time to go! Time to go!' he urged over his radio, his voice sounding stressed.

'OK, OK, we are going,' was Bracco's reply. He then suggested that they fire all their rockets first and when that was done, he came on the air again and said they still had their machine guns.

'OK,' he told De la Guardia, 'let go with the machine guns while these guys move out.'

But then, quite unexpectedly, while making the final pass, De la Guardia said that he'd been hit by ground fire. 'Hey, Bracco! Something hit me ... I can see an opening, a tear of some kind on top of the wing.

Bracco acknowledged and moved towards and below his wingman's aircraft. Once underneath he said: 'All right, yeah, you got a hit. It doesn't look too bad, you're just spilling a little fuel.'

De la Guardia didn't have to be told that the T-28 fuel tanks were like rubberised cells and that if they were punctured by ground fire, they automatically seal themselves and minimise fuel loss. But still, it was worrying, De la Guardia conceded. With that, the two pilots headed home.

But it was too late. On the final track in, the planes ran into a succession of thunderstorms that only the Congo can generate. That forced a detour, and by the time they were 80 kilometres from base it was obvious that they were not going to make it.

Mishou's last words to the pilots from the base had been something about them coming for them first thing in the morning. When his engine started coughing, De la Guardia bailed out.

'I jumped from the left side, going out head first. It was already pitch-black, right there, but I still spotted the beacon on top of the vertical fin miss me by about three metres … lucky I wasn't hit …

'On clearing the plane, I started pulling on my D-ring and it seemed ages before it finally opened. You pull and you pull some more, and then you ask yourself, where the hell is the parachute? It takes a few seconds.

'Since I had emerged head first from the aircraft, I flipped when the parachute opened. Then quite unexpectedly, the harness pulled taut against the Uzi cradled on my chest and almost broke a rib. I did see a flash somewhere ahead of me, but at some distance. It could have been something else, but I think it was when the aircraft impacted the ground.

'As I was coming down in the parachute, I looked down. That was when I saw several lightning strikes, five or eight kilometres away, illuminate the entire area around me.

'I looked down and all I could see was jungle – a pea green soup of a tropical forest that even in that bad light seemed to go on forever.'

Moments later the jungle rushed up towards the pilot and he impacted, going into the heavy foliage at an angle and crashing through the treetops before his parachute snagged. The back of De la Guardia's helmet colided with a branch, hard enough to crack the tough plastic. Total silence followed.

After a few moments the pilot regained his bearings. Slowly he began to take stock. He felt around his body and though there were bruises galore, nothing seemed seriously injured. Meantime, he found himself hanging metres above the ground, his parachute canopy stuck on a protruding branch of one of the trees. He could do nothing as the wind rustled the branches around him and rain dripped down onto his helmet.

Chapter 21
The Central Intelligence Agency's Air War in the Congo

Minutes later it was completely dark and for the first time it was impossible to see the ground. Which was when the thought hit him: how the hell was he going to get himself out of that mess and get down unharmed?

Here he was, a young Cuban student and sometime crop duster, hanging from a 30-metre forest giant in an African jungle. He was familiar enough with the flight plan they'd logged earlier to be aware that he was far behind enemy lines. Were he to be detected, they would kill him. Simple as that, only it wouldn't be quick. In Africa's remote regions, it never is.

Totally on his own, lonely and, for the first time, terrified, he knew that there was absolutely nothing he could do until it got light again. For a time he started thinking about family and friends.

The night passed slowly and more than once he asked himself what he was doing there, how he got there and why the hell he got involved.

And how had the CIA ended up hiring him to go to the Congo?

In 1966, the *New York Times* published an article where it claimed that the Central Intelligence Agency had put an 'instant air force' into the Congo a couple of years previously. This was done to support the operations of mercenary troops hired by the Congolese government to fight a rebellion.

By then America was openly supporting the Congolese government militarily, politically and economically and it was fairly common knowledge that the CIA was involved.

What was not common knowledge at the time was that Washington's paramilitary support of the Congolese had actually started long before the rebellion broke out in 1964, and that it was initially intended for entirely different purposes.

The CIA had already sent an air unit to the Congo in 1962 to help support the Congolese government against a rather modest military threat which had turned into a grave political problem for Cyril Adoula, the prime minister of that period.

In a remarkable book by Leif Hellström – a Swedish historian of considerable note – titled *The Instant Air Force: The Creation of the CIA's Air Unit in the Congo, 1962*, he tells us that a significant problem for the Congolese Central Government in the early days was that it lacked air power.

During the colonial period the Belgians operated a small force of transport aircraft and helicopters in the Congo, but most of these, as well as all their Belgian pilots, had been transferred to Katanga soon after independence.

The Congolese made a few efforts to build up an air force but none of this led anywhere, and by the autumn of 1962 there was not a single pilot, Congolese or otherwise, in the *Force Aérienne Congolaise*, or Congolese Air Force (FAC). This military arm had bought six ex-Belgian T-6 Harvard trainer aircraft in mid-1962, which could potentially be used for air support missions, but only if pilots and the requisite armaments could be acquired. And therein lay the rub, because on independence from Belgium in 1960, the Congo – a country almost as large as France, Germany and Spain together – had only six university graduates. It had no aviators – not even a single pupil pilot.

Meanwhile, to the secessionist south, the Katangese Air Force (*Aviation Katangaise*, which abbreviated to Avikat) was being steadily built up again, having been destroyed by the United Nations during fighting in 1961.

By late September that year the Avikat had ten T-6 aircraft, the same type as those bought by the FAC. But unlike the Central Government, the Katangese had hired mercenary pilots for its aircraft and had armaments in abundance, thanks in large part to Belgian mining interests who wished the dissident state to remain distant from the country's Central Government in Leopoldville, soon to change its name to Kinshasa.

This tiny air force soon began flying ground attack missions in northern Katanga in support of Katangan military operations against dissidents and supporters of the Central Government.

Durban's Peter Duffy fought long and hard for Mike Hoare's 5 Commando in the Congo (and was later recruited by Hoare for the aborted Seychelles invasion. He is seen here, centre left in camouflage with a group of his unit's irregulars near Lake Tanganyika. (Photo: Peter Duffy)

Chapter 21
The Central Intelligence Agency's Air War in the Congo

Duffy (left) with the aircrew of one of the American bombers provided by the CIA to fight Simba rebels in the north-east of the country. (Photo: Peter Duffy)

Since it was in the interest of the Congolese Central Government to be able to provide its ground troops with effective air support, it needed to find more aircraft or at least enough pilots to man its planes. Moreover, it needed to do so quickly. At about this point, the Americans stepped up to the plate, in part to stymie Soviet efforts at destabalising an entire region that stretched all the way across the African continent.

One needs to bear in mind as well that Portugal was already fighting a series of major insurrections in Angola and Mozambique, the majority of the rebels ranged against Lisbon funded and supported by Moscow. In this regard the Congo was also involved, and obviously, this alarmed some American strategists. Which was when somebody in Washington emerged with the idea that the best alternative would be to allow surrogate forces into the fray that were under total American control.

If the US government was to assist the Congolese government in countering the Katangese air threat, there are a number of ways of going about it.

The two main alternatives for the Americans were to give the assistance needed themselves or get someone else to provide it. The latter option had the advantage of reducing the risk of the United States being accused of meddling in Congo politics. In theory, the Americans might have attempted to persuade one of its allies, or some neutral country in Africa or elsewhere, to provide the Congolese with unilateral assistance.

However, even ignoring all the possible practical and political complications which could have arisen from such a move, it would likely have been difficult to find any country willing to stick its neck out in this way, especially in an extremely volatile Africa.

In practice, this option was not even seriously considered. (However, there were discussions in 1962 about Italian involvement in the setting up of a military flying school in the Congo, but this, of course, was more of a long-term project). Another possible route was to involve the United Nations, which was already heavily committed to Congolese security. The consensus at the time was that the UN had enough to worry about without adding to its problems. And anyway, the UN had become problematic.

If the US government decided to go ahead on its own, the obvious solution would be to officially send in American military forces, which would be coordinated with the Congolese at a high level. Operationally, this move had several advantages; politically there were numerous risks.

Another possible solution might have been to use as a force, which, de facto, was under US control, but not obviously so. And this is where the Central Intelligence Agency entered the picture.

By 1962 the CIA had gained considerable experience in how to organise, equip and run small air forces in remote corners of the globe. One of the immediate spin-offs from the CIA-sponsored Bay of Pigs debacle was that a cadre of expatriate Cuban pilots was now available in the USA, already with solid experience of CIA procedures.

Paramilitary operations had formed an important part of the CIA's activities for many years and Langley already had a cadre of several hundred people who carried out planning and training for clandestine operations.

Additional personnel were hired as needed, either on loan from the US military or from the 'free market' in the USA or abroad: ergo mercenaries.

Having made its decision to help and as part of an American support

Chapter 21
The Central Intelligence Agency's Air War in the Congo

programme for the Congo government, a military advisory team travelled to the Congolese capital in June 1962. It published a report a month later, which noted – much like the British and the UN also did around this time – that there were grave problems in many parts of the embattled country. It went on to suggest various options, including the military one.

As for the future, it was stated that:
- Development of such an organisation will necessitate outside training and material assistance over a period of time.
- Until the indigenous personnel can be trained and a Congolese unit organised, some arrangement will have to be made for utilisation of the available aircraft and facilities to meet Congolese operational needs.

At this stage, mid 1962, the US government was still reluctant to get directly militarily involved in the Congo, the idea being that a peaceful solution to the Congo crisis might arise. Whoever was making these deductions obviously had very little experience either of Africa, or African politics generally.

Still, efforts continued to be directed at supporting United Nations' mediating initiatives, but at somebody's insistence, a token shipment of jeeps, radios and various other items was put together and delivered to the Congolese Army a few weeks later.

By now the Congo government had taken delivery of the first batch of its new T-6 Harvard trainer/ground support aircraft and they immediately turned to the USA for help.

The American ambassador reported late August 1962 that he had met with Congolese Prime Minister Adoula, who was happy about the arrival of the aircraft but that he now insisted on getting help in finding pilots to fly the planes. Ostensibly, the ambassador remained non-committal.

A few days later he did send a reminder to Washington that Premier Adoula now had six aircraft but still no pilots.

'He may be tempted to hire no good roustabouts who might be willing to take aggressive initiative,' formed part of the message. Weeks later the ambassador made his point again.

For at least a fortnight during this critical time frame Adoula had on his desk a draft contract offered by an obscure company on the far side of the Atlantic Ocean called Air Panama. He was also advised that there was a real possibility that mercenary pilots might be hired for combat as opposed to instruction. If this happened, warned the

American ambassador, 'the effect on a national reconciliation plan would be adverse'.

Air Panama (or *Aerovias Panama SA*, to give the firm its correct name), despite its origins, was a relatively small airline in Miami, Florida. It already had a role flying charter for the UN in the Congo and was now trying to get a contract with the Congolese government.

There was talk at this point of Air Panama providing training for the FAC, presumably including support for its T-6s and the inclusion of exiled Cuban pilots. The US government looked favourably on Air Panama's proposal and, in return, Air Panama's management was willing to assist the US government. By mid September 1962, the CIA director reported that the manager of Air Panama had visited his offices 'and volunteered any use of his facilities we need'. Whether Langley ever took him up on the offer is not clear.

Late September 1962, the UN obtained confirmation that the Katangese Air Force had received a number of T-6 aircraft. This information was forwarded both to Washington and to the Congolese. Clearly, the US government was becoming increasingly concerned about developments in central Africa, particularly about the deteriorating military situation in the Congo, and especially the prospect of an unrestrained civil war, which suddenly appeared imminent.

A memorandum to President Kennedy from the State Department at this time claimed that 'our plans for the Congo are slowly sinking into the African ooze'.

There was no improvement in the situation over the next few weeks and meanwhile the Congolese government was coming under increasing political pressure from the opposition to do something about Katanga. By early October there were reports that the Soviet Union was preparing to offer military assistance directly to the Congolese government. Washington needed to act promptly.

A month later there were reports of Katangan aircraft carrying out attacks on the Congolese troops in northern Katanga and for the first time the Congolese government asked Washington directly for help. It desperately needed combat aircraft, was the gist of it, 'since only military pressure would inspire truly conciliatory action by [Katangan President] Tshombe.'

Enter Lawrence (Larry) Devlin, the CIA Chief of Station in the Congo at that time and an old friend of the author. After a lengthy discussion with Devlin about the political situation, Adoula closed the meeting by suggesting that a few good American aircraft would

Chapter 21
The Central Intelligence Agency's Air War in the Congo

Cuban pilots are stopped at a road block in Stanleyville (Kisangani today) after that city had been liberated from the Simba rebels. Most of these aviators had been recruited by the CIA in Miami. (Photo: courtesy of the Leif Hellström collection)

do more to maintain his government in power than anything else the US government might be able to do.

Devlin, who died recently, disclosed in his book that it was primarily the American ambassador in the Congo who was behind the initiative to hire Cubans. The number of telegrams from the ambassador to Washington concerning aircraft and armaments suggests that he took a very personal interest in the matter.

To find suitable personnel for its new air unit in the Congo, the CIA had turned to the group with which it had already had a history of association. Exiled Cubans living in Florida had been involved in numerous clandestine disputes on behalf of their host government, including the nefarious Bay of Pigs fiasco.

In late 1961 Luis Cosme, who had been Chief of Operations for the CIA air unit in that disaster, went to Washington to get help for the Cuban exile pilots in obtaining valid flying licences. After some

Two mercenary flown T-6 aircraft of the Katangese Air Force on a mission in the autumn of 1962. These were the aircraft the Congolese government and the United Nations were so worried about. (Photo: via Leon Libert)

discussions, the CIA agreed to pay the bill and deposited US$25,000 with the Emery Riddle School of Aeronautics in Miami. This was about adequate for training 20 pilots, which the 'pupils' got free of charge and without strings attached. It was seen as a way to say 'thank you' for services rendered in the past.

The CIA also appointed an officer by the name of George (Jerry) Sohl to keep pace with developments and to act as liaison with the Cubans.

This move also slotted in with the CIA's preference for 'foreign' personnel to be hired for this type of operation. Five pilots were initially recruited, most of them from the group training at Emery Riddle and, all but one, veterans from the Bay of Pigs.

The selection was made with the assistance of Cosme, who picked pilots known to him personally, with the contracts written up at his house. Salary was listed at US$800 a month plus expenses, and the contracts were for a six-month stretch. A single Cuban aircraft mechanic was also taken on.

Officially, the pilots were hired by a medium-sized firm called Caribbean Aeromarine Company, which had been incorporated in Florida in April 1962. Among many other activities listed in its registration, the company was said to 'employ personnel and to provide for their training and instruction in what was termed 'the operation, service, maintenance and repair' of aircraft.

In reality, Caribbean Aeromarine's paymaster was Langley and it effectively acted as a front company for the CIA – business lingo, a so-called 'proprietary'. These were (and are) companies formed for the purpose of facilitating CIA activities and there were dozens, if not hundreds of them, working in a variety of fields all over the globe.

Some were formed simply to be at hand if their expertise in a particular field was needed and more often than not, their directors and owners were local lawyers. This was apparently the case with Caribbean Aeromarine, since all three members of the board gave the same office building as their official address.

The exact date when the Cubans were hired is not known. Likely it was only two or three weeks before they travelled to the Congo. Prior to setting out for Africa, the crew was given a series of thorough checkouts on the Harvards they were scheduled to fly in Africa by a former United States Navy pilot in Miami. There was also some training in formation flying and no problems were encountered in this preliminary phase because four of the pilots had flown T-6s either in the Cuban Air Force or the Cuban Navy.

Once in the Congo – with Jerry Sohl accompanying the group as its 'manager' – the official line taken was that they were there on contract, working directly for the Congolese government. Consequently, everybody was issued with official identity documents issued by the *Armée Nationale Congolaise*.

The Cubans travelled under false passports which indicated that they were all from Guatemala, the Dominican Republic or elsewhere in the Hispanic World. It didn't work, because in no time at all, just about everybody in town knew there was a bunch of Cubans around.

Also, the Congolese tended to refer to them as *les techniciens américains* (American technicians) – implying United States origins. So it was no big secret locally that Washington had been involved in the recruitment process.

Curiously, the local Congolese media did not pick up on this anomaly at the time, though there is little question that they would have been warned off by government goons had they tried to highlight the issue. In those days it wasn't worth your life to try to ignore official warnings and, indeed, half a century later, not very much has changed…

At first, all the T-6 aircraft were based at the N'Dolo airfield in Leopoldville, where the local military also had its flying school and the Cubans were allocated a small office.

Initially, the aircraft were not armed and for a while, things went slowly. The Cubans flew fairly regularly, usually making formation flights over and around the capital to make sure that everyone knew that the FAC was now 'operational'.

Since the Hispanic crews got paid extra while in the air – so much an hour – they flew almost every day. Also, all their aircraft were in good condition and technical problems were quickly solved by the Cuban chief mechanic and his Congolese assistants.

A few days after their arrival, Sohl and the Cubans were taken to see Colonel Mobutu, the Chief of Staff of the ANC. He requested that they immediately go to Katanga to attack some Katangese troops who were in the process of besieging one of his units. Sohl argued that this was impossible – the planes were not yet fitted with arms, he explained. What he did not tell Mobutu was that his government was still eager to avoid contributing to any escalation of the ongoing military conflict. It was a futile argument because with both the Katangese and the rebels receiving foreign military support, hostilities were escalating anyway.

Finally, somebody in Washington saw light and the order was given to supply the Cuban aviation contingent with what was termed 'a reasonable quantity' of rockets, but only after 'technical details' [had been] clarified. Once more the situation was allowed to smoulder, with nothing positive emerging from the impasse.

By early December the Congo's leader Adoula was so discouraged that he claimed that his government was in ruins. He also warned the Americans that the security of his country was at stake. He went on to say that 'Tshombe was bombarding his troops and villages on a daily basis and that both the Americans and the United Nations seemed powerless to do anything about it. In particular, it rankled that he had what appeared to be an effective combat wing but wasn't allowed to use it.

So the Cuban pilots stayed 'under wraps' and the US continued to delay the delivery of aircraft rockets for their Harvards.

About then, the American ambassador made urgent representations to his bosses and urged that Washington speed up the delivery of the weapons, in large part to counter Soviet offers of military supplies. These were imminent, he declared and he suggested telling the Congolese that they were on their way. It is worth noting that by now even the American ambassador had become acutely pessimistic about the situation and actually feared a collapse of the government. He said as much in his reports home which have since been declassified.

In fact, the Congo situation was getting a lot of attention in Washington. The notes from daily staff meetings, including the one at the White House on 10 December 1962 contained the following comments:

> After a little pessimistic brooding around the table, the discussion turned to broader issues. [...] Bundy, Kaysen and Dungan said that one of the best things that could happen might be for the Congolese National Army to drop a few bombs in the Katanga from a few aircraft which the United States would furnish them for that purpose[1].
>
> The idea seemed to be that this would tend to remove a lot of the intricate complexities of the Congo problem (UN, UMHK, etc.) and perhaps reduce it to a nice clean war between Leopoldville and Elisabethville. There was a little laughter around the table at this suggestion. For example, Bundy said that 'we were all certainly a bunch of hawks, but there was an unmistakable undercurrent of seriousness nevertheless.'

United States Air Force markings are removed from a CIA-supplied bomber after arriving in the Congolese capital. (Photo courtesy of Leif Hellström collection)

By this time the Cuban pilots had been informed that they might be expected to mount an attack on the Avikat base at Kolwezi.

Once the rocket rails had been fitted to the aircraft, they were flown to an airfield some distance from Leopoldville where the pilots began practising for their attacks. Meanwhile, the United Nations also continued attempts to find additional fighter aircraft.

Although Sweden had agreed in late November to send reinforcements to its unit, this was on the condition that other nations would also contribute aircraft. In early and mid December the UN tried to persuade – among others – Greece, Iran, Italy, Pakistan and the Philippines to contribute either aircraft or crews, but negotiations dragged on with nothing substantive taking place.

Eventually the Philippines agreed to provide pilots. They would fly aircraft provided by Italy, while Iran – then still under the Shah – promised both aircraft and crews, but it was clear that neither would arrive in the Congo for several weeks.

In some of these cases the Americans were quietly providing diplomatic support behind the scenes. With regard to aircraft from Italy, Washington did, in effect, provide the aircraft as well, since these had originally been supplied to Rome as part of a US aid package and technically, the planes were still the property of the United States.

Also, the option to use US military forces was still kept open and, in fact, received a lot of attention at the time due to the worsening political situation in the Congo.

The Joint Chiefs of Staff wrote a recommendation early December 1962, stating that among other things, that body believed that 'the central issue of the Congolese problem is to keep a pro-Western regime in power.' This would remain a problem as long as the Katanga problem remained unresolved.

They therefore recommended, '[i]f required to prevent the collapse of the Central Government, [to] offer the UN a US military package consisting of one Composite Air Strike Unit with necessary support elements.'

A detailed plan was also drawn up to send a fighter squadron with eight jet fighters and two reconnaissance aircraft. In the draft of the plan, many of the woes of the country were listed, including 'the instability and administrative flabbiness' of the Adoula government and the latent threat of Soviet military assistance.

The State Department wrote just before Christmas that, 'one of the most difficult problems facing Adoula [and his government] is the handicap they face in virtual freedom of air enjoyed by Katanga Air

Force.' It was then suggested that the United Nations should destroy the Avikat on the ground, thereby indicating that air support for the Congolese obviously still had a high priority.

An American general was sent to the Congo on a fact-finding mission and one of his main tasks was to 'assess the need for a US tactical fighter squadron in the Congo and to determine how this force could best be employed to advance US objectives there.'

According to an observer close to the president, one reason for this mission was for President Kennedy to delay having to take a decision on the subject.

In the end President Kennedy agreed to send the fighter unit if the United Nations made an official request for the US to do so. This came through on the second-last day of the year. Within hours, an American fighter wing began 'planning and coordination ... for a higher headquarters tasked move of a squadron of F-84 aircraft to a classified forward operating location.'

The aircraft situation at the end of December 1962 was therefore as follows:

- The United Nations fighter force had received some Swedish reinforcements, but the Swedish unit was considered unreliable and ineffective. Additional units from other countries had been promised but would take some weeks to arrive.
- A unit of the US Air Force had just started preparations to move to the Congo from Europe to form part of the UN forces, but this too would take some time.
- The 'Congolese Air Force', i.e. the CIA air unit, had received its rocket armament and was training for a possible strike on Katanga in mid January.

Almost overnight, time had run out in the Congo. Fighting had broken out between United Nations forces and Katangese troops and when this continued, UN headquarters eventually decided to strike back.

By all accounts this was initially seen as just another 'police action' and there was no indication that the UN expected any major changes to result. Days later a Swedish fighter unit attacked the Avikat base at Kolwezi and over the next couple of days the Katangese Air Force was almost totally destroyed on the ground. The few aircraft that survived fled to Angola to enjoy the protection of the Portuguese government.

At the same time, UN ground forces moved forward and quickly captured the remaining Katangese strongholds with little or no resistance. Katangan secession formally ended on 14 January 1963.

What becomes clear with hindsight is that both the United Nations and Washington were taken by surprise by events as they rapidly unfolded. There was actually some reluctance to accept that, in the end, it had all been so easy.

The manner in which the Avikat had been destroyed surprised just about everybody because they believed that the Katangese would put up stiff resistance. Indeed, opinion in Washington at the time was that 'estimates of damage to it have been greatly exaggerated.' Even so, it was suggested that there was no longer any point in sending US aircraft to the Congo and the deployment was soon cancelled.

Implementation to send Philippine and Iranian fighter squadrons had however already been set in motion, and both units were allowed to go to the Congo, even though they were no longer needed. They stayed only a few months before returning home. The Swedish Air Force element – then the only United Nations fighter unit – remained in the Congo, before it too, was disbanded in September 1963.

With Katanga gone, there was no longer any immediate need for the CIA air unit, either. Adoula's government was relatively safe for the time being and there were no immediate internal or external enemies threatening military action.

Even so, the Cuban pilots were left in place and they continued to fly the T-6s around Leopoldville, 'to show the flag.' It was a relatively cheap way for the Americans to show support for Adoula's government. Also, with Katanga gone, the Congo situation was largely defused and there was little or no political risk involved.

Until early 1964, the situation in the Democratic Congo Republic remained more or less unchanged, apart from periodic changes of personnel. It was then that revolt against the Central Government broke out in the Kwilu province, to the east of Leopoldville. Kikwit, its capital, was to be used decades later as a staging post for the revolt led by Laurent Kabilla in unseating President Mobuto Sese Seko in 1997.[2]

The rebellion became known as the 'Mulele Revolt', after its leader, Pierre Mulele. A few weeks after the revolt started, the CIA air unit deployed to the front and subsequently flew numerous ground attack missions in support of the ANC.

In an unusual arrangement, the CIA aircraft would also fly air cover for rescue helicopters of the United Nations when these went to pick up refugees from Protestant and Catholic mission stations in remote areas. In return, the UN promised to provide a rescue service for any Cuban pilot forced to crash-land or bail out.

Later in that year, when a second, more serious revolt broke out further east in the Congo, the CIA air unit was greatly expanded and received more modern aircraft directly from Washington, again under the auspices of the Central Intelligence Agency. This expatriate group of mercenaries, for that is what they were – fought on for three more years, finally ending their security role late in 1967.

It is interesting that they lasted as long as they did in Africa. Following the Bay of Pigs debacle in 1961, President Kennedy never again placed quite the same degree of trust in large paramilitary operations as had President Eisenhower.

On the other hand, 1961 onward saw increased focus on anti-guerrilla and other peripheral or 'brush-fire' wars in the Third World. Portugal was fighting three major military campaigns in Africa and the Rhodesian War was about to take off, followed by a South African military role in Angola. This was a direct result of the Soviet Union's pledge to support so-called 'wars of liberation' around the world.

All these factors raise the question: was military intervention in the Congo at the behest of the Central Intelligence Agency necessary?

Horst Faas, the famous Vietnam photographer who died in 2012, gave the author this photo of a bunch of juvenile prospective fighters taken in Katanga's old Elizabethville (Lubumbashi today) half a century ago.

For answers, one needs to look back at recent history. For example, Southeast Asia in 1961: When the USAF carried out a covert operation in Vietnam (all the while maintaining that it was part of the effort launched by the Vietnamese Air Force), the CIA set up a series of clandestine operations in Thailand for operations over Laos.

Both operations were roughly the same size, both were intended for the same type of missions and both operated the same kinds of aircraft. In addition, that CIA operation employed mainly USAF pilots on loan. Of significance here is that the CIA was seen as just another 'tool' by the American government, in that it was an organisation on par with any of the branches of the regular armed forces. The bottom line here was the consensus in Washington at the time that sending in the CIA was not necessarily considered a very dramatic decision. It was more a question of what was most practical in each given situation.

In the Congo in 1962, using the CIA was apparently regarded as pragmatic.

Compared to CIA air operations, Washington's efforts in the Congo were relatively modest compared to other theatres of military activity such as in Asia. They were also 'uncomplicated', not least because the crews operated in what could be regarded as a 'friendly' country and had relative free rein in the capital. Moreover, the aircraft involved in all these strikes were already there and the logistics support was at hand.

At first, most of the actions could be regarded as 'window-dressing', since their aircraft lacked armament. It actually took something like two months before the planes were made combat-ready. Things might have been different had the crews been called on to actually go into combat against Katanga, but this never happened.

1 McGeorge Bundy was Special Assistant to President Kennedy for National Security Affairs and attended all relevant White House briefings, especially those involving the Congo.
2 Al J. Venter: *War Dog – Fighting Other People's Wars*, Casemate Publishers, Philadelphia, 2006, which deals with subsequent mercenary activity in Mobutu's Zaire as well as Zimbabwe's military participation in those struggles, See chapters 10–13, pp. 241–320. See also the author's experiences in the Congo in *Barrell of a Gun – A War Correspondent's Misspent Moments in Combat*, Chapters 19–22, pp. 357–400.

CHAPTER TWENTY TWO

FIGHTING HORSEMEN ON THE ANGOLAN BORDER

The men and the horses of the South African Army's Equestrian Unit was established to engage in counter-insurgency activity in some of the most difficult and remote terrain along the frontier with Angola. It was also one of the toughest units in the force for the simple reason that in order to belong, you had to be damn good at what you did.

It had started out as a routine patrol. Just another operation similar to the dozens of others undertaken by the South African Army patrolling close to the Angolan border in the Ovambo tribal area.

But this was different, a pursuit op, a chase. The tracks were fresh – two, perhaps three hours old. And the pursuers (the unit with whom I was embedded) was catching up fast. By late afternoon the distance between hunter and hunted was even less. As the youthful lieutenant in command explained – he had turned 21 just weeks before I arrived at his bush base – there was no time to stop for a break. Contact was near, he stressed.

The tracks led towards a school, another of the officers intimated. Could it be that the guerrilla group was using the place as a base? The issue rankled, because if there were children there, the pursuers would have more problems…

Lieutenant Barnard spurred his horse as the patrol approached a cluster of low buildings. Without hesitating, he signalled towards the bulk of his horsemen following only paces behind – about 18 of them – to cut across the flank. By a prearranged signal he told them to take up positions behind the school. If the quarry was around, the mounted unit would limit the option of retreat. If not, then who knew what would happen…

Lieutenant Johan Louw of the SA Army's mounted unit takes his men through their paces at their operational base near the Angolan frontier. (Photo: Author)

The young officer and two of his men rode on towards the school at full gallop. One of the horses gave a nervous quiver: we could see, even from a distance, that the animals sensed tension. The entire scenario was like something out of an old John Wayne movie.

Then it happened. As the lieutenant charged through a clump of low bushes, the adversaries came within sight of each other. There were three insurgents and each was armed.

Both groups reacted instinctively, or rather, as they had been trained to do. Barnard spurred his horse and pushed forward at a gallop. The enemy broke and ran, one of the group heading off at a tangent across open ground. His comrades chose the safety of numbers and used their carbines to herd a bunch of school children around them as they ran for safety. Their objective was a patch of dense scrub at the far end of the compound.

Lieutenant Barnard drove his charging horse after the lone runner. He called for the man to stop, but the man fled, clearly in blind panic. Within seconds Barnard had reached the man, who quite unexpectedly turned and raised his Kalashnikov.

Lieutenant Barnard didn't hesitate, his 9 mm pistol already in his hand. Before the guerrilla could fire, the South African had shot him through the neck … The man was dead before he hit the ground.

Chapter 22
Fighting Horsemen on the Angolan Border

Meanwhile, with a crowd of schoolkids crowding their focus, Barnard's comrades were finding things more difficult. One of the mounted soldiers was tempted to try a long shot at the two fleeing insurgents, but the milling schoolchildren presented too great a risk. As he said afterwards, an innocent child could easily have been hit.

But, as the last two guerrillas finally broke free of their makeshift shield and ran for the safety of the scrub, one of the horsemen did manage to get off a swift volley: an entire magazine was fired at the fleeing man and a blood trail picked up by trackers a short while later confirmed that one of the raiders had been wounded.

Lieutenant Barnard ordered a brief inspection of the area. Judging by a sheaf of documents taken from a pack abandoned by the insurgents it was clear that the trio were part of a much larger insurgent group, all of them SWAPO, or in the lingo, the Soviet-backed South West African Peoples Organisation.

Barnard was now faced with a difficult decision: did he go after the larger group which had perhaps a couple of hours start, or did he settle for the more certain – but smaller target – of the two surviving infiltrators?

He chose the former option.

One of Lieutenant Louw's mounted patrols checks out a village in a remote area. This kind of work could be dangerous with some of the units ambushed and two of the troopies attached to the unit killed when their horses tripped anti-tank mines. (Photo: Author)

Although there were only two hours of daylight left, the lieutenant pushed his troopers hard. By sunset the main body of the enemy was just ahead and as he admitted afterwards, the option of following a fairly distinct spoor in the dark looked tempting. Instead, Barnard chose to make camp rather than face the possibility of running into a night ambush. In any case, the men and horses were beat – they had been up since dawn.

It was a good decision. Later searches indicated that the insurgent group – now only a few kilometres ahead of the pursuing cavalry troop – had set up a large ambush. Clearly, they had expected the chase to continue and instead of an expected platoon of the enemy, subsequent radio intercepts suggested that the real figure was closer to 60.

But the drama was not over yet, not by a long chalk. When the South Africans failed to take the bait, the guerrillas decided to backtrack and make a pre-emptive strike of their own. For those men were members of SWAPO's distinctive 'A-Team' – each one of them tough, aggressive, bloody-minded and very well trained indeed. Also, they had the death of a comrade to avenge.

The attackers hit the South Africans' temporary base shortly after one in the morning. Emerging stealthily out of the darkness, the guerrillas laid down a heavy blanket of tracer fire, punctuated by the heavier blasts from RPG-7 rocket launchers. The lieutenant radioed through to headquarters and asked for backup, a gunship perhaps, but he was refused: there was nothing that could be done to help, which didn't exactly come as a surprise. He'd need a casualty or three to have that happen.

Also, the South Africans had not been caught napping. Wide-awake sentries had alerted the troop even before the terrorists had opened up and every one of Lieutenant Barnard's men was retaliating throughout the duration of the nine-minute firefight.

Once the shooting started to waver, it appeared that the other side might be withdrawing, which was just as well because three South African cavalrymen had been wounded, none seriously. The lieutenant had taken an AK bullet hit in the arm; another man had dropped with a slug in the leg, while the third casualty was hit by shrapnel, probably from an RPG.

The horses hadn't been so fortunate; nine of the animals had to be put down the next morning, which took place before the Puma helicopter arrived to lift out the wounded and those members of the unit left without mounts.

The insurgents did not go unscathed. There were at least two

Chapter 22
Fighting Horsemen on the Angolan Border

A singular advantage was that the horses were able to cover considerable distances under what were sometimes extremely difficult conditions, particularly in the rainy season. Also, the unit moved silently through bush country where the sandy soil masked its approach. Trouble was, arrangements always had to be made to bring fodder in should the animals be taken far from base. (Photo: Author)

more wounded, one seriously. Part of a limb was found near the guerrillas' original attack position.

In terms of the amount of time spent on the border and the number of contacts made with the enemy, South Africa's fighting horsemen comprised one of the most active units in the Operational Area. Yet it was curious that during the course of the first year, the Equestrian Unit – as it was officially known – had only one man killed in action. He died in a landmine blast, triggered by his horse.

It was an enormous blast, as might have been expected when a Soviet TM-57 anti-tank mine has been triggered. The blast – tailor-made by Moscow's engineers to destroy heavy armour – vaporised much of the animal while the rider lost both his legs and died within minutes.

Catastrophic, was how the death of that youthful soldier was later described by Lieutenant Johan Louw, an equally young officer who originally hailed from Pretoria. As he explained, the unit had been crossing a fairly remote area where an insurgent group had been particularly active.

'We were moving diagonally and there were perhaps 12 or 15 horses ahead of the man. Yet, when it was his turn to cross one of the many tracks they passed across, his horse triggered the mine … simply put, it was a stroke of bad luck.'

397

Barely a day went by on patrol that the unit did not make contact with 'Local Pops' – troopie lingo for the local population. These people were not always friendly, which usually suggested a SWAPO presence nearby. (Photo: Author)

As he recounted, the blast could just as easily have been set off by any man in his troop, himself included: 'It was really something that only happens in wartime – obviously the fellow's number came up ...'

While still operational, the Equestrian Unit remained relatively successful. It was rare for the guerrillas to directly confront these mounted pursuers. They would wait in ambush rather than try to outrun the horses, especially once they became aware that there were horsemen on their trail.

The speed at which South Africa's bushveld cavalry operated can be judged from just one example ... one spoor was already 24 hours old by the time Lieutenant Louw and his men picked it up just before dawn. Before nightfall – roughly 12 hours later – the cavalry had caught up with the fleeing SWAPO group and a running firefight ensued. The insurgents, totally unaware that a ragged bunch of cavalrymen were on their heels, were caught totally off-guard.

Time and again the men and horses of the Equestrian Unit proved they can move at an incredible speed when they have need to. On one particular follow-up operation they moved at a canter for 70 kilometres in seven hours – across the kind of difficult, sandy terrain that is symptomatic of this dense bush country that adjoins the former Portuguese colony.

The mounts, mostly of the traditional Afrikaner *Boerperd* breed, were exceptionally hardy and, like their riders, exceptionally fit. According to Louw, his men were soon acclimatised to the harsh and often demanding conditions in the Operational Area.

'They can even adapt to situations where water is scarce – which is quite often,' he told me.

A general shortage of potable water in the border combat zone was one of the reasons why the men were not expected to shave while on patrol. 'I'd much rather the guys carried more ammunition and extra water bottles than shaving kits,' he commented. Such 'business first' attitudes obviously worked, because the unit averaged a kill on each of its contacts in the six months prior to my own visit.

Despite the 'cavalry' tag, the horses were not used in actual combat unless it could not be helped. Rather, they were regarded by their commanders more as a means of transport, taking their riders into a position where, having dismounted, an action might take place and where helicopter support might be called in by radio. Once a firefight was on though, the riders reacted as normal infantry.

Most of the men conceded that operating with horses presented some peculiar sets of problems.

Said one: 'The animals are extremely sensitive and often act as an excellent early warning system. But at the same time, their snorting and stamping can create difficulties, especially when we're on an operation in open bush country that demands silence.

'There have been times when we've been seconds away from a contact and a horse has whinnied and immediately exposed our position. But by then we're pretty well spread out – which is one of the reasons we take so few casualties.'

After spending a week on ops with a mounted unit, it didn't take long for me to sense an uncanny understanding between animals and their riders. Each man was solely responsible for his own horse and it was not unusual to see troopers coaxing their animals through difficult conditions, almost as though they were helping a friend which, of course, they were.

On several occasions I watched the men water their horses before drinking themselves. It was the same with fodder; first the animal, then the rider.

One consequence of this intimacy between man and beast was the heartbreak some of the soldiers felt when their horses got injured or killed. Some of the men had to be relieved of combat duty until they were able to get over their grief. Then, after a suitable period, they'd get another horse ... and, obviously, the war would go on.

As with men attached to other specialist fighting units, it was apparent from the start that it took a somewhat unusual kind of person to become an Equestrian Rifleman. Lieutenant Louw – then only 21 years old and today one of the top landscape architects and developers in the country, handling projects simultaneously on three continents – maintained that it was not necessary for a man to have had previous riding experience.

'It helped, of course, but if your heart was set on the Equestrian Unit and you were prepared to go the distance, we'd suss you out soon enough. It was enthusiasm that went with the job that we looked for among the applicants.'

The training was rigorous, he stressed. The riders were required to complete a six-month basic training course at the Equestrian Centre at Potchefstroom and then spend several months in the Angolan border area for intensive counter-insurgency training. Only then, with all that behind them, were the youngsters granted full operational status.

One of the tougher demands was that unit members had to be prepared to spend 15 months on active duty and, clearly, far away from home. That meant that there was little time off from bush operations, apart from rest periods for their horses. Lieutenant Louw, for example, celebrated his 20th and 21st birthdays between forays in the bush.

His 21st birthday was highlighted by a 'cake' made from a watermelon, on which were perched 21 matches. His unit enjoyed a quick barbie and a cup of *mahango*, the local Ovambo beer – revolting stuff if you've never tried it before – to wash it all down.

Trainees were given good instruction on how to care for their animals in the field, and how to get the best out of each one of them. The recruits also had to learn the rudiments of bush veterinary procedures because while on operations in the bush, it was seldom that the troop was within call of a vet. Most important, the riders had to know what to feed their mounts: forage was brought in whenever the unit operated out of a static base, but there were many times when the mounts simply fed off the land.

Said Lieutenant Louw: 'in winter, when the country becomes dry and arid, it's a helluva business ... it can get extremely tough.

'But we manage, for no other reason than because we have to.'

CHAPTER TWENTY THREE

THE ALGERIAN CONNECTION

Algeria's historical role in ousting France – its former colonial overlord – from North Africa half a century ago, has played a powerful role in the subsequent overthrow of several modern-day oligarchs in nearby states. The civil war that followed the departure of the French spawned Salafism in a region that had never experienced this kind of Islamic extremism before.

There is some similarity in the nature of the struggle for freedom in Algeria and what has since taken place in Tunisia, Libya and Egypt. Though the level of violence was more acute, a similar strain of radical politics and nationalist sentiment came into play, accentuating, in a sense, the eternal Third World gulf between the haves and the have-nots.

However, it would be as misleading to compare the battle of Algiers of the 1950s with yesterday's revolts in Tripoli or Cairo as it would be to attempt to draw a parallel between Northern Ireland and Vietnam.

Bloodshed, violence, revolution, liberal protest, the abhorrence of brutality and increasing bitterness are all there. But the most important element throughout has been the degree of commitment. As we have seen in Syria today, and even within the Intifada uprising in Israel, contemporary Arabs show a superabundance of commitment when they believe that their cause has the blessing of Allah, often on both sides of the same front line.

All these uprisings have manifested basic guerrilla war concepts. Syria's revolt has devolved into a full-scale war that is likely to persist; much as did the revolution in Libya until the tyrant Muammar Gaddafi was killed. So too, with Algeria. But then the war that followed needs to be seen from the point of view of the settlers, the *pieds noirs* (colloquially Black Feet or French civilians).

The Algerian war of the fifties proved to be something of a watershed in the cycle of European colonial politics. It was the first conflict of the modern period involving a major European power in Africa. It was also the first war that was militarily and politically 'lost by an imperial force': consequently it set the pattern for a frenzy of political activity in dozens of other African states eager to reject European rule. (Photos: Author)

Walter Laqueur, the acclaimed military historian and strategist, once observed that the situation in Algeria might have been different if France had still been the 'mastodon' it had formerly been. By the time that Charles de Gaulle began to prepare for the independence of Algeria, France had already killed 200,000 Arabs, and the French were certainly capable of continuing the war for a while longer. 'But where would it all lead?' asked Laqueur.

'The army, seeing no further than the next *djebel*, did not want to be deprived of its victory. It had only one remedy; to break the bones of the *fellaghas*. But this would merely lead to a new war in five or ten years, and by that time the Arabs would be even weightier in numbers.'

More important still, and fundamental to the end result, was that Algeria was actually part of metropolitan France. The distance between Algiers and Marseilles is not much greater than from London to Frankfurt. We know now that when the crunch eventually came, most of the million-odd Frenchmen in Algeria, the *pieds noirs*, simply cut their ties and went home. As a result, the Algerian economy nearly collapsed, and ever since Algerians have been queuing in tens of thousands to leave the country for which they fought so bitterly.

Chapter 23
The Algerian Connection

It is not generally realised that while France lost about 2,000 of its troops in the Algerian War, local Arab recruits played only a subordinate part in the conflict, and often defected en masse to the 'terrorist' enemy. Once independence had been achieved, Algeria entered its second, internecine stage of violence when these 'collaborators' were slaughtered in their thousands, in spite of assurances to the contrary at the final Evian agreement which brought peace to North Africa.

The Algerian War was still further complicated by differences on religion. To most of the Muslim rebels – who were regarded as little short of fanatics by their European masters – they were waging a jihad against an infidel power. Also, Algeria's conflict sometimes deteriorated into spates of vindictive retribution that spawned bloodshed of horrific proportions. At times, senseless torture was the norm rather than the exception. In the same way, the rebel *Jabhat at-Tarīr al-Waṭanī*, or in French, the *Front de Libération Nationale* (FLN) took few prisoners; those that they caught were usually tortured first, in a bid to gain information about their compadres, and then murdered.

Everyday life in Algeria under the French had a lot to do with the war that finally brought independence. The Colonial French rarely included the Arab community in national sporting activities, such as they were. A token Arab player would make the local (white) Algerian team and Arab football teams were rarely pitted on a national basis against French teams. In fact, it is historically correct to aver that in Algeria, under French administration, the Arabs were generally regarded as physically inferior to the average French macho.

The lack of social contact between the settlers and the Arabs in North Africa was almost total. It manifested itself constantly. One of the most obvious examples was the absence of intermarriage between Europeans and Algerians. Such unions took place at the rate of less than a hundred a year. Sexual encounters between Europeans and Algerians were limited to the furtive meetings of homosexuals and the commercial transactions of prostitutes.

To understand properly what happened in Algeria a couple of generations ago, it is necessary to look back in history.

The French entered Algeria in 1830 with a punitive military expedition against the Dey of Algiers, the recognised ruler of a state which for years had maintained diplomatic and commercial relations with several European countries. After the surrender of the Dey, Paris waged a relentless pacification campaign – lasting 17 years – against the indigenous Arabs and Berbers, who were fighting to retain the land that they had inhabited for centuries and their Islamic way of life. The conquered territories were subsequently divided into three French *departements*, which juridically constituted an integral part of France.

No other colonial power ever interfered, and Algeria remained French until it became independent.

French settlers in Algeria, who began to arrive during the pacification, were soon joined by others from Spain and Italy, who subsequently received French citizenship. This melting process was roughly similar to what occurred among Dutch, German and French settlers in South Africa.

As was the case in other African countries that had been settled by European colonials, the Algerian issue was bedevilled by the question of what to do with the natives who greatly outnumbered the settlers. Paris, believing in the French mission *civilisatrice*, initiated several efforts and took limited steps over the years to assimilate its Algerian Muslim subjects as full French citizens.

First the handful willing to abandon their personal status under Islamic law, then the special categories of educated Muslims; and finally, in 1947, all Algerian Muslims nominally became full Frenchmen. Early metropolitan French policies, in other words, resembled British policies that entailed a qualified franchise for Africans.

The colons, or colonists, however, always stubbornly resisted all attempts to grant the Arabs anything like complete equality. Not merely did they wish to monopolise their special privileges; they considered the Muslims inferior; not because of their colour (which was little different from their own) but because of their vulgar contempt for Arab culture and religion.

When Paris made it brutally clear that it would never consider letting Algeria be anything other than part of France, young Arab militants who subsequently formed the FLN began planning guerrilla actions. The FLN theoretically welcomed non-Muslims who shared its aspirations, although it focused on the Arab-Muslim heritage of Algeria and its solidarity with others in the Arab world.

In truth, the FLN turned to violence because there was absolutely no hope of attaining its goal of independence through peaceful negotiations.

Throughout the period of French occupation of North Africa, Arab opposition to rule from Paris was never far from the surface. Many of P.C. Wren's stories about the French Foreign Legion, which kept generations of schoolboys in the English-speaking world enthralled

Chapter 23
The Algerian Connection

– myself included – were based on actual exploits by the Legion in the Algerian Sahara. Uprisings were brief and bloody, and they were equally brutally suppressed.

By the end of World War II, the position of France in North Africa had been weakened, and a serious insurrection – known as the Setif bloodbath – broke out in 1945. Nationalist forces alleged that 20,000 Arabs were killed by the French. Official reports give the number of about 1,500 rebels shot by security forces. Walter Laqueur believes that the real figure is probably between 5,000 and 8,000. That was a dangerous conflagration, and it would undoubtedly have drawn the attention of the United Nations if it had been in existence at that time.

The events at Setif made an indelible mark on the minds of the Arab people of Algeria. Although they were in fact responsible for the uprising, which left little more than 100 French dead, with many more injured and women brutally raped, including one old lady of 84, they considered the French 'over-kill' to be out of all proportion to the events that caused it.

The Algerian poet Kateb Yacine wrote: 'It was at Setif that my sense of humanity was affronted for the first time by the most atrocious sights. I was 16 years old. The shock that I felt at the pitiless butchery, which caused the death of thousands of Muslims, I have never forgotten. From that moment on my nationalism took definite form.'

The War

There was certain logic in the choice by the FLN of 1 November 1954 for the launch of their 'jihad' against the French in Algeria. It was the eve of the Christian festival of All Saints' Day, and most of the devout *pieds noirs*, it was assumed by the FLN leaders, would be off their guard. At least the vigilance of the police would be relaxed. The settlers themselves assumed (just as the Israelis did just before the Yom Kippur War in 1973) the Muslims would surely respect the sanctity of a religious holiday.

They did not. The country had already been divided up by the FLN into six *Wilayas* or autonomous military zones, and there were attacks in each of them. Some were the work of a small group of armed men; in other areas, such as Biskra, a group of rebels attacked the police station half an hour before the predetermined hour of three in the morning.

The attack on the barracks at Batna went off roughly as planned, but not before its occupants were aroused by alarm bells and flashing lights. Two of the guards, 21-year old Chasseurs, were mowed down because peace-time regimental orders required that their rifles should be unloaded and their ammunition sewn up in their pouches. They were the first military personnel to be killed in the war.

The first officer was cut down by machine-gun fire as he emerged from his quarters in the small garrison at Khenchela. He was a Spahi, Lieutenant Gerard Darneau. Other attacks took place at the Ichmoul lead mine where the guerrillas intended to seize a quantity of explosives, but failed. It was the same at the tiny gendarmerie post of T'kout and in the Tighanimine Gorge a few hours later. The local bus travelling between Kiskra and Arris was ambushed and a loyal *caid* or government functionary was shot. Two young French teachers were wounded in the attack.

There were five targets in Algiers: the radio station, a fuel depot, the telephone exchange, the gasworks and a warehouse belonging to a prominent French politician. All five attacks were frustrated, largely because the attackers were ill-trained and badly equipped. Similarly in Oran, none of the groups fulfilled their objectives. One of the attacks, launched prematurely, found the authorities on their guard, and by morning eight insurgents had been killed, six of them with weapons in their possession.

Elsewhere in Algeria the attacks took on a similar pattern, some of them successful, many others not, largely because of a lack of modern weapons. A few of the attackers were armed with knives. Ben Bella later said that the FLN began the rebellion with between 350 and 400 firearms, 'and virtually nothing heavier than a machine gun'.

Most of the bombs that exploded on All Saints' Day were primitive devices made locally by inexpert artisans. Only months later did military supplies begin to arrive in Algeria from Morocco and Tunisia.

The British historian Alistair Horne tells us that not a weapon at that time (or for several years to come) came from the communist bloc; nor, with the slender resources of the FLN, was more than a modest quantity of guns acquired elsewhere abroad. Therefore, from the start of hostilities, the theft of French arms from depots or their recovery on the battlefield became a prime military objective. A French doctor reported later that most of the wounds he treated in the early days had been inflicted by hunting rifles and shotguns.

It is notable that the French had been warned as early as six months before the first attacks that an offensive by a group of rebels was being prepared. The office of the Governor General even received

Chapter 23
The Algerian Connection

Clockwise from top left: French Army conscripts take a breather in the interior of Algeria. Helicopters quickly became a valuable adjunct to the kind of colonial military operations initiated by Paris. General Charles de Gaulle, the French President of the time, takes the salute on his arrival in Algiers. It was he who eventually 'pulled the plug' on French military operations in North Africa when he became aware that a political solution to the war was the only option. French 'Special Forces' go into battle in Algeria from a modified *Sikorsky* and, *Agusta Bell-47s* were widely deployed in Algeria as the war progressed. They operated mainly out of Boufarik and Oran bases near the coast. (Photos: Author)

a warning from an informer that this was about to take place, but it was apparently filed away in some pigeonhole and retrieved only after the attacks had taken place.

Once the first attacks had happened, the French reacted with a purpose. The Commander-in-Chief in Algeria, General C. de Cherritre, had about 55,000 soldiers at his disposal, though few were ready for action, since most of the best French counter-insurgency forces were either still in French Indo-China or on the high seas on their way home.

According to Jacques Chevallier who wrote *Nous les Algeriens* (1958), De Cherritre reckoned that he had fewer than 4,000 usable combat troops in the entire country when the revolt began. There was only one helicopter in Algeria at the time and eight Junkers bombers of World War II vintage. While there were 60,000 Algerian troops in the French Army, many of them were serving 'at home'. These were immediately branded collaborators and became a prime target of the insurgents throughout the war; their families sometimes suffering a worse fate than the men themselves.

However, reinforcements soon arrived. By the end of that year, the French Prime Minister, Mendès-France, had sent 2,000 more troops and twenty companies of riot police. It took little more than three weeks for an extensive counter-insurgency operation with artillery and air support to get underway.

Then, curiously, terrorist attacks on Europeans stopped as suddenly as they had begun.

Many suspects were rounded up, various Arab organisations were proscribed, offices were raided and documents confiscated. Large numbers of innocent people fell into the bag.

It is also surprising that the Algerian revolt raised little public interest in Europe, comparable, say, to Israel's Intifada of late 1987 and 1988, though memories of Hitler's War was still fresh in the minds of most and few wished to dwell on a new spate of violence that didn't directly affect their interests.

Alistair Horne observed: 'On the ground, the physical reaction or over-reaction was predictable. It was predictable, not specifically because of the *pied noir* mentality, but because this is the way an administration caught with its pants down habitually reacts under such circumstances; whether it were the British in Palestine, Cyprus or Northern Ireland, the Portuguese in Mozambique or the French in Indo-China.

'First comes the mass indiscriminate round-up of suspects, most of them innocent but converted into ardent militants by the fact of their imprisonment; then the setting of faces against liberal reforms designed to tackle the root of the trouble; followed finally, when too late, by a new progressive policy of liberalisation.'

In spite of the accumulation of forces, the war began slowly. At first, the rebels were astonished at the fury of the French response, although much of this stemmed from the indignation of the settlers over the fact that the Arabs should reject a colonial system that was so obviously of benefit to all.

Few French residents of Algeria were aware of the hardships suffered by the *fellah*, the indigenous population. That included widespread unemployment, and often less than rudimentary education and medical facilities for most Arabs. They were also insensitive to the almost irreconcilable political differences between the French and the Arabs.

To most French people in Algeria, it was fine to have Algerian Arabs working as menials on the farms or in the factories at wages none of them would consider on the mainland, or as domestic servants, but any notion of integration on any other basis was not to be considered.

Some settlers demanded the immediate execution of all captured members of the FLN. A local senator demanded that 'the evil be pursued where it be found and the ringleaders rooted out...' He insisted that security measures be increased and called on his metropolitan associates to create the political atmosphere to launch 'the proper solution' to the rebellion. Obviously, the response of Paris paid dividends. Between 2 November 1954 – the day after the revolt began – and early February the following year, not a single *pied noir* was killed by insurgents.

In stark contrast, terrorist attacks against the Algerian population continued unabated. It was the typical Third World pattern of coercion by violence to make it very clear to the Algerian people that to be associated in any way with French authority meant an unpleasant death. The population was being terrorised into supporting the revolution in much the same way as black dissidents in South Africa used the 'necklace' to bring the populace in line with revolutionary activities.

Public opinion in France, meanwhile, was almost totally behind the settlers. Even the socialist François Mitterrand, then Minister of the Interior, was a supporter of the status quo. 'Algeria', he said, in a catchword that was to be repeated endlessly, '*is* France'.

The guerrilla war that followed began hesitantly in 1955. Apart from sporadic acts of violence, most of the country was peaceful.

As John Talbot says in his book *The War without a Name – France in Algeria 1954–1962*: 'For at least a year after All Saints' Day, three of the district chiefs (of the six *Wilayas* or command structures) had almost no followers or weapons under their control. Violence was confined almost entirely to the three *Wilayas* of eastern Algeria, from the outskirts of Algiers to the Tunisian frontier. The western *Wilayas* from Algiers to Morocco were, for months, nearly as peaceful as Paris on a Sunday morning. For most of the war the Sahara saw more oil prospectors than guerrillas.'

'By the end of 1955, as a result of concerted undercover work and the deployment of mainland forces, coupled to a strengthening of security throughout the country, most of the original members of the FLN had either been killed or jailed.'

But by then the war had gathered some momentum. Repression was first replaced by some measure of reform, but it was generally agreed that it made little impression on either the settlers or the Algerians. Although the FLN had few successes, its mere existence was enough to force Paris to deploy huge numbers of men.

The French Air Force was expanded and prepared to start its programme of bombing and strafing selected targets. But that was to come later. And when it did, leaflets were usually dropped in advance to give the local people warning of the attack in time for them to seek shelter. The air force dropped thousands of warnings on *fellah* settlements in the interior.

With the arrival of the vaunted 25th Airborne Division, the first French Paras led by the legendary Colonel Ducournau who had recently returned from Indo-China, set up headquarters in Arris in the Nementcha mountains near the Tunisian border. Following the same principles that he had applied in Southeast Asia, Ducournau decided immediately to apply Mao's maxim of 'merging with the people like fish with the water' and pursuing the rebels in their own strongholds. But this was not an easy task: the Paras had some success, but many failures.

In retrospect, what disconcerted the FLN command was that after the first attacks, most *pieds noirs* resumed their way of life as if nothing had happened.

There was no mass exodus back to France and in France itself the war was relegated to the inside pages of the press.

Precautions had to be taken, of course. After the first acts of terrorism in Philippeville and Bone in the east and the increase in military aid from Tunisia and, indirectly, Egypt to the FLN, no one travelled anywhere without an escort. Six months after the All Saints' Day attacks, insurgent actions averaged about 200 a month. That included road ambushes, isolated attacks on farmers and their property, cutting down telephone poles, shooting members of the local militia on leave and occasional skirmishes with the army.

A year later these figures had increased significantly. According to official reports they rose to 900 in October 1955, to 1,000 in December and to more than 2,500 in March 1956. Much of this activity was due to the opening of what was termed The Second Front.

By the beginning of 1957, almost 30 months after the outbreak of hostilities, FLN guerrilla fighters were active in five of the six *Wilayas*, the forces in the west having linked up with their compatriots in the east on the high plateau between Saida and Tiaret. At that stage the French estimated that there were between 15,000 and 20,000 members of the FLN, although these figures included sympathisers and 'night-time guerrillas' who would carry on with their normal jobs during the day and fight in the dark hours.

The FLN command claimed double that number of loyalists; war always results in hyperbole. But even 4,000 guerrillas raised from a community of almost ten million could hardly be regarded as a nation in arms.

Chapter 23
The Algerian Connection

The first deployment of helicopters in combat. (Photo: Author)

Gun-running increased enormously. As the FLN hierarchy made headway in Algeria, so its influence spread beyond the borders. More money was contributed by friendly Arab states and more weapons made available for the fighters. At the same time the revolutionaries, even during the most favourable times, never had enough modern weapons for every man. Settlers and soldiers were being beaten or knifed to death right to the end of the struggle.

Gradually the war turned from 'hard' targets such as police barracks and patrols to 'soft' civilian objectives and the so-called 'Muslim friends of France'. These might include *caids* or village constables or even lower functionaries such as postmasters and tax collectors.

A fundamentalist influence also acted strongly on the rebel forces. Muslims were forbidden to smoke or drink. Penalties were severe; first offenders had their noses or ears cut off and for a second offence FLN cadres would inflict what the army called 'the Kabyle smile' – slitting of the throat.

The FLN also turned to economic sabotage, maiming and killing of cattle, the uprooting of vines and poisoning wine vats. Dogs were often found with their throats cut. In May that first year, four French civilians caught unarmed on their farms had their throats cut.

In August 1955, there were the massacres at Philippeville. A group of rebels convinced several hundred peasants that the hour of their deliverance was at hand. Armed with axes, knives, sickles and other implements, the mob set upon settlers and Algerians alike.

At the small pyrites extracting town of El Halia, Algerian miners slaughtered European overseers and their families. Some were hacked to death, others were disembowelled, still more had their throats cut while their arms were pinned behind their backs. It was a gruesome report that arrived on the desk of the French Governor General in Algiers. About 150 people were killed, about half of them settlers.

The French army and the Foreign Legion arrived on the scene while the massacre was still going on. In reprisal they killed over 1,000 Algerians, including women and children, and took many more prisoners, some of whom later died in custody, although this was strenuously denied by the authorities. The worst fears of the French settlers were being realised.

In Paris, meanwhile, arguments developed between the two factions: the one was opposed to greater violence, and the other all for using maximum force to put down the rebellion.

The French government maintained that France was facing a revolt of French citizens. They were rebelling against their own government. It was stated that in Algeria the army was not fighting a war but conducting what was called 'operations for the maintenance of order'.

There were a few parallels with what was then happening in Malaya. The British, like the French, never referred to 'communist terrorism' in Southeast Asia as a war, but rather as an 'emergency'. This fiction was adopted because to place the country on a war footing would have enormously increased Lloyds' insurance premiums and would have had many other undesirable results. The same motives operated in Algeria also. After all, it was argued, for Algerians to rebel against their own government was to put them *hors la loi*.

In April 1955, accordingly, the government, with parliamentary assent, declared a state of emergency in Algeria, which, although curtailing civil liberties, stopped short of actual war.

In France nearly 10,000 reservists were recalled to active service, and there were plans to delay the release of about 100,000 conscript troops, many of whom had already seen active service in Southeast Asia.

After the Philippeville massacres, 60,000 reservists were recalled, and a week later another 120,000 conscripts due for discharge were told that they would be kept under arms. And so it went on, until by 1960 half a million French troops had been concentrated in a country several times the size of France, which was then passing through the most difficult period of its post-war history.

What made the situation in Algeria different from August 1914, when most men of military age gladly rallied to the *tricolor*, was that

Chapter 23
The Algerian Connection

fighting in Algeria, in the minds of most, was certainly not defending *la patrie*. The enemy was not battering at the gates of Paris.

The extent to which the war had grown is shown by statistics issued at the time by the French Ministry of Defence. During 1955 the number of French troops in Algeria increased from about 80,000 to nearly 200,000. A year later, in the autumn of 1956, a third of the entire French armed forces were on active service in Algeria. This was no longer a limited, holding operation to suppress a few disaffected 'rebel groups running wild on the fringe of the Sahara'. The FLN had grown to its full strength.

Meanwhile, the conflict intensified. The government of the time, under Guy Mollet, acknowledged that by the end of 1956 France had committed more than 400,000 men to North Africa. As George Armstrong Kelly stated in *Lost Soldiers: The French Army and Empire in Crisis, 1947–1962* (Cambridge, Mass. 1965), there were 'perhaps as many as twenty soldiers for every FLN guerrilla in the bush'.

Less than ten per cent of this force did the fighting. The main task of the majority was to protect the persons and property of settlers and Algerians, to keep the main roads and rail links safe and open and to protect strategic installations from FLN sabotage. The task of the rest, perhaps between 30,000 and 40,000 men, was to hunt down the cadres of the FLN. The term 'search and destroy', long familiar to those who have followed the wars in El Salvador, Vietnam, Rhodesia, Namibia and Angola originated with the French in Indo-China. It became typical of the classic guerrilla struggle in Algeria and by early 1957, one out of every three Europeans in Algeria wore a French uniform.

The Battle of Algiers

The square mile of the Casbah in Algiers has often been the subject of films and books. It charmed tourists and filmgoers alike long before the war, and independence brought its quota of socialism and xenophobia. With its narrow, twisting streets, great walls and mysterious passageways, even now it is not unlike casbahs of Rabat, Casablanca and Meknes in Morocco or of Tunis.

The enigmatic Casbah has always been a place of intrigue and secret drama; the setting of the romantic but fictitious Pepe le Moko.

It was not surprising, therefore, that the FLN should choose the Casbah in Algiers, with its 100,000 Arab inhabitants, as the place to carry the war from the *bled* to the towns. It was regarded by the FLN as an autonomous zone with three branches: intelligence, military and financial. For most of 1956 conflict had been limited to the countryside; the urban or third phase of guerrilla war had begun.

Who fired the first shot in the Casbah remains a subject of regular debate. The FLN maintains that it was the French Paras, and it may well have been, though even Alistair Horne says that it is an over-convenient assumption.

The Algiers network was run for the FLN by Saadi Yacef, the son of a Casbah baker who was said to have worked for the French as a double agent. Yacef was competent and dedicated. Within a year he had about 1,500 operators reporting to his various commanders, many of them westernised Arab boys and girls who had grown up and been educated with the sons and daughters of French *pieds noirs* and who might have passed as French.

Many of the girls, such as Zohra Drif and Sarnia Lakhdari, both law students in their early twenties, were attractive and often dressed stylishly in Western garb. Drif was a stunner; she turned many heads, French and Arab. She was also passionately opposed to French rule. She called Hitler's invasion of France in 1940 God's revenge on the Frenchmen for what they had done to the Muslim people of North Africa.

This devotee of André Malraux, with his pre-war ideal of a terrorist as the archetypal 'solitary, heroic individual' had all the characteristics of a potential killer. She preferred to use bombs and was a member of an elite squad of about 50 revolutionaries created specifically for that purpose, nearly all of them young.

The FLN Algiers Autonomous Zone began making bombs early in 1956. The authorities were aware of it and did what they could to stop it, but with little success. They were fully occupied trying to trace groups of Yacef's assassination squads roaming the streets killing civilians. On 19 June 1956 after the execution of two inveterate terrorists, one of them a cripple, the order came from the FLN Central Command to 'take the war to the people'. Between 21 and 24 June, Yacef's squads shot 49 civilians in the streets of Algiers.

Then, on 10 August, an immense explosion ripped through the Casbah, killing about 70 Arabs. At first the authorities gave out that a bomb-making factory had blown up; later a *pied noir* counter-terrorist cell hinted at responsibility, but that also has never been thoroughly investigated. However, it had the effect of giving a new dimension to the war.

A month later Yacef brought before him the women Drif and Lakhdari and a more recent member of the group, Djamila Bouhired.

Chapter 23
The Algerian Connection

He gave them the task of placing three bombs that contained about two pounds of explosives each in the heart of French Algiers; one at a popular milk bar on the corner of Place Bugeaud; another at the cafeteria in the elegant Rue Michelet, much frequented by members of the smart set; and the third in the terminus of Air France near the centre of the town. Because of a faulty timer, the third bomb failed to go off.

The carnage inflicted by the other two bombs was appalling: there were three deaths and about 50 injured, including children. Most of the victims were young people who had nothing to do with the war or its ultimate course. Naturally, the settlers reacted violently.

The Algerian bombs were not complex Russian SPM limpet mines or other sophisticated devices such as those being used in Syria or Afghanistan today. The metal casings were often roughly welded pipes or machine parts put together in tiny factories in the Casbah. Yacef's bomb-maker was a chemistry student, Taleb Abderrahmane, operating in a secret laboratory, but the products, so simply fashioned, were effective enough.

Soon the Algerian conflict spread and intensified from August to December 1956. According to one French literary source 'bombings, shootings, stabbings, and destruction of property soared from about four incidents at the beginning of January 1956 to fifty in July, almost hundred in September and to roughly four each day in December'.

Yacef's agents were active everywhere: in cloakrooms, municipal offices, buses, cinemas, restaurants, sports pavilions; and that was apart from direct attacks on French government establishments.

The authorities in France became increasingly disconcerted by these events in their nearest colony. The press had become more vociferous, and some sections of society were shocked at the disclosure that some French nationals, though only a few at that stage, had gone over to the FLN. There were several intellectuals, mainly associated with Algiers University, including Professor André Mandouze, Professor of Literature, who gathered together a core of FLN sympathisers. There was also a prominent *pied noir* surgeon, Pierre Chaulet, who, with his wife, carried out numerous operations on wounded members of the FLN, often under very difficult conditions. Both were later discovered and had to flee to Tunisia. They returned only after Algerian independence to settle permanently in the country, although it is said that they soon fell foul of the new order.

Local settlers would have been even more disconcerted if they had known that one of the members of Saadi Yacef's bomb-laying teams was a French student at Algiers University, Danielle Mine. She was discovered much later, when it was too late to do anything about her.

In Algeria at that time it was clear to everyone that the country had become untenable. A new face and a new approach were needed to fight the worst urban terrorism that Europe had seen since the end of World War II. But revolutions were breaking out all over the world. Castro had just landed in Cuba from the ship whose name was later to decorate the masthead of the national newspaper, *Granma*.

Amid some of the worst atrocities in Algiers, General Raoul Salan arrived. He was a man who was to be associated with the tragedy of Algeria until the very end, and afterwards, from exile in Brazil. Salan was the most decorated French soldier. He had served in various campaigns and had been awarded the British CBE and the American DSO, as well as a long row of French medals. In 1954 it was the sombre visage of Salan that had presided over the defeat of the French in Indo-China.

The press in Algiers quickly christened him the Proconsul, although those who knew him better called him *le Mandarin*. He was probably the most competent French soldier yet to have entered the war, also ambitious, but he avoided official ceremonies. His job was to fight, and he made no secret of the fact that he preferred visiting units in the field to receptions.

Salan needed to know about the war he was fighting from the men doing the work. He had always worked that way; and even if his fellow officers were suspicious of his professed vagueness about political ideas and accused him of being a socialist, a freemason and an opium-smoker (all of which charges he rejected with disdain), he quickly stepped into the shoes of the departing Commander-in-Chief in Algeria, General Lorillot.

There was no question that it was a formidable job facing the man. Within sight and sound of his office, people were being killed. In retaliation the *pieds noirs* were sometimes more brutal than the FLN. They asked no quarter and gave none. Algiers had become an almost lawless battleground. The country was now encumbered with a military apparatus of almost half a million men, and although the FLN was being rooted out of some of its lairs by the army, they were still getting results. This was terrorism in its purest form.

Some of the terrorist attacks were mindless. After the 74-year-old Froger, President of the Federation of Mayors of Algeria had been assassinated; the FLN placed a bomb in the cemetery that would have caused further damage if his cortege had arrived in time. The

Chapter 23
The Algerian Connection

colons ran wild. Furious *pieds noirs* hauled innocent Arabs out of their cars or assaulted them in the streets. They left three dead and 50 injured.

Looking back on recent history, we can see that that was exactly the reaction that the FLN wished to provoke. They wanted mobs to go on the rampage; to loot, to kill and inflame passions to such a degree that Arab and French Algerians would never talk to one another again, far less administer the country together at some future time. They wished to make Algeria ungovernable, to force the French to concede that it was a lost cause. Of course they succeeded in the end, and that is why the Algerian revolt is always held up by radicals to prove what sheer brutality can achieve.

On 7 January 1957, Lacoste decided that a more rigorous approach was necessary. He summoned General Salan and the recently arrived commander of the elite 10th Para Division, General Jacques Massu. He told them that the 1,500 police in Algiers had proved themselves incapable of handling the situation and that after two years of limited hostilities, the situation had deteriorated almost to a level of anarchy. The strike force of the newly 5,000 airborne troops would step in and stop the riot.

The Paras had the job of restoring order in a hilly seaside conurbation, then roughly the size of an average European or American city. It appeared an impossible prospect.

To keep a stable and permanent presence in the Casbah was totally different from patrolling the streets of the rest of Algiers. But with so many stories of FLN atrocities against the French and so many of their fellow countrymen who had fallen victim to terror, the Paras went to work.

In North Africa indiscriminate assassination was followed by systematic torture and brutal and thorough techniques of interrogation. Neither was troubled by humanitarian scruples. They went to the very limits of means that security forces of a civilised country could use.

The Paras employed a subtle system of control from the beginning. The Casbah had been divided into sectors by the FLN. It was likewise segmented by the army in its own fashion. Each area, each block, each tenement building came under the command of an officer or an NCO, and it was he who made direct contact with the inhabitants.

Once the system was devised and every French soldier was aware of his duty, the senior occupant of a block of flats was ordered to report to army headquarters. Usually this person had achieved a position of authority because of political associations. Some were outspokenly pro-FLN; others were more discreet. Having been taken to HQ, this 'man of confidence' was told that from then on he would be held responsible for any activity that might take place in the building or block. If any acts of terrorism were linked to it he would die and one of his children, or his wife, would die first.

All the way up the line the system was put into effect. French undercover agents had a free hand in bringing in suspects. Proof of association with the FLN was not necessarily a *sine qua non*; anyone who was even vaguely suspected of anti-government activity in the past fell into the net. Many suspects died while being interrogated.

Clearly, the measures were draconian. Ultimately they caused so much revulsion that the European (especially the French) and American press and TV exposed the brutalities and injustices and helped to bring the war to an end. These iniquities were no less repressive and repulsive than those imposed by the occupying Germans 20 years earlier. Since memories die hard, the French establishment came under fire for sanctioning such atrocities. Yet it was no worse than what the FLN were doing, and it is to the discredit of the liberal press that they ignored the one and sensationalised the other.

But, as the Nazis had shown, violence is very often a most effective retaliation. While the Paras tended to contrast the disgusting business of fighting terror with terror in the towns, with what some of them called 'the purity of fighting in the *bled*', there was no doubt that the two tasks were incompatible. Some of the more horrible episodes were then and later written by men who had actually taken part in the military security programme.

It also resulted in more French civilians, both in France and Algeria, going over sympathetically to the FLN. There were even some soldiers, men of conscience, who deserted to the other side, although they were only a small minority, and if their bona fides were not entirely satisfactory, they were put to death, often in cruel fashion, usually after being accused of spying for Paris. To be shot outright in some Algerian backwater rather than tortured to death was more than could be hoped for.

The undoing of some of these idealists was what was called the 'flit test'.

A man was either wholly for the FLN or he was against. Everything was painted emphatically in black and white. There were no greys.

Therefore, if a man who had no obvious reason to do so wished to be associated with the movement, he was required to display his hatred for the system by killing somebody who belonged to the

Chapter 23
The Algerian Connection

governing machinery – usually policemen. Young idealists on the run from the French army were hardly likely to exchange one form of savagery for another, and most refused to do any more killing. They had seen enough. Consequently, they were regarded as infiltrators, and few were admitted to the ranks of the FLN.

The FLN, of course, was aware that the French often used bogus deserters to infiltrate their organisations. It had been a regular practice in Southeast Asia, but it did not meet with much success in Algeria.

Meanwhile, in Algiers the Paras were having some notable successes. They would act on the flimsiest evidence. A man found with money in his pocket would be accused of carrying or collecting funds for the FLN. Under some 'persuasion' he would eventually disclose to whom he paid the money. The next man would be tortured until he named names, and so on up the line. It was a simple but effective system, and it brought results. Torture was the army's answer to terrorism.

Also, the soldiers worked quickly. Any piece of information was acted upon immediately, sometimes even before a man's family knew he had been picked up. Surprise was vital to the success of the operation, and it achieved the kind of results that the police within the strictures of the laws of the Fourth Republic had never been capable of.

The army was also methodical. It was answerable to no one, and it devised its systems carefully; areas were cordoned off with barbed wire and regular searches were made. The fact that the Casbah was compact and difficult to control also worked against the FLN; it was a small tactical area that could be worked through, slowly and thoroughly. Gradually the insurgents lost their edge and it was only a question of time before they lost the battle for Algiers.

By such methods did the Paras gain the mastery of the Algiers Autonomous Zone. They recovered weapons, deprived the FLN of its funds, arrested leaders, stopped recruitment of more insurgents and nearly stopped the bombings, shootings and stabbings. By mid April, less than four months after General Massu had faced the Governor General in his office, he was able to remove every regiment but one from Algiers.

The war was not yet over. With the army out of the way, Saadi Yacef cranked the system up again and started a new wave of bombings and killings. But the new order was short-lived; the 10th Division was brought back to Algiers, and by mid September the two principal coordinators of the rebellion, Yacef and his lieutenant Ali la Pointe, were captured and killed. If means justified the ends, then France had certainly achieved a remarkable success. By October acts of terrorism amounted to only one a month.

Foreign reporters in the country noted at the time a curious anomaly. On the one hand the Paras were performing miracles in re-establishing the old order and were lauded as the 'Saviours of Algiers'. On the other, there was much friction, especially in rural areas, between the colons and the army. Soldiers who were doing most of the work guarding the livestock, buildings, possessions and family of the farmers against terrorism were regarded by the settlers as no better than a necessary nuisance. They manifestly despised those conscripts who chose to work with Arab communities in a bid to alleviate problems.

Additionally, there was little fraternisation except where it was necessary. Although there were exceptions, French civilians rarely went out of their way to make those responsible for their safety comfortable. They regarded the half-million metropolitan troops almost as an army of occupation.

The soldiers, for their part, regarded the colons as selfish ingrates. The troops were often accused of doing too little to stop the spread of revolt. Sometimes the soldiers intervened to stop French farmers killing suspected Arabs and, of course, that provoked yet more animosity.

An appalling massacre of two dozen young French conscripts at a village 80 km south-east of Algiers on 4 May 1956 brought the reality of the Algerian war home to Frenchmen. Until then the conflict had been relegated to the inside pages of most newspapers. After only two weeks in the country, a small patrol of young conscripts, most of them from Paris, were ambushed at point-blank range by one of the insurgent leaders known locally as Ali Khodja, a deserter from the army.

The youngsters were no match for the tough FLN regulars. Within minutes most of them were dead. A handful remained alive and while they were being beaten and bound, several of the bodies were barbarously mutilated. Some were disembowelled, others had their testicles cut off and stones stuffed into ventral cavities. Only one man survived the experience. He was later rescued by a Para strike force in a fight in which the only other French soldier taken alive by the band was killed.

The event was big news, not only in France but also in the rest of Europe and the United States. In France, at last, Algeria had become headlines. This was the worst single loss of the war so far: nearly all the boys who died were hardly out of their teens. The army, for once candid in its communiqué, admitted that they had been brutally massacred.

About the same time the first reports of torture by the French army in Algeria began to creep into news reports, usually as a result of some young conscript baring his soul while on home leave. No one would speak publicly about such atrocities, and reports were usually discreetly phrased for fear of prosecution. But as the hints and whispers became more widespread, the public began to take notice. It horrified some and delighted others, who believed that the excesses of the FLN should be returned tenfold.

In clandestinely published tracts, reservists told what they had seen in Algeria of the use by the army of the sun, water, beatings, deprivation of food and water and even more horrifying examples such as electric wires attached to genitals, soda bottles forced into the vagina and anus of victims, finger and toenails pulled out with pliers and the local version of the rack, bodies contorted by ropes and weights and bones snapping under pressure. In many cases torture and resultant death were regarded as little more than cold-blooded acts of reprisal. And, if nothing more, the French army did prove itself extremely efficient at extracting information under severe duress.

The government reacted, of course. Newspapers of liberal tendency were scrutinised. Any mention of torture was forbidden. London's *Economist* of 27 July 1957 reported that in some cases 'squeezing the press' meant that 'for some editors police visits were as routine as visits from the postman'.

About that time there also began the first discreet, even furtive, attempts to negotiate an end to the conflict directly with the FLN. By March 1956, Guy Mollet had already sent his first 'peace mission' to Cairo, led by the Foreign Minister, Christian Pineau, who made a direct approach to President Nasser to put out what was termed at the time 'feelers for conversations' with the rebel movement.

A series of altogether five such meetings took place in 1956 in Cairo, Rome, Belgrade and even the FLN headquarters in Tunis. Naturally, all were hidden under a cloak of secrecy, for it would never have been acceptable to the French public to discover at that early stage that while their boys were dying for 'a just cause' in Algeria, their government was actually breaking bread with terrorists.

Alistair Horne in his book *A Savage War of Peace* maintains that Ben Bella considered, even so early, that 'peace was within reach'.

Mollet, in an interview with Horne later, thought otherwise. He said: 'Even if Ben Bella had not been sequestrated, I doubt whether things would have turned out very differently, because the FLN never accepted our basic theses that there should be, first of all, a ceasefire.' As Horne concludes: 'No one will ever know.'

The war dragged on. Despite losses, the French position in Algeria was far stronger than it had been a short while previously in Southeast Asia. Moreover, Algeria was not a distant colony but, in theory, an integral part of Metropolitan France.

Algeria had no jungles or forests where the rebels could hide and the French Air Force could easily spot rebel concentrations. Most importantly, most Frenchmen at the beginning of hostilities were all for the war, it was only later, as more and more attention by the mass-communications media was focused on the conflict, that the public was gradually worn down by an incipient form of war weariness that also characterised the American embroilment in Vietnam.

Algeria had become the first of the 'media' wars and France paid a heavy price as a result.

For the French there were some serious problems in the offing. It was not that the members of the FLN were a monolithic party like the communists in Vietnam – there was much internal strife between the various rebel cadres – but they did have the advantage of safe borders to cross when the going became tough and sanctuary in the neighbouring countries of Tunisia, Libya, Egypt and Morocco. Walter Laqueur, in his book *Guerrilla*, actually considered that the FLN would have been defeated but for external support.

The single biggest problem facing Paris was that the French dared not attack the rebels in their cross-border sanctuaries in neighbouring states.

As Laqueur says: 'However much the generals might rave, they were powerless to pursue the enemy. Even a minor air attack against an FLN base on the Tunisian side of the border (Sakiet Sidi Yusuf) provoked a major international scandal; a massive attack was altogether unthinkable, since the French government felt it could not commit such an affront to world opinion.'

Since then, the United States (in Vietnam), the Israelis (throughout the Middle East and the Maghreb), and South Africa (in Angola, Mozambique, Zambia and Zimbabwe) have emphasised the right of any nation under attack from beyond its own borders to retaliate.

Although the 'right of hot pursuit', as it is usually called, is not codified in any statute book, its frequent and effective application over the past half century has practically established its validity in most seats of power – in the West, at least.

More serious, in the Algerian war effort was the inherent weakness of the French government to get to grips with some of its problems. The country was passing through its most difficult period since the end of World War II; there was no real leadership until De Gaulle arrived on the scene and no stable day-to-day government; with the result that the succession of crises in Paris inevitably affected the situation in Algeria.

Keeping several hundred thousand French soldiers on active duty in North Africa was also costing France a billion dollars a year; money it did not have. No wonder, therefore, that the conflict gradually lost support at home. When De Gaulle made his first conciliatory remark that possibly force was not the answer to the Algerian problem, the cumulative sigh of relief throughout France was almost audible.

Yet, at the end, the war was closely run. While the French army had at first underestimated the extent of the rebellion, they very quickly brought in the men and systematic measures to deal with the menace and the FLN rebels lost the initiative. The rebels were further hampered by the fairly secure Morice Line along the Tunisian border, which made infiltration from outside difficult; and by the *regroupement* of villages and which, in effect, 'denied water to the guerrilla "fish"'.

Walter Laqueur says that by 1961 the number of *fellaghas* inside Algeria was down to about 5,000 men, scattered in small groups.

The situation was not much better for the French, although they always put on a brave front, especially when the press was about. According to Laqueur: 'If FLN morale was low, among the French it was at breaking point.'

They could not keep huge garrisons indefinitely in all the main towns and huge mobile reserves besides. There were 20,000 insurgents concentrated in Tunis, beyond the reach of the French, and the European population of Algeria was up in arms against the *defaitistes* in Paris.

By now the military commanders in Algeria were paying less and less attention to orders from Paris. In short, when General De Gaulle took over, France was on the verge of civil war and the danger did not pass for several years.

The FLN succeeded in obtaining diplomatic recognition from about 20 countries, including Russia and China. They had set up a government in exile, with the result that when the time came to meet the French face to face at Evian, they could do so with the confidence and the effective backing of their own masses.

The end came seven years after the beginning of the struggle, and half a million Frenchmen in uniform were sent home. Tens of thousands of people had been killed. More than a million people were uprooted, and Algeria became a dictatorship where the rule of law was at least as severe as it had been at the height of the war. Socialism was adopted and now, well into the New Millennium, it is interesting to look at the results of nationhood in Algeria compared with what might have been if the country had accepted the French offer to make Algeria a real, not merely theoretical, part of France.

If the rebels had accepted, Algeria would now certainly be in the European Common Market; and what a different situation that would have created for 1992.

There are still 6,000 Frenchmen living in Algeria and more than two million Algerians in France. One might well ask: what was it really all about?

BIBLIOGRAPHY

Abbas, Ferhat, *Guerre et Revolution d'Algerie*, Paris, 1962.
Behr, Edward, *The Algerian Problem*, London, 1961.
Bell, J. Bowyer, *The Myth of the Guerrilla*, New York, 1971.
Crozier, Brian, *The Rebels*, London, 1960.
Crozier, Brian, *The Morning After*, London, 1963.
Henissart, Paul, *Wolves in the City: The Death of French Algeria*, New York, 1971.
Horne, Alistair, *A Savage War of Peace, Algeria, 1954–1962*, Macmillan, London, 1977.
Massu, Jacques, *La Vrai Bataille d'Alger*, Paris, 1971.
O'Ballance, Edgar, *The Algerian Insurrection, 1954–1962*, London, 1967.
Ortiz, Joseph, *Mes Combats*, 1964.
Talbott, John, *The War Without a Name: France in Algeria 1954–1962*, Faber and Faber, London; 1981.
Werth, Alexander, *The Strange History of Pierre Mendes – France and the Great Conflict over French North Africa*, London, 1957.

CHAPTER TWENTY FOUR

THE GREAT ZAMBEZI RIVER

Africa has innumerable attributes, but not one is as compelling as the Zambezi riverine system. Though it passes through regions that lack the kind of almost impenetrable triple-tiered jungle found along the Congo or the Amazon rivers, this 2,400 km stretch of water can be as wild, primitive and as dangerous a backwater as either.

I've been on lion hunts in Matetsi in the old Rhodesia, warthog hunts with my .45 ACP pistol in Namibia (and believe I still have the record on that one) as well as two buffalo hunts with Harry Selby at Xugana in Botswana's Okavango Delta – though strictly as an observer. For all that, the trip down the lower Zambezi a few years ago was one of the best safaris I've done.

Even though I've visited grander and better-known African attractions like Serengeti, Maasai Mara, Chobe, the enormous Selous Game Reserve and others, the attraction of this great river is always elemental. M'Tondo, where it all happened for us, lies in a remote, isolated corner of south-central Africa where roads exist, but just!

As the crow flies, it is about 40 minutes by air from Lusaka, the Zambian capital, but it took us more than five hours by road. Once off the main drag, only an SUV will cover the distance all the way to the lodge, across a muscle-driven vehicle ferry and more game guards than we'd anticipated.

We got to M'Tondo late afternoon and what a revelation it was. There were no phones, no TV, no radios and certainly no computer link-up. We were greeted by raw African bush ... and an awful lot of that though accommodation at the lodge was sumptuous, even if we had to take our own grub.

The lodge – an old Colonial farmhouse built between the wars – sits fairly high up, is framed by a small cluster of baobabs and overlooks the river as well Zimbabwe's Mana Pools reserve across the way. We arrived with the river in full spate and I reckon that the Zambezi, at that point, must have been about a mile across. There were two low islands in the middle of the river well within our view – long strips of land studded with reeds and rushes – that seemed to attract a variety of wildlife. There were more hippos and crocs than you'd like to think about while elephants swimming against the current from the far bank were a regular feature, usually after lunch ...

On the opposite bank and with our binoculars, we could follow the antics of a lot of game including huge herds of buffalo, more impala than you could count and an astonishing variety of other animals, including lion. After dark, you couldn't miss their growls – a low series of 'greeuw ... greeuw ... greeuw' calls – punctuated by an occasional roar.

There were no humans on that side of the river, except for the occasional group of open-boat enthusiasts who would make their way downstream, sometimes under armed guard, because of hippo. Occasionally they'd land on one of the islands and make camp for the night, or having decided that the position was too exposed, perhaps chose another location at the water's edge a bit downstream. My view was that camping out on open sand – with nothing between a bunch of flimsy tents and water – was taking a bit of a chance.

Though the national park on the Zambian side lies another hour of tough driving along a rutted track, there was wildlife everywhere around M'Tondo. We were greeted by a herd of elephant long before we reached our destination and still more at the airstrip a few hundred metres from where we slept.

These beautiful creatures were constantly around the lodge, sometimes keeping us awake at night as they shredded bushes and trees around the main structure while feeding. Lots of little ones too, some quite tiny and one or two so small and unsteady that they could only have been weeks old.

When the herd crossed to the islands to feed, baby elephants would grab the tails of their mothers and hang on. It was both quaint and lovely to behold.

The same with the hippo in that location. We had three or four pods of these noisy hulks which we could view from the porch – at least 80 or 100 of the beasts all told. They really came to life after dark, displaying a gusto that disturbed with their snorting, blowing and farting that sometimes went on till dawn. We were kept awake with the noise and it sometimes became bothersome because they would emerge from the river to feed within a stone's throw of the lodge.

Chapter 24
The Great Zambezi River

Some visitors tended to regard these night-time romps as enchanting, but they were actually bloody noisy. It was also the case when these cumbersome animals would shoot great dollops of crap five or six metres into the air, which they did each time they came ashore. The result was that all the foliage along the riverbank was covered in hippo shit, in places a foot thick. They did so during daylight hours on the islands in front of M'Tondo as well, always a spectacle...

There was also hyena around, not many, but enough to be bothersome. We'd only hear their absurd cackles after dark, often fairly close to where we were seated around the braai. Then we'd joke about the possibility of an attack, but it had never happened, though, clearly, the event could be quite traumatic to someone who had never experienced it before. Somebody spoke of it as the discordant call of the bush.

There was no missing the occasional 'cough' out there in the dark somewhere. It was a distinctive and chilling sound and signified leopard. That was a concern, especially when these big cats might have been just out of sight along the same bank of the river where we were perched.

Then, the following morning as we trudged the bush, you couldn't miss their tracks. On our last evening at M'Tondo we heard a kill, probably a baboon being taken by one of the big cats. The poor creature gave out a mighty shriek and then all of Africa fell silent. The event didn't deter the hippos from resuming their cacophony soon afterwards...

Crocs were a problem along the length of the river. I watched some native fishermen in their dugouts on several afternoons and to my mind it was a precarious way of making ends meet. While some of the men in their tiny boats fished with their nets, one member of these four- or five-man groups would furiously beat the water with his paddle to keep 'flat dogs' away.

Not long before I visited M'Tondo, wildlife writer Steve Edwards wrote about Katy Reeves, a young American boater who was completing a canoe journey downstream towards the Mozambique border with her father and sister and who was snatched from her boat by a very large crocodile. The event that took place in August 2003 was cathartic and people along the river still speak of it with awe[1].

Steve Edwards tells us that Stretch Ferreira and Doug Carlisle, two of the more experienced old pros of the bush who were guiding Jack Reeves and his two daughters on a canoeing safari, saw it all.

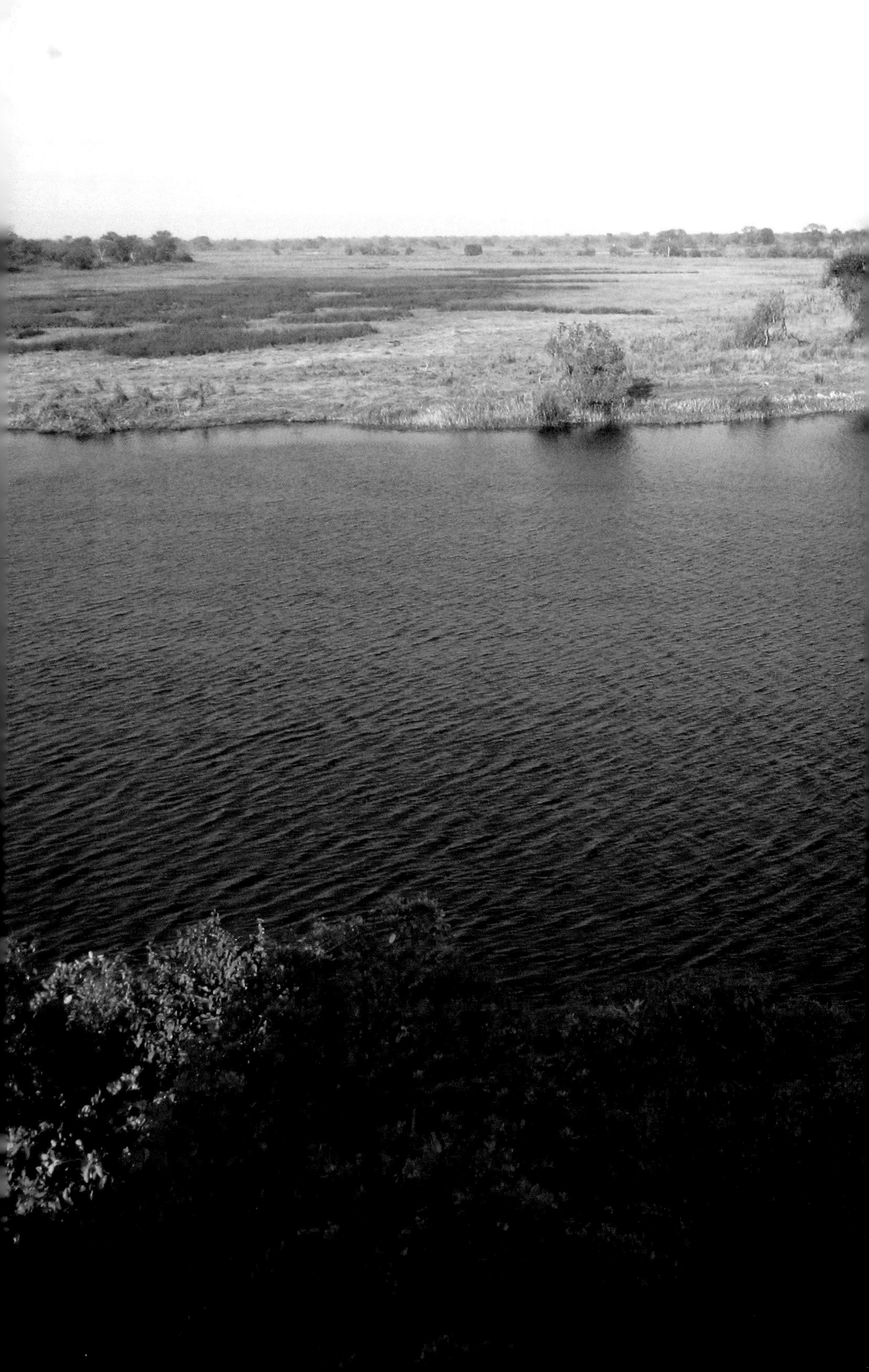

The upper reaches of the great Zambezi River emerge from a remote region adjoining the Congo. Part of the river flows through southern Angola and is joined later by its major tributary, the Kafue, home to one of the finest game parks on the African continent. (Photo: Caroline Castell)

Describing the incident, Stretch recalled afterwards that they were drifting downstream 'when I saw this large crocodile near the bank. To give the crocodile access to deep water, both canoes headed for shore and the creature submerged.

'The canoe carrying Stretch and Jack Reeves was slightly ahead of the second canoe, with Doug Carlisle and Katy and Carrie Reeves on board. Then, quite suddenly and without warning, the croc lunged from the water and attacked Doug's canoe, which immediately listed over.

'As the boat started to right itself, the crocodile – whose head had remained out of the water throughout – snatched Katy from her seat on the canoe and almost capsized it. Moments later it reappeared again on the surface with Katy in its jaws, and then started to swim into deeper water. At this point it released the American, who managed to struggle to the surface twice.

'By now Stretch had swung his canoe around and was frantically paddling towards Katy. As he drew close, the girl's father reached out in an attempt to grab hold of his daughter, but the crocodile attacked again and pulled her under. In desperation Stretch fired his handgun into the water: he'd hoped that the concussion might force the predator to release the girl.'

Stretch Ferreira remained in the vicinity for some minutes, but there was no further sign either of Katy or of the croc.

Edwards recalls that the search continued until noon the following day, when one of the other men located and shot two large crocs in the area. Brought ashore and cut open, their stomach contents revealed body parts of Katy Reeves. Stretch, who had spent many years conducting canoe safaris, said that the attack was 'unprecedented.'

Contrary to the official Zambian tourist line, there have been numerous attacks on boats over the years and Steve Edwards lists a bunch in his article. Like the one in November 2004, when a South African kayaker's boat was attacked by a croc, probably a territorial male. This time it was the boat that was bitten and not the man. He managed to reach shore and abandoned his trip.

Then in the summer of 2012 reports started coming through of a rogue croc that had been killing villagers fishing on the river just beyond Mpata Gorge and perhaps an hour downstream by boat from M'Tondo. The area lies adjacent to the confluence of the Zambezi and Luangwa rivers and by the time I was told of it, the croc had killed 14 villagers.

Apparently the animal had learned that it was fairly easily to tip over the villagers' shallow-bottomed pirogues with its tail and once the fishermen were in the water, it would grab a victim and make off. The situation became so serious that the fishing village was finally abandoned and its inhabitants moved to another area downstream. These days, most reports from companies that offer tourist services along the Zambezi are likely to warn their guests about overactive hippos threatening to attack boats, but they will rarely mention crocs.

The presence of hippo in most of Africa's great rivers has been accepted as a given for centuries. Indeed, there is hardly a river safari that does not experience a couple of charges along the way, and when that does happen, it is because there are juveniles about.

The truth is that when a hippo attack is driven home, the results can be disastrous, which underscores the reality that on the African continent, hippos kill far more humans than crocs.

Indeed, while diving in Lake Tanganyika with Peter Sachs in the 1990s – we spent some weeks making a documentary for the SABC on Burundi and dived fairly regularly south of Bujumbura – our constant fear was that a rogue hippo might approach our group while we were in the water. As we were to see for ourselves, these animals were regarded as a threat to all lone boats on the lake.

Our only source of comfort was the fact that we were diving with scuba gear at depth, though obviously, if any hippos did arrive on the scene, a stage would be reached when we would have to surface...

For all that, there were no guns in our three-man party that spent a week at M'Tondo early in the new millennium. The group included my granddaughter, Rachel, who I fear, seems to have inherited some of her grandpa's recklessness.

The lodge, I discovered, was rustic and charming and, for Africa, quite unique because there were no African settlement anywhere near the place. That meant that poaching was at a minimum.

When it was taken over by my old pal, former professional hunter and historian Hannes Wessels, he let the adjacent chalets fall into disrepair. What was left of the original structures was still in place when we visited M'Tondo, with walls and plumbing still intact and just waiting for new thatched roofs to be laid. I made a point at the time that he would first need to get rid of the mambas and cobras that had moved in; there were snakes aplenty at M'Tondo, but that is the way things are along almost the entire length of the river.

The kind of peace and tranquillity encountered today, according to Hannes, belies its earlier history where brigands, poachers, adventurers and soldiers played a role against a backdrop of colonialism, political intrigue and power plays. At the turn of the last century, the legendary figure of Major Hannes Pretorius (aka 'Jungleman') roamed this wild territory in search of ivory, and referred to as Zambezia by some of the earlier visitors.

It was there in abundance in a region that had only been settled by Europeans a few years before.

In the Pretorius autobiography[2], this veteran African traveller remarked that 'life is held cheaply in Zambezia.' He added that 'feuds, punishments, barbaric rites, tribal wars, cannibalism, slave raids – all take constant toll of the population.' Interestingly, that comment was made a century after slavery had been abolished by the British and the colony named Northern Rhodesia, as it was called then, fell under British control.

Pretorius was not the only European in the area. A Portuguese desperado was ensconced on nearby Kanyemba Island, which he had converted into a minor fortress. On the run from both the Portuguese and Rhodesian police, he had killed several Portuguese Askaris who had been sent to arrest him and return him shackled to Lourenço Marques for his arraignment. He succeeded in ingratiating himself with the local chief, took several black wives and lived out his life on the river. The number of light-skinned locals still in evidence today remains a testament to his virility.

Photo: Johan Corbane.

Chapter 24
The Great Zambezi River

By all accounts, wrongly accused of complicity in the murder of Paramount Chief Chiawa, Hannes Pretorius was implicated and sentenced to death by burning. He left the area in haste and headed north into German East Africa or, more commonly at the time, Tanganyika, something which took place shortly before the Great War.

Between the two great wars, following in the tradition of Cecil John Rhodes's 'Grand Design' to connect Africa under the auspices of British authority by rail 'from the Cape to Cairo', much of the area along the Zambezi River, and further north, was administered by British Colonial authorities and a relative peace settled on the area.

A licence system was introduced which allowed hunting to continue, but it was controlled, as with other areas, by a government agent who called himself a commissioner. The area was rich in game and, as one visitor to the area expressed it, 'black rhino were as common as goats.'

Man-eaters were common and the Northern Rhodesia Game Department was frequently called in to deal with these predators, especially when they made serious inroads into indigenous livestock. One of these commissioners was H.M. Taberer, whose family later came to play a major part in the development of the tobacco industry in both Northern and Southern Rhodesia.

Following the end of World War II and the emergence of several prominent African politicians like Kwame Nkrumah in the Gold Coast (soon to become Ghana) and Dr Hastings Banda in Nyasaland (subsequently Malawi), pressure began to mount on the European colonial powers to abandon their African possessions. In the late 1950s, Britain started to limit its colonial control, and a decade later, Northern Rhodesia became Zambia and its first President was an illustrious schoolteacher who had started to dabble in politics. His name was Kenneth Kaunda.

For wildlife on the Zambezi River, this was not good. On Kaunda's watch – as a ruler, the man quickly showed his hand as a demagogue and as with Zimbabwe a generation later – European interests came under fire. Hunting and national parks were targeted because the facilities they offered were more popular with whites than Africans. Consequently, game controls collapsed, corruption was endemic throughout the country and poaching almost became the norm.

Therefore, with the onset of the Rhodesian War, the Zambezi Valley became a battleground as well as transit zone for 'liberation fighters' who crossed the great river to launch their guerrilla struggle.

At a mile across, and forming the largest sheet of falling water in the world, the magnificent Victoria Falls is one of the natural wonders of the world. Called Mosi-oa-Tunya – 'the Smoke that Thunders' – by the locals, it is best experienced in full flood during Southern Hemisphere winter months. (Photo: Caroline Castell)

Chapter 24
The Great Zambezi River

During the course of the war many of the rebel fighters, fresh from training camps in Tanzania, Egypt, Libya, the Soviet Union, Cuba and elsewhere, were sometimes forced to swim the river at night. Obviously, crocodiles took a toll.

Rhodesian Special Forces responded with cross-border raids that included lacing roads, tracks and paths with mines (both anti-tank and anti-personnel, many of them captured and of East European manufacture).

When the war finally ended in 1980 there had been an enormous amount of damage done.

For one, a substantial body of rhino had been wiped out and the elephant population severely depleted. Rhino horns and ivory were dispatched to the coast by poachers for transhipment to Asia, the Middle East and India, some for dagger handles and horns ground down to powder and used as aphrodisiacs for randy Chinese. It was a dreadful example of greed and a total lack of compassion.

It was about then that Farley Winson, a British national, arrived in Zambia. One of his missions was to gain the confidence of President Kaunda, or KK, as he was referred to in the media and who was said to be 'open to ideas'. With the Zambian economy hitting new lows following the collapse of the copper price, KK was looking for a quick fix.

Farley Winson explained to the Zambian president that if he were to acquire titles to significant stretches of land in the Zambezi Valley, he would be able to develop a process which would enable him to transform grass into diesel fuel. In an astonishing display of naiveté, the President believed the trickster and as a consequence, 'Zambezia' became a reality.

Clearly, KK was delighted at the prospect of Zambia becoming self-sufficient in fuel. Even more so when he visited the estate and his car was fuelled with diesel that had allegedly been extracted from grass. It was all fraud of course, but for a while the ruse worked and Winson made a packet. When the authorities finally tumbled to the scam, the expatriate Brit fled the country.

Once more, the future of the Zambezi Valley was put on the back burner, at least until KK started to campaign for the next elections: the president feared that the Winson saga would become a political weapon that might be used against him and his instructions were clear: remove all traces of the grass-to-fuel imbroglio.

It was then that another larger-than-life figure came to the rescue. This was Lew Games, head of one of Africa's largest hunting safari concerns and he saw opportunities in the great natural valley that had once been home to millions of animals. In fact, Games had just recently emerged from a bitter encounter with the Tanzanian authorities who had accused him of running a hunting company along the Mozambique border as a front for South African Intelligence.

But Lew Games was no Winson. He had spent most of his life hunting and in later years turned his attention to conservation. With the help of a colleague, he acquired a property along the river and set about saving what was left of the animals that had not been poached. In effect, he created an extremely efficient environment for the re-generation of wildlife.

The task was daunting. Almost all wildlife along the stretch of river where he had made his home had been wiped out. In his estimate there were perhaps 15 impala left of what had been hundreds of thousands only a few decades before. The rest of the game was transitory and seasonal, moving in and out of the Luangwa region, but because the herds had been hunted so hard in the past, most animals fled at the first hint of a human presence.

Thanks to Games, together with the support of the local chieftainess and her people, large tracts of Zambezi has recovered, if not all its former primeval bounty, a substantial part of it. It helped, too, that new and effective game laws were instituted and staff hired to counter poaching. We were to see some of these people manning the gates on our way into M'Tondo.

With protection re-established, game has returned in abundance and the elephant population has flourished, to the point where culling has been considered to limit numbers.

Lew Games died in 2002, but his spirit remains strong. So do many of the animals along the Zambezi that he did so much to save.

Of the four great rivers of Africa that include the Nile, the Congo and the 4,200 kilometre Niger, the Zambezi appears to have attracted many of the earliest adventurers who were prepared to put pen to paper. This quite substantial group included an intrepid a bunch of African, European as well as Arab explorers, the latter usually more involved in slave trafficking than in recording new discoveries.

Most of those who tried to plot the Zambezi's meandering 2,700 kilometre course that takes it and its tributaries through six countries and today includes two of Africa's great lakes – Kariba and Cahora Bassa in Mozambique – invariably started their journeys at the coast, sometimes as far north as Bagamoyo, a good two day's march from Dar es Salaam in what was then Tanganyika.

Over centuries, fever, hostile natives and animals took a terrible

Chapter 24
The Great Zambezi River

toll. As we have seen, there are crocodile and hippo along the length of the river, almost all the way north to the insignificant little spring that bubbles up between the roots of a small copse of trees in Zambia's Mwinilunga District, where that country conjoins with Angola and the Congo.

Along its course, there is always something of interest taking place, from the annual flooding of the Barotse Plains over the rockier Ngonye watershed, all the way down to the mile-wide Victoria Falls not far from where the river touches first Botswana and then Zimbabwe. Along the way it is joined by several other rivers, the Kavango out of Angola, Chobe, Kafue River and finally, the still-untamed Luangwa.

Because the river fringes on so many countries, cross-border traffic has created a series of traditions of its own. In southern Africa, there are those who regard the Zambezi as little more than a conduit for smuggling goods. It is certainly that way at Kazungula, about 90 minutes by car upstream from Victoria Falls at the confluence of the Chobe and Zambezi rivers.

At Kazangula, upstream from the Zambian town of Livingstone, the ferries come across from Botswana at regular intervals. Though a relatively short journey across the Zambezi, it all adds charm to travelling in these parts. (Photo: Caroline Castell)

Because Kazungula has what some regard as the busiest ferry traffic on the African continent, there are those who do nothing else but circumvent the law. Many of these profiteers are caught, but few are ever brought to trial: almost to a man (and woman) they work what is referred to as 'the system'.

In a sense, what goes on at Kazungula is a microcosm of the economy of many African states. Botswana, Zambia and Zimbabwe all have their own border facilities along the river and each one of them systematically follows protocol, guarding their borders and, after dark, padlocking their figurative gates each night.

This symbolic locking-up process is of little consequence to great numbers of operators who use the fragile security system to their own advantage. Fishermen and smugglers use their dugouts with abandon, moving from country to country, visiting friends, suppliers and customers.

The river god – it is known as Nyami-Nyami – keeps an eye on things, they will tell you if you quiz them about their lifestyle. They will confide that it is known to slumber a lot, only waking furiously when irritated and one or more people are lost in the river, sometimes to crocs, other times when boats capsize and the incumbents are drowned.

Size does not matter to Nyami-Nyami, they say, pointing to the fact that dugouts as well as large steel ferries have sunk or 'been made' to capsize. Other river craft sometimes simply disappear at his whim, they reckon.

With such a temperament, one might have suspected Nyami-Nyami to be female. But no, every local will tell you quite adamantly, he is a man-god because he has a sense of humour.

They will recall that one evening there were three ferries all nicely moored alongside for the night, real mariner style. The next morning one of the craft had disappeared. There was no explanation, the local harbour master was told, it was just not there. Obviously, the ferry master was puzzled and he sent some of his crew to ask around. They all came back and said that nobody had seen or heard anything.

Of course, many meetings followed, the police were summoned and calls made across the river to the other border posts. Still nothing...

Somebody observed that the Zambian police believed that Nyami-Nyami might have been involved in the disappearance, but he omitted this from his official report to headquarters in Lusaka because, as everybody was aware, Zambia is a Christian country and witchcraft has been banished.

Finally, a report was submitted to the office of 'Opee', Zambian jargon for the Office of the President, and it then emerged that the chief of customs thought that Nyami-Nyami must have had something to do with the missing ferry.

The Kazungula chief of customs did write a report in his official capacity, but then he followed that with another, addressed to the ever-vigilant Zambian secret service.

And to this day, nobody knows what happened to the missing ferry.

Crossing the border at Kazungula is always an experience. It is also a delightful trip travelling north towards Zambia because the roads are excellent and Botswana long ago learned, to its own advantage, to cater for the visitor.

The ferries run constantly from both banks and for those who haven't had this African experience, it is a delight. Your fellow travellers are likely to be a mixed bunch, with a sprinkling of smugglers among them, but then they know the ropes. That becomes clear when you arrive on the Zambian side of the river and they move to one side while you step up to border controls a little further ahead.

By now you would have been approached by a dozen or more operators, each one of them totally familiar with the kind of rigmarole that awaits the unsuspecting tourist. They will even exchange your money for you. The appropriate answer here is not even to think about it.

For 'a small fee' they reckon they are able to put you through both customs and immigration, but be cautious. While these 'operators' are able to ease your passage through what is always a tiresome and sometimes formidable bureaucratic morass, the process can be inordinately expensive. Essentially, they are after your money, which is fair enough, but quite a few of these cons are in cahoots with the authorities. At the instigation of your so-called 'facilitator', you might be stopped at a whim and unspecified 'fees' demanded.

Most of those caught usually pay the money and move on, especially when you are told by an official that if you do not 'comply', you will be sent back to the other side of the river. The other alternative is to wait at the frontier until morning when the 'boss' is scheduled to arrive. Meantime, you hear afterwards, he's been there all the time, in his office around the back.

Such are some of the wiles in a developing Africa where the

unsuspecting are always being separated from their cash. It is the way things are done in much of the continent.

Somebody who does the trip quite often warned that it is best to go through on your own. 'It might be slow,' he told us, but you get through in the end if you resist unreasonable demands ... they end up getting tired of you and eventually you're told to go,' he explained.

'Just have all your documents in order and that includes carnet and insurance for your vehicle.'

1 Steve Edwards: 'Crocodile Attacks', *African Hunter* Vol. 13 No. 1.
2 *Jungle Man: The Autobiography of Major P.J. Pretorius* (Resnick's Library of African Adventure), London, 2000.

Photo: Darrell Watt

CHAPTER TWENTY FIVE

A WITCHDOCTOR IN THE HOUSE

> More than half a century of traipsing around Africa has led to several notable experiences with voodoo, black magic or, as some people in West Africa like to call their beliefs, Ju Ju. These tenets go way back in traditional African culture and I learned long ago to take such things seriously, if only because those who practise these cultic traditions certainly do…

Several experiences stand out vividly over the years, first in Nigeria where I lived for almost a year in the 1960s, and 20 years later in Liberia where my film crew and I spent a month making a documentary film.

In Nigeria, I would sometimes head off into the bush on Saturdays with my expatriate buddies to escape the noise, frustrations and in-your-face thrust of Africa's most bustling conurbation. Most times we would leave Lagos and head out west to Badagry, a sleepy little fishing village not far from the Dahomey frontier. Today Dahomey is called Benin, while Badagry has had a major West Africa highway thrust through its heart.

In those distant days, there were probably more Ju Ju or voodoo shrines in Badagry than any other place I visited, and, being on the road for much of the time I was in Nigeria, I saw an awful lot of towns and villages. Badagry was different though: you couldn't walk 50 paces without spotting one of these primitive structures, usually on the street adjacent to the homes of those who built it. Most would resemble a modern-day concrete or mud-and-stone braai or barbie, perhaps a metre tall, with everything centred on a small raised edifice in the middle, often covered by a modest tin roof because it rains a lot in Nigeria.

The idea was that the 'devout' would place their offerings or sacrifices on this central platform, make their wishes or lay their curses and hope for the best. Most times, because chunks of meat or fish – or even dead birds or cats – would be among items that landed on a pile, the result was not only unedifying, it was revolting. And it stank.

I never saw anybody clean one of these shrines, with the result that one pile of putrefying debris followed another and so it went on, as long as anybody could remember.

What was peculiarly interesting about this kind of Ju Ju, is that one weekend I decided to take a couple of spools of film of Badagry for a feature I'd promised a London news agency. I went through three or four rolls of film and included quite a few shots of different shrines that dotted the landscape. On being processed, the film came out fine, except that every single frame that should have displayed a shrine came out blank. It didn't help that that same Saturday night the drums and a noisy service of sorts could be heard until the early hours from the only church in town, complete with shuttered windows and locked doors.

I never visited Badagry again, which was probably just as well as a lot of townsfolk had started to ask questions about this 'stranger with his camera … and what exactly he was doing there'.

Also, while living in Nigeria, I once took photos of two large concrete figures, a man and a woman in the kind of funerary finery that had once been prominent in Igboland and who were long dead. The effigies stood right by the side of the road, the entire panoply overwhelmed by jungle that encroached from all sides.

This time, all three photos that I took of this pair of three-metre-high statues displayed a large black patch in exactly the same position between the two heads. It was almost as if I had pointed my lens directly into the sun and it had burned straight into the negative.

I mentioned this event in *Africa Today*, one of my early books, and even used one of the photos to illustrate the apparition.[1]

A mistake often made by people who like to refer to themselves as authorities on Africa and its traditions, is to use the word 'witchdoctor' generically, as if to apply to all people involved in these kinds of spiritual, or quasi-spiritual matters. That would be almost as bad as calling a quack an MD. Historically, these medicinemen and women were referred to as sorcerers.

In the traditional southern African context, the word applies to a sangoma, or what is customarily referred to as traditional healer, even though some practitioners in other parts of Africa actually label themselves as witchdoctors and have signs alongside their stalls

Chapter 25
A Witchdoctor in the House

proclaiming them as such. Not only Africans follow these disciplines, because there are many white people inducted into these mysterious orders. The medical side often follow deep-rooted tradition that go back eons and more often than not, involves plants, berries and potions that science sometimes reveals to have the healing effect claimed by those sangomas administering them.

But even in South Africa there are those who sometimes use these powers to achieve dubious objectives.

Erin Conway-Smith reported in June 2012 that a South African trade union had been accused of using witchcraft to recruit new members.[2] She disclosed that South Africa's biggest trades union, the National Union of Mineworkers, or NUM, was battling with an 'upstart rival' for control of the Impala Platinum mine, and that union leaders were taking the witchcraft allegations very seriously.

She said that Frans Baleni, NUM's general secretary, made a statement that a rival trades union group, AMCU, was having success in attracting members at the Impala Platinum (Implats) mine because of special *'muti'*, or traditional medicine made from ingredients that can include plants and animal parts.

She went on: '*Muti* is an important practice in southern Africa, and South Africans from all walks of life seek out traditional cures for ailments ranging from rashes to erectile dysfunction, as well as for magical purposes such as bringing good fortune in love and business. Reuters entered the picture by issuing a report that in addition to *muti*, NUM's members also believed the AMCU had a 'very strong sangoma, or witchdoctor'.

Not long before that happened, a report from Michael Oti Adjei of BBC Sport – datelined Accra in February 2012 – stated that Goran Stevanovic, the coach of Black Stars, the Ghana national football team, had revealed deep divisions within his squad. He said that some players had used witchcraft against their own teammates.

The Serbian made his claim in a leaked report on the Black Stars' failure at the 2012 Africa Cup of Nations, where they were beaten by eventual winners Zambia in the semi-finals. He added that he had 'never heard of a situation when players have used it against their own colleagues ... that is a very bad situation.'

As with most pursuits, there are obviously those who sometimes push the envelope. I made a film in Togo in the 1980s and it included sequences of an enormous voodoo 'supermarket' that represented just about everything that was evil in the unfathomable world of what some folk like to call the supernatural.

Followers came from all over Africa – as well as the Caribbean, both Americas and even from those plying this relatively obscure domain in London – to buy their concoctions. On display were thousands of dead parrots, lizards, disembowelled monkey carcasses and, to my horror, the eviscerated heads of horses and some of the larger primates.

The place stank of death and I was pleased to get away. In fact, I went straight back to my hotel and had a shower. Later that evening I had another, because the reek seemed to have followed me back to my room. Talking later to some of the French expatriates who had long experience of serving in Francophonic Africa, I learned that for those with these predilections and with the right kind of money you can get just about anything you need at that Lome market, including human body parts.

I found something similar but a lot more secretive and austere in Liberia, also while filming there with Charles Norman and others who formed my crew.

There was no 'marketplace', but on travelling about the interior we discovered several areas that we were told were prohibited to 'non-believers' and white people especially. The reason, we soon discovered, was that sinister sacrifices took place at these places.

Most of the people with whom we worked or with whom we came into contact were evasive about the true purpose of these hidden rituals. One young man who became part of our group intimated that it wouldn't be worth our lives if we tried to go into forbidden areas with a camera. He also warned that most of the mountaintops in the region north-west of Monrovia were sacred.

We got him drunk one night and with a bit of prompting that involved dollars, he revealed that some of the human sacrifices were eaten and was quite candid about cannibalism in the bush, which he said was commonplace. We were sceptical at first, but a Swedish aid worker told us before we left the country that they had heard similar reports, all surreptitious.

Only years later, while covering the civil war in Sierra Leone, was I able to finally confirm that people were killing and eating each other in the neighbouring territory. Colonel Bert Sachse, a former Rhodesian and South African Special Forces operative who commanded the mercenary group Executive Outcomes during the war, told me that one of his biggest problems was in getting rebel soldiers back to his headquarters so that they could be questioned.

'We would capture two or three rebels and then send a helicopter

Chapter 25
A Witchdoctor in the House

to bring them in,' said Sachse, adding that there was invariably one or two bodies short of the original number of prisoners reported to have been taken.

'Of course I tried to stop these practices, but they were very much part of the culture in the deep jungle interior ... it was obviously something that had been going on forever,' he said. Sachse also disclosed that both sides in the war never went into battle without invoking the spirits of the dead, rites that sometimes included a witchdoctor brewing a powerful alcoholic drink which the troops were told would protect them from bullets. Government troops in Sierra Leone were issued liquor daily and were half smashed most of the time anyway.

I was to cover some of those aspects in the book I subsequently wrote about that and other African conflicts in which I had been involved, marginally or otherwise.[3]

Back to Liberia, which was very different to anything I'd previously encountered in Africa.

While out in the jungle, we'd usually make an improvised camp in one of the villages where we had been filming, but the crew was spooked by the fact that the village dead was buried right alongside the living. There were graves everywhere, mostly alongside the houses where we were supposed to sleep. An immediate result was that most of the team preferred to get their heads down in the Combi we'd hired. When bedtime came, they'd drive it up the road a hundred metres from the village, mainly to get away from what they referred to as 'the ungodly atmosphere of the place'.

I slept in one of the huts as I'd always intended to, and while no ghosts walked over my prostrate body on an improvised bed of woven mats, I didn't sleep very well either. The place was creepy.

There is no question that belief in the supernatural is as much a part of the equation in the lives of the majority of Africans as Catholicism is integral to the Vatican.

In an article about Africa, the website that deals with witches and witchcraft[4] states that different African tribes refer to witchcraft differently. The Nyakyusa tribe of East Africa refer to it as a 'python in the belly'; the Pondo tribe of South Africa as the 'snake of the women', the Xhosa tribe of South Africa believe it to be a great hairy beast. Some refer to it as a baboon.

'In southern African traditions, there are three classifications of somebody who uses magic: the *thakathi* (often improperly translated into English as 'witch') is a spiteful person who operates in secret to

While on Bazaruto Island, Luis Cardosa – seen here outside his modest cottage – was a regular companion. A former soldier in the Portuguese Army who fought in Angola, Luis finally returned to where he was born in Mozambique and given the option of joining Frelimo. He remained a banker for Frelimo for the rest of his working life and, as a loyal party member, was allowed to build himself this cottage on the island and retire there. Martha Gellhorn often dined with him.
(Photo: Author)

harm others; the sangoma is a diviner or shaman, somewhere on a par with a fortune-teller, often employed in detecting illness, predicting or advising on a person's future, or identifying the guilty party in a crime, as well as practising some degree of medicine, while the *inyanga*, usually translated as 'witchdoctor', heals illness and injury through herbalism and naturopathy, and provides customers with magical items for everyday use.

'The *thakathi* is almost exclusively female, the sangoma is usually female, and the *inyanga* is almost exclusively male.

Historically, 'witch smellers' (almost always women) were important and powerful people among the Zulu and other Bantu-speaking peoples of southern Africa. 'They were responsible for rooting out evil witches in the area, and were sometimes responsible for considerable bloodshed themselves. They wore extravagant costumes, usually including animal skins, feathered headdresses and face paint, and their hair was heavily greased, twisted in complicated designs, and frequently dyed bright red.'

The website goes on to say that the Tswana tribe of southern Africa believe there are two types of witches: day sorcerers and night witches. Day sorcerers use their magic to inflict harm through the use of herbs and other medicines, and are taken more seriously. Night witches are mainly old women who gather in small groups and then travel about bewitching the unfortunate. They do not wear clothes but smear themselves with white ashes or blood of the dead.

Similar followings are found throughout Africa, and while most believers are normal, law-abiding people, violence emerges almost as a matter of course in some societies. Indeed, according to Benjamin Radford, the American-based managing editor of the *Skeptical Inquirer*, belief in witchcraft all too often leads to murders in Africa.

In his comment in *Live Science*, Radford declared that a new Gallup poll found that belief in magic was widespread throughout sub-Saharan Africa, with over half of respondents saying they personally believe in witchcraft.[5]

'Studies in 18 countries show belief varies widely (ranging from 15 percent in Uganda to 95 per cent in the Ivory Coast), but on average, 55 per cent of [African] people polled believe in witchcraft.

'As might be expected, the older and less educated respondents reported higher belief in witchcraft, but interestingly such belief was inversely linked to happiness. Those who believe in witchcraft rated their lives significantly less satisfying than those who did not. One likely explanation is that those who believe in witchcraft feel they have less control over their own lives. People who believe in witchcraft often feel victimised by supernatural forces, for example, attributing accidents or disease to evil sorcery instead of randomness or naturalistic causes.'

Cultural belief in witchcraft has wider implications for Africans as well, from law enforcement to aid donations to public health.

'In Africa, witchdoctors are consulted not only for healing diseases, but also for placing curses on rivals. Magic (or at least the belief in magic) is commonly used for personal, political, and financial gain.

African belief in witchcraft has also led to horrific murders and mutilations in recent years.

'In 2008, a mob of hundreds of young men killed eight women and three men in two villages in rural western Kenya. The victims were accused of witchcraft – having cast spells that lowered the intelligence of the village's children. Some of the suspected witches and wizards were hacked to death with machetes, or had their throats slit before their bodies were burned.

'In East Africa, at least 50 albinos (people with a rare genetic disorder that leaves the skin, hair and eyes without pigment) were murdered for their body parts in 2009, according to the International Committee of the Red Cross.'

Radford tells us that an albino's arms, fingers, genitals, ears, and blood are highly prized on the black market, believed to contain magical powers and are used in witchcraft. In a continent of dark-skinned Africans, albinos are often the subject of fear, hatred, and ridicule. The practice of using their body parts for magical ritual or benefit was widespread in the past and in some of the remoter regions, still continues. Such attacks are particularly brutal, with knives and machetes used to cut and hack off limbs, breasts and other body parts from their screaming victims – including children.

The albino issue has festered for years in Black Africa. During colonial times, French, British or Portuguese officials tended to turn a blind eye to what was obviously a succession of human rights transgressions. In recent years though, some solid action has been taken at international level.

Even CNN hopped onto the bandwagon with Errol Barnett doing a lengthy report on the subject in October 2012, labelled 'Witchcraft in Tanzania – the Good, the Bad and the Persecution'.

As he comments, a sense of mystery and fear engulfs witchcraft and 'here faith in this specific form of African tradition can turn deadly.'

He goes on: 'People with albinism have been dismembered in western parts of the country because so-called witchdoctors perpetuate a belief that albino body parts bring great wealth.'

Interestingly, those suspected of witchcraft are also targeted; an estimated 600 elderly women were killed in 2011 due to the suspicion that they were witches, according to the Legal and Human Rights Centre in Tanzania. In fact, declares Barnett, the Pew Forum on Religious and Public life conducted 25,000 face-to-face interviews in 19 African nations and found that among them, Tanzanians hold the strongest belief in witchcraft.

It says 60 per cent of the Tanzanians interviewed believe that sacrifices to ancestors or spirits can protect them from harm, and that many Christians and Muslims incorporate elements of traditional African beliefs into their daily lives.

Barnett: 'Students at Dar Es Salaam University were reluctant to

Chapter 25
A Witchdoctor in the House

American author and former wife of Ernest Hemingway, Martha Gellhorn, at Bazaruto, seen here with one of her friends who watched over her whenever she snorkelled in deep water, which was every day. (Photo: Luis Cardosa)

talk to CNN about opinions relating to witchcraft. Some explained, even if they don't personally believe in the practice, their relatives take it seriously. Others feel one must believe in the practice for it to have any power over them. So even with a university education, some students retain some faith in witchcraft.

'Believers seeking healing regularly visit Mama Safi, a self-proclaimed "good witch", who gained her powers after being visited by spirits, she says. "I'm able to remove evil, stomach sickness, migraines, typhoid and diabetes too," she boasts. Safi conducts parts of her ceremonies in Arabic, even though she claims to have never studied it.'

Her fee ranges anywhere from US$20 to $120 depending on the service provided; expensive when you consider most Tanzanians live on less than $2 a day.'

A final word about witchdoctors, this time from an unusual source; the famous American war correspondent Martha Gellhorn who spent many years towards the end of her life in East Africa, rued

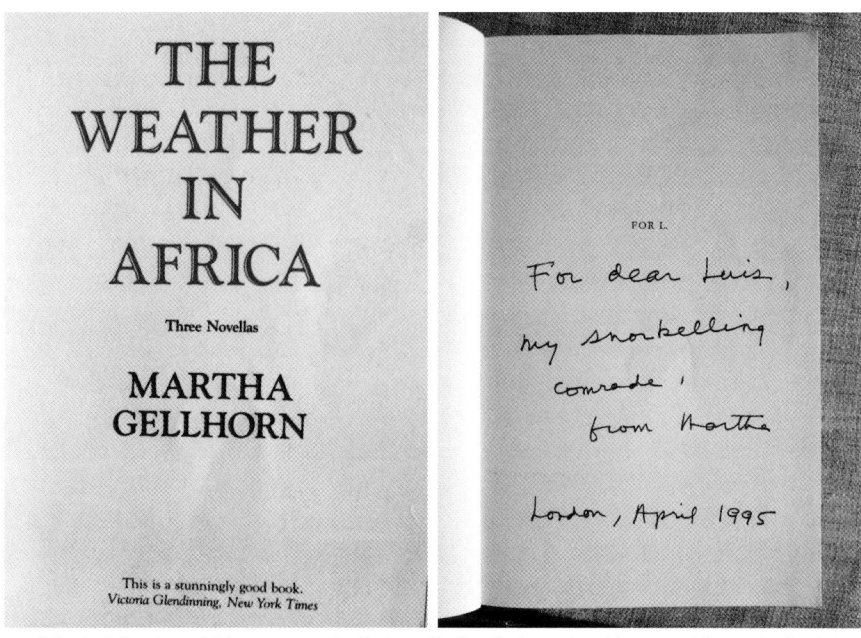

Martha's book on Africa, appropriately inscribed to Luis on the title page. (Photo: Author)

the fact that she had discovered Africa so late in life. At one stage Martha visited the island of Bazaruto in Mozambique having had her deteriorating eyesight seen to in London some months before. The treatment was a disaster and she lost almost all sight in her left eye.

Once on Bazaruto, the normally reserved and quiet-spoken Martha Gellhorn apparently decided it was payback time and I quote from what she wrote in an article for the London *Evening Standard*.[6]

'I asked Paul [Mansfield], the World Wildlife boffin, who knows everybody, to bring along a witchdoctor. My intention was revenge. After some negotiating, the witchdoctor agreed to come at 7 am. He arrived with Paul, a nice man, and two game wardens at 10 am. He was barefoot in a loose, long dirt-black overcoat and shapeless felt hat. He was very tall and looked ominous.

'Inside my cabin, he took off his hat and coat to reveal spotless white shorts and a white and pale blue-striped tennis shirt. He sat on the floor mat with his legs sprawled and said something in Chitswa, the local language. This went to a game warden who repeated it in Portuguese to the second game warden who whispered it shyly to Paul, who repeated it to me.

'"He asks what you want to know," said Paul. "Tell him it's about my eyes." Before I got further, the witchdoctor took a handful of

Chapter 25
A Witchdoctor in the House

Up and down this stretch of coast locals dry batches of fingerlings and other fish caught in their nets. Much of it is offered for sale in the markets on the mainland. (Photo: Author)

small objects like bones from a leather pouch, cupped them in his hands, closed his eyes and spoke. "He's praying to the spirits," said Paul. The witchdoctor rolled the bones, like throwing dice.

'He looked at them thoughtfully and said through the interpretation chain, "She will not be blind. She will see more or less as she does now."

'"That's nice," I said. "Now ask him to put a curse on the man who damaged my eyes so he will have the same eyesight I do."

'"You can't do that," Paul said. "He doesn't make curses. He's a *curandero*, a healer. Why not ask for something positive, like make the doctor fund a clinic here?"

'"This is not an Oxfam meeting," I said crossly.

'"All right, we can ask him how you should harm the man who harmed you. That's advice, not a curse." This was relayed to the witchdoctor who again prayed and threw the bones.

'His verdict was reported back. "He says your anger should lessen because the man is very sick in the chest and will die if not treated." This was bad news. I didn't want him dead, I wanted him handicapped.

'Thanks and handshakes all round. The fee was five dollars.

'Outside, draped in his awful coat, the witchdoctor said: "I was never before consulted by a white."

'I haven't met a lot of witchdoctors either,' I replied.

Interestingly, Martha Gellhorn was said to have learned after her return to London that the eye specialist who had botched her treatment was indeed quite ill. Very ill, in fact, because he died soon afterwards from a pulmonary disease.

Which raises the question: how did the Mozambique witchdoctor know that a doctor in faraway London was ailing…

1   Al J. Venter: *Africa Today,* Macmillan, 1974.
2   Erin Conway-Smith, *Globalpost,* June 15, 2012.
3   Al J. Venter; *War Dog: Fighting Other People's Wars,* Casemate Publishers (US and UK) 2006.
4   www.witchcraftandwitches.com/world_africa.html.
5   *Live Science,* 9 December 2009.
6   Martha Gellhorn,: 'A Spell of Coral Relief'; *Evening Standard,* London, 18 November 1995.

CHAPTER TWENTY SIX

A WEEK IN AN AFRICAN JAIL

Veteran Africa newshound Tim Lambon, originally from north of the Limpopo, was given his first media job by Al Venter when he was hired as an assistant soundman on a film shoot in Afghanistan, then under Soviet control. He went on to make a name for himself in Britain working for many of the majors, including ITN and CNN. It was while filming in Liberia during the final days of Charles Taylor's brutal rule that he was arrested in Monrovia...

Half asleep, the noise of men shouting, the clump of heavy footfalls and the rattle of rifles tend to bring ordinary mortals rather sharply to their senses. I'd just managed to pull on my boots when they burst in, a braying mob of black uniformed thugs brandishing Kalashnikov rifles, Africa's curse.

My CNN colleagues Sorious Samura, David Barrie and Gugu Radebe were already being forced out the door as I managed to snatch up my shirt and bum bag. A huge hand slapped the small of my back, grabbing my trousers and belt, dragging me towards the door. I swivelled to provide the least resistance and started running, harried by the last two goons.

Across the concrete compound, towards the gates we went. My recollection is of a silent movie in sodium pink and half-tones.

I couldn't hear what they were shouting. The gates were open and at first glance the street was 'one in the morning' deserted. Terrified, I saw four bodies lying in the road and the concomitant headline: 'Arrested journalists shot while trying to escape.' I suppressed the thought and worked on some kind of tactic for the moment.

Turning towards the left, some of the fear subsided. Toyota pick-up trucks with engines running were waiting ... no framed death yet.

But the other half of the equation was: 'Where the hell are they taking us?'

There were hands thrust into pockets to get at our possessions. I was glad for the snotty hanky I'd secreted. Nasty surprise!

On instruction, Gugu, my big Zulu soundman, and I vaulted into the truck. Sitting on the floor under the A-frame seat, I was pulling on my shirt when someone noticed the bum bag ... goodbye to all that.

'Hands on the seat!' came the order and we complied as the vehicles turned and lurched away from Liberia's National Security Agency headquarters.

Standing on the tow bar, the bruiser hanging onto the tailboard caught a glimpse of the watch on my arm.

'What's that?' he demanded.

I stayed silent and began to take it off – I'd be losing it anyway. But he couldn't wait and made a lunge, missing the timepiece as the Toyota rolled drunkenly around a corner. A moment's panic, an outstretched hand flailed fresh air. When our Toyota straightened out again, the goon grabbed the bench nearest him and held on for life, which was when he ripped the cheap old Casio from my wrist.

Something at the back of my mind smiled at this display of slapstick, it was the least of my worries.

So started a 'week of leisure', me and my colleagues as 'state guests' of former Mister (and more recently, Doctor) Charles Taylor, erstwhile president of the Republic of Liberia. This was the same man that today resides under close detention at The Hague, where the International Court of Justice found him guilty of committing crimes against humanity. A vain and petty dictator, he'd played a significant role in the destruction of his country's economy and infrastructure, his henchmen pillaging what few natural resources remained.

I'd accompanied a documentary film team to Monrovia to talk to him, in the hope of trying to establish what was going on, but Taylor, ever suspicious, wasn't eager either to see us or allow anybody access to the facilities within his government.

Instead, having allowed us to film unimpeded for nearly two weeks, the Ministry of Information – at the behest of the sinister Reginald Goodridge, Press Secretary to the President – revoked our press cards and what had been a valid accreditation. That document had clearly stated that we were allowed to film, but apparently any filming in Liberia was illegal without a nod from the top.

Once in custody, we were detained in what was blithely referred

Chapter 26
A Week in an African Jail

to as an 'Officers' Cell' at the Monrovia Central Police Station: on suspicion of being engaged in espionage.

Conditions where we were held were perhaps one step up from the rest of the inmates, which also meant that we were spared being stripped to our underpants and thrust into the inner sanctum of what was colloquially referred to as 'The Sweats'. You were incarcerated there if you argued with the police, or perhaps left a night club drunk.

The charge office for both sets of jails boasted a single 60 watt bulb and a wobbly ceiling fan.

The only piece of furniture was a counter, now turned on its side and used as an impromptu bed, supplementing a filthy foam mattress that covered much of the floor.

The problem with being assigned to the 'Officers' Cell' is just that – the officers. The worst of the nutters in black uniforms, who transgressed their own brutal code, ended up marking time in that fetid hole. Friday night when we arrived, there were six of them sprawled on the floor. We were snapped from our adrenaline-fed stupors at five the next morning when they woke up and immediately started fighting. The struggle flared from punches to cracking heads on the floor and, as suddenly as it had started, it was all over, except for shouts and hysterical laughter.

Throughout the weekend, the population of demented and drugged-up policemen ebbed and flowed, culminating with an influx of 15 or so on the Monday morning. Violence was always there, a mean and capricious spirit hovering just beneath the surface, waiting to infiltrate some crazy's head and send him into a froth over nothing.

After being arrested in more vile places than I care to recall, I've learned that the best policy is to 'present no edges'. Stand with your shoulders drooped, head forward, hands held like a penitent Presbyterian. Never sit or lie down while there is a threat or when anyone new walks into the cell. Be alert to both mood swings and undercurrents, always listening, but never overtly paying attention. Avoid eye contact and move quickly but unobtrusively away from aggressive activity.

I quickly tutored the others in these tactics and we managed to avoid much of the unfocused aggravation which engulfed the place. Reminded of 18th Century woodcuts depicting the chaos of Bedlam, I knew there was a similar element of malicious insanity in the cells where we were held and which simply had to be avoided.

After a few days among the policemen in detention, we realised that it was a safe area for drug transactions to take place. The brutal mobs of black-suited policemen who marauded the streets of Monrovia often appeared to be high when we made contact, and what we saw in prison confirmed that large amounts of cannabis and alcohol were probably to blame.

Before our detention, a warrant to search our hotel rooms had listed 'marijuana, cocaine and heroin' among the things they were looking for. I found it ironic that it was in the police station that the narcotics junkies came into their own.

The loudest and most aggressive of the Monday morning miscreants, having staked their places on the fallen counter, loosened their uniforms and took off their boots. Then they proceeded to smoke their way through at least three huge spliffs each before falling soundly asleep. The dope was a blessing, suppressing noise and aggression during our last few hours in the 'Officers' Cells'.

By then, we'd made contact with the world outside and our Counsel visited us on Monday afternoon. He insisted it was highly likely we would never be charged and anticipated our release the next day. We were heartened, but I had a sneaking suspicion our lawyers were underestimating their opponents' resolve. Sure enough, less than 20 minutes after our so-called 'protectors' left, we were taken to the steps of the court, summarily arrested and charged with 'espionage'.

Now on remand, we were moved – again under armed guard – to the Monrovia Central Prison. It was late in the afternoon when we arrived and after perfunctory processing, were marched into a long, low and very dark building. The walls were painted boot brown to a height of seven feet off the floor, the remainder and ceilings being bright yellow. There was a desultory selection of graffiti on the walls of the cell into which Sorious and I were ushered. I took a scratchy drawing of an old-fashioned helicopter on the west wall to be an omen that might signify something positive for our release. I flew choppers and the Sierra Leonean ambassador had hinted that they might use one to take us out of the country should we be freed.

High on the east wall was the single word 'Victor' which for the first few days I failed to recognise as a name. So set was I on any kind of real or imagined encouragement that I thought it was the result of someone being disturbed before they'd been able to add the letter 'Y'. Although I never underestimated how serious the charges were, and accepted that the duration of our imprisonment might be extended, I never lost faith in the team of people I knew were working in the UK for our release.

Life in Monrovia's jail was remarkably structured. The building was clean, the ablution block – though old and seriously damaged in places – was clean and the population was viceless. Smoking was not allowed and if drugs were in use, they were out of sight. This regime was maintained, not by the six or eight venerable warders who wandered around with plastic night sticks during the day, but by an internal mafia of inmates who called themselves the 'Government'. Their realm of the cell block which they controlled was plausibly named 'Republic of You-Go-Sober'.

Their 'Commander-in-Chief' or 'C-in-C', was a *mestico* of medium build, innocuously named Russell. He headed up the 15-man 'Government' that included a 'Cabinet' with, among others, Ministers of Finance, Foreign Affairs, Justice and Defence. His lieutenants were a six-and-half-foot Nigerian called the 'Godfather' and Hassan, a wiry Sierra Leonean.

We became aware of the 'Government' on our first night when someone started drumming energetically on an oil can and the clamour of the cells instantly stopped.

'This is a newsflash from Radio "You-Go-Sober"' announced the newsreader several times from the far end of the corridor. What followed was an impeccable parody of a 1950's news bulletin informing the silent inmates that because a 'Cabinet' member had been transferred, another had been appointed after a vote within the 'Government'.

There followed a series of comments as to the new incumbent's attributes and abilities from several of the senior 'Ministers' before the newsflash ended with another roll on the oil can.

It seems that the 'Government' was a self-perpetuating organism, deciding its own hierarchy through which the prison authorities apparently worked. After six in the evening, the whole block was locked down and keys to all the cells passed into the 'Government's' hands.

They were in charge until six the next morning when the uniformed officers nominally took over again. In charge of not only security, but also the economy, Russell and his team supplied us with toothbrushes (exceedingly welcome after four days), toothpaste, candles and matches, all of it at prices that, surprisingly, had not been inflated to match our status.

After supplying those few earthly needs, the 'Church of You-Go-Sober' kicked in. Brother Tobias, a perennially sunny character on crutches with round National Health-style glasses, handed out Billy Graham magazines with encouraging stories and supplied David with a Bible. David read his Exodus with zeal, no doubt dreaming of parting the Red Sea out of there.

With little else to do, the African mania for Pentecostal Christianity predominated and church services with much singing and chanting were a daily feature of prison life throughout.

Through an experience like this, I quickly learned that fear was not a constant. But given that its level was constantly fluctuating, I could dissect fear into two distinct categories. There was real concern for any kind of bodily harm which arose from what people could do to you in different places within the prison walls, like the toilets or exercise yard, and there was the dread that stemmed from us acknowledging how serious our situation was.

The first gave you that metallic taste in your mouth and made it difficult to keep control of a pen afterwards. The nightmarish ride from the NSA to the Central Police Station on the first night, for instance, was probably the biggest spike to our fear quotient.

The holding cells with their unpredictable sense of imminent violence then kept the measure of dread high. But the structured environment of the Central Prison, after an initial peak from the apprehension of something unknown, ended up pretty low on the list of scares.

The second fear, in contrast, was always in the background. It supplemented the dread of bodily harm, but even when there was no perceivable threat to one's person, this generalised level of apprehension remained omnipresent. It fluctuated with news from home, articles in the press or the non-committal prognoses of our Council.

In reality, fear was the pulse of the prisoner's morale. Our states of mind were always influenced by the statements from individuals and, by inference, whether they came true or not. It led us, after the first few days and several disappointments, to almost write off the Sierra Leonean ambassador as a genial but over-optimistic buffoon.

Initially our legal representative, Varney Sherman, looked like he might have nailed it down, but ultimately, although he came across with a great deal of flash, the system actually ran *him* and not, as he claimed, the reverse.

However, the British Consul, Brian Brewer, was always straight up and down, and while he, like us all, initially underestimated the severity of the predicament, he never spun a line that ended up disappointing.

Chapter 26
A Week in an African Jail

At a constantly low level, morale plummeted the night they trounced our Defence with our late charge and arrest. It clawed its way back slightly with the Counsel's optimism about the applicability of bail, only to plunge again when that was denied. Only after that do I think the others started to learn the trick of hoping without counting on the outcome. As the saying goes – especially when incarcerated in an African jail – never count your chickens …

When rumours that we were to be released started to circulate, we dared not hope – although the prospect seriously disturbed our sleep. Disappointment would have been unbearable. Through that long last morning and into the afternoon, we told ourselves that nothing was happening until finally, the call came, loud and clear: 'Bring your things, you're going home.'

Only then did we dare to hope.

ACKNOWLEDGEMENTS

There are many people I need to thank in creating which is the culmination of several years' work. Every one of these folk was involved in some aspect of this book.

The Protea Books production team comprised my editor Danél Hanekom and Martie Eloff who ran communications and everything else that nobody could or would touch; a very big thanks to all. A very big thank you also to Jerry Buirski and Carmen Hansen-Kruger who proofed this work from top to bottom.

Also in the picture is Nicol Stassen, who not only owns and runs Protea Books, but is a fellow author with a bunch of titles to his credit, including his most recent which deals with the South African Boers in Angola. When I originally put the idea about this work to Nicol, he didn't hesitate. *Dankie, my ou vriend!*

Actual production was the domain of Bruce Gonneau who, with the support of Jenny his wife, made what you see here before you into something tangible. Bruce has handled many of my books in the past and no question; he really is a scribbler's delight when it comes to putting together a new title.

Caroline Castell took many of the photos in this book and made a pretty good job of them all. She has also been assisting me editorially.

Next comes Fiona Capstick and her alter ego Adelino, whose vast experience as a military intelligence operative while serving in the SADF still comes in handy. Fiona was a good friend of Colonel Robert Denard even before he relocated to Pretoria after being ousted from the Comores by units of the French armed forces.

And let us not forget our mutual buddy Manuel Ferreira who, among other adventures, served under Denard on his island 'kingdom'.

My old friend Roelf van Heerden, with whom I spent time while deployed with Executive Outcomes in Sierra Leone some years ago, gave me some valuable insights into the future role of private military companies — as well as operators — in Africa's brush-fire wars. Former SAAF Alouette gunship pilot Arthur Walker put me in touch with Roelf again, soon after he'd returned from Puntland for the last time early in 2013. There he'd been involved in a series of Somali anti-piracy operations which Roelf had been running at the time.

Peter 'Monster' Wilkins – a former brigadier in the air force who, together with his delightful wife Val, spent three years as a military attaché in Washington DC, and he rates high among contributors to this work. These days, working for Durban's Starlite Aviation, his travels take him all over Africa (and to Kosovo, Marion Island and soon, to the Antarctic). Many of 'Monster's photos appear between these covers: indeed one of the colour sections is a photo essay of some of these adventures.

The same with my old compadre Neall Ellis; always around when I need him most. And Cobus Claassens, with whom I spent solid time in the Sierra Leone War, and afterwards, when he was running anti-piracy ops out of Freetown. Cobus will recognise some of his photos on these pages, including the one of us together, taken after the Battle of Biama. Thanks for your help over a very long period Cobus, and here's to your involvement again, perhaps in the sequel to *Blood Diamond*.

So too with my old *rafiki* Peter Younghusband and his irrepressible Jill, whose Spanish, incidentally, is as good as her English because she grew up in South America.

David Mannall came up trumps with one of the best chapters in the book, describing one of the seminal battles of the Angola War. That was on the Lomba River when Soviet main battle tanks matched ability and tactics against South African Ratel infantry fighting vehicles. Havana rated the Ratel as an 'inferior' fighting machine, yet, a bunch of extremely well-trained and motivated youngsters from down south completely routed the Angolan Army. Interestingly, FAPLA – as the Angolan Army was called – had stiff Cuban, Soviet and East German support, but in the end the other side had to run for their lives, abandoning their hardware and, in many instances, leaving even their uniforms and AKs on the battlefield as they disappeared into the bush.

Former SAS operative Darrel Watt did us all a lot of good when he provided the support that Caroline and I needed to write the story of Adam Buske, his professional hunter at Mushingashi Wildlife Conservatory on the Kafue in Zambia. The colour section which shows many of the African animals found there all but encapsulates conditions on the ground and along the river at 'Mushi'. I have Hannes Wessels to thank for introducing us to Darrell and Adam in the first place.

That lovely lady and fellow dive buddy from Belgium, Manya Corbane, provided several wildlife photos here.

Helena, the widow of Andre Dennison opened her files for us

and gave us a bunch of pictures – together with a stock of delightful anecdotes from the Rhodesian War. Thank you my dear, and here's to the next braai in Downe. Other Rhodesian photos came from the good offices of Chris Cocks and some diagrams and maps from Dr Richard Wood. Thanks to you both.

The 'dreaded' Peter Duffy, and our mutual pal Graham Linscott, the *Idler* columnist on the *Mercury* are also due for a few words of appreciation. Peter, while staying with Graham in Durban, gave me some excellent material and photos which covered the time he spent fighting in the Congo under the venerable Mike Hoare.

Other Congolese photos, as well as quite a few which covered the war in Biafra, were provided by Leif Hellström. A remarkable fellow, he has some of the best photo archives of these conflicts that I've seen.

The chapter on Valentine Strasser, the former head of state of Sierra Leone would never have appeared without the help of Simon Akam, who originally told us all about him in an article he did in *The New Statesman*.

I went to war on horseback with a young army lieutenant by the name of Johan Louw, today one of South Africa's leading landscape architects. His chapter adds a strong flavour of adventure to this book and hopefully I will be working with him again on his time with SWASpes.

Others who deserve thanks include my old colleague René Pélissier who I rate as the leading authority worldwide on Portugal's wars in Africa. So too with Dave Atkinson who flew helicopter gunships in the Congo for Robert Mugabe and is today training young chopper enthusiasts in Lesotho.

I asked Peter Felstead, the longest-serving editor of *Jane's Defence Weekly* for some photo material on RAF Chinook helicopters and he gave me some from his personal files. Still more came from my dear departed old friend Mohammed (Mo) Amin with whom I spent a lot of time in Nairobi. I often stayed with Amin and Dolly when visiting Kenya from the Republic and a sad day it was when he was killed in an Ethiopian passenger jet that crashed on approaching Grande Comoros after it had been hijacked by terrorists. All the more so because he had already lost an arm in the Ethiopian War.

'Sharkman' Walter and his wife Sandy Bernardis must be remembered for the help they have given Caroline and me in getting all this material together. Their dive lodge at Widenham on Natal's South Coast is still one of our favourite destinations. So is Mozambique's Bazaruto Lodge, originally run by that lovely husband-and-wife team Louis and Paulien Erasmus.

I was there for a fortnight as their guest in the summer of 2012, the idea being to gather material for a book on the archipelago – dating back to World War II, when Bazaruto served as a German U-Boat base. That book is still very much on the cards. Louis introduced me to his Mozambique namesake Luis, an old associate of Martha Gellhorn. He still lives on the island and is featured in one of the chapters dealing with witchcraft.

And at the end of it, almost none of this would have been possible without the help of the entire Troskie family. That includes Manie, Elise, Bernard and Gerhard with whom we have spent some lovely times at their home in the Pierre van Ryneveld suburb of Pretoria.

Al J. Venter
Downe, England
June, 2013

In the same series published by Protea Book House:

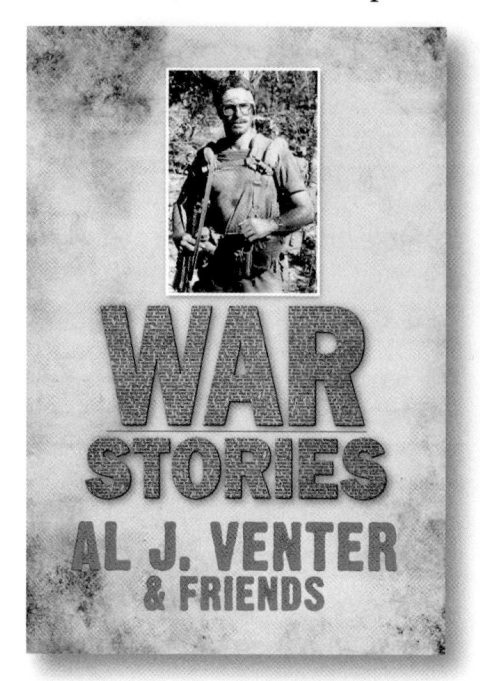

By the same author:

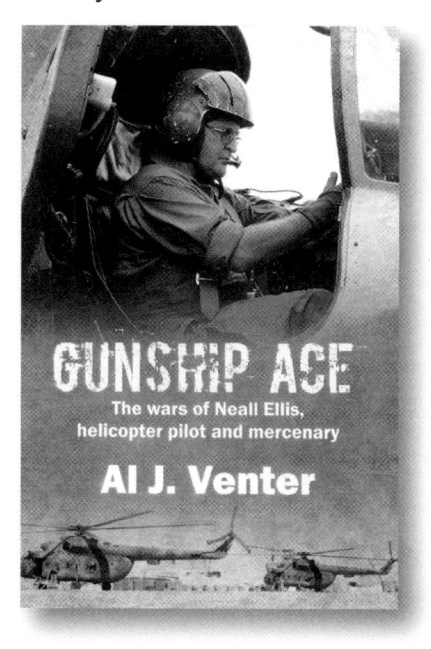